Multimedia Data Management

Multimedia Data Management

Using Metadata to Integrate and Apply Digital Media

Amit Sheth, *Editor*
University of Georgia
Athens, Georgia, USA

Wolfgang Klas, *Editor*
University of Ulm
Ulm, Germany

McGraw-Hill

New York   San Francisco   Washington D.C.   Auckland   Bogotá
Caracas   Lisbon   London   Madrid   Mexico City   Milan
Montreal   New Dehli   San Juan   Singapore
Sydney   Tokyo   Toronto

Library of Congress catalog card number: 97-76372

McGraw-Hill

A Division of The McGraw-Hill Companies

ISBN 0-07-057735-8

The sponsoring editor for this book was Scott L. Grillo, the editing supervisor was Paul R. Sobel, and the production supervisor was Sherri Souffrance.

Printed and bound by R. R. Donnelley & Sons Company.

To my parents, Pravin and Surbhi,
for their life-long active role in my progress,
and to my wife, Parul, for putting up with my work schedule.

— Amit

To Karin, Sebastian, and little Katharina
for being patient with me.

— Wolfgang

Contents

Contents

Contents

Preface

Metadata can play a very important role in the effective discovery and search, access, integration and management of a variety of digital data, whether stored as multi-media data or in independently created and managed repositories. In this book internationally known researchers discuss the what, why, and how of metadata related to various digital data such as text, audio, image, video, and mixed-media. The book aims to give a comprehensive understanding of the role metadata play in managing a variety of metadata for digital media in information systems. In addition, it also points out various challenging problems that beg for further research.

Following an introduction to the topic the subsequent chapters address the following key issues on metadata:

- What are the characteristics of the media type considered, e.g., text, image, voice, video?

- What are the various types of metadata (e.g., data or content independent, content or data dependent, representing structure or semantics) and typical examples of metadata, e.g., abstractions from raw video data?

- What is the content, the reference terms, the ontology of the metadata and its management?

- What are the strategies used for manually and/or automatically generating/extracting and maintaining metadata?

- How is metadata structured, what kind of language is used to describe the structure? What are relevant standards?

- What is the relationship between data and metadata, how is metadata stored and organized?

- How does metadata facilitate information discovery and retrieval? What role does metadata play in enabling novel and sophisticated applications exploiting digital data?

The book's intended readers are researchers and advance product developers dealing with multimedia data management and multimedia applications, database professional dealing with unstructured data and non-traditional applications, professionals in application domains (e.g., geo-spatial data, medical imaging, personal digital video) where metadata and metadata standards play major roles, and practically all librarians at higher-education or technical institutions and universities.

We would like to acknowledge the effort of the contributing authors. In particular, we would like to thank Susanne Boll for her substantial effort for integrating the chapters into the book and coordinating and preparing the final camera ready version.

Wolfgang Klas

Amit Sheth

Contributors

Gulrukh Ahanger
Multimedia Communications Laboratory
Department of Electrical
and Computer Engineering
Boston University
Boston, Massachusetts 02215, USA

Kate Beard
National Center for Geographic
Information and Analysis and
Department of Spatial
Information Science and Engineering
University of Maine
Orono, ME 04469-5711, USA

Susanne Boll
Department of Database and
Information Systems
Faculty of Computer Science
University Ulm, Oberer Eselsberg
D-89069 Ulm, Germany

Klemens Böhm
Integrated Publication and
Information Systems Institute
Dolivostraße 15
D-64293 Darmstadt, Germany

Francine Chen
Xerox Palo Alto Research Center
3333 Coyote Hill Road
Palo Alto, CA 94304, USA

Wesley W. Chu
Department of Computer Science
University of California, Los Angeles
Los Angeles, CA 90024, USA

Pamela Drew
Department of Computer Science
Hong Kong University of
Science and Technology
Clear Water Bay, Hong Kong

Farshad Fotouhi
Computer Science Department
Wayne State University
Detroit, Michigan 48202, USA

William I. Grosky
Computer Science Department
Wayne State University
Detroit, Michigan 48202, USA

Oliver Günther
Institut für Wirtschaftsinformatik
Humboldt-Universität zu Berlin
Spandauer Str. 1
D-10178 Berlin, Germany

Arun Hampapur
IBM TJ Watson Research Center, H1-D47
30 Saw Mill River Road
Hawthorne, NY 10532, USA

Contributors

Takanari Hayama
Institute of Information Sciences
and Electronics
University of Tsukuba
Tsukuba, Ibaraki 305, Japan

Chih-Cheng Hsu
Department of Computer Science
University of California, Los Angeles
Los Angeles, CA 90024, USA

Ion Tim Ieong
NCR Corporation
100 N. Sepulveda Blvd.
El Segundo, CA 90245, USA

Ramesh Jain
Virage Inc
177 Bovet Road, Suite 520
San Mateo, CA 94403, USA

Zhaowei Jiang
Computer Science Department
Wayne State University
Detroit, Michigan 48202, USA

Don Kimber
Xerox Palo Alto Research Center
3333 Coyote Hill Road
Palo Alto, CA 94304, USA

Takashi Kitagawa
Institute of Information Sciences
and Electronics
University of Tsukuba
Tsukuba, Ibaraki 305, Japan

Yasushi Kiyoki
Faculty of Environmental Information
Keio University
Fujisawa, Kanagawa 252, Japan

Wolfgang Klas
Department of Database
and Information Systems
Faculty of Computer Science
University Ulm, Oberer Eselsberg
D-89069 Ulm, Germany

William Klippgen
Excite, Inc.
555 Broadway
Redwood City, CA 94063, USA

Julian Kupiec
Xerox Palo Alto Research Center
3333 Coyote Hill Road
Palo Alto, CA 94304, USA

Thomas D. C. Little
Multimedia Communications Laboratory
Department of Electrical
and Computer Engineering
Boston University
Boston, Massachusetts 02215, USA

Jan Pedersen
Verity Inc.
894 Ross Dr.
Sunnyvale, CA 94089, USA

Peter Schäuble
Information Systems
ETH Zentrum
CH-8092 Zürich, Switzerland

Amit Sheth
Large Scale Distributed
Information Systems Lab
Department of Computer Science
University of Georgia
415 Graduate Studies Research Center
Athens, GA 30602-7404, USA

Contributors

Terence R. Smith
Department of Computer Science and
Department of Geography
University of California at Santa Barbara
Santa Barbara, CA 93106, USA

Ricky K. Taira
Department of Radiological Sciences
University of California, Los Angeles
Los Angeles, CA 90024, USA

Agnès Voisard
Institut für Informatik
Freie Universität Berlin
Takustr. 9
D-14195 Berlin, Germany

Dinesh Venkatesh
EMC Corporation
171 South Street
Hopkinton, Massachusetts, 01748 USA

Martin Wechsler
Information Systems
ETH Zentrum
CH-8092 Zürich, Switzerland

Lynn Wilcox
FX Palo Alto Laboratory
3400 Hillview Ave. Bldg 4
Palo Alto, CA 94304, USA

Jerry Ying
Department of Computer Science
Hong Kong University
of Science and Technology
Clear Water Bay, Hong Kong

Chapter

1

Overview on Using Metadata to Manage Multimedia Data

Susanne Boll, Wolfgang Klas, and Amit Sheth*

Department of Database and Information Systems,
Faculty of Computer Science, University Ulm,
Oberer Eselsberg, D-89069 Ulm, Germany
{boll,klas}@informatik.uni-ulm.de

*Large Scale Distributed Information Systems Lab,
Department of Computer Science, University of Georgia,
415 Graduate Studies Research Center
Athens GA 30602-7404, USA
amit@om.cs.uga.edu

Abstract

This chapter introduces the reader to the key role that metadata can play for managing various digital media, often also called new media, such as image, audio, and video in information systems. We present different views on how metadata can be modeled, classified, extracted, managed, and applied, to support a convenient handling of digital media. We discuss various issues on the role of metadata from different viewpoints: the application scenario perspective, the media processing perspective, and the metadata type and classification perspective. We also look at the world of standards for handling metadata.

Finally, the chapter gives an outline of this book and provides a coherent view over all the chapters. Each of the chapters and its main issue in the field is introduced in brief with respect to the concepts and issues discussed in this chapter.

1.1 The Need for Metadata in Multimedia Systems

Real applications in industry face the serious problem of how to handle large amounts of a variety of digital media. Therefore, there is a growing demand for database and information systems support in the area of modeling, management, and processing digital media. There is a need to explicitly capture a fair amount of content-information as well as application-specific semantics by means of a variety of *metadata*, e.g., multimedia indexes, attribute-based annotations, and intentional descriptions, to allow appropriate access to, selection of, and processing of digital media.

One of the key problems to be solved is the development of metadata, that is, the generation, structuring, representation, management, and proper utilization of data or information about data. While the issue of metadata has received a fair share of attention in conjunction with structured data (e.g., biomolecular data) and text documents, most of the current practices in the context of digital media and multimedia data management are still quite ad hoc.

Metadata plays a far more important role in managing multimedia data than does the management of traditional (well-)structured data or information retrieval techniques applied to text-only data. Some of the reasons for this are:

Different query paradigm. The exact-match paradigm for querying is no longer suitable or adequate for querying or retrieving various types of digital media.

Inadequate processing techniques. Content-based processing techniques are too hard to analyze, and very large data sets are often limited or inadequate.

Lacking efficiency. When a content-based search is possible, it cannot be used very frequently (e.g., for every query) for performance reasons and because of varying application- and modality-specific search criteria.

Semantics of multimedia data. Derived data and interpreted data (which may be considered a part of the metadata) as well as context and semantics (which may be easier to base on metadata rather than raw data) are of greater value when dealing with multimedia data or new/digital media (especially audio-visual data).

Let us discuss a couple of items listed above in a little more detail. Various digital media or components of multimedia data involve very large raw data volume. This has consequences on effective management and retrieval of the digital media. Content-based retrieval on raw data means that the query capabilities are limited to the number of available matching algorithms. Performance is lacking when queries are executed on large data sets. Indirect retrieval and processing, however, that use abstract information or metadata of the digital media seem to be a promising approach to enhance querying and processing and to improve response time as metadata will be of much less volume than the digital media themselves.

Semantics of multimedia data like images, video, and audio is implicit to the raw media data. By analyzing and processing, semantics can be made explicit to some extent on different abstraction levels, from feature values to knowledge-based concepts. Metadata describing this semantics explicitly may still not be sufficient for exact-match querying. For example, color distribution feature values of an image for red, black, and yellow still do not allow the conclusion that the image shows a sunset. The user's term *bar* may be ambiguous as it may match the concepts *barrier* or *pub* or *legal profession* dependent on the user's idea. A different querying paradigm is needed to allow a proper mapping of the user's ideas to the explicitly available semantics of a media object and, finally, to the raw data.

Metadata that is derived or extracted from digital media have the additional advantages of being more amenable to traditional data retrieval and manipulation techniques than the raw digital media. Examples include text annotations of images or other media or attribute-based metadata that can be managed by a structured database. These can then be easily applied or analyzed using text processing or information retrieval techniques and database management systems, respectively. For fuller exploitation of data and to provide information system interoperability it is necessary to support correlation of data. It is often more convenient and useful to identify and specify correlation at the metadata level rather than between raw data items.

In many situations metadata, as it is traditionally defined, is not sufficient for managing digital media and multimedia data. In the case of structured databases, the norm is to use schema descriptions and associated information (such as database statistics) as metadata. In the case of unstructured textual data and information retrieval, metadata is generally limited to indexes and textual descriptions of data. Richer forms of information, as conveyed by context, ontologies, and semantics, are very important here [8]. Metadata in such cases provide a suitable basis for building the higher forms of information.

With this book we try to look at the problems of *generating/extracting, structuring, representing, storing/organizing,* and *using* metadata for various digital media and multimedia data as well as their applications. We look at metadata for images, audio and speech, video, structured documents, and geo-spatial data and finally at the role of metadata in multimedia documents stored in digital libraries and in mixed-media-based information access.

For each medium, we address a variety of issues and try to give answers to questions like:

- What are the characteristics of the media type considered, e.g., text, image, voice, and video, and the application domains that provide the context for metadata-based exploitation of the digital media?

- What are typical types and examples of metadata in the context of a media type, e.g., abstractions from raw video data?

- What are the content, the reference terms, the ontology of the metadata?

- What are the strategies and techniques used for manually and/or automatically generating/extracting and maintaining metadata?

- How is metadata structured, and what kind of language is used to describe the structure?

- What is the relationship between data and metadata (e.g., size) and does this induce any implications in handling metadata?

- How is metadata stored and organized, i.e., which techniques are used to represent metadata in, for example, databases?

- How does metadata facilitate information discovery and retrieval as well as other processing of digital media?

- Are there metadata standards related to the digital media or application domain of concern and what role do standards play?

Next, we present three perspectives that govern the management of digital media and multimedia data. These perspectives evolve from or are supported by the chapters of this book, and many of the examples given are based on these chapters. The issues outlined above are addressed in the context of these perspectives, i.e., particular application scenarios, media processing techniques, and the characteristics of metadata.

1.2 The Application Scenario Perspective

We briefly discuss in the following the application areas covered by the subsequent chapters in this book with respect to metadata issues.

Image retrieval, navigation, and browsing in collections of images.
More and more application areas, such as medicine, maintain large collections of digital images. Efficient mechanisms to efficiently browse and navigate through the collections, however, are still lacking. Semantic content-based image browsing and navigation are needed instead of searching and viewing directory trees for image files such as `apwr38.gif`. An important issue is to extract images according to the user's (semantic) association and impression of an image, e.g., sunset at the sea, and not only according to mere (syntactic or structural) image features such as the color or texture. For the retrieval of images, a suitable definition for semantic equality and similarity of images is also needed. To be able to support the mapping from the users' ideas down to the raw image data, a model describing the association between users' concepts and image characteristics and semantics is needed (see for example Chapter 7).

Advances in techniques for obtaining images of the body's interior have greatly improved medical diagnosis. New imaging methods include various X-ray systems, computerized tomography, and magnetic resonance. The introduction of computerized tomography (CT) was a major advance in visualizing almost all parts of the body, particularly useful in diagnosing tumors and other space-occupying lesions. These new techniques lead to accumulation of masses of digital medical images stored in medical image archives.

For satisfying diagnosis, however, it is not sufficient to store and access a patient's CT images with the patient's record-id. Rather, suitable querying mechanisms are needed for a useful employment of the images in medical diagnosis (see Chapter 6). The questions of a surgeon to a medical image archival may be: How does my patient's tumor look compared to similar cases of brain tumors? What is the normal growth rate of a special type of brain tumor? Does the spatial growth of a brain tumor decrease with a certain drug therapy?

The images themselves do not give hints about whether they show a brain tumor or where it is located in the body. Therefore the knowledge of the spatial content of the images and the evolutionary behavior of the spatial content for a medical image (e.g., for a brain tumor) must be used or made available when processing a surgeon's queries. The result of a query should then be a collection of images that have similar spatial characteristics compared to a given image or a sequence of images showing the growth of a brain tumor over a year's time.

Searching image collections can be employed to find a starting point in a "web" of images from which the user may want to start a navigation through images and related information.

After having selected a particular image of interest, navigating through an image collection can take place, e.g., by choosing a particular part of the image that is currently being displayed. This selection can lead to associated data such as a set of related images or some other related textual information. One may also navigate in the (hyper-)textual information and may come back to the image collection via special links/hooks in the text and find an image associated with the respective textual information.

For example, an image of a person comprises various regions having semantic content, e.g., the various subregions that correspond to the eyes, lips, and nose. When viewing a media object, the related information can be investigated for learning, e.g. which person can be seen on the image. Additionally an information *location* associated with a person's image can lead to an associated building and room of the location and then "finally" to the image of the person's office (see for example Chapter 5).

Navigating image collections might also involve navigating three-dimensional (3-D) representations, e.g., of the body's interior. A sequence of CT images can be the basis of a computed 3-D graphics representation of the brain. A surgeon may navigate through this representation of the brain. She/he may select a particular volume of interest, the thalamus, and enter it, viewing it at a higher resolution to see whether there is a growth inside. The surgeon may also select a part of the 3-D representation inside a thalamus that allows him/her to view photographs of patients with similar growth, etc.

This kind of support for image retrieval, navigation, and browsing requires a lot of semantic knowledge which can be represented by means of metadata and which can be used by the retrieval, navigation, and browsing algorithms.

Video. In many domains video clips are archived digitally, e.g., in news agencies. Besides the archiving of the digitized video clips, an important issue is to browse through a collection of videos and select them either entirely or partially. A difference between searching, browsing, and navigating in videos in contrast to images is the temporal aspect. The abstract information that is added to video to support retrieval can change within the video depending on the part of the video. Furthermore, querying against a video database results in a sequence of video clips, each of which is time-dependent.

For example, nowadays we have to watch a provider's news and cannot eliminate those news items we are not interested in. Personalized news (for an example see Chapter 10), cut to special personal interest, will make a news watcher independent of the news and of the time the news is actually on air. According to a user profile, videos are searched, and those parts of the present news items are selected that fit a questioner's need. With semantic knowledge about the structure of news, newly assembled and temporally arranged news items can be composed to form a personalized news extract. The interesting issue is how to define such a user profile and how thousands of news items of a news provider can be attached metadata that in combination with a user profile allow for a satisfying mapping between the two and the successful reassembling of the personalized news.

A similar application scenario can be derived from the demand of a critic who only wants to watch those parts of a film that suffice to write a quick review of the film or the special demand of a sport enthusiast who has only time to see a sequence of all field goals of a certain football game of a certain team in order to be able to talk about the game the next day or the post-game analysis of football teams to support planning of strategies and analyze performance (for an example see Chapter 9).

Audio and speech. Radio stations collect many if not all of their important and informative programs such as radio news in archives. Often it is of interest to reuse or to refer to parts of such programs in other radio broadcasts. However, to efficiently retrieve parts of radio programs it is necessary to have the right metadata generated from and associated with the audio recordings (see for example Chapter 8). This asks for retrieval of audio that contains spoken text. One important issue here is the detection of text in the audio, i.e., speech recognition. Here problems that arise in speech recognition because of different pronunciation of words by different speakers and language peculiarities must be overcome. Another important issue is the mapping between a high-level vague query, like a textual or a query containing spoken text, to the metadata attached with the audio recordings. This calls for an organization of the metadata to support efficient query evaluation and for a query evaluation model that determines those recordings in an archive that are relevant to a user's query.

Structured document management. As the publishing paradigm is shifting from popular desktop publishing to database-driven publishing, processing of structured documents becomes more and more important. Interesting issues are the description of document structure and layout, structure and content-oriented retrieval of components of documents, full-text retrieval, presentation of document content on various output channels like print media, CD-ROMs, WWW, etc. Particular document information models like SGML (Standard Generalized Markup Language) and HyTime (Hypermedia- /Time-Based Structuring Language) introduce a lot of descriptive information, i.e., metadata, on the structure and content of documents (see for example Chapter 2). Such metadata can be used during processing for improving system performance, e.g., database configuration, and document type-specific query optimization, or for providing new functionality, e.g., higher expressiveness of query statements, integrating information retrieval techniques with database functionality, and providing query templates based on document structure or layout. Metadata can be used at various system layers, e.g., at the specification layer by means of document type definitions, for the internal representation of documents and its components including storage models and indexing, for maintaining histories of processing a document, to support declarative access and query processing, etc.

Metadata about structure can be used by the author of a news article to retrieve interesting parts of documents in a huge document archive. For a well-targeted query the document structure available via metadata can be exploited. Not only can all the documents be retrieved by the author that contain the name "Helmut Kohl" but also all documents that contain the name in their heading as this is a known structural element in the documents. Efficient retrieval is achieved by exploiting document structure as the metadata can be used for indexing, and that is essential for short query response time. A typesetter of a newspaper's title page can make use of the metadata to properly lay out the article, that is, to process the document like "Place the *title* in 18pt Helvetica at the top of the page, align the first two *paragraphs* beneath the *headline*, and let the remaining *paragraphs* follow on the next page."

Geographic and environmental information systems. Geographic and environmental information systems are used by various parties who have very special information needs. Such systems have to provide an integrated view on individual geographic and environmental data sets. Obviously, one key problem is the provision of descriptive information on the content provided to the end users and for the information system itself in order to facilitate transparent integrated access to different information sources. The problems faced in this application domain are related to some extent to the integration of heterogeneous databases (see for example Chapter 4). Approaches taken in this field deal with a significant amount of metadata for global query decomposition, global transaction management, schema integration, and management of federated information systems. Other important issues addressed are exercise of control over the degree of uncertainty and accuracy of the data. An important milestone achieved in this application domain is the availability of national and international standards for metadata frameworks (see for example Chapter 3).

Digital libraries. Digital libraries offer a wide range of services and collections of digital documents and constitute a challenging application area for the development and implementation of metadata frameworks. All digital library projects currently under development have to solve metadata issues. Most of the approaches have oriented their metadata framework toward the description of collections of digital material ranging from full text to spatially referenced data sets to multimedia material like video and audio. This allows development of a semantically rich library catalog which in turn provides for the development of rich functions for searching, retrieving, evaluating, and obtaining information. For example, the approach taken in the Stanford Digital Library project focuses on the establishment of an infrastructure for various interoperable services. Metadata therefore is used to describe services and to provide a general interoperability framework. The Alexandria Digital Library project follows the traditional library paradigm, employing many of the well-known traditional forms of metadata like thesauri and subject headings. Metadata turns out to be one of the most critical and essential ingredient for communicating information in a well-performing digital library (see Chapter 12).

Mixing various media to support information access. Access to multimedia information most often is single-media-oriented, i.e., the media type of a query is the same as of the data, or the retrieved information is of a single media type. Mixed-media access is an approach which allows for using a variety of media types in queries independent of the media type of the data (see for example Chapter 11). In other words, a single query can be used to retrieve information from data which consists of different media, or queries using different media types can be used to more precisely describe the information needs. Using word spotting techniques one can build up a time index of keywords on recorded speech (audio) or a location index of keywords on images of text. Using speaker segmentation techniques one can partition audio segments corresponding to different speakers. If additional information is available on speakers, one may be able to also identify speakers. Semantically rich information available in speech but not in text is prosodic information occurring in emphatic speech, i.e., changes in pitch, amplitude, and timing, which allows recognition of segments of speech intended to be important, at least from the speakers viewpoint. Having available these kinds of metadata one may be able to pose semantically rich queries based on a combination of the different aspects and media.

1.3   The Media Processing Perspective

Another interesting viewpoint on metadata is the kind of media processing taking place in the application frameworks. In principle, we can distinguish three types of media processing:

Generation of metadata. This kind of processing serves the purpose of generating metadata on a particular medium. It can be structured along the following lines.

- Analysis of raw material

  In many cases media objects are analyzed and metadata is generated according to the focus of the analysis. This is done very often off-line, i.e., after having recorded and stored the medium and prior to any processing which makes use of the metadata. The reason for this is the tremendous costs involved in analyzing media. Examples of this type of processing are the recognition of document structure in semi- or non-structured text, the extraction of feature values from images, segmentation of audio by speakers, recognition of scene cuts in videos, or content-based recognition of advertisement in video.

- Semi-automatic augmentation

  In contrast to the analysis of raw material, semi-automatic augmentation of media results in additional meta-information which cannot be derived from the raw material as such. It often requires comprehensive background knowledge of the context for providing additional information. Examples are the diagnostic findings of a doctor related to a computer tomography image, which are based on the doctor's experience and state of the art in medicine.

- Processing with implicit metadata generation

  The previous two types of processing are techniques for explicitly generating metadata. Alternatively, metadata can be generated implicitly when creating the raw media data. For example, a digital camera can implicitly deliver time and date for pictures or videos taken. Similarly, an SGML editor generates metadata according to the document type definition when the document is edited. In addition, processing can be guided by a *metadata creation scheme* which determines in detail, the type and organization of metadata and relationships between individual metadata items. For example, editing structured documents by using SGML editors automatically leads to metadata according to the SGML Document Type Definition (DTD) defined and used for the document. The DTD represents the *metadata creation scheme*. A similar example is the usage of specific WWW page editors which generate a lot of additional information on, for example, the page and its author according to HTML and some convention used by search engines. With the evolving new standard markup language of the Web, XML, the tendency for processing structured documents and, as a consequence, the implicit generation of metadata begins to take shape throughout the World Wide Web.

In specific application areas, many tools are already available to support generation of metadata. For example, in the field of geographic information systems a list of tools is given in [5].

Usage of metadata. By attaching metadata to media, various processing steps can conveniently use the metadata. Here, the most prominent types of processing are querying, retrieval, navigation, and browsing. These types of processing make use of metadata mostly in terms of indexing. That is, metadata is used to effectively discriminate data in order to provide for efficient processing. Furthermore, metadata can be used to allow for additional types of queries which cannot be answered by processing raw material only. This is usually the case when metadata stems from manual augmentation of media such as in the example of a doctor's diagnosis.

Maintenance of metadata. Another type of media processing affects existing, already generated and derived metadata. This usually requires updating metadata, which in turn requires explicit knowledge about the structure and semantics of metadata.

Metadata has to be updated according to changes in raw data. This may cause a new full cycle of metadata generation in order to substitute the old existing metadata on a medium. For example, if images stored in an image archive are manipulated, the feature values extracted when an image was registered in the archive may have to be recomputed. An interesting question is whether it is possible to update metadata incrementally, e.g., by performing only incremental analysis related to the modified items. For example, if the color of images changes, only color-related feature values have to be updated, but other types of analysis like the spatial placement of objects are not needed. However, incremental adding of metadata may be a problem as is known from indexing in information retrieval.

Furthermore, metadata can be updated directly without any modification of the raw material. A simple example is the correction of metadata according to the changes of semantic knowledge used for constructing the metadata, e.g., new medical findings which lead to a revision of the previous diagnosis.

1.4   The Metadata Characteristics Perspective

1.4.1   Types of Metadata

Metadata itself can be characterized and classified according to its type. In the application scenarios outlined above we can identify kinds of metadata along three dimensions: media type-specific, media processing-specific, and content-specific metadata.

Media type-specific metadata. Media types induce specific kinds of metadata, e.g., features like texture of images, frequencies in audio, font size of text, motion in video. Continuous media like audio and video have associated with them a whole lot of metadata attributes which relate to the notion of time, which static media like images and text do not have. The more specific a media type, the more specific the associated metadata attributes. For example, for speech – in comparison to audio – one can identify additional metadata items, like specific keywords present in spoken text, and speaker characteristics, like female or male, child or adult (see for example Chapter 11). In the case of video, we can have metadata that describes implementation specific properties like play-out rate, cinematographic properties like camera motion and lighting, or a time-based semantic space derived from the content of the video (see for example Chapter 10). It can be observed that media-specific metadata properties can be further differentiated along the dimensions of media processing and media content.

Media processing-specific metadata. Metadata can describe functions designed to process specific media. For example, search and retrieval functionality provided in a digital library involves metadata which relates to media objects, their contents and types, but additional metadata is intended to assist search and retrieval functions (see Chapter 12). Functions to transfer media objects over networks may also have attached metadata directing the way of transferring the media. Looking at videos (including audio) which communicate, e.g., television news, we can identify story styles, determining how media material is composed overall and how a mediator (an anchor person or reporter) interacts with the visual and aural constituents of the news message. Having such a story style explicitly identified and having it available as metadata allows further interpretation and processing of the news, e.g., a personalized filtering, diversification, and delivery of information (see Chapter 10). Another important type of media processing-specific metadata is information related to media processing performance which can be used to measure and consequently achieve desirable system performance. Similarly, meta-information about the interoperability of system components is essential to deliver the proper application functionality (see Chapter 4). In general, metadata attached to media processing functionality may be dependent on or independent of the content and type of media.

Content-specific metadata. Media objects may have associated metadata which is solely derived from the content represented by the media objects. Such information is independent of media type and media processing. It reflects the semantics of the media object in some given context. Different media objects may have identical content-specific metadata. For example, an animation of the launch of a rocket, a video and a photography on the launch of a space shuttle, and a document describing the functionality of rocket engines may share the same content-specific metadata related to the functionality of rocket engines. From this example one can also observe that the organization of metadata may be very critical. In the case of the video in the previous example, the metadata related to the functionality of rocket engines may be just a small piece of metadata associated with that video. In the case of the document this metadata could be the only one associated with the document. Obviously, granularity of metadata units and their organization in terms of, e.g., hierarchies, is an interesting issue.

Besides the characterization of metadata along the three dimensions, one can identify very specific, well-known types of metadata.

Annotations. Media objects may be annotated, which, in principle, constitutes metadata to be used further on. Annotations to a media object may be of any kind of media, although most traditional applications use only textual annotations. Annotations may relate to the media contents, the media format, processing type, temporal and spatial space associated with media objects, etc. Most often, annotations are generated as the result of an intellectual task, but they may also be generated automatically by a media analysis step.

Set of keywords. Keywords are a traditional way of providing metadata on a subject and are well known in the context of indexing. The issue with keywords is the existence of a common metric or ontology accepted by the various parties involved in the media processing. It is mandatory to apply this metric or ontology both to the identification and assignment of keywords and to the usage of keywords for processing, e.g., searching and retrieval.

Metadata on history, age, and quality of data. Metadata can include information about the history, age, and quality of media objects and/or associated metadata. The distinction between age and quality of media objects and age, history, and quality of associated metadata, i.e., a case of having metadata on metadata, is an interesting issue, but is not further discussed here.

In principle, metadata can be original information which actually existed before any media processing toward the generation of any further metadata takes place – one could also call it defacto metadata – or it can be derived through some processing. This distinction may have some influence on the further processing, e.g., some device like X-ray equipment delivers a media object in some specific format which cannot be influenced by anybody. Information about this format constitutes original metadata. If the media object is converted into some other format like DICOM or JPEG due to any subsequent processing, information about the new representation constitutes derived metadata. Medical doctors may be very sensitive to the qualitative differences of the X-ray images and may want to have access to the processing history, including the history of metadata.

We have now taken a closer look on the different types of metadata we have identified in the application scenarios. In the following we will sketch a classification of metadata.

1.4.2   Metadata Classification

Classifying metadata to get suitable abstractions aids in exploiting metadata. One of the interesting classifications appears in [2]. Another classification used in the InfoQuilt project [10] appears in [7] and is adapted by some of the chapters in this book. A summary of this classification as adapted from [8] is presented next.

Content-independent metadata. This type of metadata captures information that does not depend on the content of the document with which it is associated. Examples of this type of metadata are *location, modification-date* of a document and *type-of-sensor* used to record a photographic image. There is no information content captured by these metadata, but these might still be useful for retrieval of documents from their actual physical locations and for checking whether the information is current or not.

Content-dependent metadata. This type of metadata depends on the content of the document it is associated with. Examples of content dependent metadata are *size* of a document, *max-colors, number-of-rows*, and *number-of-columns* of an image. Content-dependent metadata can be further sub-divided as follows:

> **Direct content-based metadata.** This type of metadata is based directly on the contents of a document. A popular example of this is full-text indices based on the text of the documents. *Inverted tree* and *document vectors* are examples of this type of metadata.

> **Content-descriptive metadata.** This type of metadata describes the contents of a document without direct utilization of those contents. This type of metadata often involves use of knowledge or human perception/cognition. An example is denoting the fragrance of an image containing a flower. Another example of this type of metadata is textual annotations describing the contents of an image. This type of metadata comes in two flavors:

>> **Domain-independent metadata.** These metadata capture information present in the document independent of the application or subject domain of the information. Examples of these are the *C/C++ parse trees* and *HTML/SGML document type definitions*.

>> **Domain-specific metadata.** Metadata of this type is described in a manner specific to the application or subject domain of information. Issues of vocabulary become very important in this case as the terms have to be chosen in a domain-specific manner. Examples of such metadata are *relief, land-cover* from the GIS domain and *area, population* from the Census domain. In the case of structured data, the database schema is an example of such metadata. Another interesting example is *domain-specific*

ontologies, terms from which may be used as vocabulary to construct metadata specific to that domain.

1.5   The World of Metadata Standards

Standards are an important means to achieve common representation schemes
and interoperability of systems, and hence can play a pivotal role in exploiting
metadata. There are very many activities going on this area including

- the development of a metadata taxonomy to help structure the discourse
  on metadata,

- the development of ontologies related to metadata attributes, and description of data elements and domains in terms of naming, typing, classification, and semantics,

- the definition of a meta-model registry structure to achieve mappings
  among different meta-models, and

- the definition of generic functionality for tools for the development and
  operation of metadata bases.

1.5.1   Metadata Standards in the Context of Multimedia Systems

Some prominent standards related to metadata management and relevant in
the context of multimedia systems are summarized next.

- The ISO 11179 standard [9] addresses the specification and standardization
  of registration of data elements.

- The Metadata Coalition Interchange Standard is a joint effort of industry
  vendors and users addressing a variety of problems and issues regarding
  the exchange, sharing, and management of metadata. This joint effort
  resulted in the Metadata Interchange Specification V 1.1 [11].

- The Meta Content Format (MCF) [14] addresses the abstraction, standardization and representation of the structures used for organizing information. In order to adequately describe information organization structures,

MCF allows objects representing entities such as people, organizations and projects to be first class citizens on the same level as files, folders and Web pages. MCF is a general purpose structure description language. In addition to the syntax and semantics, it also provides a standard vocabulary for describing common objects such as people, organizations, meetings, etc. MCF is a lingua-franca schema for integrating different information sources. It does not use or provide a standard schema. Rather it provides a framework for determining which data from one schema can be automatically and dynamically converted into data in a very different schema.

- Dublin Core Metadata Element Set [3] is a consensus which represents a simple resource description record that has the potential to provide a foundation for electronic bibliographic description in the context of on-line libraries that may improve structured access to information on the Internet and promote interoperability among disparate description models.

- Standards developed by the U.S. Federal Geographic Data Committee (FGDC), e.g., Content Standards for Digital Geospatial Metadata [4] which provides a common set of terminology and definitions for the documentation of geospatial data. The standard establishes names of data elements and groups of data elements to be used for these purposes, the definitions of these data elements and groups, and information about the values that are to be provided for the data elements.

- HL7 is a standard developed by the Health Level-7 group [15] (an ANSI accredited standards developer) whose members are hospitals, professional societies, health care industry including almost all of the major health care systems vendors, and individuals worldwide. HL7 includes specifications for medical records and information management.

- UDK, a proposal for a European Environmental Catalogue, constitutes a meta-information system and navigation tool set for collections of environmental data [12, 13]. It is already in place in Austria and Germany and under evaluation in many other European countries.

- Product Data Exchange using STEP (PDES) is an American National Standard (ANS), developed by the U.S. PRO IGES/PDES Organization (IPO), which is accredited by the American National Standards Institute (ANSI). PDES [1] is an adoption of the International Standard for the Exchange of Product Model Data (STEP). STEP has been approved by more than 20 countries worldwide, including all major U.S. trading partners.

1.5.2   Related Standardization Bodies

Major standardization activities are driven by various groups including national and international standardization authorities and a coalition of industry and user groups. Some interesting bodies relevant in this context are

- The NASA/Science Office of Standards and Technology [16] aims at the evolution and adoption of data systems standards for advancing the communication of scientific knowledge about Earth, the solar system, and our universe. It participates in and coordinates standardization activities related to data archiving and exchange.

- The Metadata Coalition [17] is a joint effort of industry vendors and users, which came up with the Metadata Metadata Interchange Specification V 1.1.

- Global Change Data and Information System (GCDIS) [18], while not a primary standardization body, constitutes a collection of distributed information systems operated by United States Federal Government agencies involved in global change research. GCDIS is designed to provide comprehensive global change related data and information to scientists and researchers, policy makers, educators, industry, and the public at large. GCDIS data and information span the world and are broadly multidisciplinary. GCDIS coordinates the efforts of the participating agencies to develop the GCDIS and, hence, deals to a significant extend with metadata issues.

- X3L8 is a technical committee of Accredited Standards Committee X3 [19], which is accredited by ANSI. X3L8 establishes standards for specifying and standardizing data. The focus of the work is on establishing ways to describe data to facilitate human use and to enable intelligent computer processing. Data is described through use of metadata (data about data). Metadata issues covered by the committee include naming, identification, definitions, classification, and registration. The standards developed by the committee are used in many areas, such as Electronic Data Interchange (EDI), data administration, information management, application development for information systems, and data access/interchange via the World Wide Web (WWW) and National Information Infrastructure (NII). X3L8 is involved in the development of ISO/IEC 11179 and of the X3L8 Metamodel for the Management of Sharable Data.

- X3T2 is a technical committee of Accredited Standards Committee X3 [19], accredited by ANSI. It focuses on Data Interchange and is concerned generally with defining the data that is interchanged between a variety of entities ranging from subroutines and functions to remote applications. Obviously, there are many metadata issues involved in this.

1.5.3 Sample Standardization Projects

A partial list of interesting big projects which apply standards for the handling of metadata include

- the ESA Prototype International Directory (ESA-PID) [20], the European Space Agency's Prototype International Directory, which is an information source for rapid and efficient identification, location and overview descriptions of data sets of interest to the earth and space science research community including collections of earth observation images,

- the Environmental Data Registry (EDR) [21] of the U.S. Environmental Protection Agency (EPA), which provides information about data elements used in selected EPA systems,

- the Basic Semantic Repository (BSR) [22], a joint ISO/UN-ECE initiative, which tries to apply some kind of stable semantic reference point as a standard means of naming data elements,

- the Data Documentation Initiative (DDI) [23], developing a Document Type Definition (DTD) for an international codebook standard using the Standard Generalized Markup Language SGML, and

- the Government Information Locator (GILS) [24] identifying and describing information resources throughout the U.S. Federal Government, and providing assistance in obtaining the information.

1.6   Outline of the Book

This book consists of twelve chapters. Following this introduction we first look at the domain of document management, then at the state of the art in metadata handling in geographic and environmental applications, followed by a collection of chapters addressing metadata issues in the context of various media types, and finally we address the role and potential of metadata in the context of digital libraries.

Employment of database technology to administer documents of arbitrary type leads to a new, database-oriented view of publishing in which meta information occurs in a variety of ways. The chapter *Metadata Handling in HyperStorM* by K. Böhm focuses on the organization of metadata, the role of standards, and the storage and the usage of metadata for the processing of multimedia documents. It provides a classification of metadata as it appears in the context of multimedia documents. The chapter describes information models of standards for document interoperability, i.e., SGML/HyTime and DFR, with respect to metadata issues. It also discusses the usage of metadata for document storage, that is, how information models can be reflected within the database system. It shows how the nature of multimedia documents leads to new ways of exploiting metadata.

In the chapter *Metadata in Geographic and Environmental Data Management*, O. Günther and A. Voisard give an overview of metadata schemes and implementations in geographic and environmental information systems. Case studies include the Content Standards for Digital Geospatial Metadata of the U.S. Federal Geographic Data Committee (FGDC) and the Catalogue of Data Sources (CDS) of the European Environmental Agency. Furthermore, they discuss the UDK (Environmental Data Catalogue) project, an international software engineering effort to facilitate access to environmental data from the government and other sources, in greater detail. The chapter presents the UDK data model, its implementation as a distributed information system, and its upcoming integration into the World Wide Web.

Metadata Management for Geographic Information Discovery and Exchange by P. Drew and J. Ying looks at the role of metadata in the context of gluing together and making integrated use of existing geographic information systems illustrated by the geographic information exchange facility under construction in Hong Kong. The chapter focuses on the operational management needed to capture and transfer metadata across distributed geographic information systems. It shows how the transformation infrastructure works for the purpose of discovery and retrieval of information in different systems.

Using Metadata for the Intelligent Browsing of Structured Media Objects, by W. Grosky, F. Fotouhi, and Z. Jiang, discusses the role of metadata used in techniques for browsing and querying large image databases in an easy and efficient way. It is shown how images can be combined with textual information, establishing a kind of content-based hypermedia space, and how one can impose a virtual world metaphor on the information, which help the user to navigate through the image collection. Associative retrieval also includes navigation between a 3-D graphics representation of a virtual world and particular individual images as well as sets of images.

In *Content-Based Image Retrieval Using Metadata and Relaxation Techniques* by W. W. Chu, C.-C. Hsu, I. T. Ieong, and R. K. Taira, an approach for content-based image retrieval is proposed. The approach supports semantic query operations like *nearby* or *far away*, similarity operators, and the usage of conceptual terms. Image content is reflected by three metadata layers: at the pixel level, at the semantic level including spatial, temporal, and shape features, and at the knowledge layer. These layers provide for an integration of image representation and image content and allow for querying images by features and content.

In *A Metadatabase System for Semantic Image Search by a Mathematical Model of Meaning*, Y. Kiyoki, T. Kitagawa, and T. Hayama discuss use of metadata to provide associative search of images for a set of user-given keywords. The chapter presents a new method based on metadata for selecting images. The metadata used do not depend on the characteristics of the media, but use keywords that are associated with images based on user's impression. The approach uses various existing ontologies.

An information retrieval system that allows a simultaneous search for speech documents and text documents is presented in *Metadata for Content-based Retrieval of Speech Recordings* by M. Wechsler and P. Schäuble. It presents arguments for the use of *best-match retrieval* as opposed to *exact-match retrieval* and an approach which is based on the automatic generation of metadata to support such retrieval. It also discusses metadata organization by means of a new controlled indexing vocabulary, and its use that provides for the same retrieval effectiveness as a conventional Boolean retrieval system.

The chapter by R. Jain and A. Hampapur, *Video Data Management Systems: Metadata and Architecture*, characterizes video metadata and its usage for content based processing. Through an analysis of applications and the nature of queries, it leads to a rather comprehensive set of features (metadata items) that are included in their data model for representing video. The chapter discusses challenges of integrating video into databases and the resulting requirements for a video data model. A specific data model for describing video data and an architecture for a video data management system is presented.

Information personalization is increasingly viewed as an essential component of any front-end to a large information space. Personalization can achieve both customization of the presentation of information as well as tailoring of the content itself. In the chapter *The Use of Metadata for the Rendering of Personalized Video Delivery*, W. Klippgen, T. D. C. Little, G. Ahanger, and D. Venkatesh investigate techniques for personalizing information delivery based on metadata associated with diverse information units including video. They begin with a survey of approaches to information personalization and the requirements for this task. Subsequently, they present a characterization of the use of metadata to facilitate video information personalization.

The chapter by F. Chen, M. Hearst, D. Kimber, J. Kupiec, J. Pedersen, and L. Wilcox titled *Metadata for Mixed-Media Access* discusses a new information access paradigm which allows formulating queries in different media types than the media type of the data queried. The media considered in the chapter are speech, images of text, and full-length text. It illustrates how the combination of different media types can be used for accessing information and how metadata is automatically generated and used for supporting data access.

The last chapter, *A Framework for Meta-Information in Digital Libraries* by K. Beard and T. R. Smith, discusses the challenges of developing meta-information for digital libraries and outlines the contents of meta-information needed to support the basic search, retrieval, evaluation, and transfer functions in a digital library. The authors develop a framework for modeling meta-information in a digital library catalog. The framework provides a basis for the rational design of meta-information and for the analysis and resolution of catalog intraoperability and interoperability issues. The Alexandria Digital Library (ADL) provides specific examples of this framework.

This book represents culmination of our quest, which started with the special issue of SIGMOD record [6], in understanding the similarities and the differences in effective management of different digital media, with emphasis on the role metadata plays in achieving this objective. We hope that the effort of the distinguished authors of the following chapters leads us to good progress in our journey toward infocosm, a society in which people will have information anywhere, any time, and in many forms, for effective decision making, better learning, and more fun.

References

[1] ANS U.S. PRO/IPO. Product Data Exchange using STEP (PDES): Initial Release (Parts 1, 11, 21, 31, 41,42, 43, 44, 46, 101, 201 and 203). ANS U.S. PRO/IPO-200-1994, 1994. URL http://uspro.scra.org/catalog/ANS.html).

[2] K. Böhm and T. Rakow. Metadata for Multimedia Documents. In [6].

[3] Dublin Core Metadata Element Set: Reference Description. OCLC Online Computer Library Center, Inc., Office of Research and Special Projects, Dublin, Ohio, USA, January 1997. URL http://www.oclc.org:5046/research/dublin_core/.

[4] FGDC. *Content Standard for Digital Geospatial Metadata.* U.S. Government, Federal Geographic Data Committee, Washington, D. C., April 1997. URL ftp://fgdc.er.usgs.gov, URL http://www.fgdc.gov/Metadata/metahome.html.

[5] FGDC, Federal Geographic Data Committee. *July 1997 Survey of FGDC Metadata Tools*, FGDC, USA, July 1997. URL http://www.fgdc.gov/Metadata/toollist/metatools797.html.

[6] W. Klas and A. Sheth (eds.). Metadata for Digital Media. Special issue of SIGMOD Record, 23 (4), ACM Press, December 1994.

[7] V. Kashyap, K. Shah, and A. Sheth. Metadata for building the MultiMedia Patch Quilt. In S. Jajodia and V.S. Subrahmanian (eds.). *Multimedia Database Systems: Issues and Research Directions.* Springer-Verlag, 1995.

[8] V. Kashyap and A. Sheth. Semantic Heterogeneity in Global Information Systems: the Role of Metadata, Context and Ontologies. In M. Papazoglou and G. Schlageter (eds.). *Cooperative Information Systems: Current Trends and Directions.* Springer-Verlag, 1997, pp. 139–178.

[9] ISO/IEC. Information technology. *Specification and standardization of data elements – Part 6: Registration of data elements.* ISO/IEC 11179-6, 1997.

[10] InfoQuilt. Information Brokering for Globally Distributed Heterogenous Digital Media. Large Scale Distributed Information Systems Lab, Department of Computer Science, University of Georgia. URL http://lsdis.cs.uga.edu/infoquilt/.

[11] Metadata Coalition ([17]). Metadata Interchange Specification. Version 1.1, August 1997. URL http://www.he.net/ metadata.

[12] T. Schütz and R. Böhm. Die Datenstrukturierung des Metainformationssystems Umwelt-Datenkatalog, In H. Kremers (ed.). *Umweltdatenbanken.* Metropolis, Marburg, 1994.

[13] T. Schütz and H. Lessing. Metainformation von Umwelt-Datenobjekten - zum Datenmodell des Umwelt-Datenkataloges Niedersachsens. In A. Jaeschke et al. (eds.). *Informatik für den Umweltschutz 7. Symposium Ulm.* Springer-Verlag, Berlin Heidelberg, 1993.

[14] Meta-Content Format. URL http://mcf.research.apple.com/wp.html.

[15] Health Level-7 (HL7). ANSI accredited standards developer. URL http://www.mcis.duke.edu/standards/HL7/hl7.htm.

[16] NASA/Science Office of Standards and Technology (NOST). National Space Science Data Center (NSSDC), Goddard Space Flight Center (GSFC), Greenbelt, MD. URL http://www.gsfc.nasa.gov/nost/.

[17] Metadata Coalition. Industry Initiative for Metadata Interchange. URL http://www.he.net/ metadata/.

[18] Global Change Data and Information System (GCDIS) Group. Federal Committee on Environment and Natural Resources (CENR), Subcommittee on Global Change Research (SGCR), Subgroup of the Data Management Working Group (DMWG). URL http://www.gcdis.usgcrp.gov/.

[19] National Committee for Information Technology Standards. URL http://www.x3.org/.

[20] Prototype International Directory. European Space Agency (ESA).

[21] Environmental Data Registry (EDR). U.S. Environmental Protection Agency (EPA), Washington. URL http://www.epa.gov/edr/.

[22] The Basic Semantic Repository. URL http://www.cs.mu.oz.au/research/icaris/bsr.html.

[23] The Data Documentation Initiative. URL http://www.icpsr.umich.edu/DDI/.

[24] Government Information Locator Service (GILS). U.S. Federal Government. URL http://www.usgs.gov/gils/index.html.

Chapter

2

Metadata Handling in HyperStorM

Klemens Böhm

GMD-IPSI
Integrated Publication and Information Systems Institute
Dolivostraße 15, 64293 Darmstadt, Germany
Klemens.Boehm@gmd.de

Abstract

With a generic framework to administer structured documents of arbitrary type, metainformation occurs in a variety of ways. On the one hand, structured documents already contain metainformation before their insertion into the storage system. On the other hand, it is advantageous to furnish the storage system with additional information to extend its functionality and to improve its performance. In this chapter, based on a database-oriented view of publishing, we describe the different ways metadata are used in our framework. To this end, it also reviews how the information models of different standards for document exchange are mapped to the underlying database schema.

2.1 Introduction

By using database technology to administer structured documents, the classical perspective that publishing is essentially a linear process, as depicted in Figure 2-1, is replaced by a non-linear view, as depicted in Figure 2-2. The purpose of the HyperStorM (Hypermedia Document Storage and Modeling) project at GMD-IPSI is to evaluate OODBMS technology as a basis for hypermedia document storage. We investigate in detail how advanced database features can be exploited in this particular application scenario. For instance, this holds true for query-processing mechanisms of the underlying DBMS, in our case the OODBMS VODAK [33], to provide powerful declarative access mechanisms to the document collection. Query processing for documents steps more and more into the foreground. Namely, on the technical level, accessing a document has become trivial, basically due to the proliferation of the WWW and corresponding browsing tools. In other words, by using such technology, when accessing a document, one does not have to explicitly deal with actualities such as physical distribution of the document collection or heterogeneity with regard to documents' media types.

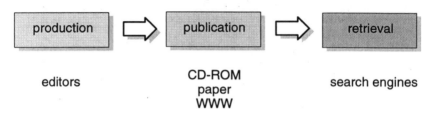

production $\Rightarrow$ publication $\Rightarrow$ retrieval

editors   CD-ROM
                            paper   search engines
                            WWW

Figure 2-1   Classical view of publishing.

When designing a database application for hypermedia document storage, a fundamental question is which information model should be supported. The *information model* or *document model* is the universe of documents' characteristics that are made explicit in the respective framework. For instance, while SGML (Standard Generalized Markup Language), [17, 9] and ODA [18] essentially allow the identification of documents' logical components, the arrangement of documents within a collection can be reflected with DFR (Document Filing and Retrieval) [19]. The HyTime-standard (Hypermedia- /Time-Based Structuring Language) [20, 26], in turn, allows the reflection of document components' semantics. From another perspective, the information model is the entirety of metainformation on documents and the document collection that are made available as well as the way this information is modeled.

The objective of this chapter is as follows: with the prototype for hypermedia document storage that has been developed and implemented as a key component of HyperStorM, we have chosen to support the information models of SGML/HyTime and DFR. In this chapter, we describe the role of metadata in the context of this framework. We will answer the following three questions:

Which metadata can be encountered? Our database application framework has served as a platform for a variety of research prototypes, including the interactive online journal 'MultiMedia Forum' (MMF) [27] and the POLAR-project ('Public Office Longterm Archiving and Retrieval') [5] where access to a collection of town-council submissions has been facilitated over public networks. Experiences from these projects have been incorporated into a classification of

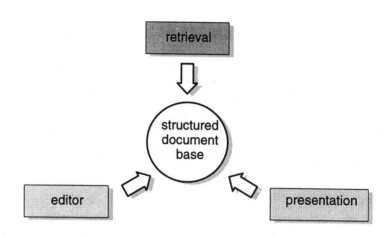

Figure 2-2 Database-oriented view of publishing.

the different kinds of metadata we are aware of. Furthermore, as our framework allows for administering documents of arbitrary type, we have examined the most important standardized (SGML-)document-type definitions. As they are the outcome of a group effort aiming for anticipation of a broad variety of scenarios, they are more likely to include relevant kinds of metadata that might not have occurred in one individual context. The document-type definition itself likewise is metainformation, and in the context of our work, the database is enriched with additional information on element types.

How are metadata stored? The answer to this question is twofold: the first part of the answer is how metadata are reflected in the respective information models. The second part is how the information model is mapped to the database schema, and how the information model impinges on the system architecture.

How are metadata used? The answer to this question is manifold, as most of the features of our framework rely on metadata. The issue will be briefly outlined in the paragraphs to follow.

In more detail, explaining how metadata is used in our framework covers a large part of this chapter. The relevant aspects include the following ones.

- Documents of arbitrary types may be administered, while at the same time explicit support for individual document types is provided [1]. In consequence, the document type has to be inserted into the database. This is one way metainformation is made explicitly available.

- The database-internal representation of document components is configurable to allow for an efficient implementation of certain basic operations on documents and the document collection [6]. The configuration specification reflects knowledge on the anticipated access patterns, e.g., which element types are frequently subject to queries. Such metadata is not included in an (SGML-)document-type definition. Rather, it must be provided explicitly by the system administrator.

- In the context of *information retrieval (IR)*, while trying to capture documents' content, search is going beyond pattern matching on the syntactical level [29]. Rather than implementing IR services as part of the database application, the approach we have pursued [32] is to integrate an existing IR system, namely INQUERY [11]. On the other hand, as opposed to our integrated system, conventional IR systems (IRSs) do not provide explicit support for documents' logical structure, and modifications of the document base in the general case are not feasible. With our approach, metadata is used to facilitate information retrieval on document components and to improve efficiency of the overall system.

- The system provides generic support for declarative and navigational access to the document base via the WWW [7]. Metainformation is exploited in both cases. With regard to navigation, a link anchor in the laid out version of the document incorporates information on the documents referenced. To ease declarative access, views on document types are in use. The view specification is metainformation.

In previous work, some of these aspects of our framework have been described in isolation. In contrast to this chapter, the role of metadata has not been explicitly elaborated. In [22] an overview of approaches where metadata on digital media is used to achieve a specific objective, e.g., to enhance browsing of structured media objects, is given. In this chapter, however, it is taken into account that our database-application framework has a large set of metadata-dependent features. By gradually extending and refining the system over time, new kinds of metadata have been incorporated or have been made explicit.

The remainder of this chapter has the following structure: in the following section, we briefly discuss how metadata can be classified. In Section 2.3, we describe how metadata are reflected with the information models of the different standards for document exchange. Section 2.4 contains a description how the different information models are reflected in the storage system. In Section 2.5, we describe how metadata is used in the context of our work. Section 2.6 concludes the chapter.

2.2 Classifying Metadata for Multimedia Documents

In this section, the different kinds of metadata for hypermedia documents we are aware of are described and classified in several dimensions. We will point out later how the metadata used in the context of our work fits into the different categories. First, metadata on documents is either *metadata on the instance level*, i.e., metadata describing individual documents, or *metadata on the type level*. As an example of the later, with SGML, documents' internal structure must be conformant to a grammar, the so-called *document-type definition* (DTD). The notion of 'document-type definition' is comparable to the notion of 'schema' in the database context. The DTD is metainformation on the type level. Metadata on the instance level can now be classified as follows [8]: metadata for the representation of media types, e.g., the coding of an object of type AUDIO; content-descriptive metadata; metadata for content classification, e.g., the level of expertise required by the reader, such as novice, advanced, expert; metadata to identify document components; metadata on document history, e.g., versioning information and status information during the publishing process.

The distinction between metadata and raw data is not always clean-cut. As an example, consider element types `keywords`, `abstract`, or `title`. Such items can be seen as metainformation as the information is already contained in the document body. From another perspective, such information may not really be redundant, as the phrasing of the title, the selection of keywords, etc., may well reflect the author's intentions, rather than being an objective and precise summary of the respective text. In consequence, an explicit distinction between raw data and metadata in the storage system may be seen as unnatural. With SGML, such an explicit distinction does not have to be made.

2.3 Document Models and Metadata

In this section, the information models that are the basis of our prototype are described with a particular focus on metadata issues. The formalisms we explicitly deal with are the ISO-standards SGML [17, 9], HyTime [20, 26], and DFR [19].

As indicated in the introduction, the answer to the question how metadata is stored with our approach is twofold. First, how metadata are modeled using the respective formalisms such as SGML and DFR remains to be described. This is the topic of this section. Second, it has to be explained how the respective information models are reflected with the storage system. This issue will be dealt with in Section 2.4.

2.3.1   The SGML Information Model

SGML is a formalism allowing the definition of exchange formats for documents. For different document types, different such formats may be defined. Within an SGML-document, logical document components, so-called *elements*, are made explicit by means of so-called *markup*. In Figure 2-3, <frontm> and <department> are examples of *begin markup*, </department> and </frontm> are examples of *end markup*, i.e., <department>Urban Development Department</department> is an element of type department.

```
<TCS>
<frontm>
<subject>Budget 1994 ...  </subject>
<department>Building Supervisory Board</department>
<department>Urban Development Department</department>
</frontm>
<body>
<submission keywords='money traffic'>
The town council ...  to be informed.</submission>
<decision>Renewing of the installations ...</decision>
</body>
</TCS>
```

Figure 2-3   Fragment of an SGML document.

The elements of a document make up a hierarchical structure. With SGML, it is important that element types cannot arbitrarily be introduced into documents, and elements cannot be arranged within the document at liberty. Rather, documents have to be conformant to a so-called *document-type definition (DTD)*, which, in essence, is a grammar. Such a document-type definition can be seen as an exchange format for documents. A fragment of the TCS-document-type definition is contained in Figure 2-4. Lines starting with <!ELEMENT... are *element-type definitions*. The regular expression within the

element-type definition, the so-called *content model*, specifies which elements may occur within an element of the respective type. For example, an element of type frontm may consist of an element of type subject, followed by at least one element of type department, etc. Besides that, elements may be furnished with attributes. Again, attributes and their type must be specified within the document-type definition, e.g., attribute keywords is an attribute for elements of type submission.

```
<!DOCTYPE TCS [
<!--Town Council Submissions-->
<!ELEMENT TCS     (frontm, body)
--Town Council (Darmstadt) Submission-->
<!ELEMENT frontm (subject, (department)+)
--frontmatter of document-->
<!ELEMENT body (submission, decision, justif?)
--body of document-->
<!ELEMENT (subject|department|submission|decision|justif)
          (♯PCDATA)>
<!ATTLIST submission keywords  NMTOKENS>
...]>
```

Figure 2-4   Fragment of an SGML document type definition.

With SGML, metadata on documents can now be modeled as follows:

- There may be elements whose content is metainformation. Such element types will be referred to as *informational element types*. Examples of such elements, given the TCS DTD, would be the list of departments involved that is contained in the FRONTM-element.

- Markup enclosing raw data is metainformation. Such markup will be referred to as *structural or non-structural markup*. Structural elements are semantically meaningful chunks of text, e.g., paragraphs, introductions, chapters, or, in the TCS DTD, submission, decision, etc. Non-structural elements are individual words or short sequences of words within structural ones.

- SGML attributes contain metainformation. In most cases, only structural elements are furnished with attributes.

- The document-type definition is metainformation. It may either be explicitly contained within the document's prologue, or it may be non-ambiguously referenced from within the document. While the first three modeling alternatives can be applied to metadata on the instance level, the document-type definition is metadata on the type level.

While structural and non-structural element types are, in essence, metainformation to identify document components, informational element types are in use to model the other kinds of metadata described in Section 2.2. Finally, with SGML, the distinction between raw data and metadata does not have to be made explicit. This may have to be taken into account when mapping the SGML information model to a database schema.

2.3.2 Metadata in Standardized SGML Document-Type Definitions

In the recent past, SGML has drawn a lot of attention, partly due to the proliferation of the World-Wide Web (WWW) and the respective document-exchange format HTML [15], which is an SGML document-type. SGML has been used to model large documents and document collections in publication environments and in the field of engineering. The advantages of SGML are particularly appealing in these application domains; in particular, consistency within and between documents is ensured. It is notably in those fields that efforts have been undertaken to come up with standardized document types. The outcome of standardization efforts is of interest in this context. Namely, one objective has been to capture all kinds of metainformation that are relevant in the context. By analyzing these document-type definitions, the quality of our classification from Section 2.2 can be assessed. Furthermore, with the standardized DTD, another objective has been to find adequate ways of modeling metadata. As a result of examining these DTDs, we should be able to confirm the list of modeling alternatives for metadata from Subsection 2.3.1. In the following, we look at the outcome of the most relevant standardization efforts in the field.

The objective of the *Text Encoding Initiative (TEI)* [21] is to provide a general interchange format for all kinds of (research) documents. The document-type definitions contain generic structural element types, e.g., `frontm`, body, `back` for horizontal structuring, but also `chapter`, `section`, `subsection` for vertical structuring, as well as generic structural element types such as `head` or `list`. In the TEI-context, the differentiation between *structural elements, crystals,* and *floating elements* is introduced, bearing some ressemblance to our distinction between structural and non-structural element types. TEI-documents have a header containing information such as the title and the author as well as the document's revision history.

Within the context of *Edgar* [28], companies send a description of themselves to the U.S. Security and Exchange Commission (SEC) once a year. Documents must conform to an SGML DTD. This DTD provides structural element types that are quite specific, e.g., `business`, `properties`, `legal proceedings`, etc.

CALS ('Computer Aided Logistics and Support') [25] is an initiative of the U.S. Department of Defense. A DTD to be used in military projects has been defined. The structural element types are similar to the ones of the TEI DTDs. Attributes contain application-specific metainformation, e.g., administrative information, the document's degree of confidentiality, etc.

The *DIN ('German Institute for Standardization')* has set up a document-type definition to record DIN standards. The structural element types introduced there are the canonical ones. Metainformation in the header is specific to this particular application domain, e.g., there is a DIN number, which can be seen as metadata on document history. Furthermore, there is administrative information, i.e., metadata for content classification, and abstracts in foreign languages.

The *AAP ('Association of American Publishers')* has come up with a set of document-type definitions to model documents within their scope. There is a math DTD (not a stand-alone DTD; it has to be included in other DTDs), an article DTD, and a book DTD. None of these DTDs is very complex and they introduce types that do not fit into our classification.

Clearly, the most prominent SGML document type is HTML [15]. Important characteristics of HTML, as compared to SGML, are the following ones:

- HTML markup does not always identify logical document components. Rather, in some cases, the layout is directly specified. Examples of such "element types" are `bf` ('boldface') or `i` ('italics').

- The element types corresponding to logical document components are generic, e.g., `head`, `body`, and do not reflect the characteristics of specific document types.

- The new versions of HTML, e.g., HTML 3.2, have an attribute META by means of which metainformation in the respective documents is made explicit. The values of attribute META primarily serve as input for Internet search engines. The HTML DTD does not define which metainformation has to be reflected, and there are no rules about how to model metainformation. While with SGML metainformation can be structured using specific markup, this is not feasible with HTML.

- HTML documents that can be accessed over the Internet frequently do not conform to the HTML DTD. While such documents can be displayed with Internet browsers, more sophisticated concepts, some of which are described in this chapter, cannot be applied to these documents.

The practical relevance of HTML, on the other hand, results from the fact that the interpretation of HTML markup by Internet browsers and Internet search engines is fixed.

Summing up, from analyzing the standardized SGML document-type definitions, we conclude that our classification of metadata from Section 2.2 is fairly complete. Furthermore, we have not encountered any modeling alternatives for metadata using SGML that have not been mentioned in Subsection 2.3.1.

2.3.3 Reflecting the Semantics of Metadata Using HyTime

With SGML, the structure of documents is made explicit. The semantics of document components, however, cannot be reflected using SGML. It is possible to leave the interpretation of metadata to an application on top of the SGML-storage system. On the other hand, the HyTime standard provides a list of element-type definitions, so-called *architectural forms*, with the following characteristics: the semantics of the architectural forms, i.e., the way the content and attributes have to be interpreted, is specified in the standard. HyTime architectural forms are type definitions to model hypermedia document components, e.g., hyperlinks or event schedules. These type definitions can be used in arbitrary document-type definitions. The advantage envisioned is that, with such DTDs being exchanged between different platforms, elements describing the processing of such documents will be interpreted in a uniform way. However, in more detail, if an architectural form is used in a document-type definition, the corresponding element-type definition does not have to be identical with the architectural form. This includes that architectural forms and derived element types may have different content models – the content of an element must conform to both –, and the range of an attribute of the derived element type may be a subset of the one from the architectural form. Further, derived element types may have another name than the architectural form, and there may be additional, application-specific attributes.

In summary, the architectural-form approach leads to a much higher degree of flexibility, as compared to a standardized DTD for hypermedia documents. On the other hand, design and realization of a database-application framework that allow the administration of HyTime documents of arbitrary type and provide adequate support for the semantics of architectural forms are complex tasks. With regard to the metadata issue, metainformation that can be modeled with HyTime could also be modeled with SGML. Rather, the difference is that for some kinds of metainformation, e.g., how to traverse a hyperlink, a standardized representation has been defined. By allowing for HyTime constructs to be used in arbitrary application scenarios, these constructs have to be fairly generic, and metainformation has to be made explicit that could have been hardcoded with more specific solutions.

2.3.4   Organizing the Document Collection Using DFR

The DFR-standard (Document Filing and Retrieval) [19] provides another information model on documents. It introduces mechanisms to structure the document collection. As opposed to SGML, documents' internal structure is not considered, i.e., documents are seen as atomic. Logical units in the DFR information model are *DFR documents* and so-called *DFR groups*. A *DFR object* is either a DFR document or a DFR group. A document is contained in a group. Each group, except for the root group, is contained in another one. The resulting hierarchical structure can be extended by means of links pointing from one group to another one in another branch of the hierarchy. So far, the information model is comparable to others, e.g., the one of a UNIX filesystem. Furthermore, DFR information services are embedded into a communication system, and the DFR standard provides operations to access a DFR archive, including declarative search mechanisms. With regard to the modeling of metadata, DFR objects have a predefined set of attributes, and they can also be furnished with application-specific ones. Information contained in these attributes is metadata. In the context of the POLAR-project (Public Office Longterm Archiving and Retrieval) [5] several document collections in the field of local public administration have been modeled using DFR. One of the resulting DFR hierarchies is depicted in Figure 2-5. In the project GAMMA, a multimedia calendar of (cultural) events has been developed as a DFR application [31]. Figure 2-6 contains a fragment of the respective DFR hierarchy. The difference to the hierarchy from Figure 2-5 is the following one: in the first example, the different steps between hierarchy levels correspond to different classifications. That is, classification on the top level is according to the different offices in the department; the classification at the bottom right reflects the document status. In contrast, in the CoE example, classification on the different levels is according to the same item of metainformation, namely, the location of the cultural event described in the respective document. The subgroups of a DFR group do not have to be a categorization of this higher group. Rather, overlappings of the subgroups are feasible, and the subgroups do not have to completely overlap the higher group. This becomes obvious with the middle level of the hierarchy in Figure 2-5, but also with the classification of Hesse in Rhein-Main area and Frankfurt in Figure 2-6. Namely, the Rhein-Main area essentially is part of Hesse, a German state, and the city of Frankfurt, which belongs to Hesse, is located in the Rhein-Main area.

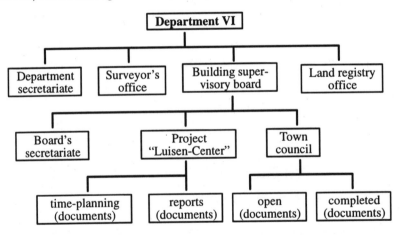

Figure 2-5   Sample DFR hierarchy.

Leaving aside the fact that new groups can still be generated with documents having already been inserted into the archive, metadata origination in the context of DFR consists of two steps:

1. The DFR hierarchy is established, and attribute values are assigned to the DFR groups.

2. The individual documents are inserted into the appropriate group.

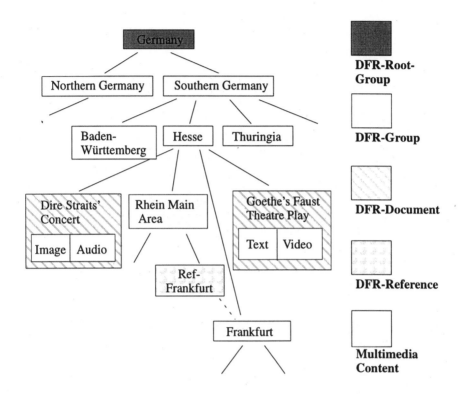

Figure 2-6 Another sample DFR hierarchy.

2.4 Using Metadata for Structured Document Storage

In the previous section, we reviewed the information models of standards for document interoperability. In this section, in order to provide the second part of the answer to the question of how metadata is stored within our framework, we describe how these information models are reflected within our system.

2.4.1 Using Metadata to Configure the Physical Representation of Documents

Our mapping of the DFR information model to the database schema is straightforward. Each DFR object, i.e., each group and each document, corresponds to an individual database object. Coming up with an appropriate representation of the SGML information model, however, is a more complex task. Basically, there seem to be the following alternatives [6, 7]: On the one hand, each document element corresponds to a database object. However, as the costs of certain basic operations, such as inserting a document into the database or retrieving a document from the database, are almost directly proportional to the number of database objects, experience shows that this approach is not always feasible for documents with a complex internal structure. On the other hand, documents' database-internal representation is an unstructured one. That is, a document is contained in a BLOB within the database. To facilitate operations on the internal structure of documents, e.g., navigation, it is feasible to parse the document to generate objects reflecting the structure dynamically [2, 3]. With this approach, granularity is on the document level when documents are modified. With the approach to structured document storage described in [24], there are index entries for each element type. They refer to the exact location within the documents where an element of the respective type starts. The disadvantage, in turn, is that, in the general case, updates are cumbersome, and a lot of index structures have to be modified.

We pursue a hybrid approach [6, 7]: a distinction is made between a logical and a physical level. In this context, the physical level is about which database objects explicitly exist. Different objects on the logical level, i.e., elements, may be contained in one single physical object. To this end, an extended identification mechanism for (logical) objects is introduced: they are not only identified by means of a 'physical' OID, but rather an OID plus an additional identifier, in this case an INTEGER-value denoting the position of the begin markup within the string. We say that "small" elements, being different logical objects that are contained in one database object, are *flat*. Elements of one type are always modeled in the same way, i.e., they are all either flat or not.

The database application allows the storage of (SGML) documents of arbitrary types. No manipulations of the database schema by hand are necessary in this context. This requirement reflects the large number of DTDs that already exist and may be designed in the future. A document-type definition has to be inserted into the database before documents of the respective type can be stored. When inserting a DTD, it is first converted into an SGML document on the syntactic level (outside the database). The resulting document conforms to a so-called *super-DTD*. This document is then inserted into the database, not the original DTD. Deciding, which element types are flat and which ones are not has to be done at this point. This task has to be carried out anew for each document type whose instances shall be administered by the database. The super-DTD instance has attributes whose values specify the configuration. They may be modified before being inserted into the database to configure the database application. For example, the super-DTD contains an element type ELEM. An instance of ELEM corresponds to an element-type definition from the (application-) DTD. The super-DTD contains the following attribute definition.

```
...
<!ELEMENT  ELEM        (ATTRIBUTE*)>
<!ATTLIST  ELEM        ...
                       FLAT    (YES|NOT|...)           NOT
...  >
```

If the value of attribute FLAT is YES, the respective type is flat. By means of the super-DTD instance, other aspects of documents' physical representation can also be configured.

In the context of inserting document-type definitions, the configuration information is metainformation on the type level that is made explicit in the super-DTD-instance. The motivation is to make insertion easier for the user [7]. The document-type definition itself is contained in the database as super-DTD instance.

2.4.2   Using Metadata to Reflect the Operational SGML Semantics

The framework should provide operations reflecting the SGML semantics, e.g., operations to navigate on and to manipulate documents' components. These operations have to be available on the logical level. For example, there is a method getFirst (e: ElementType): logical_OID that returns the first element of the parameter type within the target element. If getFirst with parameter department was sent to the frontm-element in the sample document from Figure 2-3, the database-OID and the start position of element <department>Building Supervisory Board</department> would be returned. With such operations, in order to abstract the fact whether a document component is flat or not, it must be possible to identify the structure of flat elements. A prerequisite to do so is that markup identifying the flat document components is available. This markup is metainformation, as already pointed out. This metainformation is made explicitly available within flat document components so that the document-type definition does not have to be accessed in order to non-ambiguously identify the logical structure of the document.

With SGML, an explicit distinction between raw data and metadata does not have to be made. When storing SGML documents in the database, the default is that no such differentiation is made. The physical representation, however, is configurable so that element and attribute types can be indexed. If a certain piece of metainformation on the instance level is accessed rather frequently, this can be taken into account with the physical representation.

2.4.3   Facilitating Content-Oriented Search on Document Components

It is one aspect of our work to provide information-retrieval functionality on document components [32]. When searching a document collection, there is a difference between search on the syntactic level and search for concepts on the semantic level: one aspect of search on the semantic level is that, even though a term may explicitly occur within a document, the document may not be relevant with regard to the concept expressed. For instance, if the query term is 'multimedia,' and a document contains the sentence 'Multimedia issues are not covered by this article.,' then, ideally, the document should not be retrieved. However, it will be retrieved if the search is on the syntactic level. Given a large document collection, the objective of information-retrieval systems is to quickly identify all documents that are relevant to the respective query, while going beyond pattern matching in the sense implied above. The *belief value of a document with regard to a query* is the probability that the document is relevant with regard to the query. In the IRS, documents are organized in *IRS collections*. To provide information-retrieval functionality for database content, the IRS INQUERY [11] has been loosely coupled with the OODBMS VODAK. Each database query generates an IRS collection. The query result must be a set of database objects. For each of these objects, there has to be a corresponding piece of text. These pieces of text form the IRS collection. A database object with IR functionality inherits several methods from a supertype. For example, there is a method getIRSvalue (IRSquery: STRING): REAL whose result is the IRS value of the target object with regard to the query. The IR functionality is encapsulated by such methods. The application programmer only makes use of methods from the database schema when accessing the IRS. The text of a database object does not have to be physically contained in a property. Rather, to allow for a higher degree of flexibility, the text is retrieved by method get-Text(): STRING. While the method's signature is fixed, its implementation has to be provided by the programmer of the respective database schema.

These coupling mechanisms have now been applied to our database application for structured document storage: an IRS collection contains elements of a specific type. Text is now stored redundantly in the database and the IRS. For example, there may be collections INTRODUCTION, SECTION, etc. With the coupling, it has been taken into account that elements may be represented by logical database objects, which are not necessarily identical with the physical database objects. The initial configuration for which element types of IRS collections are available is specified in the super-DTD instance, in analogy to the specification which element types are flat and which ones are not. Further ways in which metadata are used in order to provide IR functionality are described in Section 2.5.

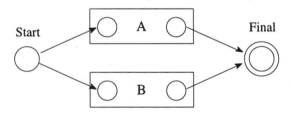

Figure 2-7 Sample automaton.

2.4.4 DTD Representation

As pointed out before, the document-type definition is metainformation. On the one hand, this metainformation is contained in the database in the super-DTD instance, as just described. Furthermore, for each content model, when the DTD is inserted into the database, a corresponding finite automaton is created. The automaton in Figure 2-7 corresponds to the content model (A|B). The automata are generated using an extension of the DREAM parser [13]. They are not persistent. Experience shows that fairly simple content models may already lead to a large number of edges and states. The number of database objects, however, has to be minimized for efficiency reasons. With our implementation, every time the database server is started, the automata have to be generated anew in main memory. In addition to the automata, a table containing the 'included-in'-relation for the respective DTD is maintained: the table is not persistent and may have to be regenerated. We say that *an element type* B *is directly included in an element type* A if B occurs in the content model of A, i.e., if an element of type B may occur in the content of one of type A. In a nutshell, the relation 'included-in' is the transitive closure of the relation 'directly included-in.' One reason why these automata and tables are generated is to ensure consistency in case a document is modified. Furthermore, these structures are the basis for DTD-based query optimization, as described in Section 2.5.

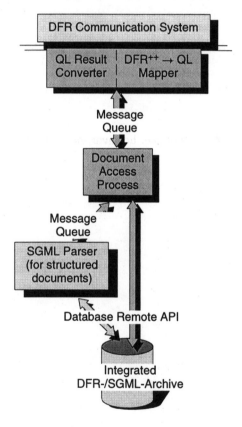

Figure 2-8   Architecture.

2.4.5   System Architecture

We conclude this subsection with some remarks on architectural issues. We look at the integrated SGML-/DFR-database application framework where access is in accordance with the DFR-standard. The overall architecture is depicted in Figure 2-8. Insertion of documents into the database is controlled by an SGML parser. The parser recognizes the logical structure of the document to be inserted. It then invokes a sequence of database operations that generate the database-internal representation. Figure 2-8 shows that the server consists of several components. The rationale behind this is to become more platform-independent. For performance reasons, the parser and the server run on different platforms. The component 'DAP' (Document Access Process) now fulfills the following purpose: certain basic operations, such as create, copy, delete, etc., are part of the DFR standard. create takes as a parameter the group into which the newly created document is to be inserted, copy is provided with information on the target group, etc. At a first level of analysis, one wants to provide these operations as part of the (logical) method interface of the database server. We do not see, however, how this could be accomplished, as create is not a database-internal operation. To this end, an additional layer is inserted in the overall architecture on top of the parser. This interface provides all the DFR operations. Thus, there is an abstraction from the fact of whether an external component, such as the parser, is invoked, or the operation is directly passed on to the database server, as is the case with most of the other DFR operations.

2.5   Using Metadata in HyperStorM

In this section, we give an overview of past or ongoing aspects of the Hyper-StorM project where metadata is used. Even though a large number of issues are related to declarative access, they are presented as individual issues so that they can be presented in a more structured way.

2.5.1   Higher Expressiveness of Query Languages

With metainformation on documents or document components being available, queries can be better focused. This includes the following issues: search in document components only of a certain type or with certain other characteristics, search for documents where document components are arranged in a certain

way, search for document components instead of entire documents only, search
for documents belonging to DFR groups with certain characteristics. In any
case, metadata for document component identification is exploited.

With regard to such query languages, there is the general problem that expressive query languages are also more complex. In consequence, while such query
languages meet the demands of experienced users, beginners or occasional users
may be ready to dispense with some of the expressiveness for ease in expressing
information needs. The conclusion we have drawn is to offer more than one
query mechanism. In more detail, there are the following alternative ways of
expressing information needs [7]:

- The VODAK Query Language [33] being an OQL-like query language [10]
  allows to incorporate methods from the database schema into the queries.
  For example, with the sample query

  ACCESS p0
  FROM e0 IN ElementType, p0 IN e0 → getElements()
  WHERE (e0.ETName =='SUBMISSION')
       AND p0 → hasAttrValue ('KEYWORDS', 'traffic')
  all elements of type SUBMISSION whose attribute KEYWORDS has value traffic is returned.

- A language similar to the PAT-query language [30] is available. For example, the query 'SUBMISSION' selects all elements of type SUBMISSION, the
  query 'ATTR_SELECT (SUBMISSION, KEYWORDS = 'traffic')' is equivalent to
  the above query.

- *Query templates* are document-type-specific query forms that are generated automatically from the DTD and a so-called *query-template specification*. Query-template specifications must be checked for conformance to
  the DTD before they can be used. Query templates can be seen as views
  on the document-type definition. The query in Figure 2-9 is equivalent to
  the above example.

The first mechanism (OQL) is the most expressive one. For evaluation, both
PAT-like query terms and query-template input are mapped to OQL-query
terms with our system. The second mechanism (PAT) allows the retrieval of sets
of elements only, and it lacks certain features such as aggregation and the notion
of position. The set of queries that can be formulated using the query-template
approach is relatively limited [7]. However, the user does not have to know the

Figure 2-9 Sample query form.

modeling, the syntax of a query language, or the respective document-type definition to express his or her information needs. With the second approach, however, the user must be familiar with the query language and the DTD. With the OQL-mechanism, the user must also know the underlying modeling. Thus, using query templates to express information needs is the easiest way. On the other hand, as knowledge of the underlying modeling is required to formulate OQL-queries, this is not a practical approach for most users.

Metainformation allows for more precise queries in the sense indicated above. With regard to query templates, their specification is metainformation on the type level.

2.5.2   Specifying Physical Characteristics of Documents to be Retrieved

In addition to document characteristics mentioned in the previous paragraphs, other document characteristics likewise may be important for declarative access. For instance, consider the case that, in a distributed environment, a client is configured so that it only supports certain codings for datatype VIDEO. In this case, it may be advantageous to specify such restrictions on the data to be retrieved ahead of time, before the data is transported to the client. As another example, the user may only want to see multimedia documents whose size does not exceed a certain threshold value. There are the following differences between these two examples: while the information about the coding has to be made explicit in advance, metadata on physical document characteristics, e.g., their size, can be computed by the storage system, and it is not necessary to model it using, say, SGML or DFR. However, the database schema must provide operations to compute and retrieve such metainformation. For example, the schema contains a method getSize, returning the size of documents and document components. Such methods may now be incorporated in OQL queries. Analogously, the PAT-like query language can be extended in this respect. Just as there are operators such as ATTR_SELECT or CONTENT_SELECT, there may be a new operator SIZE_SELECT, e.g., SIZE_SELECT (INTRO, > 100). The query template likewise may contain entry fields to specify physical characteristics of documents to be retrieved. With SGML and DFR, it is left to the user which metainformation is made explicit and how it is modeled. On the other hand, the physical document characteristics relevant for declarative access have to be anticipated when designing the database application, e.g., by having respective methods as part of the database schema.

2.5.3 Using Metadata for Query Optimization

Metainformation can be used to accelerate declarative access to the document collection. One aspect that is important in the HyperStorM context is to use knowledge of the underlying document-type definition. The approach can be compared to using knowledge of the database schema for query optimization with conventional database systems. While in this general case query optimization mechanisms have to be generated anew for each database schema, our objective is to automatically evaluate the underlying document-type definition.

In order to optimize declarative queries with VODAK [4], the Volcano optimizer generator [14] is used. It allows the generation of rule- and cost-based algebraic query-optimizer modules from a query algebra and corresponding transformation rules. The rules may reflect application-specific knowledge, in particular the semantics of methods. Furthermore, application of rules may be subject to arbitrary conditions. The algebra operators are concrete algorithms associated with cost functions. Within the optimization, an algebra expression is mapped step by step into the optimal equivalent expression according to the given rules.

The following example illustrates which optimizations are feasible. The example is based on this element-type definition.

```
<!ELEMENT AUTHOR  (SURNAME, NAME)>
```

An element of type AUTHOR must contain one of type SURNAME, followed by one of type NAME. Further, suppose that this is the only content model containing element type SURNAME. To continue the example, consider query

SURNAME INCL-IN AUTHOR

All SURNAME-elements contained in an AUTHOR-element are to be selected. Based on the DTD-information, it suffices to select all SURNAME-elements, as each SURNAME-element must be contained in an AUTHOR-element.

We now consider (PAT-)algebra expressions consisting of one operator and say which optimizations are feasible that simplify the structure of the expression.

A INCL-IN B. The query selects all elements of type A that are contained in one of type B. If an element of type A is always contained in one of type B, the expression is equivalent to A. If an element of type A is never contained in one of type B, the expression is equivalent to EMPTY.

A INCLUDS B. The query selects all elements of type A that contain one of type B. If an element of type A always contains one of type B, the expression is equivalent to A. If an element of type A never contains one of type B, the expression is equivalent to EMPTY.

ATTR_SELECT (A, attrName, regex). The query selects all elements of type A where attribute attrName contains the regular expression regex. If elements of type A do not have an attribute of type attrName, the expression is equivalent to EMPTY.

ID-REFER (A, attrName, B), ID-REF-BY (B, attrName, A). The first query selects all elements of type A, referencing one of type B with their attribute attrName. If A does not have an attribute of type attrName of type IDREF or IDREFS, the expression is equivalent to EMPTY.

For expressions containing more than one operator, further optimizations are feasible. Consider the expression

EDITOR INCLUDS (SURNAME BEFORE NAME)

It returns all EDITOR-elements containing a SURNAME-element that, in turn, occurs before a NAME-element. The expression may be simplified to EDITOR IN-CLUDS SURNAME or even EDITORS, even if expression SURNAME BEFORE NAME cannot be simplified according to the DTD.

As pointed out in Section 2.4, given a DTD, there are automata corresponding to the individual content models and tables reflecting the containedIn-
relationship between element types. Operations on these structures are part of
the framework. For example, there is a method isExclusivelyContainedIn (X: ElementType, Y: ElementType): BOOL. It returns TRUE if an instance of the first
element type is always contained in one of the second type. For example,
isExclusivelyContainedIn (SURNAME, AUTHOR) returns TRUE, while isExclusively-
ContainedIn (SURNAME, NAME) does not. Using this method, a rule can be
formulated (using a pseudo-notation) reflecting one of the above cases:

isExclusivelyContainedIn (X, Y) $\Rightarrow$ X INCL-IN Y $\equiv$ X

On the left hand side of the arrow, there is the condition; on the right hand
side there are the equivalent query terms.

With regard to the implementation of method isExclusivelyContainedIn, it is sufficient to access the containedIn-table. In other cases, the automata must be
directly accessed.

Depending on the overall query size and on the size of the document-type
definition, the condition 'isExclusivelyContainedIn (X, Y)' may be checked fairly
often during query optimization. Hence, an efficient implementation of the
method is mandatory. This is one reason why both automata and tables are
cached within main memory.

Measures described so far have the effect that the structure of query terms is
simplified. However, it may also be advantageous to transform queries using
knowledge on the DTD so that their structure is not simplified; in some cases
it may even become more complex. Suppose the sample DTD contains the
element-type definition

    <!ELEMENT AUTHORS AUTHOR+>

Then, for instance, it may be advantageous to replace expression

    SURNAME INCL-IN ((ATTR_SELECT (AUTHOR, ...)))

with expression

    (SURNAME INCL-IN AUTHORS) INCL-IN ATTR_SELECT (AUTHOR, ...)

if there is an index for all SURNAME-elements that are contained in an element
of type AUTHORS, but not for SURNAME-elements contained in an element of
type AUTHOR. It may be advantageous to have additional operations with high

selectivity and low costs. In other words, by means of the additional operator, there is a preselection that justifies the structural extension of the query term. Difficulties with that kind of optimization are the following ones: first, the equivalent expressions have to be enumerated. With a rule-based approach, only one equivalent expression can be generated by means of a transformation rule, rather than a set of expressions. Second, the costs have to be modeled in an adequate way. If there is a preselection, the following selection might be less selective. This interdependency between selections has to be captured in the cost model.

As a summary of this item, we observe that a sophisticated representation of metadata, in this case the document-type definition, may be worthwhile.

2.5.4   Content-Oriented Search on Multimedia Document Components

As explained in Section 2.4, IR functionality has been made available by means of a loose coupling. With the underlying IR system being one for text, the coupling cannot directly be applied to elements with multimedia content. To facilitate information retrieval on multimedia document components to some degree, in literature there has been the suggestion to use adjacent (textual) document elements as a substitute and to do text retrieval on them instead [12, 16]. With a generic approach to structured document storage, i.e., documents of arbitrary type can be administered, the adjacent document components remain to be specified. This specification must be carried out on the type level, as it cannot be done individually for large document collections. It is reasonable to use the super-DTD-instance for this purpose. Adjacency of document components, as described above, is a characteristic of element types themselves, not their physical representation, and this aspect of element types' semantics remains unchanged over time if the document-type definition is not altered.

In a first step, the super-DTD is furnished with an additional attribute DERIVE.

```
<!ATTLIST DERIVE (SELF|SUBSEQ|ALLSIBS) SELF>
```

This attribute specifies how method getText retrieves the text of the target element. SELF is the default value. With this attribute setting, the execution of getText is the usual one, namely, concatenating the leaves of the subtree rooted at the target element. For multimedia document components, the value may be set to SUBSEQ, i.e., the text of the following element is assumed to be the element's textual representation, or to ALLSIBS, i.e., the text of all sibling elements is taken. More sophisticated ways to model adjacency of document components on the type level are conceivable, in particular in order to take into account documents' secondary structure.

Metainformation in this context is used in two ways. First there is the specification which element types shall be administered by the IR system. The adjacency information, e.g., the setting of attribute DERIVE for individual element types, also is metainformation.

2.5.5 Document Rendition and Ease of Navigation

The separation of documents' layout and their logical structure is a main advantage of formalisms such as SGML. Compared to conventional approaches, a high degree of flexibility with regard to the layout of documents is ensured: conversion to a layout format may be context-dependent. With our approach, conversion of documents to an output format takes place within the database. Conversion is specified by a stylesheet that is read from file. Conversion is based on the logical document markup and is driven by the conversion specification, both of which are metainformation. Alternatively, it seems feasible to retrieve SGML documents from the database, and to use any conversion tool that is commercially available to generate the laid out version of the document. The reason why conversion is realized within the database-application framework is to allow for a flexible rendition of hyperlink anchors, as described in the next paragraphs, and an efficient implementation of these mechanisms.

When navigating through the document collection with conventional systems, the following problems may arise [7]: *navigation failure* occurs if the reader is unable to access the document referenced by a hyperlink anchor, either for technical reasons, or because the link is outdated. *Expectations vs. Actual Content* is the effect that the context of the hyperlink anchor brings up certain expectations of the reader regarding the content of the document referenced that, however, are not matched by the actual document. *Lost in Hyperspace* refers to the phenomenon that the reader, while browsing the document collection, may loose orientation. In principle, these problems can be mitigated if the laid out version of a hyperlink anchor bears information on the documents directly and indirectly referenced. With our approach, the stylesheet specifying the conversion may contain a database query. In the laid out version of the document, the query results are displayed together with the hyperlink anchor. This allows information on documents referenced to be made available that, otherwise, the reader could only obtain by downloading the document. Consider the document fragment from Figure 2-10. The value of attribute REFERENC of element ANCHOR is a reference to the sample document from Figure 2-3.

```
In the <ANCHOR REFERENC='redevelopment'>submission from June 7th,
1994,</ANCHOR> it is argued that, due to the backlog of the
residents and the demands of the newcomers, housing space is
strongly needed.  It seems realistic to assume that approx.
600 appartments can be constructed each year in the years to
come.  Further, it is supposed that the majority of these
appartments, approx.  350 appartments...
```

Figure 2-10 Fragment of a document containing a link anchor.

In one particular conversion specification, it may be stated that elements of type DEPARTMENT from the document referenced are displayed together with the corresponding link anchor. The laid out version of the sample document from Figure 2-10 would then look as in Figure 2-11. Metainformation to be displayed may have been explicitly modeled using SGML or DFR. It may also be information computed at runtime, such as physical characteristics of documents or extraction of keywords.

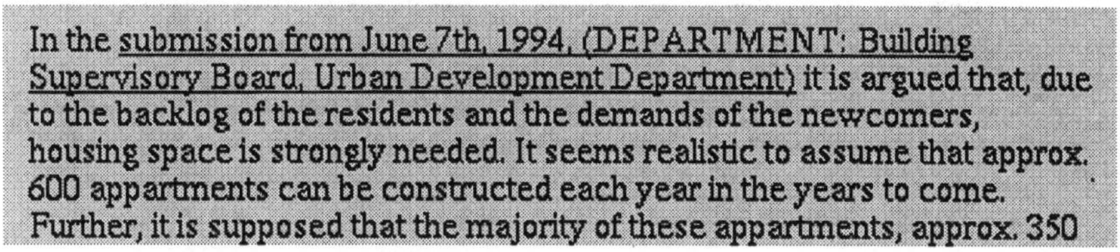

In the submission from June 7th, 1994, (DEPARTMENT: Building Supervisory Board, Urban Development Department) it is argued that, due to the backlog of the residents and the demands of the newcomers, housing space is strongly needed. It seems realistic to assume that approx. 600 appartments can be constructed each year in the years to come. Further, it is supposed that the majority of these appartments, approx. 350

Figure 2-11 Fragment of laid out version of sample document.

With such sophisticated approaches to link anchor rendition, document conversion may become arbitrarily complex and time-consuming. The usage of database technology in this context has the advantage that conversion output may be materialized within the database, and consistency of this materialization is ensured by the DBMS. In other words, conversion has to be carried out anew only when a relevant portion of the database content is modified.

2.6   Conclusions

While our system administers documents of arbitrary type, it provides for advanced functionality, e.g., flexible conversion to a layout format or arbitrary views. To cope with these requirements and to enable an efficient implementation of such functionality, metadata is made explicit in a variety of ways, and mechanisms to insert metadata into the system have to be created. The respective description has been the objective of this chapter. With more specific approaches, i.e., only documents of a limited set of types can be handled, metainformation does not have to be made explicit, but, rather, tends to be hardcoded into the system.

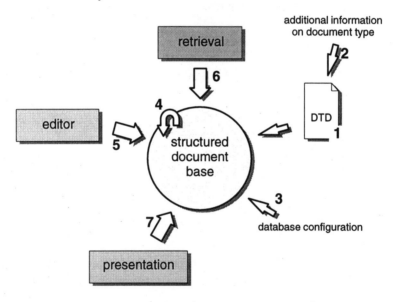

Figure 2-12   Database-oriented view of publishing revisited.

In this chapter, various categorizations in the context of metadata have been introduced: There is a differentiation between metadata on the instance level and metadata on the type level. On the instance level, metadata has been classified in accordance to the nature of the information. The various modeling alternatives of metadata both within and outside of the respective information model have been described. We have given a comprehensive overview of the ways metadata is used within our framework.

In Section 2.1 it has been pointed out that the classical view of publishing becomes a database-oriented one by using new technologies. In Figure 2-12, the different ways metadata are part of our framework are visualized. A DTD that itself is metainformation (1) can be furnished with additional information (2). The information about how the database-internal representation of documents of a certain type should look can also be specified in this way, but it can also be directly communicated to the database (3). Other metainformation can be computed and administered by the storage system itself (4), e.g., information on document history. Authors and editors make metainformation explicit, e.g., by including it into the document using the mechanisms described before, by defining DFR groups and assigning documents to them (5). Metainformation is also used for declarative access to the document base (6) and for conversion to a layout format (7).

In essence, with regard to the different ways of metadata being used within our framework, the following differentiation is feasible: metadata are used to extend the functionality of the system or to improve efficiency of existing features. This is reflected in Table 2-1.

Extended functionality	improved performance
deriving IRS values for MM elements	configuration information
query templates	DTD-based query optimization
layout, hyperlink rendition	
higher expressiveness of query languages	

Table 2-1 Classifying the different ways metadata are used within our framework.

Another important way metadata can be used is to facilitate access to heterogeneous information sources. While concepts for the general case are already available [23], applying them to this particular application scenario, i.e., structured documents, still remains to be done. In more detail, one may want to provide homogeneous access mechanisms both for heterogeneous document structures within the database as well as a part of the documents being outside of the database.

References

[1] K. Aberer, K. Böhm, and C. Hüser. The Prospects of Publishing Using Advanced Database Concepts. In Christoph Hüser, Wiebke Möhr, and Vincent Quint (eds.), *Proceedings of Conference on Electronic Publishing*. John Wiley & Sons, Ltd., April 1994, pp. 469–480.

[2] S. Abiteboul, S. Cluet, and T. Milo. Querying and Updating the File. In R. Agrawal, S. Baker, and D. Bell (eds.), *Proceedings of the International Conference on Very Large Data Bases*. VLDB Endowment, Dublin, Ireland, 1993, pp. 73–84.

[3] S. Abiteboul, S. Cluet, and T. Milo. A Database Interface for File Update. In *Proceedings ACM SIGMOD*. ACM Press, 1995, pp. 386–397.

[4] K. Aberer and G. Fischer. Semantic Query Optimization for Methods in Object-Oriented Database Systems. In *Proceedings of International Conference on Data Engineering*. IEEE Computer Society, 1995, pp. 70–79.

[5] K. Böhm et al. DeTeBerkom Project POLAR – Public Office Longterm Archiving and Retrieval; Modelling and Archiving of Files and Structured Documents. Technical report, GMD-IPSI, IGD/ZGDV, March 1995.

[6] K. Böhm, K. Aberer, and W. Klas. Building a Configurable Database Application for Structured Documents, 1997. Accepted for publication in Multimedia – Tools and Applications.

[7] K. Böhm, K. Aberer, E.J. Neuhold, and X. Yang. Using Metadata for High-Quality Access to the Document Base, 1996. Accepted for publication in VLDB Journal.

[8] K. Böhm and T. Rakow. Metadata for Multimedia Documents. *SIGMOD-Record, Special Issue on Metadata for Digital Media*, 23(4), December 1994, pp. 21–26.

[9] M. Bryan. *SGML*. Addison-Wesley, 1992.

[10] R. G. G. Cattell (ed.). *The Object Database Standard: ODMG-93*. Morgan Kaufmann Publishers, 1994.

[11] J. P. Callan, W. B. Croft, and S. M. Hardig. The INQUERY Retrieval System. In *Proceedings of the Third International Conference on Database and Expert Systems Application*. Springer Verlag, 1992, pp. 78–83.

[12] W. B. Croft, L. A. Smith, and H. R. Turtle. A Loosely-Coupled Integration of a Text Retrieval System and an Object-Oriented Database System. In N. Belkin, P. Ingwersen, and A.M. Pejtersen (eds.). *Proceedings of the Fifteenth Annual International ACM SIGIR Conference on Research and Development in Information Retrieval.* ACM Press, 1992, pp. 223–232.

[13] T. Göttke and P. Fankhauser. DREAM 2.0 User Manual. Technical Report 660, GMD-IPSI, St. Augustin, 1992.

[14] G. Gräfe and W. J. McKenna. The Volcano Optimizer Generator: Extensibility and Efficient Search. In *Proceedings of the International Conference on Data Engineering.* IEEE, Vienna, Austria, 1993, pp. 209–218.

[15] HyperText Markup Language (HTML). Available under URL http://www.w3.org/pub/WWW/MarkUp/.

[16] D. J. Harper and A. D. M. Walker. ECLAIR: an Extensible Class Library for Information Retrieval. *The Computer Journal*, 35(3), 1992, pp. 256–257.

[17] *Information Technology – Text and Office Systems – Standardized Generalized Markup Language (SGML)*, 1986.

[18] *Information Technology – Text and Office Systems – Office Document Architecture (ODA) and Interchange Format*, 1989.

[19] *Information Technology – Text and Office Systems – Document Filing and Retrieval (DFR)*, 1991.

[20] *Information Technology – Hypermedia/Time-based Structuring Language (HyTime)*, 1992.

[21] *Guidelines for Electronic Text Encoding and Interchange*, April 1994. URL http://etext.virginia.edu/TEI.

[22] SIGMOD-Record Special Issue on Metadata for Digital Media. ACM SIGMOD, ACM Press, 23(4), December 1994.

[23] E. Mena et al. OBSERVER: An Approach for Query Processing in Global Information Systems based on Interoperation across Pre-existing Ontologies, 1996. Accepted for publication at in Proceedings of First IFCIS International Conference on Cooperative Information Systems (CoopIS'96), pp. 14–25.

[24] M. T. Özsu et al. An Object-Oriented Multimedia Database System for a News-on-Demand Application. *Multimedia Systems*, 3(5-6), 1995, 182–203.

[25] U.S. Department of Defense. Markup Requirements and Generic Style Specification for Electronic Printed Output and Exchange of Text. MIL-M-28001A, 1990. Washington, D.C.

[26] S. J. De Rose and D. G. Durand. *Making Hypermedia Work.* Kluwer Academic Publishers, 1994.

[27] Klaus Süllow et al. MultiMedia Forum – an Interactive Online Journal. In C. Hüser, W. Möhr, and V. Quint (eds.), *Proceedings of Conference on Electronic Publishing.* John Wiley & Sons, Ltd., April 1994, pp. 413–422.

[28] U.S. Securities and Exchange Commission. *EDGAR File Manual: Draft User's Guide for Electronic Filing with the U.S. Securities and Exchange Commission,* 1994.

[29] G. Salton and M. J. McGill. *Introduction to Modern Information Retrieval.* McGraw-Hill Book Company, first edition, 1983.

[30] A. Salminen and F. W. Tompa. PAT Expressions: an Algebra for Text Search. *Acta Linguistica Hungarica,* 41(1), 1994, 277–306.

[31] H. Thimm and T. Rakow. A DBMS-Based Multimedia Archiving Teleservice Incorporating Mail. In W. Litwin and T. Risch (eds.). *Proceedings of First International Conference on Applications of Databases.* Lecture Notes in Computer Science 819. Springer Verlag Berlin Heidelberg, June 1994, pp. 281–298.

[32] M. Volz, K. Aberer, and K. Böhm. Applying a Flexible OODBMS-IRS-Coupling to Structured Document Handling. In *Proceedings of the 12th International Conference on Data Engineering.* IEEE Computer Society, New Orleans, 1996, pp. 10–19.

[33] VODAK V 4.0 User Manual. Technical Report 910, GMD-IPSI, St. Augustin, April 1995.

Chapter

3

Metadata in Geographic and Environmental Data Management

Oliver Günther and Agnès Voisard*

Institut für Wirtschaftsinformatik
Humboldt-Universität zu Berlin
Spandauer Str. 1, D-10178 Berlin, Germany
guenther@wiwi.hu-berlin.de

*Institut für Informatik
Freie Universität Berlin
Takustr. 9, D-14195 Berlin, Germany
voisard@inf.fu-berlin.de

Abstract

Metadata is used increasingly in geographic and environmental information systems to improve both the availability and the quality of the information delivered. The growing popularity of Internet-based data servers has accelerated this trend even further. In this chapter, we give an overview of metadata schemes and implementations that are common in this domain. Case studies include the Content Standards for Digital Geospatial Metadata of the U.S. Federal Geographic Data Committee (FGDC), and the Catalogue of Data Sources (CDS) of the European Environmental Agency. Another activity that we will discuss in somewhat greater detail concerns the UDK project, an international software engineering effort to facilitate access to environmental data. The UDK (Environmental Data Catalogue) is a public meta information system and navigation tool that helps users to identify and retrieve environmental data from the government and other sources. In 1995, first versions of the UDK were made available in Austria and Germany; several other European countries are currently evaluating the system. We will present the UDK data model, its implementation as a distributed information system, and its integration into the World Wide Web.

3.1   Introduction

The preservation of the environment has become a major public policy goal throughout the world. Governments are concerned more than ever about their environmental resources and are establishing policies to control their consumption. Citizens take a greater interest in the current and future state of the environment and adapt their ways of living accordingly. As a result of these political developments, there is a major demand for environmental information and appropriate tools to manage it. Recent legislation reflects this trend. According to a recent directive of the European Union, for example, almost all environmental data that is stored at public agencies has to be made available to any citizen on demand [4]. As the last few years have shown, the tendency to exert this right is rising steadily. There is, for example, an increasing demand for up-to-date information on air quality in inner cities, on water quality in coastal regions, and so on. In addition, new legislation requires companies to provide an increasing amount of data about the environmental impact of their products and activities.

Given the amount and complexity of environmental data, these new information needs can only be served by using state-of-the-art computer technology. *Environmental information systems* are concerned with the management of data about the soil, the water, the air, and the species in the world around us. The collection and administration of such data is an essential component of any efficient environmental protection strategy. Vast amounts of data need to be available to decision makers, mostly (but not always) in some kind of condensed format. The requirements regarding the currency and accuracy of this information are high. While the information technology required for this task is rarely domain-specific, it is often important to select and combine the right tools among those that are available in principle. This requires a thorough knowledge of related developments in computer science, as well as a good understanding of the environmental management tasks at hand.

A particular need exists for convenient navigation aids that help users to take advantage of network-based, distributed information, regardless of their computer literacy. Starting from some environmental query or problem formulation, such navigation aids should help users to localize the relevant data sets and to retrieve them quickly and in a user-friendly manner. An essential prerequisite for both navigation and data transfer is the availability of appropriate *metadata*, i.e., data about the format and the contents of the data. The key idea is to enhance data sets by concise descriptions of themselves in order to improve both the speed and the accuracy of related search operations. The metadata serves as a kind of online documentation that can be read and utilized by appropriate tools as well as by human users. Note that there is no intrinsic distinction between data and metadata; it is rather a question of context whether a given data item represents metadata or not.

In this chapter, we will discuss the question of metadata in geographic and environmental data management in greater detail. Section 3.2 gives a more elaborate definition of metadata and shows how metadata can be integrated into a traditional data management architecture. Sections 3.3 through 3.5 describe several concrete approaches to metadata management. Section 3.3 presents the U.S. initiative to create a National Spatial Data Infrastructure (NSDI); this includes discussions of the Spatial Data Transfer Standard (SDTS) and the FGDC Content Standards for Digital Geospatial Metadata. Sections 3.4 and 3.5 continue with descriptions of two European systems: the Catalogue of Data Sources of the Environment (CDS) and the German and Austrian proposal for a European Environmental Data Catalogue (UDK). Section 3.6 concludes with a summary and an outlook on future work.

3.2 Metadata and Data Modeling

Our further discussion is based on a *three-way data model* that distinguishes between environmental objects, environmental data objects, and environmental metadata (Figure 3-1). The term *environmental object* is used to describe the real-world objects making up the environment. This includes natural entities, such as lakes and biotopes, as well as artifical objects, such as factories or highways. Nesting or overlaps between environmental objects are common. Each environmental object is described by a collection of *environmental data objects*, which are abstract entities that can be handled by computers or directly by decision makers. A typical environmental data object would be a series of measurements that captures the concentration of a certain substance in a river (the corresponding environmental object). Each environmental data object is in turn associated with one or more *metadata objects* that specify its format and contents. The documentation of the measuring series described above would be a typical example. It may include data about the spatial and temporal scale of the measurements, the main objectives of the project, the responsible agency, and so on.

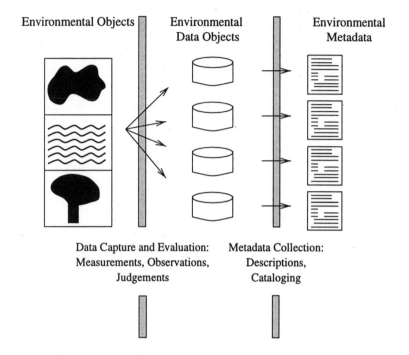

Environmental Objects | Environmental Data Objects | Environmental Metadata

Data Capture and Evaluation: Measurements, Observations, Judgements

Metadata Collection: Descriptions, Cataloging

Figure 3-1 Three-way object model of environmental information systems.

The data flow in many environmental applications closely resembles the data flow in classical business applications. It can be structured into four phases: data capture, data aggregation, data storage, and data analysis.

1. The first phase, *data capture*, concerns the collection of environmental raw data, such as measurement time series or aerial photographs. In this phase, the great variety of environmental objects is mapped onto a collection of environmental data objects, which have a structure that is much simpler and more clearly defined. There is a variety of ways to perform such a mapping, including measurement and observation, but also value-based judgment.

2. In the second phase, *data aggregation*, this raw data is condensed and enriched in order to extract entities that are semantically meaningful. In the case of image data, for example, this includes the recognition of geometric primitives (such as lines and vertices) in an array of pixels, the comparison of the resulting geometric objects with available maps, and the identification of geographic objects (such as cities or rivers) on the

picture. The information can then be represented in a much more compact format (in this case, a vector-based data format, as opposed to the original raster data). Measurement time series also need to be aggregated and possibly evaluated by means of some standard statistical procedures. The aggregated data is then stored in a file or a database.

3. In the third phase of *data storage*, one has to choose a suitable database design and appropriate physical storage structures that will optimize overall system performance. Because of the complexity and heterogeneity of environmental data, this often necessitates substantial extensions to classical database technology.

4. In the final *data analysis* phase, the available information is prepared for decision support purposes. This may require access to data that is geographically distributed, stored on heterogeneous hardware, and organized along a wide variety of data models. The data analysis is typically based on complex statistical methods, scenarios, simulation and visualization tools, as well as institutional knowledge (environmental legislation, user objectives, etc.). Only the synthesis of these different inputs allows us to judge the state of the environment and the potential of certain measures, both planned and already implemented.

The overall objective of this complex data flow is to provide decision support at various levels of responsibility. Figure 3-2 uses the symbol of the pyramid to demonstrate this idea. The last three phases of the data flow correspond to a bottom-up traversal of the pyramid. Data can be used throughout that traversal for decision support purposes. While the data in the lower part of the pyramid tends to be used for local, tactical tasks, the upper part corresponds to strategic decision support for the middle and upper management.

Metadata may be *collected* at any of the four phases of the data flow and built into the corresponding data structures. As Kashyap et al. point out in [18], much of the data produced during data aggregation and storage is already metadata, starting with simple database schema information up to high-level semantic abstractions of the available data sets. While collection has been mostly manual so far, the automatic extraction of metadata is increasingly becoming an option; Drew and Ying give a concrete example in Chapter 4 of this volume.

As for the *use* of metadata, it is mainly taking place in the data analysis phase and fulfills a variety of purposes:

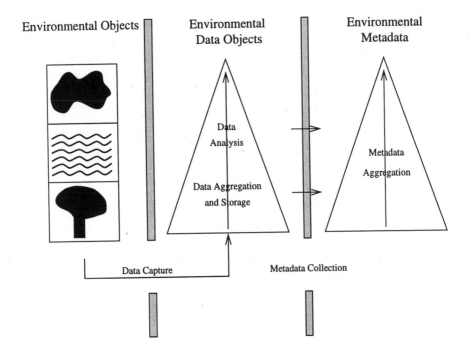

Figure 3-2 Data flow in environmental information systems.

- Computerized environmental information systems are able to collect and process much greater amounts of data than anybody could have thought of only a few years ago. Automatic data capture and measurement results in terabytes of new data per day [2]. Even in processed form, this kind of data is impossible to browse manually in order to find the information that is relevant for a given task. Modern information retrieval tools allow the automatic or semi-automatic filtering of the available data in order to find quickly those data sets one is looking for. Metadata forms an important foundation of these tools by serving as a condensed representation of the underlying data. As such, it supports browsing, navigation, and content-oriented indexing.

- Environmental data management is extremely *heterogeneous*, both in terms of hardware and software platforms. Data is organized according to a wide variety of data models, depending on the primary objectives of the particular agency in charge. Metadata can help to overcome these heterogeneities by specifying the platforms on which a given data item is located. This way, appropriate conversion routines can be introduced (semi-)automatically, wherever necessary.

- Environmental data is frequently *uncertain*. Metadata can be used to specify the accuracy of a data item, so users can judge from the metadata whether the corresponding environmental data objects are relevant for their current needs.

- Metadata can also help to *inventory* existing data holdings, to unify naming schemes, and to record relationships between different data items and data sets. This aspect of metadata has recently become very popular as one of the core functionalities of *data warehouses* [16].

The concept of metadata is not new. Online documentation of programs and data sets has been in common use for many years. Machine-readable metadata has also been known for a long time, in particular in the context of relational databases, where the internal database structure (the *database schema*) is typically represented in a relational format itself. What is new is the more systematic approach to providing machine-readable metadata, and the trend to standardize metadata in certain application areas.

For the subsequent discussion, it is useful to distinguish between two kinds of metadata [28]. The term *denotative metadata* is used to refer to the kind of metadata that describes the logical structure of a data set; a relational schema would be a typical example. The term *annotative metadata*, on the other hand, is used to describe data that provides content-oriented context information, such as the documentation of the measuring series described above. Following Melton et al. [28], further examples of annotative metadata include "information in scientific notebooks, instrument logs, manuals, and reports that document the platform and instrument conditions, the operational environment, interferring sources of noise, and that uniquely identify the software and computer platforms used for analysis, modelling and simulation." In the remainder of this chapter, we will concentrate on annotative metadata and use the term metadata in that sense. It should be noted here that other researchers have presented different ways to classify metadata; Kashyap et al. give an overview of related work in this volume [18].

The relevance of metadata for the management and analysis of complex data sets has been pointed out early on by McCarthy [26] and pursued further in the area of statistical and scientific databases. Siegel and Madnick [36] built on those ideas, concentrating on possible applications in financial data analysis. The IEEE Mass Storage Systems and Technology Committee has sponsored several metadata workshops whose results are available on the Web (URL http://www.llnl.gov/liv_comp/metadata/metadata.html). The use of metadata in geographic and environmental information systems is of a more recent nature [34]. Lately, however, there has been broad agreement that metadata are a crucial factor to improve both the quality and the availability of geographic and environmental data. Several conferences on spatial databases and geographical information systems (GIS) have devoted parts of their program to metadata [15, 5, 6], and there has been a variety of workshops dedicated exclusively to metadata management in the geosciences and the environmental sciences [27, 28].

In terms of practical consequences, metadata technology is increasingly being integrated into commercial GIS. Most commercial systems have always maintained some basic metadata on the objects to be administered. *ARC/INFO*, for example, generates and maintains metadata on the spatial registration, projection, and tolerances of a coverage or grid [7]. Every time one creates a coverage, the system creates a set of metadata files, including the TIC file (containing data about the coverage's coordinate registration), the LOG file (tracking all ARC operations performed on the coverage), and the BND file (containing the coordinate values that denote the outer boundary or spatial extent of your coverage). There is also denotative metadata giving some schema information of the INFO tables that contain the non-spatial data components.

The practical use of metadata, however, is extending much beyond this somewhat narrow scope. One trend is to collect more information about the detailed content of the data. Vendors typically choose some bibliography-style format to represent this information; conformity with the FGDC Content Standards (see Section 3.3.2) is increasingly required. The ARC/INFO component *DOCUMENT.AML* [7] is a typical example of such a tool.

Another trend is to describe the history and quality (also called *lineage*) of data sets and their sources in more detail. *Geolineus* of *Geographic Designs Inc.* is a typical tool for this purpose [12]. Geolineus represents the data in a GIS by means of dataflow diagrams, where coverages and grids are shown as icons. Icons along the top of the diagram represent the *source data* on which the GIS is based. Icons further down represent data layers that were *derived* with spatial analysis operations like *BUFFER* or *INTERSECT*. Finally, icons at the bottom of the diagram represent *products*, i.e., derived data items that represent the final steps in a GIS application. Geolineus shows the type of data in the corresponding layer for each icon and maintains command histories for each coverage. The system allows the storgae of documentation about each layer in a frame-based format.

In Chapter 4, Drew and Ying describe a concrete approach to use metadata in order to provide uniform access to a heterogeneous collection of GIS and spatial databases. Based on metadata about those systems and their contents, their *GeoChange* system serves as a navigation and access tool. To a large extent, it is non-intrusive, i.e., it can be implemented on top of an existing collection of independent systems without major changes to the underlying architectures and implementations.

Other trends in metadata management include the inclusion of more spatial elements in the metadata itself [35] and the use of metadata to describe and access not only other data sets, but also models and algorithms [23].

Parallel to these application developments, metadata management has become a focus in an increasing number of government R&D projects. Besides the efforts described in the following sections, there has been a project by the European Space Agency (ESA) to develop an online geosciences metadata system, called the *ESA Prototype International Directory* [39]. At about the same time, the United Nations Environmental Program (UNEP) has started a project on the *Harmonization of Environmental Measurements (HEM)* [19]. Also actively involved in the harmonization of environmental data in research and monitoring is the International Council of Scientific Unions (ICSU), represented by its Scientific Committee for the Problems of the Environment (SCOPE) and its Committee on Data for Science and Technology (CODATA) [1]. The Norwegian *SAMPO* project uses ARC/INFO's *ArcView* to catalogue its spatial data holdings [29]. The Austrian Ministry of the Environment has developed a *Central European Environmental Data Request Facility (CEDAR)* [33]. Other efforts include the *CIMI* system of the Dutch Ministry of Transportation, Public Works and Water Management [22], the Australian *FINDAR* system [17] and the New South Wales Department of Conservation and Land Management's *Data Directory* [31, 30].

Coordination between this great variety of efforts is difficult. As we will show in Section 3.4, the newly founded European Environmental Agency will have an important role to play here. One promising effort concerns the development of a common European geodata standard. With strong support from the European Center of Normalization, Germany's and Belgium's Geographic Data Files (GDF) are generally considered the frontrunner [32]. Further standardization is required, however. Environmental phenomena do not stop at national borders. In this domain, international cooperation on a broad scale is essential for making progress.

3.3 The U.S. National Spatial Data Infrastructure (NSDI)

Since the early 1980s, the U.S. Government has been working intensively on creating a National Spatial Data Infrastructure (NSDI). A major motivation for this effort was to abolish the notorious incompatibilities among the internal formats used by various government agencies. Examples include DLG, TIGER/Line, and GRASS of the U.S. Geological Survey, DIGEST and the Vector Product Format (VPF) of the Defense Mapping Agency (DMA), and DX90 of the National Ocean Service. The parallel use of such a variety of standards led to considerable expenses to the taxpayer that could at least in part have been avoided.

Most of the early efforts on NSDI were coordinated by the U.S. Geological Survey, an agency under the supervision of the U.S. Department of the Interior. One of the first major results was the development of the *Spatial Data Transfer Standard (SDTS)*, a Federal Information Processing Standard to facilitate the online exchange of spatial data [37]. The goal is to accommodate different spatial data models, to preserve topologies, and to maintain even complex relationships, as data is transferred across different computer platforms and software systems. Other than many existing standards (such as VPF), the SDTS is not an exchange format. It rather provides guidelines that need to be translated into a native application-specific format before they can be used. Most GIS vendors provide interfaces and tools for that purpose [8].

Since 1990, the NSDI efforts have been coordinated by a working group called the *Federal Geographic Data Committee (FGDC)*, which is composed of representatives of the Departments of Agriculture, Commerce, Defense, Energy, Housing and Urban Development, the Interior, State, and Transportation; the Environmental Protection Agency; the Federal Emergency Management Agency; the Library of Congress; the National Aeronautics and Space Administration; the National Archives and Records Administration; and the Tennessee Valley Authority. The committee is chaired by the Department of the Interior, represented by the U.S. Geological Survey.

In May 1994, the FGDC published a draft for the new *Content Standards for Digital Geospatial Metadata* [11], which was later approved by the National Institute of Standards and Technology as a Federal Information Processing Standard. The implementation of the standard is based on the Executive Order 12906, "Coordinating Geographic Data Acquisition and Access: The National Spatial Data Infrastructure," which was signed on April 11, 1994, by President

Clinton [38]. In addition to providing a long-needed political foundation for the NSDI, the order requires all government agencies to use the FGDC Content Standards for documenting all new geospatial data it collects or produces as of April 11, 1995.

While both the SDTS and the FGDC Content Standards refer to metadata about spatial data, they have distinctly separate functions. The SDTS is a language for communicating spatial data across different platforms without losing any structural or topological information. The FGDC Content Standards, on the other hand, specify the kind of annotative metadata that federal agencies are required to collect on a spatial data set they maintain. The only two sections that both standards have in common concern data quality and the data dictionary information; we will discuss this in detail later on.

3.3.1 The Spatial Data Transfer Standard (SDTS)

The Spatial Data Transfer Standard (SDTS) [37] was designed to facilitate the online transfer of the full range of geographic and cartographic data. Both vector and raster data of a large variety of data models can be exchanged across heterogeneous hardware and software platforms using the SDTS. The standard is structured into three main parts; the subsequent presentation follows the overview of Fegeas et al. [10].

1. *Logical Specification*

   This part contains the logical specification of the entities and data objects used to describe different GIS data models. It consists of three major sections in turn and provides guidelines on how spatial and nonspatial objects (simple or composite) are to be organized, named, and structured.

   The first section presents a conceptual model of spatial data. It describes the real world as a set of "entities" (cities, rivers, factories, etc.), each characterized by attributes, which are assigned attribute values. The model then goes on to define a set of zero-, one-, and two-dimensional spatial objects (such as points, lines, and polygons) and the relationships between entities and spatial objects.

   The reader should take notice of the particular use of the term "entity," which in this standard has been chosen to describe a real-world phenomenon, whereas the term "object" is reserved for the digital representation of an "entity." In analogy to the standard entity-relationship literature, the term "entity type" is used to describe a set of similar entities; in that context the single entities are also called "entity instances." The term "feature," finally, which is still very common in the geoscientific community, is here defined as both a real-world entity and its object representation, i.e., as the superclass of the classes "entity" and "object."

The second section of part 1 is devoted to data quality. It specifies five portions of a data quality report: lineage, positional accuracy, attribute accuracy, logical consistency, and completeness. The lineage portion describes source and update material (with dates), methods of derivation, transformations, and other processing history. Positional accuracy is concerned with how closely the locational data represent true locations. Attribute accuracy is similarly concerned with non-locational descriptive data. Logical consistency refers to the fidelity of encoded relationships in the structure of the spatial data (e.g., the degree to which topological relationships have been verified). The completeness portion includes information about geographic area and subject matter coverage. Note that large parts of this second section of part 1 are replicated in feature group 2 (data quality information) of the FGDC Content Standards.

The third section of part 1 constitutes the largest portion of the whole standard; it specifies detailed logical transfer format constructs and specifications for SDTS transfer data sets. An SDTS transfer is organized into modules with records, fields, and subfields. Thirty-four module types are specified as detailed field and subfield record layout specification tables, designed to include many kinds of information: global, data quality, feature and attribute data dictionary, coordinate reference, spatial object, and associated attribute and graphic symbology information. The data dictionary portion, which conveys the meaning and structure of entity and attribute data, is divided into three module types: definition, domain, and schema. Parts of the data dictionary portion are replicated in feature group 4 (entity and attribute information) of the FGDC Content Standards.

2. *Data Content Registry*

This part provides data content standards by specifying a model for the definition of spatial entity types, attributes, and attribute values. The underlying idea of this part of the standard is that there is a need for common definitions of spatial features (resp. entities). In that sense, this part is nothing but a thesaurus. It contains a list of about 200 topographic and hydrographic entity types with 244 attributes, plus a list of about 1200 terms that are in a synonym or subtype relationship to any of those standard or primary terms. It is foreseen by the designers of the standard that this section will be subject to continuous updates and extensions.

3. *Physical Structure*

This part specifies the implementation of the transfer using the ISO 8211 international standard for information interchange. The ISO standard itself is embedded into the SDTS to ensure that data can be transferred to any computing environment. The U.S. Geological Survey has developed a public domain software function library to assist in encoding and decoding SDTS data into ISO 8211 format.

It is important to keep in mind that the SDTS and ISO 8211 are separate standards. ISO 8211 is an international data exchange format that can be used to transfer any type of data, not just spatial data. ISO 8211 provides a means of transferring data records and their description across heterogeneous hardware and software platforms. It requires, however, that the *content* and the *meaning* of the data records are defined by the user. In that sense, the SDTS can be considered a user of ISO 8211.

The SDTS is designed such that parts 1 and 2 are independent of part 3, which is specific to ISO 8211. If necessary, the SDTS could replace part 3 by another version that uses a different implementation format without affecting parts 1 and 2. ISO 8211 was chosen so that the SDTS could use an existing general-purpose transfer standard rather than having to develop a new SDTS-specific format. It is designed to work for any media, including communication lines. ISO 8211 is self-describing. An ISO 8211 file (called a *Data Descriptive File (DDF)*) contains both data and the description of the data. The *Data Descriptive Record (DDR)* is fixed; it contains the structure and description of the data. The *Data Records (DRs)* are of variable size; they contain the actual data. There is always one DDR in a file, and one or more DRs.

Given the great complexity of the standard, the designers also introduced a concept called *profile*, which is a kind of customization of the standard for a particular data model. If a new data model is to be supported, the interested parties may specify those options of the standard that are needed to support that data model. This subset of options can then be submitted for approval as its own Federal Information Processing Standard and, once approved, is added to the SDTS as a new SDTS profile.

Currently, there exists a *Topological Vector Profile (TVP)* for vector data with full and explicit topology. Another profile that is about to be approved is a raster profile for image and gridded data. Under consideration are further vector profiles for network/transportation data, for nontopological nautical chart and hydrographic data, and for CAD data.

3.3.2   The FGDC Content Standards for Digital Geospatial Metadata

The FGDC Content Standards define metadata as *data about the content, quality, condition, and other characteristics of data.* They structure the spatial metadata into the following seven groups of features. Only the first (identification information) and the last feature group (metadata reference information) are obligatory; the remaining ones are optional.

1. *Identification Information*

   This feature group contains the basic meta information about a given data set, including:

   - Textual description

   - Information about the time period described

   - Spatial reference: A minimum bounding rectangle is required. Optionally, one can provide a more detailed polygonal description.

   - Keywords: They can be freely chosen, but need to be associated with a term from the relevant thesaurus. One keyword about the theme of the data set is obligatory. Optionally, one can provide further keywords that refer to the theme, the space, or the time corresponding to the data set in question.

   - Person or organization to contact for more information about the data set (optional)

   - Access constraints and security information (optional)

   - Information about the technical representation of the data set: special software, operating system, file name, data set size (optional)

2. *Data Quality Information*

   This feature group contains general information about the quality of the data set. In addition to an assessment of the accuracy and consistency of the data, this includes metadata about the data source ("lineage") and about completeness.

   Note that this feature group replicates the content (but not the structure) of the SDTS's data quality section (part 1, second section).

3. *Spatial Data Organization Information*

   This feature group contains information on which mechanism was used to represent spatial information in the data set. At this point the standard supports a generic mechanism to represent raster data, and SDTS and VPF to represent vector data. The SDTS section is based on part 1 of the SDTS specification.

The fact that both SDTS and VPF were included explicitly shows how the designers of the standard sometimes had to sacrifice conciseness and clarity in order to obtain approval from all participants. It was not possible to move all government agencies toward a single standard for representing vector data. Among other reasons, this is mainly due to large amounts of essential legacy data, whose conversion would exceed the available resources of the respective agencies.

4. *Spatial Reference Information*

This feature describes the projection and coordinate system used (e.g., *Mercator* or *Miller_Cylindrical*).

5. *Entity and Attribute Information*

This feature group allows the user to describe the information content of the data set using the entity-relationship model. The SDTS's data dictionary information is captured in this feature group. There is common agreement that this section of the standard is too superficial and should be redesigned in future versions of the standard.

6. *Distribution Information*

This feature group contains information about the distributor of the data set and about options for obtaining it. The distributor usually corresponds to the contact person/organization listed in the identification information (see 1.). The order information includes data about the possible modes of communication (modem, e-mail, etc.) and about the transfer formats used (e.g., the ARC/INFO Export format, the Initial Graphics Exchange Standard (IGES), or ASCII).

7. *Metadata Reference Information*

This obligatory feature group serves for storing what could be called "meta-metadata." This includes information about the last update of the metadata, the latest and the next review of the metadata, the party responsible for the metadata, as well as access and security constraints.

In summary, the FGDC Content Standards represent an impressive effort to establish a uniform way to document digital geospatial data sets. While mainly targeted at the description of geographic data, it also provides a solid basis for an environmental metadata system. Such an extension would entail a more detailed semantic framework, especially with regard to theme-related information.

3.4   The Catalogue of Data Sources for the Environment (CDS)

The European Union (EU) has been working on similar issues, especially since the 1994 foundation of its European Environmental Agency (EEA), located in Copenhagen. In comparison to the American activities, the EEA efforts have a wider focus, concentrating not only on spatial data, but on environmental data in a more general sense. On the other hand, the results obtained so far are not nearly as concrete as the FGDC recommendations described above.

The ultimate goal of the EU activities is the implementation of an integrated European environmental information system. Based on the results of a previous project called *CORINE CDS* (1985-1989), the EU recently commissioned a study entitled "Catalogue of Data Sources for the Environment – Analysis and Suggestions for a Meta-Data System and Service for The European Environment Agency" [9]. An essential result of this study was the (hardly surprising) insight that the construction of a European environmental information system from scratch is neither economically feasible nor politically viable. Many member countries already have some kind of national environmental information system. A European system should take advantage of part of these developments and attempt a bottom-up integration of the systems that are already functional. Devised as a *meta* information system, CDS would only store descriptions of data sets that are locally available.

The study recommends the simultaneous realization of the following two architectures:

- a standalone variant that is updated periodically based on current information from the member countries;

- a networked variant, which has online connections with a variety of national catalogs and which is only usable in connection with those.

Since the study was written (1993), the percentage of computers that are networked, usually including some connection to the Internet, has increased considerably. The first architecture option seems therefore obsolete. In turn, it should be made sure that the central catalogue provides some base functionalities independently of the current state of the national catalogs and the connections to them. This can easily be achieved by making local copies of a subset of the metadata periodically. For distribution and update purposes, the study recommends the usage of CD-ROMs. Once again, the usage of the Internet instead will probably be a matter of course by the time a CDS system will be operational. The data should be stored in a relational database system, with text fields playing an important role. The language problem shall be alleviated, if not solved, by using a multilingual thesaurus. The GIS functionalities of the proposed CDS system are only rudimentary; more complex spatial functionalities are referred to an external GIS instead.

The study does not propose a concrete format for the metadata, comparable to the detailed specifications of the FGDC or the UDK (see Section 3.5). The authors suggest instead the formation of some synthesis of the existing proposals of the member countries and of the United States. Of course, such a fusion is bound to produce semantic discrepancies and even incompatibilities. To minimize those, the study proposes to focus the synthesis on eight major classes of entities. The three most important classes listed in the study are

1. Institution
2. Activities/Projects
3. Products

The remaining five entity classes serve to represent secondary information about the entities in classes 1, 2, and 3:

4. Addresses
5. Stations
6. Communication
7. People/Persons
8. Data Sets

It seems somewhat questionable whether a single-layer taxonomy like the one above would ever be able to capture the extreme heterogeneity that resulted from a synthesis of the environmental data and metadata schemes throughout Europe. On the one hand, there will always be entity types that do not fit into the given scheme. On the other hand, there has to be a formal mechanism to refine a given entity class in order to serve the local requirements of a particular agency in an optimal manner. A multi-layer taxonomy, i.e., a class hierarchy with an inheritance mechanism, seems to be much better suited for this purpose. The UDK system described in the following section is an example of where such a class hierarchy approach has been introduced successfully.

3.5   The UDK – A European Environmental Data Catalogue

The *UDK (Umwelt-Datenkatalog = Environmental Data Catalogue)* is a meta information system and navigation tool that documents collections of environmental data from the government and other sources. These data sets may be available either online or by request to the responsible data administrator. Potential users of the system include government agencies, industry, and the general public. The UDK helps them to get answers to the following questions:

- Which relevant information is principally available for a given problem?
- Where is this information stored?
- How can this information be retrieved?

The UDK design presented in this section is the result of several years of research and development [24, 25]. In 1990, the Environmental Ministry of the State of Lower Saxony launched a research project with funding from the German Federal Environmental Protection Agency. Two years later, an international working group was formed to oversee the UDK design and its further development into a practical software tool. In 1994, Austria passed an Environmental Information Law that introduced the UDK as the official navigation tool for all environmental information on record. In 1995, the first version of the UDK was made available in Austria and the German states of Baden-Württemberg and Lower Saxony; other German states will follow. The UDK is currently also under evaluation by several other European countries, including Switzerland, Italy, Sweden, and Norway.

3.5.1   The UDK Object Model

The UDK is based on a three-way object model that is very similar to the data model described in the introduction (Figure 3-1). In the UDK we distinguish between environmental objects, environmental data objects, and UDK (meta) objects. Each real-world environmental object is described by a collection of environmental data objects. Each environmental data object is in turn associated with exactly one metadata object that specifies its format and contents.

On the screen, each such *UDK object* is represented by one or more screen layouts; see Figure 3-3 for an example. The first screen layout contains some

administrative information (object name, object ID, and keywords), a text description, and the address of the agency that is responsible for the maintenance
of this UDK object and the underlying environmental data object. The second
screen layout contains some more technical information about the environmental data object. This includes detailed data about the information content, the
capturing method and its accuracy, the spatial extent, and the validity of the
object. Spatial information can be specified using either coordinates, or (as in
this example) denominations of administrative entities.

UDK objects may exist for environmental data objects at various aggregation
levels simultaneously. Consider, for example, a national groundwater database
that contains a large number of measurements from all over the country. There
is one UDK object representing this database as a whole. In addition, however,
there may be one UDK object each for the measurements from a certain county,
there may be UDK objects representing the measurements from a particular
station, and there may even be UDK objects that represent single measurements. There may also be UDK objects for groupings that are orthogonal
to this primary aggregation hierarchy, such as UDK objects representing the
measurements that were taken in a given month.

There are two reasons for this great flexibility in defining UDK objects at various levels of aggregation. First, powerful aggregation facilities are crucial for
improving the usability and acceptance of a system like the UDK. Empirical
studies have shown that the overwhelming number of queries in such a context
refer to aggregated data rather than detailed source data. For example, citizens
may be concerned about the ozone concentration in their neighborhood on a
certain day; it is rather unlikely that they would want to know the exact concentration at a certain measuring station at an exact time. Second, aggregation
semantics differ greatly between different user communities. Some people may
have to aggregate over time, others over space, and yet others by topic. In
order to appeal to a large user community, the UDK system must be able to
accommodate those different needs.

Although it is therefore desirable to handle the creation (and deletion) of UDK
objects with great flexibility, the decision to create a new object has to be based
on a cost/benefit analysis, depending on the particular applications a user has
in mind. The effort to create and maintain a UDK object is not negligible. Recent empirical data suggests that creation takes an average of one person-day.
Maintenance involves not only the occasional update of attributes but also the
dynamic tracking of semantic associations between UDK objects and the corresponding environmental data objects; see Section 3.5.3 for further details. At
this time, most of the related work is performed by specialized personnel from

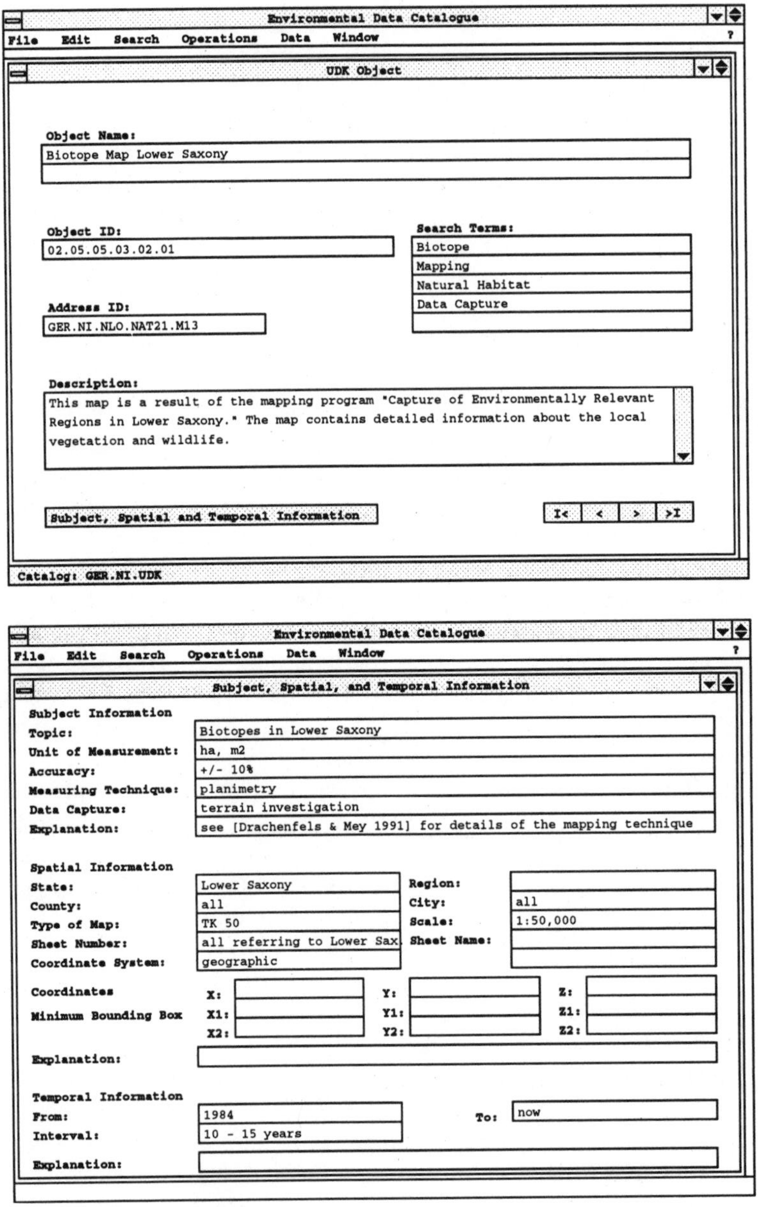

Figure 3-3 Two screen layouts representing a UDK object.

higher-level government agencies or consulting firms, and therefore is relatively expensive. It is unlikely that the work can be delegated to less qualified support staff in the near future. The idea to leave the creation of UDK objects to local domain experts (biologists, chemists, etc.) is also unrealistic at the present time. The process is still too technical and time-consuming for someone who is not a UDK expert.

Up to now, UDK objects have been identified by their position in the *primary tree*, a directed graph whose nodes correspond to the UDK objects and whose edges represent responsibilities of agencies and departments for particular sets of UDK objects, as well as part-of-relationships between large data collections (e.g., a groundwater database) and their components (e.g., the data sets corresponding to particular measuring stations). This approach to identify objects is unsatisfactory for a variety of reasons. Most importantly, UDK objects may lose their identity when they are relocated in the primary tree due to some reorganization (such as the transfer of a department from one ministry to another). In this case, the objects that were relocated have to be recreated under a new ID at the new location. As an alternative, we are currently investigating the possibility of using *object identifiers (OIDs)*, a concept well-known from the domain of object-oriented databases. OIDs are created by the system; they are usually not visible to the user. To guarantee universal uniqueness, the generation of the OID is usually based on the CPU number, as well as the current date and time of day.

3.5.2 UDK Object Classes and Inheritance

To structure the wide variety of UDK objects, and to facilitate both their capture and their administration, we recently presented the first proposal for a *UDK class concept* [14]. There we distinguish between seven classes of environmental data objects:

1. project data (construction projects, environmental impact studies, etc.)
2. empirical data (measuring series, laboratory data, etc.)
3. data about facilities (factories, buildings, etc.)
4. maps
5. expertises and reports
6. product data
7. model data (simulations, etc.)

For each of these seven classes of environmental data objects there is a corresponding UDK class that contains the UDK objects describing them. Each UDK class corresponds to a screen layout that is used for the capture and administration of the corresponding UDK objects. The bases for this pragmatic proposal were the user requirements that were stated during the first few months of UDK data capture. Obviously, this classification needs to be reviewed and possibly extended from time to time to reflect changes in user requirements. We feel it is important, however, that the above top-level classification reflects a consensus of all UDK participants.

Another extension that is currently planned concerns the *vertical* structure of this classification. In particular, we intend to turn this flat class structure into an object-oriented class hierarchy that allows the inheritance of object attributes. The hierarchy should be structured as follows.

- The root of the hierarchy (level 0) consists of the generic class *UDK_Object* with four obligatory attributes: the unique object identifier (OID), the object name, the date when the object was last modified, and the agency (or the person) that is responsible for the object. Optional attributes, such as a textual description, may be included as well. Note that this generic class is not an abstract class, i.e., it may contain objects that are not included in any of its subclasses.

- Level 1 contains a relatively small number of classes that represent a consensus between all UDK participants. Currently, this level corresponds to the seven classes described above. Changes at this level are subject to negotiation between the UDK member countries.

- On the subsequent levels of the hierarchy, participating countries or agencies are free to introduce additional subclasses depending on their particular requirements. This kind of flexibility is important not only for efficiency reasons but also for gaining acceptance throughout the intended UDK user community, especially in government agencies at the national and local levels.

Class attributes are inherited along this class hierarchy in an object-oriented manner. This includes the possibility to upgrade selected attributes from being optional to being required. It also means that attributes that are specific to a certain subclass, but not to its superclass(es), can be masked out when looking only at the superclass. For example, consider a particular topographic map m and its UDK object U_m. m is an element of the class *topographic_map*, which is a subclass of the class *map*. If one now looks at the UDK object U_m through the screen layout corresponding to the class *map*, one only sees the attributes of *map*. The additional attributes that may have been introduced to describe *topographic* maps (as a special case of general maps) are not visible in this case.

This feature, which is typical for object-oriented environments, is a crucial element of standardization in the presence of application-specific extensions on the class hierarchy levels 2 and below. Any tool that is supposed to work at the national (or international) level across particular agencies or user communities can rely on the availability of the attributes defined at level 1. Maintenance and version management are other issues that need to rely on a stable class and attribute structure at the higher levels of the object hierarchy. It is therefore important to take organizational and technical precautions to make sure that users observe this principle throughout user-specific extensions and increasingly complex class structures. The technical details of the implementation of these lower hierarchy levels are still under discussion.

3.5.3 Semantic Associations Between UDK Objects

Orthogonal to the class hierarchy described in the previous section, the UDK offers users the ability to connect *concrete UDK objects* with each other in a hypertext fashion. The resulting structures are directed graphs whose nodes correspond to UDK objects and whose edges represent semantic associations between them or between their respective environmental data objects. The semantics of those edges may vary; we will later propose a type system for edges to make this aspect more explicit. Note that those semantic nets are completely independent of the class hierarchy described in the previous section. While the nodes of the class hierarchy are *UDK object classes*, the nodes of the structures described in the following represent *concrete UDK objects*.

The most important graph structure is the *primary tree* or *primary catalogue*. Each UDK object corresponds to exactly one node of this tree structure, i.e., there is a 1:1 relationship between primary tree nodes and UDK objects. The links in the upper part of the tree serve to represent responsibilities of agencies and departments for particular sets of UDK objects. The agency that is in charge of a UDK object has to make sure that its information is correct and up to date. It is also responsible for the creation and deletion of UDK objects in the associated subtree(s). In the lower part of the tree, the links are used to represent part-of relationships between large data collections (e.g., a groundwater database) and their components (e.g., the data sets corresponding to particular measuring stations). The example given in Figure 3-4 depicts the UDK objects related to a groundwater database. Here the solid arrows make up the primary tree; their semantics varies between "is-responsible-for" (in the upper part of the tree) and "is-an-aggregation-of" (in the lower part).

Depending on particular user requirements, there may also be *secondary catalogs* to represent other semantic associations. Like the primary tree, a secondary catalogue is a directed graph whose nodes each correspond to exactly one UDK object. Other than in the case of the primary tree, however, the resulting structure does not have to be a tree. Note also that a UDK object can be referenced by any number of secondary catalogs. There is a 1:n relationship between UDK objects and secondary catalogue nodes: each UDK object can be a node in any number of secondary catalogs, but each secondary catalogue node refers to exactly one UDK object.

A typical application of a secondary catalogue concerns the representation of additional aggregation relationships that are not represented in the primary tree. In Figure 3-4 these kinds of associations are pictured as dotted arrows. These kinds of links are often useful to refer users first to relevant aggregated data sets before, upon request, giving them access to more detailed data. Another application of secondary catalogs is the construction of personal association structures. The "debate" association in Figure 3-4 (dashed line) is an example of such a structure. For such structures the system does not require users to restrict themselves to a tree structure. Similar to the freedom one has for linking pages in the World Wide Web, any directed graph structure is permitted, including graphs with cycles. The idea is to give UDK users maximum flexibility to connect and associate the various information items making up their working environment. With an attractive user interface, this option should be of great interest to a large group of users. What is important is that it has to be reasonably easy to create personal UDK objects and links. Furthermore, it is essential that those "personal" structures can be isolated from the public part of the UDK, so users can build confidential structures that are visible just for them or for their team.

In summary, it is important to note that the links connecting UDK objects may have a great variety of semantics. These different types of links need to be made explicit in the UDK by a labeling scheme. Users should have the option to choose the types of links they want to see at a given time. This would allow them to see a UDK object in a variety of contexts and to switch back and forth between those different representations. On the screen this could be supported,

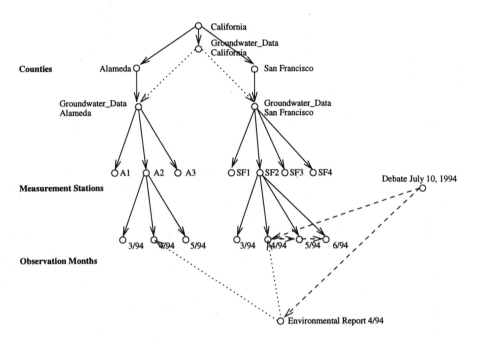

Figure 3-4 A selection of UDK objects and associations to represent a groundwater database.

for example, by different colors and drawing modes for different types of links (Figure 3-4).

3.5.4 The Future of the UDK

The UDK is a meta information system and navigation tool that documents collections of environmental data from the government and other sources. Given the extreme success of the World Wide Web (WWW), we expect a significant amount of this kind of data to be available via the Web in the very near future. At this point there is no question that the Web is the most promising option to follow the spirit of the EU guideline and to make environmental information *really available* to anybody who is interested. The UDK could play a major role in helping users to navigate in this overwhelming information pool, to identify which data is relevant for a given query, and to retrieve it fast and in a user-friendly manner.

Austria and several German states have recently released WWW implementations of the UDK (see http://www.wiwi.hu-berlin.de/~guenther/udk.html for
URLs). Access is mainly keyword-based. The result of a search is a list of
relevant UDK objects. More details on a particular object are available by
checking it and sending the marked-up form back to the server. A CGI script
then retrieves the corresponding additional attributes. Partly due to backlogs
in data entry, however, most UDK objects are much less elaborate than the
detailed example given in Figure 3-3.

HTML links between UDK objects or to environmental data objects are rarely
used in those implementations. Instead one can request the ancestor and de-
scendants of a given UDK object in the primary catalogue. This is done by
means of another form-based markup mechanism, similar to the one described
above. Further details of the implementation and related issues have been
described by Kramer et al. [20, 21].

A somewhat different approach for a WWW implementation of the UDK was
suggested in [14]. Here, each UDK object corresponds to exactly one Web
page. HTML links are used to implement primary and secondary catalogs
and to establish connections to environmental data objects. In our view this
architecture leads to a much more flexible and user-friendly implementation.
A corresponding realization is currently under consideration for the German
Federal version of the UDK.

3.6   Conclusions

The goal of this chapter was to show how metadata is becoming increasingly
popular in geographic and environmental information systems. It can improve
both the availability and the quality of the information delivered. The growing popularity of Internet-based data servers has accelerated this trend even
further. After a general discussion of the term metadata and of the question
how to integrate metadata into traditional information system architectures,
we have discussed several case studies in detail. Particular emphasis has been
put on the U.S. efforts to build a National Spatial Data Infrastructure, and on
several European projects to integrate environmental information processing at
the national and international levels.

Despite the remaining heterogeneities and inefficiencies, the outlook seems positive. The ubiquitous trend toward open systems as well as the rise of the World

Wide Web are two recent developments that will greatly improve the way we manage geographic and environmental information. Users will have faster and more comfortable access to ever greater amounts of information, and metadata will be an essential component of the underlying software architectures.

Finally, we envision an increasing number of applications where metadata is used to administer not only simple data sets but also complex software tools, such as domain-specific aggregation methods or environmental simulation models. In those applications, the metadata will be used for two purposes: (1) to find the appropriate software tool for a given problem, and (2) to apply the tool to a given data set over the Internet without having to port the software to a local machine. Our own MMM project [13] is one example of a software architecture that supports this paradigm.

Acknowledgments

Thanks to Pamela Drew, Ralf Kramer, Ralf Nikolai, Helmut Lessing, Jan Röttgers, Thomas Schütz, Amit Sheth, Walter Swoboda, and Jerry Ying for helpful comments. Thanks also to Jean-Marc Saglio, who hosted the first author's stay at the École Nationale Supérieure des Télécommunications in Paris, where parts of this work have been completed.

References

[1] C. Bardinet, J. E. Dubois, J. P. Caliste, J. J. Royer, and J. C. Oppeneau. Data processing for the environment analysis: a multiscale approach. In *Space and Time in Environmental Information Systems*, Marburg, Metropolis-Verlag, 1995.

[2] W. J. Campbell and R. F. Cromp. Evolution of an intelligent information fusion system. *Photogrammetric Engineering and Remote Sensing*, 56(6): 867–870, 1990.

[3] P. Drew and J. Ying. Metadata management for geographic information discovery and exchange. In W. Klas and A. Sheth (eds.), *Managing Multimedia Data: Using Metadata to Integrate and Apply Digital Data*, McGraw Hill, 1997.

[4] Council of the European Communities. Council Directive (90/313/EEC) of 7 June 1990 on the freedom of access to information on the environment. *Official Journal of the European Communities*, L158: 56–58, 1990.

[5] ESRI (ed.). *Proc. 11th ESRI User Conference.* ESRI Inc., Redlands, CA, 1991.

[6] ESRI (ed.). *Proc. 15th ESRI User Conference.* ESRI Inc., Redlands, CA, 1995.

[7] ESRI. Metadata management in GIS. Technical report, ESRI Inc., Redlands, CA, 1995. URL http://www.esri.com/resources/papers/papers.html.

[8] ESRI. SDTS – Supporting the Spatial Data Transfer Standard in ARC/INFO. Technical report, ESRI Inc., Redlands, CA, 1995. URL http://www.esri.com/resources/papers/papers.html.

[9] European Environmental Agency. Catalogue of data sources for the environment. Kopenhagen, Version 930831, August 1993.

[10] F. G. Fegeas, J. L. Cascio, and R. A. Lazar. An overview of FIPS 173, the Spatial Data Transfer Standard. *Cartography and Geographic Information Systems*, 19(5), 1992.

[11] FGDC. *Content Standards for Digital Geospatial Metadata.* U.S. Government, Federal Geographic Data Committee, Washington, D.C., 1994. URL ftp://fgdc.er.usgs.gov.

[12] Geographic Designs Inc. Online documentation of Geolineus 3.0. Santa Barbara, CA, 1995. URL http://www.geodesigns.com/gl_desc.html.

[13] O. Günther, R. Müller, P. Schmidt, H. K. Bhargava, and R. Krishnan. MMM: A Web-based system for sharing statistical computing modules. *IEEE Internet Computing*, 3(1), 1997.

[14] O. Günther, H. Lessing, and W. Swoboda. UDK: A European environmental data catalogue. In *Proc. 3rd Int. Conf./Workshop on Integrating GIS and Environmental Modeling, National Center for Geographic Information and Analysis (NCGIA)*, Santa Fe, New Mexico, January 1996.

[15] O. Günther and H.-J. Schek (eds.). *Advances in Spatial Databases.* Number 525 in LNCS. Berlin/Heidelberg/New York, Springer–Verlag, 1991.

[16] G. Hallmark. The Oracle warehouse. In *Proc. 21st Int. Conf. on Very Large Data Bases*, 1995.

[17] D. Johnson, P. Shelley, M. Taylor, and S. Callahan. The FINDAR directory system: a meta-model for metadata. In D. Medykyj-Scott, I. Newman, C. Ruggles, and D. Walker (eds.), *Metadata in the geosciences*, pp. 123–137, Loughborough, Great Britain, 1991.

[18] V. Kashyap, K. Shah, and A. Sheth. Metadata for building the MultiMedia Patch Quilt. In S. Jajodia and V.S. Subrahmanian (eds.), *Multimedia Database Systems: Issues and Research Directions*, Springer Verlag, 1995.

[19] H. Keune, A. B. Murray, and H. Benking. Harmonization of environmental measurement. *GeoJournal*, 23(3): 249–255, 1991.

[20] A. Koschel, R. Kramer, R. Nikolai, W. Hagg, and J. Wiesel. A federation architecture for an environmental information system incorporating GIS, the World Wide Web, and CORBA. *In Proc. 3rd Int. Conf./Workshop on Integrating GIS and Environmental Modeling, National Center for Geographic Information and Analysis (NCGIA)*, Santa Fe, New Mexico, January 1996.

[21] R. Kramer and T. Quellenberg. Global access to environmental information. In R. Denzer, D. Russel, and G. Schimak (eds.), *Proc. 1995 Int. Symposium on Environmental Software Systems*, International Federation for Information Processing (IFIP), pp. 209–218, London, Chapman and Hall, 1996.

[22] R. Kuggeleijn. Managing data about data. *GIS Europe*, 4(3): 32–33, 1995.

[23] R. Lenz, M. Knorrenschild, C. Herderich, O. Springstobbe, E. Forster, J. Benz, W. Assoff, and W. Windhorst. An information system of ecological models. Technical Report 27/94, GSF, Oberschleissheim, Germany, 1994. URL http://www.gsf.de/UFIS/ufis/ufis_publ.html.

[24] H. Lessing. Umweltinformationssysteme - Anforderungen und Möglichkeiten am Beispiel Niedersachsens. In A. Jaeschke, W. Geiger, and B. Page (eds.), *Informatik im Umweltschutz*, Berlin/Heidelberg/New York, Springer-Verlag, 1989.

[25] H. Lessing and T. Schütz. Der Umwelt-Datenkatalog als Instrument zur Steuerung von Informationsflüssen. In L. Hilty, A. Jaeschke, B. Page, and A. Schwabl (eds.), *Informatik für den Umweltschutz*, Marburg, Metropolis-Verlag, 1994.

[26] J. McCarthy. Metadata management for large statistical databases. In *Proc. 8th Int. Conf. on Very Large Data Bases*, 1982.

[27] D. Medykyj-Scott, I. Newman, C. Ruggles, and D. Walker (eds.). *Metadata in the geosciences*. Loughborough, Great Britain, 1991.

[28] R. B. Melton, D. M. DeVaney, and J. C. French (eds.). The Role of metadata in managing large environmental science datasets. In *Proc. SDM-92*, Richland, WA, 1995. Pacific Northwest Laboratory. Technical Report No. PNL-SA-26092.

[29] K. Mikkonen and A. Rainio. Towards a societal GIS in Finland - ArcView application queries data from published geographical databases. In ESRI (ed.), *Proc. 15th ESRI User Conference*, Redlands, CA, 1995. ESRI Inc.

[30] D. Miller and K. Bullock. Metadata for land and geographic information - an Australia-wide framework. In *Proc. AURISA'94*, pp. 391–398, Sydney, Australia, 1994.

[31] D. Miller and B. Forner. Experience in developing a natural resource data directory for New South Wales. In *Proc. AURISA'94*, pp. 391–398, Sydney, Australia, 1994.

[32] F. Ostyn. The EDRA - fueling GIS applications with required geographical information. In ESRI (ed.), *Proc. 15th ESRI User Conference*, Redlands, CA, 1995. ESRI Inc.

[33] W. Pillmann and D. J. Kahn. Distributed environmental data compendia. In *Proc. 12th IFIP World Computer Congress*. Elsevier, 1992.

[34] F. J. Radermacher. The importance of metaknowledge for environmental information systems. In O. Günther and H.-J. Schek (eds.), *Advances in Spatial Databases*, number 525 in LNCS, pp. 35–44, Berlin/Heidelberg/New York, Springer-Verlag, 1991.

[35] D. Seaborn. Database management in GIS: Is your system a poor relation? *GIS Europe*, 4(5): 34–38, 1995.

[36] M. Siegel and S. Madnick. A metadata approach to resolving semantic conflicts. In *Proc. 17th Int. Conf. on Very Large Data Bases*, 1991.

[37] U.S. Geological Survey. Spatial Data Transfer Standard (SDTS). Reston, VA, 1992. URL http://sdts.er.usgs.gov.

[38] U.S. Government. Coordinating geographic data acquisition and access: The national spatial data infrastructure. Washington, D.C., April 1994. U.S. Executive Order 12906.

[39] D. R. F. Walker. Introduction to metadata in the geosciences. In D. Medykyj-Scott, I. Newman, C. Ruggles, and D. Walker (eds.), *Metadata in the Geosciences*, Loughborough, Great Britain, 1991.

Chapter

4

Metadata Management for Geographic Information Discovery and Exchange

Pamela Drew and Jerry Ying

Department of Computer Science
Hong Kong University of Science and Technology
Clear Water Bay, Hong Kong
pamela.a.drew@boeing.com
jying@cs.ust.hk

Abstract

Geographic information plays an important role in the effective planning and development of large infrastructure projects; this is especially true in the rapidly developing regions of South East Asia. Correct and useful metadata descriptions of existing geographic information systems (GIS) are key to the discovery of what geographic information is available, and how to extract it for use in new applications. This chapter gives an overview of the management and use of metadata in a geographic information exchange facility under construction in Hong Kong. We present which types of metadata are useful to describe and communicate with heterogeneous GIS registered in the system, the distributed architecture and system components used to organize and translate the information between GIS, and the internal structures designed to support the user in the iterative and *ad hoc* process of metadata mining for the purpose of resource discovery and information retrieval.

4.1 Introduction

Traditionally, metadata has been defined and managed as a static view (i.e., database schema) about source information. The definition of these views was driven mostly by the need to support users in the process of discovery and assessment of information sources. However, the combined effects of an explosion in the amount and types of information available, and the advent of wide-area networks to interconnect pre-existing information sources, is changing the scope and role of metadata management.

In this expanded role, metadata models and their management systems should facilitate system-level interoperation, rather than just providing a static abstraction of source data. As more and more information becomes available in digital formats, metadata models should include information that will allow computers to connect to the source and extract requested data (or metadata) directly.

The objective of the GeoChange project at Hong Kong University of Science and Technology is to create a distributed information management architecture and related services to facilitate the discovery, selection, and retrieval of multiple, third-party geographic information sources across wide-area networks. An important task in this endeavour is to define a metadata architecture that will support system-level interoperability. Because autonomy of the third-party sources is a requirement, the metadata is maintained at the source, and is, therefore, also inherently distributed and heterogeneous just like the base geographic information.

The metadata architecture of GeoChange intersects and builds upon two important areas of research. One area is research on heterogeneous database management systems [1, 2] in which many proposals for related problems, such as schema integration, have been made. Indeed, schemas of databases are metadata. However, little has been done to analyze how other types of metadata that describe an information resource should be managed in unison with schematic metadata.

The other area is research on distributed object management and related architectures for interoperability, such as CORBA [3, 4, 5]. Systems based on these architectures have many advantages, including encapsulation, reuse, and dynamic binding of object services to implement interoperability. Yet, the details of how information exchange between heterogeneous data management objects should be performed are not specifically addressed; programmers are left to devise ad hoc solutions in the methods of the interoperating objects (or systems). The GeoChange metadata architecture is an attempt to bring the results of each of these areas to bear on the definition of an object-oriented architecture which specifically addresses how to manage metadata of heterogeneous systems for the purpose of information exchange.

This chapter is an operational view of metadata management in GeoChange. First, we give an overview of the system architecture in Section 4.2, followed by a discussion of the different types of metadata captured in a GeoChange metadatabase in Section 4.3. Section 4.4 presents how a metadatabase view is created via a systematic derivation process between information systems; Section 4.5 then describes a set of operational MetaObjects from which instances of the derivation process and information exchange can be created. Section 4.6 reviews how metadata can be queried and mined in a GeoChange server to support information resource discovery and base data retrieval. We then conclude with a discussion of the system prototype and a GeoChange application available on the World Wide Web.

4.2   System Architecture

The GeoChange architecture can be partitioned into three major subsystems: the GeoChange Local Registers, the GeoChange Server, and the GeoChange Service Interface, as denoted with the shaded areas in Figure 4-1; the bold dashed lines surround the GeoChange information infrastructure. Each of these subsystems can be distributed over a wide-area network and use a Common GeoChange Data Format (CGDF) for information exchange. Corresponding to these systems, we characterize three types of GeoChange users: the Data Provider, the GeoChange Administrator, and the Data Inquirer. Briefly, we describe each subsystem in turn; for a more thorough description please see [7].

First, there is a set of pre-existing geographic information stores each residing in geographically disparate locations and running on a variety of platforms. Each GIS interfaces with a GeoChange Local System Register (denoted Register in Figure 4-1), via its data manipulation interface, e.g., API or Data Interchange Format (DIF). The register consists of Data Import and Registration Processes. Using these processes, metadata can be semi-automatically extracted from the local system and stored in the GeoChange Server; base information can also be retrieved using these registration wrappers.

Second, there is a GeoChange Server which consists of several subsystems that coordinate the information flow between Local System Registers and Service Interfaces. It is important to note that while metadata and data are listed separately in Figure 4-1, they are treated uniformly in terms of representation and manipulation languages; they are only listed separately for clarity since metadata does serve many different roles in GeoChange from the base datasets.

Third, there are the Service Interfaces through which Data Inquirers, or their applications, access a GeoChange Server. Each Service Interface consists of Exploration and Export Processes. These processes enable end-users to browse the GeoChange metadatabase and extract information from various parts of regis-

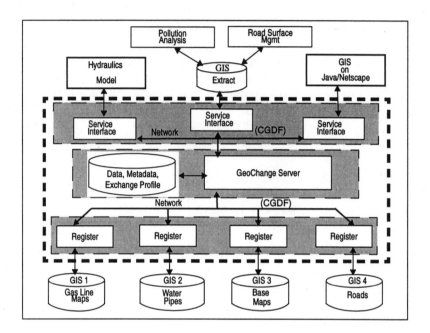

Figure 4-1 GeoChange system architecture overview.

tered sources into their own application format. Similar to the Local System Register, a Service Interface uses the CGDF to communicate with a GeoChange Server.

4.3   What to Represent

GeoChange metadata can roughly be divided into *system-specific* metadata, *domain-specific* metadata, and *instance-specific* metadata. System-specific metadata includes information required to extract data from a particular GIS API, and descriptions of other system capabilities, or utilities that GeoChange can use to facilitate geographic information translation. Figure 4-2 shows samples of two system-specific metadata entries. On_file_type stores which import and export file types are available for a particular GIS; for example, a *shape file* is a data translation standard that can be used to export data from the commercial GIS ARC/Info [8]. Similarly, each GIS has capabilities to translate between coordinate systems; these are captured in on_coord_conv. This information is used in planning the translation of datasets from disparate GIS into a new coordinate system requested by a Data Inquirer. Wherever possible, GeoChange defers data translation until retrieval time and delegates the conversion process to the local GIS, thereby reducing the workload at the server and distributing the processing as much as possible.

```
on_file_type

File type    File type name    File ext    System type    File info
shape        shape_file        shp         ARC/Info       ESRI universe file fmt
gina26       gina_26           gina        VISION         SHL imprt/exprt v2.6
gina30       gina_30           gina        VISION         SHL imprt/exprt v3.0


on_coord_conv

System type        Coordinate System
VISION             HK80GRID, AL_CONIC, OBL_MERC, MERCATOR, LAT/LONG
ARC/Info           MERCATOR, LAT/LONG
```

Figure 4-2 Sample system-specific metadata.

Domain-specific metadata relates to information particular to the geographic information application domain. This includes geo-referencing information such as scale, projection, region boundary, and coordinate systems. It also includes commonly used vocabulary of GIS models, such as Roads and Buildings, that is sometimes referred to as the ontology of the metadatabase [9]. The ontology serves a special purpose in that it provides the language of discourse for users of a GeoChange server: it is a knowledge-base of terminology with which users can pose queries to the metadatabase. The system itself also references this knowledge-base to perform correlations of metadata from different GIS registered with a server.

An excerpt of these pre-defined data types, units, and classifications in the GeoChange model is given in Figure 4-3. Noteworthy is the distinction between category types (on_category) and classifications (on_class). Category types give a large-grained view of different feature types, such as electricity features, frequently represented in a GIS as layers or themes. Classifications, on the other hand, give more fine-grained representation of the major categories: these classes are sometimes combined in a GIS to create a theme. Because each GIS varies in how it manages these distinctions, and because users may also organize classes of features into different layers, GeoChange does not enforce any particular organization beyond mapping the source information roughly into the GeoChange ontology.

Lastly, instance-specific metadata describes attributes about a particular data source such as its owner, its size, and creation date, as well as system-oriented

on_unit_type

Unit type	Unit name	Unit abbv	Unit info
METER	meter	m	Metric System (meter)
FEET	feet	ft	feet
SQ_METER	sq_meter	m2	Metric System (Square meter)
SQ_FEET	sq_feet	ft2	square feet

on_entity_type

Entity type	Entity name	Entity info
POINT	point	a point in space
LINE	line	a line in space
POLYGON	polygon	a polygon in space
NODE	node	a node on a network

on_category

Cat type	Cat name	Cat info
ROAD	road	road
ELEC	elec	elec
BLDG	bldg	bldg

on_class

Class type	Class info
TOWER	Tower Building
CHURCH	Church Building
POLICE	Police Station
FIRE	Fire Station
RESIDENTAL	Residental Building
COMMERICAL	Commercial Building
CABLE	Electricity Cable
TRANSFORMER	Electricity Transformer
SWITCH	Electricity Switch
ROAD	Roadway
HIGHWAY	Highway
TUNNEL	Tunnel

Figure 4-3   Sample domain-specific metadata: the ontology.

metadata, such as the network protocol for communication and the IP address of the data source. User-defined schemas, which augment pre-defined system specific schema and formats, are captured. This class of metadata also includes constraints that can be used as filters to limit the data that can be imported into a GeoChange server. For example, a Data Provider can limit the datasets by restricting the boundary within a region or ranges over a temporal period.

Figure 4-4 shows excerpts of metadata definitions captured about each source at the system level of granularity. For each system, an entry in the source _descriptor tracks information such as the system name, its coordinate system, and its coverage extent (the outer boundaries of the region mapped). An entry in system_descriptor captures metadata about the capabilities, or more precisely, the permitted operations on the local GIS. These include allowable access operations and the types of files which can be imported and exported from the system. System_coord_conv lists the types of coordinate systems that the particular GIS can interpret and produce. If a system registers that it has coordinate conversion capabilities (Y) in the system_descriptor, then its specific translation capabilities can be derived by cross-referencing the system_coord_conv metadata. Similar metadata entries about what file types can be imported and exported in a particular GIS are kept as well.

```
HK_source_descriptor

Source id  Source name  Coord type  Ext xmin  Ext ymin  Ext xmax  Ext ymax
1          elec_clp     HK80GRID    802230    810750    860550    846140
2          works        HK80GRID    801200    800790    861560    847150
3          transport    HKLat/Long  345355    367230    450320    257311
```

```
HK_system_descriptor

Source id  System type  ret  ret cost  crt  crt cost  imp/exp  coord conv
1          VISION       Y    5         Y    9         Y/Y      Y
2          SDE_TYPE     Y    4         N    0         N/Y      N
3          ARC/Info     Y    7         N    0         N/Y      N
```

```
HK_system_coord_conv

Source id              Coord type
1                      HK80GRID
1                      AL_CONIC
1                      AUSTGRID
1                      MERCATOR
```

Figure 4-4   Sample instance-specific metadata (system-level).

While registered source GIS will most likely disallow capabilities (N) such as the create operator (crt), target GIS need to allow such operations so that GeoChange can populate them with requested extracts. This information, combined with the import/export capabilities, is used by GeoChange to determine which GIS can support a user request (retrieve, import, or export), and if permissible, how to execute, and possibly, optimize a particular request. When appropriate, costs are associated with these capabilities to aid in the query planning and data translation process.

Figure 4-5, on the other hand, lists metadata excerpts which capture information about datasets within each system. Dataset_descriptor captures information about a particular dataset such as its category type; cat_type is an example of a field through which the GeoChange ontology is mapped onto the local GIS. Other instance-specific information, such as dataset name, is captured as well.

HK_dataset_descriptor

Source id	Dataset id	Dataset name	cat type
1	1	road	ROAD
1	2	elec	ELEC
1	3	bldg	BLDG
2	1	road	ROAD
2	2	roadann	ROAD
2	3	bldg	BLDG
2	4	bldgann	BLDG
2	5	hwy	ROAD
2	6	hwyann	ROAD
2	7	contour	CONTOUR
2	8	contourann	CONTOUR

HK_dataset_table

Source id	Dataset id	Class type	Table id	Table type	Table name
1	1	ROAD	1	F	feat_road
1	2	ELEC	1	F	feat_elec
1	3	BLDG	1	F	feat_bldg
1	1	ROAD	2	U	udf_Road
1	1	HWY	3	U	udf_Highway
1	2	CABLE	2	U	udf_Cable
1	2	TRANS	3	U	udf_Trnsformr
1	3	BLDG	2	U	udf_Building
2	1	ROAD	1	F	feat_road
2	2	ROADANN	1	F	feat_roadann
2	3	BLDG	1	F	feat_bldg
2	4	BLDGANN	1	F	feat_bldgann
2	5	HWY	1	F	feat_hwy

HK_dataset_table_def

Source id	Dataset id	Table id	Field id	Field name	Data type
1	1	2	1	name	char(30)
1	1	2	2	last_open	date
1	1	2	3	status	char(3)
1	1	2	4	type	char(5)

Figure 4-5 Sample instance-specific metadata (dataset-level).

Dataset_table and dataset_table_def describe the base data tables and the fields of the base tables, respectively; since the current implementation of GeoChange relies on the relational data model (details of the prototype implementation are summarized in the concluding section), the representation of the source information in GeoChange is a relational data view. Many contemporary GIS use some of these data model concepts in their API even though the underlying system is not always supported by relational database technology.

There are two main types of tables typically specified in a GIS: those that represent the spatial data which represents features on a map (coded F in the sample metadata) and those that capture descriptive, or annotational, information about those features (coded U in the sample metadata). For example, a river's name and its average depth are stored in a user-defined table (U), whereas the spatial information which grounds the line that represents the river in real world coordinates is stored in a system-defined table for feature (spatial) data (F). For each feature table, there can be any number of user defined tables, and referential integrity constraints between them are maintained.

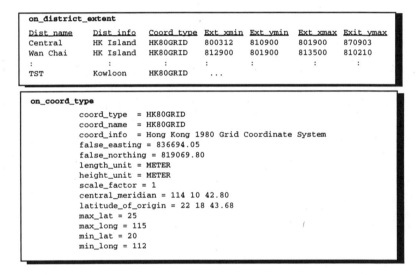

Figure 4-6 Sample metadata about a community GeoChange server.

And lastly, in addition to the instance-specific information for each local system, each GeoChange server must maintain a small amount of instance-specific metadata with respect to itself: this metadata is particular to the community (registered GIS) that it manages. For example, a GeoChange server specifically designed for the Hong Kong Community must maintain a small knowledge-base about the boundaries of particular districts in Hong Kong as most queries will be region (district) based. For the purpose of its own internal geoprocessing, it should also maintain its own coordinate system standard to which external datasets can be translated, merged (when possible), and presented to the Data Inquirer in the Metadata Browser. Figure 4-6 gives examples of this type of metadata.

In addition to this regional metadata, each GeoChange server can store metadata views about itself just as any other registered GIS. This allows GeoChange servers to be composable: one GeoChange server can become the source for another. This is similar to the hierarchy of information brokers that can be maintained in the Internet information resource discovery system, Harvest [10].

4.4   The Steps of Information Exchange

The previous section describes the types of metadata available to users of GeoChange for the purpose of GIS discovery and retrieval. The focus of this section is the system organization used in the GeoChange infrastructure to manage the derivation and translation of the metadata, and base data, from the source systems into the GeoChange metadatabase. The same infrastructure is used to support the extract, merge and export of geographic information into a target GIS. Hence, the mechanisms described here support interoperability of heterogeneous GIS.

Figure 4-7 summarizes the steps required to translate information in each phase of the GeoChange interoperability process. There are four different views of information created: Import Views, GeoChange Views, Selection Views, and Export Views. Import Views represent the data and metadata schema of the local systems. They provide the first level of translation in the information exchange process. In this step, a data model conversion from the local system to the GeoChange data model (e.g., the same data model of the CGDF) is performed. Concretely, this can be a translation from a GIS API (which inherently defines a data model, schema, and access methods) into a relational database representation. The box surrounding the respective data model of each system (the local GIS and GeoChange) represents the mapping procedure required to perform this translation. Its primary purpose is to eliminate any data model differences from the local systems while preserving their original information content in GeoChange. Import Views are the representation of the local GIS in the System Registers.

Second, GeoChange Views are collections of standardized records to which different Import Views can be translated; the instance-specific metadata tables presented in the previous section are partial examples of the metadata part of a GeoChange View. It is important to emphasize that GeoChange is literally a meta-metadatabase in that it is a database which organizes access to base data and the metadata about the base data. As a database itself, it contains

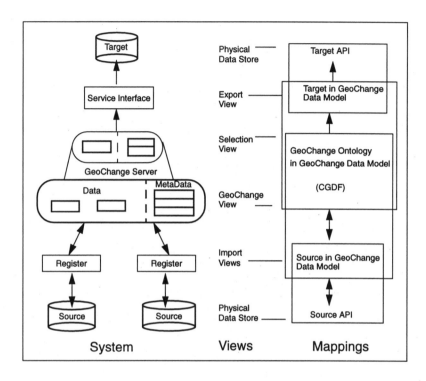

Figure 4-7 Correspondence of mapping between views in the system architecture.

metadata about metadata (and base data). Further, while each local system is captured in these common registration records (CGDF), the GeoChange metadatabase is not an integrated schema for the source systems. Instead, it is a federated architecture [1] that provides a common language in which each source GIS can be described; the Data Inquirer is still presented with the different backend systems registered with the server in this common language.

To create this meta-metadatabase, the Import Views are mapped into the GeoChange Views. However, the base data and the metadata are not handled uniformly, as summarized in Figure 4-8. The data mapping is a one-to-one correspondence from each source dataset provided by the local systems to the GeoChange View; each dataset of a local system will be represented in a separate CGDF record in the GeoChange View as depicted by the solid lines in Figure 4-8.

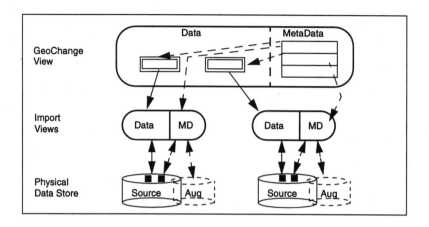

Figure 4-8   Derivation of data and metadata for a GeoChange view.

On the other hand, the metadata part of the GeoChange View summarizes, or wraps, the local system metadata into one metadatabase; the GeoChange View metadatabase can be described, in distributed database terminology, as a mixed fragmentation of the metadata parts of the Import Views. The mixed fragmentation, combined with the ontology and minimal regional metadata which summarizes a particular GeoChange server itself, creates a GeoChange metadatabase as presented in the previous section. The metadatabase also derives parts of the metadata (e.g., the schematic metadata) from the data part of the GeoChange View; in particular, the dataset_table and dataset_table_def presented in Figure 4-5 are examples of schematic metadata that can be used to query the local GIS for base data. Since schematic metadata describe base data, it is depicted as the outer boundary of the double edge rectangle in the GeoChange View data records of Figure 4-8; the metadata derivation relationships are depicted by the dashed lines.

Third, Selection Views represent the set of data which the Data Inquirer has chosen for extraction. Selection Views are formed in the same common language as the GeoChange Views. The Data Inquirer can create a Selection View by simply selecting a subset of a GeoChange View. Hence the mapping between these views is in effect a subview of the GeoChange View; no data model or schema translation is required. A Data Inquirer's Selection View can then be further refined to tailor it to the target schema (e.g., data from heterogeneous systems can be merged) during export.

And fourth, Export Views represent a Data Inquirer's selected metadata (and data) set in terms of a GeoChange representation of the target system's metadata and data models. It is analogous to the Import View created during the registration process and requires the inverse mapping step to translate from the schema of the Selection View into the schema of the Export View. From the Export View, the information is then translated from the GeoChange data model into the target GIS data model and schema using the target GIS API. Similarly, the export process, an analogous, but inverse, mapping procedure to the import process, is executed.

4.5   GeoChange MetaObjects

The reader may have noticed a pattern in the previous discussion of step-wise translation of information between heterogeneous systems. We abstract from these steps and identify a set of MetaObjects that provide an object-oriented model of what system components are needed to implement information exchange in this architecture; they are shown in Figure 4-9. Two primary types of MetaObjects are templates and views. GeoChange Templates are abstract (or deferred) classes, in object-oriented terms, which provide reusable structures that capture the basic metadata requirements of the GeoChange model and that can be specialized to represent different physical representations, e.g., an ARC/Info GIS.

There are three types of templates: System Templates, Common Templates, and Mapping Templates. The first two, System and Common Templates, map onto metadatabase storage components in a GeoChange architecture, i.e., the source and target GIS, and the GeoChange Server. These templates also provide the definition for the various views described in the previous section. In summary, the Import and Export Views are the first and last interface, respectively, between GeoChange and the physical representations (e.g., API) of the local systems; hence these views are implemented using System Templates.

Similarly, the Common Template provides the basic definition for the two views, GeoChange View and Selection View, that are kept in the GeoChange server. Since the Common Template is an abstract class in an object model, it can be specialized to represent the metadata model of choice; in our current experiment, it is specialized to the Common GeoChange Data Format (CGDF). By abstracting the metadata metamodel in this way, it is relatively easy to change the metadata model according to whatever GIS metadata standards are emerg-

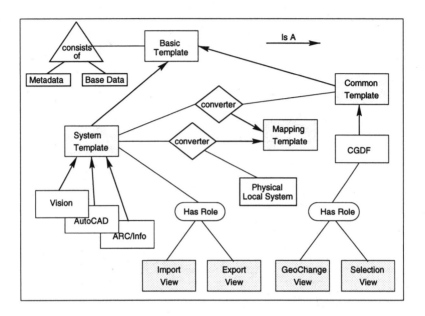

Figure 4-9 Metamodel of GeoChange metadata objects.

ing [11, 12]. Hence, the focus of this work is on the infrastructure to capture and manage a metadata model rather than the specific schema of a metadata model itself. The CGDF defined from this Common Template is based on our experimental experience in modeling several GIS systems.

The Mapping Templates manage conversions between System Templates and Common Templates: for each specialized class of a System Template, e.g., ARC/Info, a specialized class of a Mapping Template (denoted as converter in Figure 4-9) is created which translates from the schema of the specialized System Template into the schema of the specialized class created from the Common Template, e.g., a CGDF specification. Therefore, an example of a Mapping Template is an ARC/Info-to-CGDF converter. Further, since GeoChange provides uniform data manipulation for both metadata and base data, each of the metadatabase storage templates inherit from a Basic Template class which contains canonical definitions for each type of information. We illustrate each kind of template and their instantiations in the following subsections.

All of the template definitions and instances created from them are the declarations stored in the meta-metadatabase. In the same tradition as a single site DBMS, these reusable structures, and the catalogs that can be created from them, are stored in a repository within the GeoChange server. Because it is a meta-metadatabase, we refer to this repository as the MMDB.

4.5.1   System Template

Each specialized System Template is a model of a type of GIS, e.g., Vision, that GeoChange supports. As shown in Figure 4-9, it consists of a (base) data view and a metadata view. A data view template is the default data representation of a system. For example, for the GIS, Vision [13], a data view template may simply consist of a feature table definition and an associated feature attribute table definition. An example excerpt of the data part of a Vision System Template is shown in Figure 4-10.

```
DATA VIEW:

$Vision_Features (
            feat_num        NOT NULL        number(10);
            type            NOT NULL        number(2);
            feat_code       NOT NULL        char(5);
            layer           NOT NULL        number(5);
            network         NOT NULL        number(5);
            length          NOT NULL        number(38,8)
            ix_s                            number(38,8);
            iy_s                            number(38,8);
            ix_e                            number(38,8);
            iy_e                            number(38,8);
            ix_min                          number(38,8);
            iy_min                          number(38,8);
            ix_max                          number(38,8);
            iy_max                          number(38,8);
            pt_count                        number(10);
            area                            number(38,8);
            text                            char(255);
            sdata                           BLOB;
);
```

Figure 4-10   Sample data vision system template.

On the other hand, a metadata view template stores information about the data in the GIS. It includes the ontology in the database, and user-defined data definitions not included in the GIS system standard. It is typically composed of two parts. One part is the metadata that can be extracted directly from the GIS itself; Figure 4-11 contains an excerpt of the types of information that can be extracted from Vision, for example. It includes most of the domain-specific and some of the instance-specific metadata required to populate a GeoChange View.

```
METADATA VIEW (API):
$(source_descriptor) (
     source_id          NOT NULL      char(10);
     coord_type         NOT NULL      char(10);
     extent_xmin                      number(38,8);
     extent_ymin                      number(38,8); ...);
$(layer_info) (
     source_id          NOT NULL      char(10);
     coord_type         NOT NULL      char(10);
     extent_xmin                      number(38,8);
     extent_ymin                      number(38,8); ...);
$(network_info)   (
     network            NOT NULL      number(5);
     layer              NOT NULL      number(5);
     name               NOT NULL      char(30);
     type               NOT NULL      char(1);
     description                      char(80); ...);
$(user_define_table)  (
     layer              NOT NULL      number(5);
     feat_code          NOT NULL      char(5);
     description                      char(80);
     primary_name                     char(30);    );
$(attribute_info) (
     field_id           NOT NULL      number(10);        // sys gen
     table_name         NOT NULL      char(30);
     field_name         NOT NULL      char(30);
     data_type          NOT NULL      char(1);
     length             NOT NULL      number(10);
     decimal                          number(3);
```

Figure 4-11   Sample metadata vision system template.

The other part is that metadata which is not directly extractable from the GIS such as system capabilities. In this case, an augment is created; the Vision System Template augment is shown in Figure 4-12. Augments must always be populated manually by the Data Provider; automatic augment population for certain types of metadata is a topic of future work. Note also that since each GIS provides different types of metadata via its API, the design of which metadata resides in the augment and which is in the metadata part of the metadata System Template will vary from GIS to GIS. The examples given here are particular to Vision by way of illustration. Further, the augments, while ostensibly under GeoChange control, are treated uniformly as if they were stored in the local system. For example, during retrieval, GeoChange

makes queries against the backend systems and their augments; it does not
keep materialized views, or copies of the data, locally in the GeoChange server.

```
METADATA VIEW (AUGMENT):
$(source_descriptor)(
     source_id      NOT NULL    char(10);
     source_name    NOT NULL    char(10);
     source_info                char(255);
     dbms_name                  char(64);
);

$(system_descriptor) (
     source_id      NOT NULL    char(10);  // sys gen
     system_name    NOT NULL    char(64);
     system_info                char(255);
     ret            NOT NULL    char(1);   // retrieve
     ret_cost                   number(2);
     crt            NOT NULL    char(1);   // create layer
     crt_cost                   number(2);
     upt            NOT NULL    char(1);   // update
     upt_cost                   number(2);
     del            NOT NULL    char(1);   // delete
     del_cost                   number(2);
     drp            NOT NULL    char(1);   // drop layer
     drp_cost                   number(2);
     import         NOT NULL    char(1);   // file import
     export         NOT NULL    char(1);   // file export
     sp_idx_cap     NOT NULL    char(1);   // spatial index
     coord_conv     NOT NULL    char(1);   // coord conversion
);
```

Figure 4-12   Sample augment for metadata vision system template.

The GeoChange metadatabase in effect then, with a very few exceptions, is
simply a gateway or filter to the source metadata. We take this approach
to maintain the integrity of the metadatabase with respect to the source. In
a GeoChange environment, Data Providers can change their source and augments, and, hence, copies of it could become out of synchronization without
appropriate measures. Of course, it may be more tractable to make copies
of certain portions of metadata in the GeoChange server itself for performance
reasons; in this case, replicated data management techniques tailored to operate
in a wide-area network should be applied.

Also note that field and table names preceded by a $ are variables which are
bound when the template is instantiated (for a discussion of how parts of this
naming process can be automated, see [6]). For example, the $Vision_Feature

```
METADATA Electricity GIS
elec_clp.S.source_descriptor
source_id = "1"
coord_type = "HK80GRID"
extent_xmin = 802230
extent_ymin = 810750
extent_xmax = 860550
extent_ymax = 846140
```

```
elec_clp.S.layer_info
```

layer	name	description
1	"road"	"Road information"
2	"elec"	"Electricity information"
3	"bldg"	"Building information"

```
elec_clp.S.network_info
```

network	layer	name	type	description	connectivity name
1	1	"road"	NAN	"road network"	"road_net"
2	1	"hwy"	NAN	"highway network"	"hwy_net"
:					

```
elec_clp.S.user_defined_table
```

layer	feat code	description	primary name
1	"rd"	"Road"	"Road"
1	"hwy"	"Highway"	"Highway"
2	"e_cable"	"Cable"	"Cable"
2	"e_trans"	"Transformer"	"Transformer"
3	"bldg"	"building"	"building"
:	:		:

```
elec_clp.S.user_defined_attribute_info
```

field id	primary name	field name	data type	length	...
1	f_road	feat_num	n	10	
2	f_road	feat_code	c	5	
:	:	:	:	:	
20	Road	feat_num	n	10	
21	Road	name	c	30	
:	:	:	:	:	
26	f_elec	feat_num	n	10	

Figure 4-13   Metadata populated for vision system template on electricity GIS.

table could be instantiated to form a table called Lightning in a GIS kept by an electricity company which stores the recorded lightning strikes in Hong Kong. Figure 4-13 gives an example of an instantiation of the metadata part of the Vision System Template, and some sample metadata to populate it; the base data part is not shown for brevity. The reader should be able to recognize from this example which parts of the metadatabase entries presented in Figures 4-4 and 4-5 are derived from this source GIS.

4.5.2 Common Template

Common templates are abstract classes that can be specialized to create the common registration record format for a particular GeoChange server. Similar to the System Template, it has a data and a metadata part. An excerpt of the Data Common Template is shown in Figure 4-14. The $Common_Feature table provides information for feature extraction, but it does not provide enough information about the geographic features, such as length, area, and extent, that are useful for discovery and assessment. Fortunately, these feature attributes are usually derivable from the base data represented in the $Common_Feature table. We create a separate table called $Common_Feature_Attributes for such information, an excerpt of which is also shown in Figure 4-14. All systems' feature attributes are mapped to this container. If the system does not provide some of the attribute information explicitly, geoprocessing utilities within the GeoChange server may be able to derive (calculate) the attribute from the raw data. However, for those cases that cannot be covered, there are null values, or *holes*, in a CGDF record for a particular attribute of a GIS dataset.

```
$(Common_Feature) {
            fid             NOT NULL        number(10);
            entity_type     NOT NULL        number(10);
            numofpts        NOT NULL        number(5);
            sdata                           BLOB; );
```

```
$(Common_Feature_Attributes) {
            fid             NOT NULL        number(10);
            cat_type        NOT NULL        number(10);
            class_type      NOT NULL        number(10);
            length                          number(38,8);
            area                            number(38,8);
            network                         number(10);
            min_x                           number(38,8);
            min_y                           number(38,8);
            min_z                           number(38,8);
            max_x                           number(38,8);
            max_y                           number(38,8);
            max_z                           number(38,8);
            angle                           number(10);
            text                            char(255);
            cr_date                         number(10);
            cr_uid                          number(10);
            cr_gid                          number(10);
            mod_date                        number(10);
```

Figure 4-14 Example data common template.

Much of the metadata part of a Common Template (CGDF) definition was
introduced in the discussion of instance-specific metadata in Section 4.3. For
example, the source_descriptor, system_descriptor, dataset_descriptor,
dataset_table, and dataset_table_def are all examples of the metadata part
of a CGDF. As mentioned in Section 4.4, each of these tables is a mixed fragmentation over the Import views of the source GIS. To create this distributed
schema, a fragmentation attribute is added to each metadata Import View so
that the metadata manager can distinguish from which view a particular piece
of metadata is retrieved. For instance, the source_id attribute in the instance-
specific metadatabase tables serves this purpose; it is mapped to the local system augment table in the Import Views. Another key part of the metadatabase
materialization is the definition of the mapping template which specifies which
fields in the Import Views are assigned, and potentially combined, to create
the field entries in the metadatabase in the GeoChange server.

4.5.3   Mapping Templates

A specialized Mapping Template is a collection of conversions, i.e., a conversion
object, which translate between fields in different views; per the GeoChange
MetaObject model of Figure 4-9, these mappings either convert from local
system interfaces to Import Views, from Import Views to GeoChange Views,
from Selection Views to Export Views, or from Export Views to a local system
interface. In the most simple case, an entry in a Mapping Template will be
a one-to-one mapping between fields. In addition, any data type or value
conversion can be specified in the entry. One-to-many mappings, in which
a number of fields are used to calculate the value of a destination field, are
also supported; the $Common_Feature_Attributes are typical fields for which
many-to-one field mappings are required. A sample mapping template is given
in Figure 4-15.

```
$mapping (
     source_field_id    NOT NULL    number(10);
     dest_field_id      NOT NULL    number(10);
     type_convert_to                char(30);
     value_convert_to               char(30);
     type_convert_fm                char(30);
     value_convert_fm               char(30);
);
```

Figure 4-15   Sample mapping template.

Parts of an instance of a mapping definition between a VISION System Import View and a GeoChange View are listed in Figure 4-16. In the first entry, the dataset_name in the GeoChange View is created by a simple assignment from the name attribute in the layer_info table of the Vision Import View. In the second entry, the dataset_id in the GeoChange view requires a data type conversion from the layer identifier in the Vision Import View; this mapping process also triggers some internal bookkeeping procedures which uniquely identify all datasets within a GeoChange server. And in the third entry, the dataset's category type in the GeoChange View is derived by mapping the source's metadata into the GeoChange ontology (e.g., mapping the local dataset name hk_road into the type, ROAD, defined in the GeoChange ontology (on_category)).

```
System = template_table.$(layer_info).name
Common = table.dataset_descriptor.dataset_name
type_convert_to = NULL
value_convert_to = NULL
type_convert_fm = NULL
value_convert_fm = NULL
```

```
System = template_table.$(layer_info).layer
Common = table.dataset_descriptor.dataset_id
type_convert_to = STR()
value_convert_to = register_dataset_id(source_id,layer)
type_convert_fm = VAL()
value_convert_fm = register_layer_id(source_id, dataset_id);
```

```
System = template_table.$(layer_info).name
Common = table.dataset_descriptor.cat_type
type_convert_to = NULL
value_convert_to = cat_type_lookup(name);
type_convert_fm = NULL
value_convert_fm = NULL
```

Figure 4-16 Sample mapping entries: Vision-to-GeoChange.

Once the registration and mapping procedures are complete, a GeoChange metadatabase can be materialized via these mappings between views. For example, the metadatabase presented in Figures 4-4 and 4-5 can be generated this way.

4.6   Using the Metadatabase

There are two main activities which the metadatabase supports: browsing and extraction. This section gives an overview of the processing steps and some additional internal structures required to support each.

4.6.1   Browsing

Core to all Data Inquirer activities is query processing support. GeoChange query processing can be partitioned into two major classes of queries at the metadata and base data levels, though the user can transcend these level seamlessly. We term these classes of queries *meta-queries* and *base-queries*, respectively. In the following subsections, we summarize the query processing steps for each class of query.

Meta-Queries

We use the term meta-query to refer to requests to the metadatabase which supports the user in the discovery and assessment of datasets registered in a GeoChange server. For instance, the user could submit the following query[1]:

> Find the names, system types, and coordinate systems for all
> GIS that have "ROAD" datasets available in the area "Central".

This query requires a correlation of the concept *Road* to the dataset types provided in the source systems; for now, the GeoChange server manages this procedure as a straightforward table look-up in the GeoChange ontology, but more sophisticated concept space correlation can certainly be applied [9, 14]. An equivalent statement, using SQL-like syntax, on the GeoChange View is:

```
Select   SD.Source_id, SD.Source_name, DSD.Dataset_name,
         SysD.System_type, SD.Coord_type
   from  HK_dataset_descriptor as DSD,
         HK_source_descriptor as SD,
         HK_system_descriptor as SysD
  where  DSD.Cat_type = ROAD
```

---

[1] Central is the *Wall Street* of Hong Kong.

and   DSD.Source_id = SD.Source_id
and   SysD.Source_id = SD.Source_id
and   Within_Extent("Central",
          SD.Ext_Xmin, SD.Ext_Ymin, SD.Ext_Xmax, SD.Ext_Ymax)

This federated query must be decomposed into several sub-queries that can be executed at local sites. First, the global query is parsed and the mapping instances, such as those presented in Figure 4-16, are retrieved from the MMDB. Figure 4-17 summarizes the views and derivations between them to produce the end-user query result.

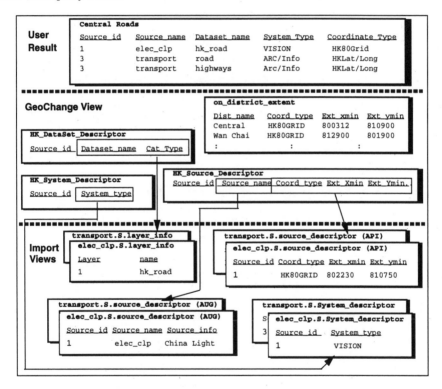

Figure 4-17 Metadata derivation path for "Find all systems with ROAD data".

Each of the GeoChange View tables is automatically decomposed into the corresponding fields in the Import Views across the local systems and appropriate query operations are performed to materialize the result. For example, HK_source_descriptor is created by a semi-join operation over HK_dataset _descriptor with those items with the ROAD category type as the selection criteria. HK_source_descriptor's tuples are materialized through a vertical fragmentation over the corresponding API portion (e.g., Coord_type, Ext_Xmin, etc.) and augment portion of the metadata (e.g., Source_name) in the Import Views. Data_set_descriptor illustrates another way in which data conversions are used: the same source attribute, layer_info.name, stored in the Import View is used to derive two different attributes, Dataset_name and Category_type, in the global dataset description (i.e., HK_dataset_descriptor). These two different conversion functions are specified in an instance of the mapping template in Figure 4-16.

Analogous to the data mappings, function calls in the GeoChange View can also be translated into functions calls supported in the local GIS. Indeed, a goal of GeoChange is to reuse existing facilities of GIS for data translation and conversion as much as possible. In this example, the Within_Extent function call can be decomposed into a set of equivalent calls at the local GIS. The result of the data mapping and decomposition process from the global query to the example electricity GIS, in SQL-like syntax, is:

```
Select   layer, name
   from   elec_clp.S.layer_info,
          elec_clp.S.source_descriptor as SD
   where Match_Type ("ROAD", name)
   and   Within_Extent("Central",
              SD.Xmin, SD.Ymin, SD.Xmax, SD.Ymax);
```

Metadata Mining for Resource Discovery and Base-Queries

In addition to meta-queries, a Data Inquirer can also query the source GIS for base data. To support dynamic access to autonomous information sources, GeoChange must provide facilities that allow the user to explore the information space to discover the necessary metadata to pose *ad hoc* base-queries. These facilities should support mining of metadata about the local systems, for the purpose of query formulation and execution, and seamless navigation between metadata and data views. This is in contrast with the alternative, and more traditional, heterogeneous database approach in which all base data are integrated into a global schema; this alternative is unsuitable for the GeoChange infrastructure since a primary goal of the system is to facilitate information discovery from disparate and autonomous sources. This section summarizes the steps involved in exploratory and iterative query processing and the internal structures designed to support it.

Suppose a Data Inquirer wanted to retrieve the following information:

List all the names and last excavation dates of the roads in the Electric Company's Dataset that have been unearthed since January, 1994.

This request can be processed through a sequence of iterative queries. At each step, the corresponding SQL statement and interim result is given based on the sample metadatabase values shown in Figure 4-17; highlighted data elements in each result are the selections used to refine the query path as the search continues.

Step 1 Uniquely identify all information sources with the appropriate class of information (e.g., ROADS); this is essentially the same query presented in previous section.

```
Select    DSD.source_id, DSD.Dataset_id,
          SD.Source_name, DSD.Dataset_name
from      HK_dataset_descriptor as DSD,
          HK_source_descriptor as SD
where     DSD.Cat_type = ROAD
and       DSD.Source_id = SD.Source_id
```

RESULT: Central Roads			
Source_id	Dataset_id	Source_name	Dataset_name
1	1	**elec_clp**	**hk_road**
3	1	transport	road
3	2	transport	highways

Step 2 Discover the proper terminology required to submit queries to the Electricity database to get more detail about the ROAD information:

1. First find a probable base data object, e.g., table[2], in the source:

---

[2]We use relational data model terms in the example, but this process applies equally to any structured data model.

```
Select          class_type, table_name, table_id
from            HK_dataset_table
where           source_id = 1 and dataset_id = 1
```

```
RESULT: Tables in Electricity (elec_clp)
class type    table name    table id
ROAD          feat_road     1
ROAD          udf_Road      2
```

2. Find what attributes are available for that object:

```
Select          field_id, field_name, data_type
from            HK_dataset_table_def
where           table_id = 2
```

```
RESULT: Attributes for User Defined Roads Information
Field id    Field name    Data type
  1         name          char(30)
  2         last_open     date
  3         status        char(3)
  4         type          char(5)
```

Step 3 Formulate the base-query against the source using the discovered meta-data. In SQL-like syntax, this query is:

```
Select          name, last_open
from            elec_clp.C.hk_road.udf_Road
where           last_open > 1993/12/31
```

This query would be translated into a sequence of *gql* calls, the API of Vision. The base-query result is shown below:

```
RESULT: Electricity Company Road Data
Road name    Last open
Queens Rd    3.1.94
Pedder St    4.1.96
```

Query Composition Hierarchy

To support this kind of process, GeoChange maintains a four-level query composition hierarchy which maps onto search variables that must be grounded at each interim step to generate executable queries; the levels of this hierarchy and the query variables bound at each level are depicted in Figure 4-18. The levels of the hierarchy are an abstraction of the major information objects in the GeoChange metadatabase: information sources, the datasets within each source, the objects (i.e., tables in a relational model) which comprise the datasets, and the attributes of the objects. At each level, there is a designated variable for which the user must supply a value to traverse to the next lower level in the hierarchy; the user can select these values from the result set generated by a query executed in the previous level of the hierarchy. As the user traverses down the hierarchy, the information space is made correspondingly more narrow.

Level	Query to Generate Binding Values	Bound Variable
Source	(select * from Source_descriptor)	NULL
Dataset	(select * from Dataset_descriptor)	Source_id
Object	(select * from Dataset_table)	Dataset_id
Attribute	(select * from Table_def)	Table_id

Figure 4-18   Four level hierarchy.

For example, in the first level of the hierarchy, the user can choose from any source registered in the source_descriptor metadata object; the free variable to be bound is the source_id. This reduces the scope of the search to the datasets of information in the selected source or sources. The next level requires that, in addition to a source_id, a dataset_id must also be bound. The last two levels in our example of table and field follow similar rules.

This composition hierarchy motivates the design of an internal data structure, called the *state structure*, which is used by the query processor to pose queries on the metadatabase. Figure 4-19 shows an example state structure for the previous base-query formulation example. Each node, depicted by the shaded boxes, tracks its level in the hierarchy, its unique identifier within that level (a level can have more than one node), the values assigned to the bound variable for that node, and pointers to nodes in the next lower level of the hierarchy.

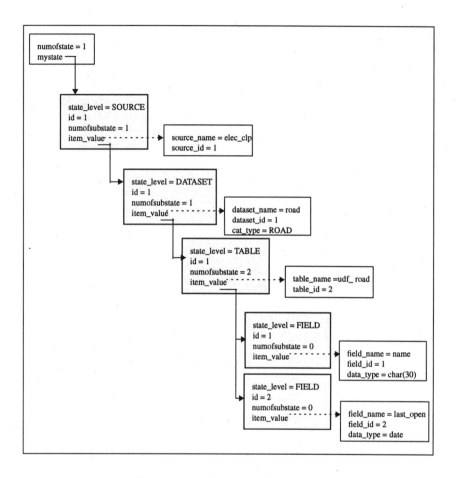

Figure 4-19   Example state structure.

Conceptually, the binding of the free variable in each level of the hierarchy can be thought of as requiring the execution of a query on the metadatabase. For example, the user could create the first two levels in the hierarchy by first selecting a source_id from the result set of a query for all registered sources and then selecting a dataset_id from the result set of a query for the datasets in that particular source. It is also possible for the user to formulate queries that will create and bind more than one level at a time. For example, the first two levels could both be automatically created and filled when the user executes the single query shown in the first step of selecting the Road dataset in the running example. The iterative query and bind process are repeated until the field level is complete, after which a query on the base data can be submitted to the local GIS. At each step, the user can place specific conditions on the query, e.g., select the roads unearthed since a certain date.

In a typical browsing session, a user will percolate up and down the composition hierarchy until the desired information is found. To support this process, a State Manager dynamically controls the state structure for each user's browsing session. For example, if a user finds a particular search path unfruitful, he or she can backtrack either to the top of the hierarchy or to some intermediary node. In this process, the user can indicate the components of the query to be discarded; internally the State Manager deallocates the corresponding state nodes.

Similarly, a user may wish to build a more complex query based on some previously discovered information (and corresponding state structure for the query); the new query could require join operations across datasets or tables, which potentially reside in heterogeneous sources. In this case, branches are formed in the state structure for different access paths to each set of base data. Hence, the state hierarchy is somewhat akin to a specialized query tree that can be incrementally constructed or destroyed and conforms to the composition hierarchy rules.

Lastly, the reader can note that the class of queries executed to *populate* a state structure are exactly those we refer to as meta-queries; this is the set of queries which return results about the information sources. On the other hand, queries *generated from* a populated state structure result in base data retrieval: the results will be data from within the local GIS. Base data retrieval requires that at least one state node at the TABLE level be complete; queries generated from the next higher level will result in a meta-query, e.g., a set of table definitions will be retrieved.

4.6.2   Export Process

By browsing the metadatabase, the user can discover the exact type, format, and content of the systems registered with a GeoChange server. If required information is found, GeoChange supports a 2-phased extract process. The first phase is to create a Selection View. Since Selection Views are also special-izations of the Common Template, they are selected subsets of CGDF records from a GeoChange View. For example, the user may specify that the data described by the the result of the metadata query as presented in Figure 4-17 become his or her Selection View. The details, and difficulties, which arise in merging heterogeneous geographic information are beyond the scope of this chapter.

The second phase is the translation process from a Selection View to the Export View of the target GIS; since this process is exactly the inverse of the import process, we only summarize it here. First, the Data Inquirer can select a System Template appropriate for the target GIS. Just as in the case of import, a specialization of this System Template, which accounts for any additional user-defined information, can be created; this defines the Data Inquirer's Export View. This target GIS is then registered with GeoChange: that is, GeoChange is made aware of the system-specific and instance-specific metadata required to communicate with it. In addition, an instance of an appropriate Mapping Template (e.g., CGDF-to-ARC/Info) is created that will perform the translation for this particular pair of Selection and Export Views.

Notice an important implication of the GeoChange metadata architecture: if the Data Inquirer makes no alterations to the Mapping Template class, the translation of information and export of it into the target GIS can be entirely automated (provided appropriate conversion functions, such as coordinate system conversion utilities, are available either in GeoChange or in the participating GIS). Even if the Data Inquirer makes some alterations, a large part of the work is already done by the GeoChange infrastructure. Further, by separating the interoperability model into distinct objects, each of which performs a narrowly defined part of the overall task, the modeling and execution of information exchange between multiple GIS are simplified.

4.7   Status and Summary

This chapter has given an overview of the management and use of metadata in a geographic information exchange facility; at its core is a distributed and heterogeneous metadatabase derived from the source GIS. A three way classification scheme of what types of metadata are needed, and a step-wise translation process of the metadata between heterogeneous GIS, were given. Based on this analysis, a set of reusable MetaObjects which capture the metadata model and the translation process were identified; these objects package the interoperation process into understandable and simplified steps. Using the metadatabase derived with these objects, a user can discover what geographic information is registered with the system using an iterative and *ad hoc* query process supported by facilities that allow transparent navigation between the metadata and base data of the source GIS. By supplying the appropriate MetaObjects much, if not all, of the extract process of metadata and data can be automated. The domain of geographic information is used as an experimental platform; however, most of the design principles of this metadata architecture are general and can be applied to any application domain.

The prototype implementation of the GeoChange facility is a combination of two commercial systems. One is InterViso [2], a heterogeneous database management system that supports the core distributed data management features of GeoChange. It provides the basic system architecture for parts of the reusable data translation facilities, query decomposition and translation, and communications software. Because its federated schema is based in the relational data model, the first instance of the GeoChange CGDF is also based in the relational data model. The other implementation component is the Spatial Database Engine [15], a database engine with geoprocessing functions. It provides a geoprocessing substrate for the GeoChange metadatabase and browsing facilities.

The first demonstration scenarios of the GeoChange prototype involve the translation and merging of source databases extracted from ARC/Info, Vision, and AutoCad provided by the Hong Kong GIS community. It is used to supply information to an "Open Road Notification" application that conveys what utilities (e.g., electricity lines, sewage pipes, etc.) are uncovered whenever a road surface is opened. Based on this experience, we will further refine what metadata should be captured in GeoChange and its most effective use in a wide-area, geographic information exchange environment.

Acknowledgments

This research is supported Hong Kong University Grants Council Research Infrastructure Grant RI93/94.RC01 and Sino Software Research Center Grant SSRC94/95.EG10. The GeoChange project has also enjoyed support, in part, from Data Integration, Inc., Environmental Systems Research Institute (ESRI), the Hong Kong Government Works Branch, Systems House, Inc., and various Hong Kong utility companies. Special thanks also to Duncan McInnis (HKUST) and the other project team members, Philip Lei and Lyman Do, for their help in the implementation of the GeoChange prototype.

References

[1] A. Sheth and J. Larson, "Federated Database Systems for Managing Distributed, Heterogeneous, and Autonomous Databases", ACM Computing Surveys, Sept. 1990, Vol. 22, pp. 183-236.

[2] M. Templeton, H. Henley, E. Marcos, and D. Buer, "InterViso: Dealing With the Complexity of Federated Databases Access", VLDB Journal, April 1993, Vol. 4, No. 2, pp. 287-317.

[3] L. Liu and C. Pu, "The Distributed Interoperable Object Model and Its Application to Large-scale Interoperable Database Systems", Proc. of the 4th International Conference on Information and Knowledge Management, Maryland, Nov. 1995.

[4] F. Manola, S. Heiler, D. Georgakopoulous, M. Hornick, and M. Brodie, "Distributed Object Management", International Journal of Intelligent and Cooperative Information Systems, March 1992, Vol. 1, No. 1, pp. 127-142.

[5] OMG, "The Common Object Request Broker: Architecture and Specification, revision 2.0", Object Management Group, July 1995.

[6] P. Drew and J. Ying, "A Metadata Architecture for Multi-System Interoperation", First IEEE Metadata Conference, Maryland, April 1996.

[7] P. Drew and J. Ying, "GeoChange: An Experiment in Wide-Area Database Services for Geographic Information Exchange", IEEE Advances in Digital Libraries, Washington D.C., May 1996, pp. 14-23.

[8] S. Morehouse, "The ARC/Info Geographic Information System", Computers and Geosciences: an International Journal, 1992, Vol. 18, No. 4, pp. 435-443.

[9] V. Kashyap, K. Shah, and A. Sheth, "Metadata for Building the Multimedia Patch Quilt", Multimedia Database Systems: Issues and Research Directions, S. Jajodia and V.S. Subrahmaniun, Eds., Springer Verlag, 1995.

[10] T. Berners-Lee, et. al., "The HARVEST information discovery and access system", Proc. 2nd Intl. World-Wide-Web Conf., 1994, pp. 763-771.

[11] Federal Geographic Data Committee, "Content Standards for Digital Geospatial Metadata", March 1994.

[12] R. G. Fegeas, J. L. Cascio, and R. A. Lazar, "An Overview of FIPS 173, The Spatial Data Transfer Standard", American Congress on Surveying and Mapping, Dec. 1992, Vol. 19, No. 5.

[13] SHL VISION* Solution, "VISION System Reference Manuals", Systems House Inc., March 1995.

[14] H. Chen, B. Schatz, D. Ng, J. Martinez, A. Kirchhoff, and C. Lin, "A Parallel Computing Approach to Creating Engineering Concept Spaces for Semantic Retrieval: The Illinois Digital Library Initiative Project", IEEE Transactions on Pattern Analysis and Machine Intelligence, Special Issue on Digital Libraries: Representation and Retrieval, 1996.

[15] ESRI, "SDE", URL http://www.esri.com/products/sde/sde.html, ESRI, 1995.

Chapter

5

Using Metadata for the Intelligent Browsing of Structured Media Objects

William I. Grosky, Farshad Fotouhi, and Zhaowei Jiang

Multimedia Information Systems Group
Computer Science Department
Wayne State University
Detroit, Michigan 48202, USA
grosky@cs.wayne.edu

Abstract

We discuss various techniques to make the browsing and querying of large image collections easier and more efficient and demonstrate how images may be combined with a standard textual database schema in such a way as to make the browsing of these images relatively straightforward. We discuss how, in certain domains, one can also impose a virtual world metaphor on the information through which the user can navigate without difficulty. This is an example of what we call a *virtual world database*. In such databases, associative retrieval includes two-way navigation between a 3-D graphics representation of a virtual world and particular images, as well as between sets of images.

5.1 Introduction

Interacting with a multimedia information system is quite different from interacting with a standard text-based information system. In any such system, the real-world objects which comprise its domain are directly represented through their properties and indirectly represented through their relationships to other real-world objects. In text-based systems, however, all properties and relationships are presented in a textual format to the user. In standard relational systems, each real-world object has a unique textual identifier and has properties whose values can be textually presented. Even in object-oriented systems, which allow the representation of more complex properties, such as those which are set or sequence valued, or those whose values are other objects, information is presented in a textual format.

In a multimedia information system, however, there exist representations of objects which are not textually based. These representations consist of portions of images (static visual representations of objects), videos (dynamic visual representations of objects), and audios (aural representations of objects). When these representations are included in the domain of an information system, they can be used in two distinct fashions: as real-world objects themselves, hereinafter called *media objects*, having properties and participating in relationships, one can treat them as one treats other first-class objects and seek to gain information about them; or, as user-recognizable surrogates for the real-world objects which comprise their content, one can use them in the process of seeking information about the corresponding non-media objects which they represent.

Concentrating on the second case above, we work under the assumption that any information concerning a media object which can be used to infer information regarding its content (i.e., the corresponding non-media objects which it represents) is an example of *content-based metadata*. Media objects are rich in information concerning the non-media objects which they represent [4], the most important of this information being the identity of the given non-media objects. This information may be gleaned in three ways: manually, where a user specifically inserts into the system that, say, a particular region of an image is a visual representation of the person *Bill*; automatically, where the system itself uses various feature matching techniques to derive a similarity between a media object m_1, which represents an unknown non-media object e_1, and another media object m_2, which represents a known non-media object e_2, the result being that e_1 and e_2 are actually identical; and semi-automatically, where the system works in conjunction with user initiated actions to identify the contents of a media object.

Knowing the identities of the various non-media objects which are represented by a media object is quite powerful. By seeing or hearing a media object, the user of a multimedia information system can gain information, through his or her own knowledge, concerning the represented non-media objects which may not be explicitly modeled by the system. Even if all such information is explicitly represented in the system and is capable of being queried on and textually answered, simply viewing or hearing the appropriate media object can invoke an emotional reaction not possible via a simple textual interface.

For this reason, a system which would allow a user to intelligently browse through a collection of media objects would serve a very useful purpose. We are developing two such approaches to this problem which we here illustrate for large image collections. The first approach is called *Content-Based Hypermedia (CBH)*. In this approach, we demonstrate how images may be combined with a standard textual database schema in such a way as to make the browsing of these images relatively straightforward. Each image will become a node in a hypermedia network. This creates another problem, however. As in any large hypertext or hypermedia system, it is quite easy for the user to become lost [15, 18]. To overcome this, we show how, in certain domains, one can impose a virtual world metaphor on the information through which the user can navigate without difficulty. This is an example of what we call a *virtual world database*.

A quite common behavior in image databases is exploratory associative retrieval followed by a query on the contents of a particular retrieved image. This behavior may be described as follows. Exploratory associative retrieval can be represented by a sequence of images $i_1, ..., i_n$, where i_k, for $2 \leq k \leq n$, is in some relationship to i_d, for $d < k$. A simple form of this behavior has $d = k - 1$. In this case, the user views an image, recognizes a particular image region as representing some non-media object, knows that this non-media object is in a particular relationship with other non-media objects, and requests the system to view all media objects, in this case images, containing a representation of the latter non-media object. Concentrating on one of the latter images, the user repeats this process many times until, finding the right image, the user asks a query concerning its contents.

Content-based hypermedia supports associative retrieval via two-way navigation between sets of images. In virtual world databases, however, associative retrieval includes two-way navigation between a 3-D graphics representation of a virtual world and particular images, as well as between sets of images.

The remainder of this chapter is organized as follows. In Section 5.2, we discuss content-based hypermedia for images. We describe the technique we use to model data in order to make it browsable, explore our approach to browsing, which we call *metadata mediated browsing*, indicate how metadata is used in the important concept of *similarity*, present the overall architecture of our system, and discuss various research topics connected to our approach, concentrating on indexing techniques for similarity browsing using content-based metadata and approaches to clustering which generate higher-level metadata to help the user browse more effectively. Virtual world databases are discussed in Section 5.3, where we introduce the concept of a virtual world database and present an object-oriented data model for a generic system. We then discuss issues in browsing through such databases. We introduce various indexing techniques for similarity browsing in Section 5.4. Finally, in Section 5.5, we present our overall conclusions.

5.2   The CBH Data Model

5.2.1   Specification

The use of CBH can best be understood through the definition of a *CBH-schema*, which is nothing more than an object-oriented schema over non-media objects which has undergone a transformation which will shortly be explained. An object-oriented schema consists of various hierarchical structures which we can classify into three domains. These are the *class hierarchy*, the *nested object hierarchy*, and the *complex object hierarchy*. The *class hierarchy* is a hierarchy of classes in which an edge between a pair of classes represents an *is-a* (specialization/generalization) relationship; that is, the subclass is a specialization of the superclass and the superclass is a generalization of the subclass. The *nested object hierarchy* is a hierarchy of classes in which an edge between a pair of classes represents either an *is-part-of* (aggregation) or an association relationship. Finally, the *complex object hierarchy* is the union of the nested object and class hierarchies. Thus, an edge between a pair of classes represents an *is-a*, *is-part-of*, or an association relationship. The class hierarchy and the nested object hierarchy are viewed as special cases of the complex object hierarchy.

To transform our original object-oriented schema into a CBH-schema, we first add a class of images. Each image is actually a complex object, comprising various regions having semantic content. Similarly, each such region, itself, may be decomposed into various subregions, each having some semantic content. This decomposition follows the complex object structure of the non-media objects represented by the given regions. That is, if non-media object o_2 is a part of non-media object o_1, and o_1 has a representation r_1 appearing in some image (as a particular region), then, cases exist where r_1 would have a component r_2 which is a representation of object o_2[1]. For example, a window is part of a building. Thus, the region of an image corresponding to a building may have various subregions, each of which corresponds to a window. We call these image regions having semantic content *semcons* (iconic data with semantics).

---

[1]This would not be the case where r_2 is occluded in the particular media object or is just not visible due to the placement of the sensor with respect to the three-dimensional non-media object o_1.

To the resulting schema, we now add a class of semcons. We note that this class *is-part-of* the class of images. Attributes of this class of semcons are based on various extracted features such as shape, texture, and color, which are used for determining when one semcon is similar to another, and thus represents the same non-media object. We note that semcons as well as their attributes are considered as metadata.

To each non-media class, we then add a set-valued attribute *appearing-in*, which leads from each instantiation of that class to the set of images where its corresponding semcon appears[2]. We also add an attribute *represents* to the class of semcons which leads from each semcon to the non-media object which that semcon represents. We note that a non-media object can be an instantiation of one or more classes. If S is the original object-oriented schema, the resultant schema, S_{CBH}, is now defined to be the CBH-schema corresponding to S.

Informally speaking, it is now possible to view an image, specify a particular semcon within this media object, and find out information concerning the non-media object corresponding to this particular image region. For example, viewing an image of Professor Smith, it is now possible to navigate to a set of images containing representations of the students of Professor Smith. We now explain how this is accomplished from the user's viewpoint.

5.2.2 Browsing Data and Metadata in CBH

In our system, browsing data or metadata is done in a uniform fashion. Browsing in a populated database under schema S_{CBH} is quite different than it would appear from the previous definitions, however. We recall that the user is browsing only through media objects. To implement this look and feel of the system, we give the implication to the user that each non-media object in a given class of S_{CBH} is replaced by the set of media objects in which the given non-media object appears. More formally, if class C in schema S and class C_{CBH} in schema S_{CBH} are two corresponding classes, as far as the user is concerned, the set of instantiations of class C_{CBH} consists of the union of the sets *appearing-in(i)*, for i an instantiation of class C in schema S. The reality of the implementation is, of course, quite different.

Whenever viewing a particular media object, the user can choose a particular semcon r for further examination. One of the actions the user can carry out

---

[2]Technically speaking, *appearing-in* also carries information concerning where in the image the given semcon is located.

is to see the value of any attribute a defined over a non-media object with respect to one of the, perhaps, many classes it can be an instantiation of and the given semcon represents. This is accomplished in the CBH-schema $\mathcal{S}_{CBH}$ by calculating $represents(r).a$, after selecting the desired class. If the value of this attribute is a simple data type (e.g., integer, real, or string), this value is textually presented to the user. If, however, this attribute's value is another (non-media) object, the user is allowed to browse through a set of media objects, each of which contains a representation of this latter non-media object. This approach easily generalizes to set-valued attributes. In a similar fashion, the user can follow an association (relationship). For example, if semcon r is chosen by the user and the non-media object $represents(r)$ participates in a binary relationship with a collection, S, of other non-media objects, then the user is allowed to browse through the set of media objects, consisting of each media object which contains a representation of a non-media object from the collection S. See Figure 5-1 for a browsing path from an image of a person *Bill* to an image of Bill's office and how it is mediated by particular relationships among corresponding non-media objects.

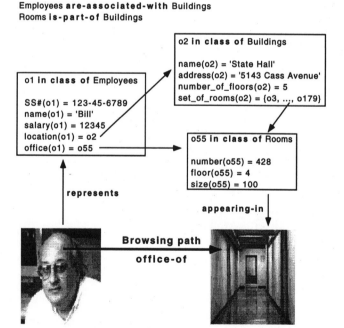

Figure 5-1   An example browsing path between media objects.

When a particular semcon is chosen, the user views a scrolling menu of choices, which includes each attribute and relationship in which the non-media object represented by the particular semcon participates. Through the use of filtering commands, the user will be able to navigate through paths composed of many relationships and attributes and restrict the collection of media objects at the final destination. For example, choosing a particular semcon which is an image of person *Joe*, a filtering command of the form **self.co-worker.residence, where self.co-worker.residence.city** = 'Livonia', will take the user to a collection of media objects which represent the residences of co-workers of *Joe* who live in Livonia.

The most likely browsing scenario is the use of metadata as an aid to browsing the data itself. A ubiquitous example of this is to navigate along *similarity* paths. Such a path would proceed from a given semcon to the set of image objects containing semcons similar to the given semcon[3]. An illustration of such navigation would be to proceed from the image of a particular person to a set of images of persons having similarly shaped eyes. Supporting such a browsing path critically depends on techniques for robust metadata generation in the form of image features, as various sorts of features matching approaches will be utilized. These browsing paths are much more complicated to support than those mentioned in the previous paragraph and utilize iconic indexes in their implementation [5, 6, 7]. We discuss these indexes in more detail presently.

Metadata, itself, may also be browsed through for various reasons. An illustration of this is when metadata is an intermediate point on a browsing path which otherwise contains some data items. One such situation is when the chosen semcon is the entire media object. Then the allowable attributes and associations over which browsing and filtering are allowed are the ones defined for the class of images in schema S_{CBH}. An example browsing path would be to proceed from a given image to the set of all images photographed by people living in the same city as the person who shot the given image[4]. Another example of browsing through metadata occurs when the user, for whatever purpose, views the output of an image processing routine on a given image. This may be done in an environment where CBH is being used as part of a testbed for image interpretation researchers.

---

[3]The hope is that the non-media objects which two similar semcons represent are identical.
[4]The identity of the person who shot a given image is, of course, metadata.

Chapter 5

5.2.3   The CBH Hypermedia Web – Metadata Mediated Browsing

A user would view CBH as a linked collection of media objects having certain recognizable portions which correspond to non-media objects modeled by the information system. By choosing a certain portion of an image, the user would be able to find out various property values of the corresponding non-media object, as well as navigate to other media objects which represent non-media objects in various relationships with the given non-media object. These media object portions are the semcons, a type of metadata which mediates a natural, user-centered navigation style enabling the user to discover properties and relationships among the modeled non-media entities. We call this navigation style *metadata mediated browsing.*

In our approach, the user's starting point in this web is akin to a web page, where we use clustering techniques [13, 12] to construct various higher-level groupings (higher-level metadata) of media objects which the user might be interested in viewing. We discuss various clustering techniques presently.

A question arises as to how the user actually chooses the appropriate media portion (semcon). One semcon may contain another and clicking a mouse over the contained semcon may also indicate that the user wants information concerning the containing semcon. For example, clicking a mouse over *Joe's eyebrow* may indicate that one wants information on *Joe, Joe's head, Joe's face,* or *Joe's eyebrow.* Each of these may be non-media objects modeled in the system. For example, instead of asking for representations of the residences of co-workers of Joe who live in Livonia, as in the previous section, one may want to browse all representations of persons with similarly shaped eyebrows.

Thus, there must be a way for the user to indicate which level of resolution is wanted. In our approach, media objects are capable of being packed and unpacked into their component semcons at any arbitrary level of resolution. We will be experimenting with various approaches of doing this, one of which will be highlighting the boundary of the appropriate semcon so the user will know which level of resolution the system will choose for a particular mouse click. Also, since a non-media object can be an instantiation of many classes, the user will be able to choose the class in which to view a particular semcon. This corresponds to the notion of *role* in relational systems.

As one can see from the previous discussion, CBH is hypermedia-based. What is new is that CBH will allow navigation to be initiated from metadata in the form of media components and is formally based on an underlying object-oriented database schema. A related and quite interesting hypertext system, which does not concentrate on media objects, is that of [3], which is based on a generalization of the entity-relationship data model. Current hypermedia systems [9, 10, 14] lean more to presentation issues rather than browsing media objects by content (an exception is [11]) and generally treat each media object as a single entity, so that the anchor point of a link must be the entire media object. These systems also do not discuss such issues as index design to make browsing and filtering more efficient. There are, however, quite powerful formal models of hypertext [8] which, though not delving into all the details necessary to implement our approach, are compatible with it. In particular, the concept of *resolver* and *accessor* functions, as presented in the Dexter model [8] seem suited for implementing *similarity* paths.

5.2.4 System Architecture

Figure 5-2 illustrates the logical architecture of the CBH database module, the most important component of our overall system. Conceptually, this module consists of a standard alphanumeric database, a semcon database, a feature database, and a media object database. Physically, of course, all this information can be stored in a single database. The standard alphanumeric database holds information concerning the non-media objects which are being represented in our system, while the uninterpreted media objects reside in the media object database. Metadata reside in the semcon database and the feature database. We note that features which reside in the feature database are properties of semcons.

Upon inserting a media object into our system, the appropriate semcons must be identified. While our present goal is to completely automate this process, our version of CBH utilizes a semi-automated approach. The user must roughly outline the various semcons utilizing a mouse. This rough outline will then be refined utilizing various image processing tools. Depending on the nature of the semcon, various features will then be automatically extracted. The user then has a choice: either to explicitly indicate to the system the corresponding non-media object which that semcon represents, or to invoke a user-mediated similarity match which finds the set of non-media objects which this semcon could possibly represent. In processing this information, the system must efficiently store the location and shape of the given semcon. For images, we are using a linear quadtree-like file structure to indicate each semcon's spatial extent.

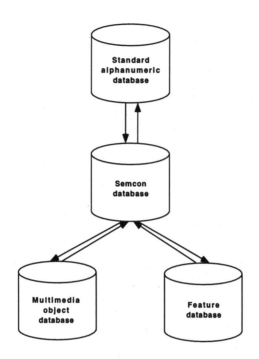

Figure 5-2 CBH database module architecture.

5.2.5 Generating Higher-Level Metadata through Clustering

Our system can be viewed as a network of data-containing components (nodes) connected by links. By the term *node*, we mean every instantiation of all classes which comprise the CBH-schema $\mathcal{S}_{CBH}$, and by the term *link*, we mean every relationship that can exist between the different classes which comprise the CBH-schema $\mathcal{S}_{CBH}$. The user gains knowledge through browsing the network. Knowledge is stored not only in the individual nodes but in the relationships between linked nodes (another form of metadata). Users make individual paths through the network based on their own interests, allowing for less cumbersome structuring of the information. The users have more direct contact with the information, and are more involved with structuring the information in their own way, compared to a traditional database system.

It is unreasonable to expect each user to adapt to the underlying structure of the network. Rather, the network should adapt itself to each user. As hypermedia networks grow larger and larger, the ability to make them more personal becomes ever more important. It is easy for users to become lost among the nodes of a hypermedia network, especially when the relationships between the nodes are not natural to the user. Allowing users to have their own view of the information reduces this information overhead.

We have previously implemented methods of autonomously monitoring a user's progress through a hypertext document and collecting information about his or her travels [13]. This information has been used to help the user navigate through the hypertext, as well as to generate clusters (using genetic algorithms and neural networks) and personal views of the document [12].

Clustering allows for higher-level concepts (metadata concerning ways of categorizing a group of nodes rather than a single node), allows the breaking of a single larger hypermedia network into appropriate modules, allows for views over the network, and allows the user to make changes at the cluster level without affecting the hypermedia network itself. Current clustering techniques in hypermedia systems are either structurally driven, where the connectivity of the nodes delineates the clusters, or concept driven, where the keywords (either in the content of the nodes themselves or in the meta-information about each node) delineate the clusters. Structurally driven clustering does not take into account how the user navigates through the nodes and links. Concept driven clustering has difficulty if the hypermedia network contains foreign languages or non-textual items. Both techniques rely heavily on the network's authors. We feel, however, that the user should really be involved in the clustering process. Each user sees different relationships between data and a hypermedia network should allow users to mold the hypermedia information to their personal needs. See Figure 5-3.

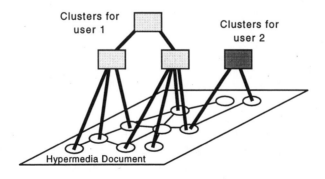

Figure 5-3   Conceptual hypermedia clustering.

In [12], we have used a genetic algorithm to delineate the clusters. Finding an optimal clustering of the nodes in a hypermedia network is equivalent to checking every partition of the set of nodes. As this is an exponential problem, it is too costly to find the optimal clustering for a network with more than a few nodes. Using an adaptive algorithm, we have found a very good clustering within a reasonable amount of time.

Metadata in the form of node clusters are generated by representing the user's tour through the hypermedia by a list of items, each item being a regular-expression-like string of the form

$$CNID : (PNID((CAID.weight - NNID@)^+),)^+,$$

where CNID is the identifier of the current node (media object), PNID is the identifier of the previous node (media object), CAID is the identifier of the current anchor (semcon), NNID is the identifier of the next node (media object), and weight is an integer indicating the number of times a particular path segment was traversed.

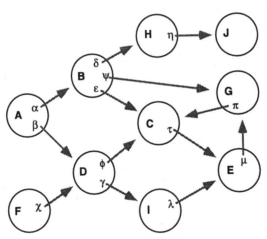

Figure 5-4 Graphical representation of a hypermedia web.

For example, consider the graphical representation of a hypermedia web as shown in Figure 5-4, where arabic letters represent node identifiers and Greek letters represent anchor (semcon) identifiers. Each time the user browses through a particular hypermedia web, he or she creates a path (a sequence of nodes visited and anchors activated). The set of paths that a user has taken, which is shown in Figure 5-5, may be graphically represented as shown in Figure 5-6.

WEB represents the hypermedia system CBH, itself, where each path begins and ends. The list data structure which captures this information is shown in Figure 5-7. These lists are then used by the genetic algorithm discussed above. In this algorithm, the payoff function is composed of two separate partial payoff functions: weight similarity and neighborliness. Weight similarity promotes clusters containing nodes with similar weights, while neighborliness promotes clusters containing neighboring nodes. We have also experimented with a neural network approach to this problem.

$$\text{WEB} \rightarrow A\beta \rightarrow D\gamma \rightarrow I\lambda \rightarrow E \rightarrow \text{WEB}$$
$$\text{WEB} \rightarrow A\beta \rightarrow D\phi \rightarrow C\tau \rightarrow E \rightarrow \text{WEB}$$
$$\text{WEB} \rightarrow A\alpha \rightarrow B\delta \rightarrow H\eta \rightarrow J \rightarrow \text{WEB}$$
$$\text{WEB} \rightarrow F\chi \rightarrow D\gamma \rightarrow I \rightarrow \text{WEB}$$

Figure 5-5   The paths a user takes through the hypermedia web.

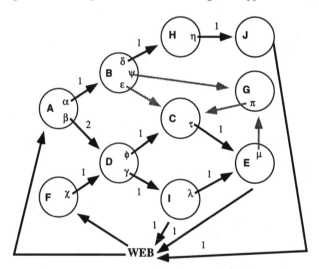

Figure 5-6   Graphical representation of the paths.

A: WEB(α.1–B@β.2–D@),
B: A(δ.1–H@),
C: D(τ.1–E@),
D: A(γ.1–I@φ.1–C@), F(γ.1–I@),
E: C(WEB.1–WEB#), I(WEB.1–WEB@),
F: WEB(χ.1–D@),
H: B(η.1–J@),
I: D(λ.1–E@WEB.1–WEB@),
J: H(WEB.1–WEB@)

Figure 5-7   List representation of the paths.

5.3   Virtual World Databases

5.3.1   Motivation

A neurosurgeon is browsing through the results of various MRI and PET scans
of a patient's brain. The interface metaphor is that of navigating through a very
realistic 3-D graphics representation of the imaged organ, a virtual brain. The
surgeon navigates to a particular volume of interest, the thalamus, and enters
it, viewing it at a higher resolution than before [1, 17]. Seeing what he thinks
is a growth inside this substructure, the surgeon uses his mouse to highlight a
particular set of voxels in the 3-D representation which comprise this growth.
A pull-down menu is then presented to him, one of its choices allows him to
view photographs of patients with similar growths. Clicking his mouse over the
chest area of a particular patient shown on one of these photographic images,
the surgeon is presented with a pull-down menu; one of its choices allows him
to view information concerning some surgical procedures done on this area of
the patient, including an image of the physician who carried out the procedure.

An image exploitation expert is browsing through the results of several months
of information gleaned from intelligence reports and satellite imagery concerning a foreign air base. The interface metaphor is that of navigating through a
realistic 3-D graphics representation of the air base in question as of a certain
date in the past. This representation comprises roads, buildings, aircraft, and
people. The expert navigates to a certain building, enters it, and goes to a particular office. Seeing the representation of a person behind a desk, the expert
clicks his mouse over this person. A pull-down menu appears, one of whose
choices is that of viewing all known photographs of the person whose office this
is. One of these photographs shows the person standing next to an aircraft.

Clicking his mouse over the aircraft, the expert is able to find the type of this aircraft and to view images of the factory where the aircraft was built. Then, clicking his mouse over a particular part of this factory in one of these images, the expert then chooses to place himself inside a 3-D graphics representation of the factory at the given location. Navigating around the periphery of the factory, the expert stops at a certain point and examines the external portion of the factory from a certain viewpoint. He is then able to view images of the factory taken from this same or closely related viewpoints.

These scenarios illustrate how the construction of a virtual world can be used as an integrating metaphor for browsing large image collections. Browsing unaided through a large collection of images can be a harrowing experience. Unless there is some structure imposed on the collection, the user is forced to sequentially examine each image in turn, an almost impossible task for a storage device containing upward of 50,000 images. The challenge of an image database is to put enough structure on an image collection so as to efficiently support user behaviors which range from goal directed queries to exploratory associative retrieval.

5.3.2   Specification

Virtual world databases have the two characteristics of *completeness* and *immersivity*. They must be able to hold complete information about real objects; all features within the problem scope must be included. For example, to represent the brain thalamus in a medical domain, not only should such features as its name, size, and color be stored in the information system, but also other features which describe the thalamus in different aspects, such as its three-dimensional volume representation, its functionality, and even some sample images. Multiple data structures must be used to represent all this information. Some features can be represented using a single simple attribute and some need to be represented by media objects such as images, audios, videos, and three-dimensional graphics.

Immersivity refers to the fact that the information should be saved in a manner which can be effectively navigated by users. Mechanisms for *dive-into* navigation have to be offered in a virtual world database. This type of navigation has many aspects, such as spatial look-and-feel and semantic hypertext navigation. These two characteristics indicate that a virtual world database is quite different from other existing information systems. The utilization of a combination of techniques from spatial databases, multimedia databases, and object-oriented databases is unavoidable.

Informally, a virtual world database can be considered to be composed of several layers: a *hierarchical hypervoxel layer*, an *object layer*, and a *media layer*.

A hierarchical hypervoxel space (HHVS) is a series of three-dimensional hypervoxel spaces (HVS) organized in a hierarchical structure. Each HVS is used to simulate a real-world three-dimensional space at a certain level of detail. A descendent of one HVS in the hierarchy represents the detailed structure of a tiny volume in the parent HVS. Each HVS is composed of voxels, where each voxel contains object reference links and some property fields. The purpose of an HHVS is to not only describe the shape and position of certain objects, but to serve as a unidirectional link from Cartesian real space to the object space. With this linkage, the HHVS is also the key structure for spatial navigation. Using a virtual car as an example, once the car is loaded into an HHVS, clicking any point can lead to the display of the parts you are touching. In a medical environment, such queries as what entity is in a certain area of the brain, what features it has, and what it looks like can be answered with this unidirectional linkage within the HHVS. Since certain anatomical structures might be too small to be viewed in one HVS, traversing up and down through the HVS hierarchy will change the query resolution. See Figure 5-8 for an illustration of a parent and child hypervoxel space.

The object layer is used to manage non-media objects. Each non-media object has a hidden attribute which points to voxels inside several HVS's within an HHVS. This linkage together with the linkage described above form bidirectional linkages between objects and an HHVS. Both real-world objects and semantic information are managed in the object layer.

For this paper, the media layer consists of images, semcons, and the related links between them and non-media objects as described in the preceding section.

Figure 5-9 shows a more detailed object model diagram for a generic virtual world database using the notation of [16].

The domain class is used to hold information describing a particular domain. For efficient organization, information concerning the real world is classified into different domains. The reason for this is that the same overall environment can have differing views. For example, in vascular surgery, a neurosurgeon is interested in the structures of arteries, veins, and other related anatomical information of the brain, whereas for epilepsy surgery, he is more interested

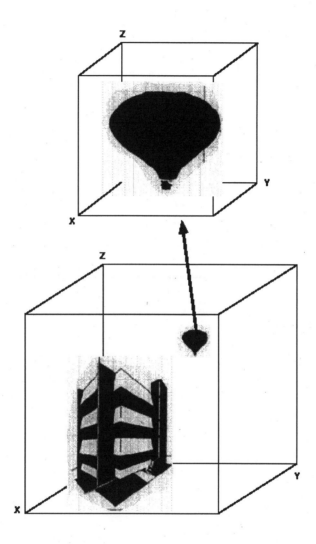

Figure 5-8   Parent and child hypervoxel spaces.

in the various electronic signals which emanate from the brain. The domain class is organized in a domain hierarchy. This means that one domain can contain multiple sub-domains, and one sub-domain can be part of several other domains. Since a virtual world database presents a 3-D navigable spatial interface, each domain should contain one instance of a 3-D coordinate class as its base coordinate system. Besides the aggregation association between dif-

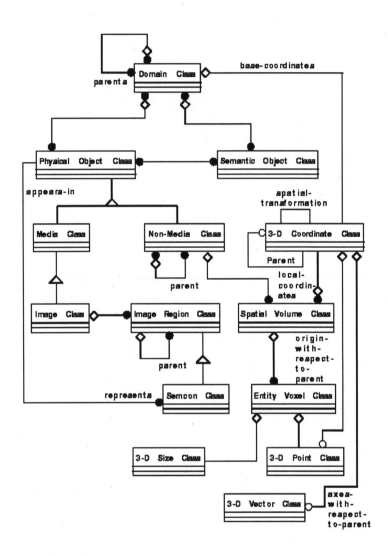

Figure 5-9   A generic virtual world object-oriented data model.

ferent domains, there also exists a base coordinate transformation association between different domains, so that spatial information in different domains can be converted bidirectionally. This association is actually part of the associated 3-D coordinate class and is hidden from the user. Each domain also contains a set of physical objects and semantic objects.

Based on the fact that a virtual world database is trying to model a real-world environment and that one of the most important aspects of physical objects in the world is their spatial characteristics, a 3-D coordinate class is necessary. Each domain as well as each physical object are defined in their own local 3-D coordinate system. A given 3-D coordinate system is composed of an origin and three orthonormal vectors which represent the three cartesian axes. Every coordinate system except that of the root domain is defined relative to a parent coordinate system.

The physical object class is designed to hold information about real-world objects. One physical object can be part of many domain classes. Physical objects have a class structure as well as participate in various associations with each other. This is indicated by the semantic object class, wherein a physical object can participate in many different semantic constructs and a given semantic construct can be instantiated for many physical objects. A physical object can be a media object or a non-media object. For this discussion, media objects consist just of images. An image consists of many regions, some of which are semcons. Regions can contain many subregions. A semcon represents a physical object, while a physical object can appear in many semcons. We note that this includes the case where a media object contains representations of other media objects, such as a photograph of a photograph. Non-media objects can contain other non-media objects and a non-media object can be contained in many other non-media objects. Non-media objects also contain a spatial volume object, which we now discuss.

A spatial volume object represents the spatial extent of a given non-media object. It is defined with respect to a given 3-D coordinate system. A spatial volume object consists of many voxels of the same given resolution, called *entity voxels*. This resolution is based on the given application requirements. Each entity voxel has a corresponding 3-D position and holds various sorts of information regarding the real-world object of which it is a part. This information can include gray-level values, colors, and shading parameters for surface rendering. Each entity voxel has a given position relative to the 3-D coordinate system corresponding to the spatial volume object which contains the given voxel. It is possible for the same non-media object to have many corresponding spatial volume objects. An example of this occurs in a medical domain where the brain is reconstructed from MRI as well as CT data.

A spatial volume object for a given non-media object can differ from a spatial volume object for another non-media object and even from another spatial volume object for the same non-media object. This occurs when the entity voxels are of different sizes and/or locations as well as when the information contained within corresponding voxels differs. Also, when the user is navigating in a virtual world, there may be many copies of the same real-world physical object. Thus, when the user is navigating in a virtual world containing many individual non-media objects, the different spatial aggregations and/or copies of each object must be transformed to a common voxel space. This is shown in Figure 5-10, where a spatial hypervolume object is the common voxel space. This object consists of many hypervoxel objects, similar to the structure of a spatial volume object, which contains many entity voxels. Each hypervoxel object points to the spatial volume objects for each non-media object which physically fills this region of 3-D-space. For example, a given hypervoxel object may point to the spatial volumes corresponding to the brain thalamus, the brain itself, the head of the person whose brain this is, and finally the person.

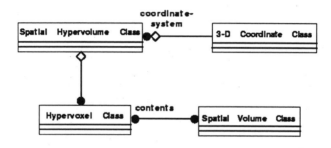

Figure 5-10   A generic object-oriented data model for a common voxel space.

5.3.3   Immersive Browsing of Large Image Collections

In browsing a virtual world database, the user is navigating through a virtual 3-D graphics representation of some physical reality. Thus, the given image collection must first be embedded in some virtual environment. Then, for a subset of the real-world objects appearing in the image collection, an object-oriented schema S must be constructed corresponding to the information through which one would like to browse. These objects are called *self-describing*. Some, if not all, of these real-world, non-media objects will also have a virtual world 3-D graphics representation, corresponding to given spatial volume objects. Other non-media objects, which have no schema-based information associated with them, and which may or may not occur in any of the images, can also have a virtual representation corresponding to a spatial volume object. Although these latter non-media objects have no associated schema-based information associated with them, they serve the purpose of making the virtual world complete and consistent for browsing purposes, and are called *non-self-describing*. As an example, consider a set of images of employee's offices. The self-describing objects could be the employees and certain types of office furniture, while the non-self-describing objects could be the office building, the hallways in the building, and the elevators in the building.

We now enhance schema S as described in Section 5.2.1, resulting in a schema we call S_{VW}. In a browsing session, the user is navigating through a spatial hypervolume object containing the 3-D graphics representations of both self-describing and non-self-describing real-world physical objects and is also able to view the image collection. We give the implication to the user that each self-describing non-media object in a given class of S_{VW} is replaced by the set of images in which the given non-media object appears, along with any of its 3-D graphics representations. More formally, if class C in schema S and class C_{VW} in schema S_{VW} are two corresponding classes, as far as the user is concerned, the set of instantiations of class C_{VW} consists of the union of the sets *appears-in(i)*, for i an instantiation of class C in schema S, together with the union of the sets *spatial-volume(i)*, for i an instantiation of class C in schema S, where *spatial-volume(i)* is the set of spatial volume objects corresponding to instantiation i. The reality of the implementation is, of course, quite different.

When viewing a particular image, the user can choose a particular semcon, r, for further examination. One of the actions the user can carry out is to see the value of any attribute, a, defined over a non-media object with respect to one of the, perhaps, many classes of which it can be an instantiation, and which the given semcon represents. This is accomplished in the VW-schema S_{VW} by calculating *represents(r).a*, after selecting the desired class. If the value of this attribute is a simple data type (e.g., integer, real, or string), this value is textually presented to the user. If, however, this attribute's value is another (non-media) object, the user is allowed to browse through a set of images or 3-D virtual worlds, each of which contains a representation of this latter non-media object. This approach easily generalizes to set-valued attributes. In a similar fashion, the user can follow an association (relationship). For example, if semcon r is chosen by the user and the non-media object *represents(r)* participates in a binary relationship with a collection, W, of other non-media objects, then the user is allowed to browse through the set of images or 3-D virtual worlds, consisting of each image or virtual world which contains a representation of a non-media object from the collection W.

In a similar fashion, when viewing a virtual world, the user may choose a particular hypervoxel for further examination. The user then has to choose among all the self-describing non-media objects whose spatial extent includes the given hypervoxel. Once the choice is made, beyond the capability of navigating as in the preceding paragraph, the user can also choose to view those images which include projections of the given hypervoxel. A further choice allows the user to view an image of the virtual world scene from the same viewpoint as in the virtual world itself.

When a particular semcon or hypervoxel is chosen, the user views a menu of choices, which includes each attribute and relationship in which the corresponding non-media object participates. Through the use of filtering commands, the user will be able to navigate through paths composed of many relationships and attributes and restrict the collection of media objects at the final destination.

With a good design, the most likely browsing scenario would be to use the virtual world to navigate to a place of interest and then to start browsing particular images of self-describing non-media objects which are represented at this location. A particular interesting browsing scenario would then utilize *similarity* paths, as previously mentioned. Such a path would, as before, proceed from a given semcon to the set of image objects containing semcons similar to the given semcon. An illustration of such navigation would be to proceed from the image of a particular person to a set of images of persons having a similarly shaped mouth. Supporting such a browsing path critically depends on techniques for robust metadata generation in the form of image features, as various sorts of feature matching approaches will be utilized. These browsing paths are much more complicated to support than those which utilize more straightforward types of filtering commands which use standard relational operators on attribute values and utilize iconic indexes in their implementation [5, 6, 7].

5.4   Indexing for Similarity Navigation Using Content-Based Metadata

We have previously examined two classes of approaches for retrieving image regions based on similarity. One class of approaches deals with the design and manipulation of indexes for shape-based similarity retrieval [5, 6, 7]. The other set of techniques is concerned with the representation of image spatial knowledge in order to retrieve image regions based on the similarity of spatial relationships among the various objects appearing in the given images [2]. Since, for images, a semcon is region-based and may have a complicated spatial structure, both of these approaches may be used to efficiently find matching semcons.

More specifically, we have proposed a data-driven, shape-based similarity retrieval approach utilizing local feature-based iconic index structures. Given any structural feature-based shape representation technique and a quantitative method to measure the similarity (or difference) between any two features, a feature index tree can be created. Such a tree can be in main memory [6] or in secondary memory [7]. Given a feature of the input image, the best matching feature in the feature index tree can then be efficiently found. Since each feature indicates which semcons it is contained in, and, in turn, each semcon indicates the media object it is contained in, we can utilize this tree to efficiently generate a set of media objects to navigate to for a particular *similarity path*.

In these implementations, each feature description is considered to be atomic. When a particular feature is found in an image, various semcons are hypothesized to be present in the image. We have shown mathematically and have experimentally verified, however, that under some very general assumptions, an index based on hierarchical features is more computationally efficient than one based on non-hierarchical features [5]. Since we have seen that semcons may contain other semcons, a natural hierarchical structure to feature construction exists. We are now applying our preceding work to this new environment.

The type of semcon we have been discussing up to now has been static. That is, a semcon is considered to be a region of a single image. There is also the notion of a *dynamic* semcon, which is a sequence of corresponding regions in a video. We believe that by using this notion, certain dynamic behaviors can be characterized, such as walking and dancing. Constructing indices for these types of semcons presents a very interesting research problem.

The above indexes do not utilize spatial relationships among features and subfeatures, however. We believe that such spatial relationships are quite important in an image database environment. Not only do entities in an image have spatial relationships with each other, but complex features consist of simpler features in given spatial relationships.

Such spatial relationships are notoriously difficult to completely describe in general. We have recently formulated an approach to this problem which is incremental in nature. Our technique allows multiple layers of description of the spatial relationships among a set of points or regions, each successive layer being more detailed than the previous layer. There are many ways of formulating our approach and we are currently conducting various experiments to see which approach leads to better behavior in particular environments.

Each formulation is based on the successive decomposition of 2-D space into quadrants and counting and/or identifying the number of points or regions in each quadrant, until each subquadrant contains a single point or region. The different approaches are related to where the origin of the decomposition is, the directions of the axes, and whether the points lose their identity or not.

We are also exploiting our previous work in spatial indexing [2] in the design of our system. This work presented a spatial access method which utilized a data structure called an SB^+-tree, which is based on a B^+-tree. The motivation behind this research is that such a structure will allow commercial databases an access method for spatial objects without a major change, since most commercial databases already support a B^+-tree as an access method for text data. The SB^+-tree is a hybrid of existing spatial access methods. For each axis of the space, a set of index points is generated, an index point being created whenever a new minimum bounding rectangle begins or ends. These index points are then used to create the corresponding SB^+-tree. The number of SB^+-trees generated is dependent upon the number of dimensions of the approximation of the spatial object. We have developed an algorithm for performing a spatial join between two spatial relations using the SB^+-tree. Through simulation, it is shown that the use of an SB^+-tree in performing such a join is much better in performance than that of an R-tree.

5.5   Conclusions

We have presented the outline of several approaches for content-based browsing of media objects and have shown how our previous work in indexing techniques for image and spatial databases, as well as in clustering techniques for hypermedia networks, lend themselves to the implementation of such a system. Metadata is central to the approach we have taken as it mediates the user-centered navigation style which this system supports. More specifically, the semcon class of metadata mediates any type of navigation, while the feature class of metadata mediates the navigation along *similarity* paths. We call this type of navigation *metadata mediated browsing*.

We have also argued that a virtual world is an integrating metaphor for browsing large image collections. Such a virtual world is a very natural representation of the environment in which the images were constructed. It should be very easy for the user to navigate to a location of interest and view whatever images he or she desires. This environment provides a very interesting mechanism for determining an entry point into an image collection. Once such an entry point is found, the user can then navigate through the image collection utilizing the semcon structure of the self-describing non-media entities as well as the hypervoxel structure of the familiar virtual world. With the possibility of utilizing similarity paths in any browsing scenario, the user has a quite powerful system at his or her disposal.

The challenge will be to design meaningful virtual worlds for given domains. We are currently implementing a virtual world database in the domain of neurosurgery of the brain. While a particular domain, such as touring through a particular city, may seem relatively straightforward to implement, some designs may hold the interest of the users better than others and be easier to use. This is another situation where the cooperation between scientists and artists may be extremely profitable.

References

[1] A. Aiken, J. Chen, M. Stonebraker, and A. Woodruff, "Tioga-2: A Direct Manipulation Database Visualization Environment," Proceedings of the Twelfth International Conference on Data Engineering, 1996, pp. 208-217.

[2] A. Ibrahim, F. Fotouhi, and S. Hasan, "SB^+-Tree: An Efficient Index Structure for Joining Spatial Relations," International Journal of Geographical Information Systems, Volume 11, Number 2, 1996, pp. 163–182.

[3] F. Garzotto, P. Paolini, and D. Schwabe, "HDM - A Model-Based Approach to Hypertext Application Design," ACM Transactions on Information Systems, January 1993, pp. 1–26.

[4] W. I. Grosky, "Multimedia Information Systems," IEEE Multimedia, Spring 1994, pp. 12–24.

[5] W. I. Grosky and Z. Jiang, "Hierarchical Approach to Feature Indexing," Image and Vision Computing, June 1994, pp. 275–283.

[6] W. I. Grosky and R. Mehrotra, "Index-Based Object Recognition in Pictorial Data Management," Computer Vision, Graphics, and Image Processing, 1990, pp. 416–436.

[7] W. I. Grosky, P. Neo, and R. Mehrotra, "A Pictorial Index Mechanism for Model-Based Matching," Data and Knowledge Engineering, 1992, pp. 309–327.

[8] F. Halasz and M. Schwartz, "The Dexter Hypertext Reference Model," Communications of the ACM, February 1994, pp. 30–39.

[9] L. Hardman, D. C. A. Bulterman, and G. van Rossum, "The Amsterdam Hypermedia Model: Adding Time and Context to the Dexter Model," Communications of the ACM, February 1994, pp. 50–62.

[10] K. Hirata, Y. Hara, N. Shibata, and F. Hirabayashi, "Media-based Navigation for Hypermedia Systems," Proceedings of the Fifth ACM Conference on Hypertext, 1993, pp. 159–173.

[11] K. Hirata, Y. Hara, H. Takano, and S. Kawasaki, "Content-oriented Integration in Hypermedia Systems," Proceedings of the Seventh ACM Conference on Hypertext, 1996, pp. 11–21.

[12] A. Johnson and F. Fotouhi, "Applied Clustering of Hypermedia Documents," Information Systems Journal, Volume 21, Number 6, 1996, pp. 459–473.

[13] A. Johnson and F. Fotouhi, "Automatic Touring in a Hypertext System," Proceedings of the IEEE International Phoenix Conference on Computers and Communications, April 1993, pp. 524–530.

[14] D. Lucarella, S. Parisotto, and A. Zanzi, "MORE: Multimedia Object Retrieval Environment," Proceedings of the Fifth ACM Conference on Hypertext, 1993, pp. 39–50.

[15] X. Pintado and D. Tsichritzis, "Satellite: Hypermedia Navigation by Affinity," In A. Rizk, N. Streitz, and J. Andre (eds.), Hypertext: Concepts, Systems and Applications, Cambridge University Press, 1990, pp. 274–287.

[16] J. Rumbaugh, M. Blaha, W. Premerlani, F. Eddy, and W. Lorensen, Object-Oriented Modeling and Design, Prentice-Hall, 1991.

[17] A. Woodruff, P. Wisnovsky, C. Taylor, M. Stonebraker, C. Paxson, J. Chen, and A. Aiken, "Zooming and Tunneling in Tioga: Supporting Navigation in Multidimensional Space," Proceedings of the IEEE Symposium on Visual Languages, 1994, pp. 191–193.

[18] M. Zizi and M. Beaudouin-Lafon, "Accessing Hyperdocuments through Interactive Dynamic Maps," Proceedings of the ACM European Conference on Hypermedia Technology, 1994, pp. 126–135.

Content-Based Image Retrieval Using Metadata and Relaxation Techniques

Wesley W. Chu, Chih-Cheng Hsu, Ion Tim Ieong*, and Ricky K. Taira**

Department of Computer Science
University of California, Los Angeles
Los Angeles, CA 90024, USA
wwc@geneva.cs.ucla.edu

*NCR Corporation
100 N. Sepulveda Blvd.
El Segundo, CA 90245, USA

**Department of Radiological Sciences
University of California, Los Angeles
Los Angeles, CA 90024, USA

Abstract

In this chapter, a metadata approach is proposed for content-based image retrieval. A three-layered data model is introduced which consists of a Representation Layer (RL), a Semantic Layer (SL), and a Knowledge Layer (KL). Raw images and segmented objects (represented in contours) are represented in the RL. Hierarchical, spatial, temporal, and evolutionary semantics of the image content are captured in the SL. This layer mimics the user's conceptual view of the image content. *Shape model(s)* and *decomposition techniques* are introduced for extracting features for differently shaped image objects. Knowledge of image feature characteristics is presented in the KL. An instance-based conceptual clustering technique is used to cluster conceptually similar image objects and features. A hierarchical knowledge representation, called *type abstraction hierarchy*, is used to represent the clustering of similar images based on a common set of features. A knowledge-based spatial evolutionary query language, KEQL, is developed to provide spatial and evolutionary constructs to query the image content with conceptual terms and approximate predicates. The knowledge base is used to relax query conditions when no answer or no satisfactory answer is returned. Further, the knowledge base is used to interpret the high-level conceptual terms and approximate predicates.

Using an object-oriented database, the proposed data model and query processing methodology have been implemented for a medical image database system at UCLA to demonstrate the validity of the metadata approach for retrieving medical images by features and content.

6.1 Introduction

Advances in medical imaging systems have revolutionized the acquisition of human images, providing views of cross sections and physiological states using a variety of modalities, including X-rays, computed tomography (CT), magnetic resonance (MR), etc. Currently, a medical picture archival and communication system (PACS) infrastructure is operational at UCLA to provide efficient archival, retrieval, communication, and display of the large repository of digital medical images [20, 39]. The digital image data is acquired automatically by PACS which contains two optical disk library units, each with a capacity of one terabyte. At present, image retrieval in these systems is based on file names or artificial keys such as *patient hospital identification numbers*. There is a need to retrieve the images by content. For example, in therapy treatment planning, the therapist is often interested in retrieving historical cases which demonstrate diagnostic image features (object shape, size, location, extent, clustering patterns, etc.) similar to a current study of interest.

The knowledge of the spatial content of a medical image is important in surgical or radiation therapy of brain tumors since the location of a tumor has profound implications for a therapeutic decision. The evolutionary behavior of a tumor is important when studying the treatment-response effects to various therapies. Also, the temporal characteristics of image features help describe the behavior of disease processes. For example, what is the normal growth rate of tumors for a given classification of patients? How does this growth rate change with various regiments of drug/radiation therapy?

Several approaches have been proposed to retrieve images in pictorial databases. Features of image objects are often used to index the images. In such systems, retrieval is based on the indexed features [17]. The information retrieval approach [34, 35] transforms the image and the query into signatures. The query is answered by matching the signatures. In addition, there are approaches which store boundaries of image objects using minimum bounding box representations [36, 18]. Since a bounding box is merely an approximation of the boundary of the original image object, representing the image object with such structures may not allow the user to retrieve all the answers that satisfy the query specification. Image objects can also be represented in point sets [31]. Spatial relationships among the image objects are dynamically determined through pixel-level manipulation during query processing. The orthogonal relationships among objects can also be encoded into a 2D string [5]. As a result, user queries concerning the orthogonal relations of the objects can be answered.

In addition, there are attempts to answer approximate queries concerning spatial objects. QBIC [29] uses object features such as *area* and *circularity* to retrieve similarly shaped objects. VIMS [1] retrieves similar images by relaxing feature values of the image based on the standard deviation of the features.

Existing approaches to image retrieval often focus on a specific application domain and have limited query capabilities [17, 5, 34, 29]. A layered model has been proposed to represent the *raw features* and *qualitative features* of video images (see Chapter 9). Biological objects *evolve, fuse, split,* and change their spatial orientation over time. Few approaches support temporal spatial query answering [31] or temporal evolutionary query answering [11], and none support spatial evolutionary query answering. This is due to the lack of appropriate metadata that captures the spatial and evolutionary nature of image content for supporting image retrieval.

To remedy such shortcomings, in Section 6.2, we propose the use of metadata to capture image content and knowledge for supporting spatial evolutionary query answering on image content. The metadata includes:

1. *Raw-image-level metadata* for providing the characteristics of the raw images and pixel-level description of the image content (e.g., contours of interested image objects)

2. *Spatial, shape, temporal, and evolutionary metadata* for modeling the spatial, shape, temporal, and evolutionary characteristics of the objects in the images

3. *Knowledge-level metadata* for representing the knowledge of spatial, shape, temporal and evolutionary characteristics of the image content

Section 6.3 describes our feature extraction of images for querying. Section 6.4 presents the modeling of medical image content with semantic-level metadata. A knowledge-based spatial evolutionary query language (KEQL) for expressing user queries is introduced in Section 6.5, and knowledge-level metadata for intelligent interpretation of image features and content is discussed in Section

6.6. The knowledge-based query processing is provided in Section 6.7, and finally the system implementation is provided in Section 6.9.

6.2   A Multi-layered Metadata Model for Representing Image Content

A three-layered model is used to organize the image metadata which consists of the Representation Layer (RL), the Semantic Layer (SL), and the Knowledge Layer (KL) (see Figure 6-1).

Raw images and contours of the objects in the images are stored in the RL. Related images are organized and stored in various stacks for efficient access [6]. The RL includes two types of metadata: (1) characteristics of the acquired raw images and (2) contours of query-able objects in the images. The characteristics of raw images (e.g., pixel width, dimensionality of images, the height and angle that a brain MR image is taken, number of slices in an MR image set, the spacing between two MR image slices, the machine and technician acquiring the images, etc.) are contained in the header of the (medical) image.

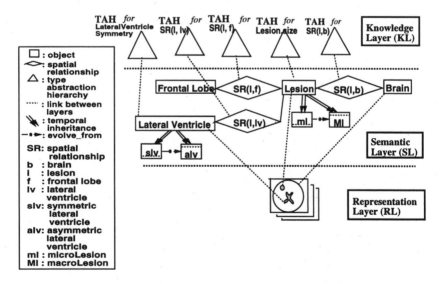

Figure 6-1   Modeling of metadata for image features and content.

The SL stores metadata for object features and spatial relationships among objects. Techniques are developed to describe the shape of objects and their spatial relationships (e.g., *Joined, Disjoined*, etc.) and evolutionary relationships (e.g., *Evolve, Split, Fuse*). An object-oriented approach is used to model the features extracted from the contours of interested objects. The model allows us to express spatial, temporal, and evolutionary objects. The metadata about these query-able objects and features are domain-dependent and application-dependent.

The knowledge layer (KL) stores the knowledge-level metadata for supporting approximate and conceptual query answering on image content. An instance-based conceptual clustering technique, MDISC [9], is used to cluster image objects based on user-specified conditions (e.g., shape descriptors and spatial relationships). The clustering of image objects is represented in a hierarchical knowledge structure, called Type Abstraction Hierarchy (TAH) [9], for supporting query answering involving similar-to predicates, spatial semantic operators (e.g., *Nearby* and *Far_Away*), and conceptual terms (e.g., *Large* and *Small*). These knowledge structures provide domain-dependent ontologies for approximate and conceptual terms used in querying image content. These metadata also help restrict the vocabularies in querying spatial, temporal, and evolutionary object features.

6.3 Feature Extraction

6.3.1 Object Segmentation

Traditional image segmentation approaches are broadly categorized as based on intensity discrimination [3] or edge detection [2].

The intensity approach assumes that a fundamental relationship exists between the pixel intensity and the physical substrate. Theoretically, imaging instruments are measuring specific physical properties such as tissue relaxation time, electron density, or atomic number. However, numerous studies have shown that factors such as field inhomogeneity, instrumentation noise, and partial volume effects all contribute to pixel intensity fluctuation and create uncertainty in discrimination [3]. Thus, simple global thresholding methods usually fail due to inherent image noise [33].

Current edge-detection-based work shows some degree of success [26], but in general requires user interaction. Most edge-detection systems cannot discriminate between true object edges, noise edges, and edges originating from, for example, a second overlapping structure. A fundamental understanding of the nature of the basic signals and hence, edge characteristics, is somewhat lacking. Some success has been gained by the use of multi-scale edge analysis [25]. The overall strategy is that noise-free edges can be obtained from a coarse scale, while a true edge location is obtained from a fine scale. However, analyzing the multi-scale behavior of edges is generally done by using heuristic rules. Visual interpretation plays an important part in correlating edges in different scales as well as in making decisions on determining a true or false edge. A lack of rigorous means for performing multi-scale edge analysis as well as parsing has seriously limited the effectiveness of these kinds of methods for automated segmentation. Most of the successful semi-automatic image segmentation methods used in image management systems fall into this category, such as active contouring [13] and liquid transforms [29] where the coarse contour or seed point is manually provided.

Most recent work in segmentation of anatomic objects involves model-guided knowledge-based methods. The important features of the model-guided, knowledge-based image segmentation approaches include [24]:

1. Physical models of each target image object (e.g., brain, lateral ventricle, cranium) are maintained within an attached knowledge-base which include:

   - Compositional models: These models identify what substructures are part of a larger superstructure. These compositional models allow the segmentation system to first localize larger superstructures in the image and leverage on important landmarks of these superstructures to localize more specific target substructures. (e.g., localizing the brain cranium constrains the spatial searching of lateral ventricle).

   - Gray-level models: These models provide statistical information regarding the expected gray-level distribution of various tissue components (e.g., brain gray matter, brain white matter, cerebral spinal fluid, bone, background, common artifacts) within a medical image superstructure (e.g., brain and hand).

   - Shape models: A shape contour analyzer decomposes complex object contours into more fundamental lines and curve segments. It is used by the system to verify that contoured objects conform to the general expected shape of the target object.

2. Object-oriented organization allows the system to attach specific process-ing methods, relationships, rules and data for each target object (e.g., brain objects, tumor objects, and hand objects).

3. Object models are used to identify important landmarks on object contours [16].

4. Models are used to verify the expected shape of extracted contours and localize any errors signifying gross difference between object shape and extracted contour shape.

6.3.2   Extracting Shape Features via Decomposition

Shape is an important property for retrieving images. Global shape mea-surements such as area and perimeter only provide a coarse description of shape. In QBIC [29], global shape descriptors such as *circularity* are used with area and perimeter values to describe the shape of image objects. Global shape descriptors such as *curveness, rectangularity, compactness, direction, elongatedness,* and *eccentricity* [38] provide certain approximate shape mea-sures for contours of relatively simple shapes (i.e., shape without irregular in-trusions and/or protrusions). However, for contours of complex shapes (i.e., shapes with irregular intrusions and/or protrusions), these descriptors do not provide sufficient expressive power for describing their specific shape content [23]. Therefore, we propose a *landmark-based decomposition technique* to de-compose complex-shaped contours into shape descriptive substructures based on the content-related landmark(s) in the images.

Landmarks are characteristic points in an image which are easily recognizable on all images and can be used to decompose *every* instance of the complex object into descriptive substructures (e.g., the tips and webs of a hand are the landmarks for decomposing a hand contour for detailed shape description of a hand). Landmark points in a contoured object can be obtained, for example, by matching model segments with corresponding data segments as described in [16] and [24].

With the landmark identified, the complex-shaped contours are decomposed into shape-descriptive substructures. The shape content of the complex-shaped object can be represented by the simpler shape and spatial relationships of the decomposed substructures. Attributes of the substructures can be common spatial characteristics (such as area, length, and width) or shape descriptors

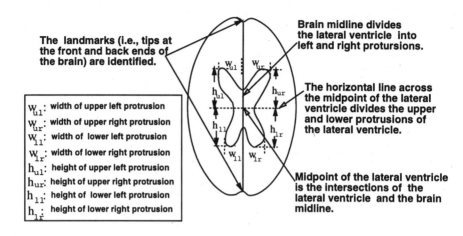

Figure 6-2 For more precise shape description, the shape model decomposes a lateral ventricle into four natural substructures: upper left substructure, upper right substructure, lower left substructure, and lower right substructure.

of the decomposed substructures. Capturing these attributes provides a more precise description on the shape of the image objects.

The lateral ventricle is used as an example object to illustrate landmark-based decomposition in studying the shape symmetry of the lateral ventricle. In medicine, the symmetry of the lateral ventricle is observed using the two tip notches of the brain contour as the landmarks. The brain contour is modeled using the *shape contour model* to automatically identify the two tips. Then the lateral ventricle can be decomposed into four substructures as shown in Figure 6-2 to study the symmetry of lateral ventricle. We can express the symmetry aspect of the lateral ventricle via the relative shape among these decomposed contours. In Figure 6-2, the height and width of the four components of a lateral ventricle are used to construct a *shape feature* to describe the left to right symmetry of the lateral ventricle as (upperLRWidthRatio (w_{ul}/w_{ur}), upperLRHeightRatio (h_{ul}/h_{ur}), lowerLRWidthRatio (w_{ll}/w_{lr}), lowerLRHeightRatio (h_{ll}/h_{lr})). The *left to right symmetry* of the lateral ventricle is an important shape feature for detecting various brain diseases [15].

6.3.3 Extracting Spatial Relationship Features

The primary concerns for a quantative description of spatial relationships include:

- Containment relationships which describe the relative position and locations of contact between a pair of objects. The detailed containment characteristics are further quantatively captured by features such as ratio of overlap, ratio of area, the shortest distance between their contours, etc.

- Directional relationships describe the directional characteristics between objects. These directional features can be quantatively captured by features such as relative distance of centroid on x *axis, y axis*, and z *axis*, respectively.

Based on anatomical knowledge and physician diagnosis, the spatial relationships of an object with respect to its surrounding objects can be derived; we shall call them the *primary spatial relationships* of the objects. We use primary spatial relationships to represent the semantics of the images in the data model. In addition, the relationships of abnormal objects discovered in diagnosis with respect to their adjacent objects are also kept in the system. Due to the relatively small number of abnormal objects found, we only need to maintain a small fraction of spatial relations in the system.

The number of spatial relations for n objects in an image is on the order of $O(n^2)$. Storing all the spatial relations not only increases the storage but also lengthens the time needed to search for the objects. To limit the size of storage of spatial features and relations, only those most frequently inquired about are stored in the system. There is a storage/response time trade-off as to what spatial features and relations need to be stored.

6.4 Modeling of Objects in Medical Images

The metadata in the semantic layer (SL), which models the temporal, spatial, and evolutionary aspects of the image objects, is detailed in the following sections.

6.4.1   Representing Image Objects

Objects and their contours in the images are identified by segmentation software. Features and content representing object characteristics are extracted
and represented in the data model. Similar image objects are classified in the
same class. For example, the object class defined for the micro-lesion in our
Gemstone implementation is:

```
Object subclass 'Microlesion'
    instVarNames: #['diameter',
        'volume', 'eventTime', 'contourPointer', 'imagePointer']
    constraints: #[ #diameter, Number],
        #[ #volume, Number],
        #[ #eventTime, DateTime],
        #[ #contourPointer, Contour],
        #[ #imagePointer, Image].
```

Microlesion is a subclass of Object. The clause instVarNames defines the
following attributes: diameter, volume, eventTime, contourPointer, and
imagePointer for object Microlesion. The constraints defines the type of
each attribute. For example, volume and diameter are of type Number.

MicroLesionSet is an object class in which each instance is a Microlesion,
as shown in the following:

```
Set subclass 'MicroLesionSet'
    constraints: MicroLesion.
```

If an image in the database contains a micro-lesion, then there is an object
instance in MicroLesionSet corresponding to that micro-lesion which is represented by its features. An object class is created for each type of identifiable
object in all the images. Thus, such data structures provide a framework and
guidelines to extract features from all images. The object instance maintains
links that point to its contours and images. The collection of all feature values
constructs a *feature database.* These pre-computed feature values in the feature
database enable the conceptual feature clustering and also speed up the image
retrieval by feature and content.

Our data model extends the object-oriented model and introduces new constructs to describe the spatial and evolutionary behavior of objects.

object feature	conceptual terms
lesion.size	*small, medium, large*
lesion.roundness	*circular, non_circular*
lesion.surface	*smooth, coarse*
lateral_ventricle.left_to_right_symmetry	*upper_protrusion_pressed_to_the_right,* *upper_protrusion_pressed_to_the_left,* ...
...	...

Table 6-1   A shape feature description table for the brain.

6.4.2   Modeling Shape

The proposed landmark-based decomposition technique provides an effective quantitative shape description when the image objects have limited numbers of shape components. The decomposed objects provides sufficient image content to retrieve specifically or similarly shaped image objects. Further, with image classification algorithms, such as MDISC [9], conceptual terms can be defined to describe a shape feature. The *shape feature description table* (Table 6-1) lists the conceptual terms for describing the shape features. Thus, users can use conceptual terms for describing a specific shape in a query: for example, *"retrieving images with lateral ventricles whose upper protrusion are pressed to the right"* (see *Query 3* in Section 6.5 and the MTAH defining *upper protrusion pressed to the right* in Color Figure-1).

6.4.3   Modeling Spatial Relationships

Modeling spatial relationships merely by simple semantic constructs such as *separated* and *connected* is insufficient to express real-life spatial relationships (as illustrated in Figure 6-3). Additional parameters are needed to describe the spatial relationships more precisely. A set of required spatial relationship features should be specified by domain experts. Parameters are provided to describe the topological relationships between two objects (as shown in Figure 6-4). More important parameters for distinguishing the subtypes under a category are placed first in the list, and parameters used in the higher branches may also be used in their descendant branches. In Figure 6-4, Bordering means that only the surfaces of the two objects are joined (i.e., $r_c > 0, r_j = 0$); Invading implies their areas are joined (i.e., one of the object is deformed by the other, $0 < r_j < 100\%$), and Circumjacent implies a full containment (i.e., one

spatial relationship	representative features	defined semantic terms
SR(l,b)	$(x_c, y_c, r_a), (a_i)$	Slightly_Occupied, Extremely_Occupied
SR(l,f)	(x_c, y_c, r_j)	Slightly_Touching, Intimately_Touching
SR(l,lv)	$(\theta_c, d_c, x_c, y_c)$	Nearby, Far_Away
...	...	...

Table 6-2 A spatial relationship description table for the brain lesion (l: lesion; b: brain; f: frontal lobe; lv: lateral ventricle).

object fully contains the other, $r_j = 100\%$). The *required constructs/operators* are necessary for every spatial relationship. A *spatial relationship description table* (as shown in Table 6-2) lists the available parameters and semantic terms for describing the spatial relationships between two objects. The values of these spatial relationships are stored in the database.

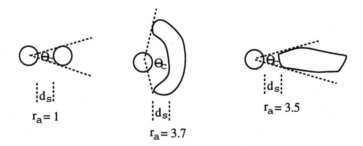

Figure 6-3 An example showing that merely using semantic operators (e.g., *SEPARATED*) and/or single measurement (e.g., the *shortest distance (d_s)*) is insufficient to capture the spatial relationship of two objects. We need additional features such as *angle of coverage* (θ_c) and *ratio of area* (r_a) to classify the illustrated spatial relationship.

This spatial modeling approach captures the containment and directional aspects of binary spatial relationships. Containment describes the relative position and possible *joining* relationship among objects while direction aspect describes the directional relationships from one contour to the other. The constructs for the spatial relationships are as follows:

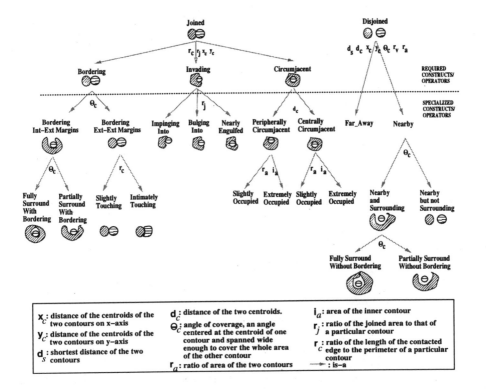

Figure 6-4 An ontology of spatial relationships (represented in a generalization hierarchy) for different topological categories between two objects (with the representative icons shown) for oncological medical images. The parameters under a branch classify the subtypes under that category.

1. No containment

- **Disjoined:** This spatial construct is used to describe two objects that are separated from one another. (For example, the micro-lesion is disjoined from the lateral ventricle as shown in Figure 6-8). The relationships under this construct are further quantified by the spatial relationship features such as d_s, d_c, r_a, and θ_c.

  The values of these spatial relationship features can be conceptually classified via clustering algorithms such as MDISC [9] to derive the meaning of the corresponding semantic terms under the DISJOINED category, such as NEARBY and FAR_AWAY. The reason for using an instance-based clustering algorithm to define these corresponding semantic terms is that the semantics of these detailed spatial relationship terms are context-dependent (e.g., the meaning of NEARBY in astrology is different from its meaning in medicine).

- **Bordering**: Two objects contact one another at one or more locations. Bordering is a significant event in the medical domain. The relationships under this construct are further quantified by spatial relationship features such as r_c and θ_c.

2. Containment

- **Circumjacent**: An object contains another object (e.g., a microlesion develops inside the brain, as shown in Figure 6-8). The relationships under this construct are further quantified by the spatial relationship features such as d_c, r_a, and i_a.

3. Partial Containment

- **Invading**: This spatial construct is used to describe one object that invades the other, which causes an object to deform. The relationships under this construct can be further quantified by the spatial relationship features such as r_j and d_c.

The directional information of spatial relationships is captured by spatial relationship features such as the relative distance of the centroids of two objects on the x-coordinate (denoted as x_c), on the y-coordinate (denoted as y_c), and on the z-coordinate (denoted as z_c).

To model a spatial relationship, domain experts need to identify the containment categories of the modeled spatial relationship. Spatial relationship features are then identified to describe the spatial relationship according to the topological categories of the two objects.

For example, in an image with a lesion and lateral ventricle, the spatial relationship instance between the lesion and lateral ventricle is classified as an instance of the class SR(lesion,lateral_ventricle). The containment relationship covers the DISJOINED and BORDERING categories and requires θ_c, d_c, x_c, and y_c as the features to describe this spatial relationship. Color Figure-2 shows an image classification hierarchy for the images in the database. The hierarchy is generated by MDISC based on the collected values of spatial relationship features of SR(lesion,lateral_ventricle) instances in the database.

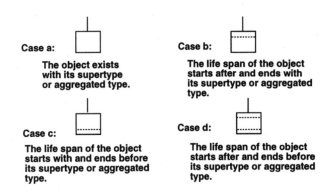

Case a:
The object exists
with its supertype
or aggregated type.

Case b:
The life span of the object
starts after and ends with
its supertype or aggregated
type.

Case c:
The life span of the object
starts with and ends before
its supertype or aggregated
type.

Case d:
The life span of the object
starts after and ends before
its supertype or aggregated
type.

Figure 6-5 Temporal object constructs.

6.4.4 Temporal Relationship Object Constructs

Let us now consider the modeling of inter-object temporal relations. The constructs that represent the temporal relationships between an object and its supertype or its aggregated type are shown in Figure 6-5. These temporal relationships define how the characteristics of the supertypes are temporally inherited. **Temporal inheritance** deals with the way time-dependent characteristics of a supertype are inherited by its subtypes. The general rule is that an object may only inherit characteristics from other objects which exist in its own space-time domain [11].

To illustrate the use of the temporal relation object constructs, we apply them to the model describing brain lesion growth. For example, the life of a lesion includes its development from a micro-lesion to a macro-lesion. The temporal inheritance between these object types is expressed in Figure 6-6.

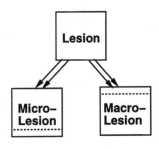

Figure 6-6 Temporal object constructs of lesion. Double arrows imply inheritance (is_a) relationship.

6.4.5   Evolutionary Object Constructs

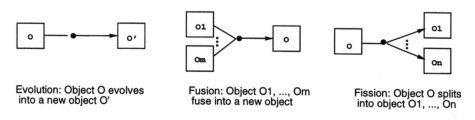

Evolution: Object O evolves   Fusion: Object O1, ..., Om   Fission: Object O splits
into a new object O′   fuse into a new object   into object O1, ..., On

Figure 6-7   Evolutionary object constructs.

Existing approaches for modeling object evolution involve maintaining object versions [22]. We enhance these basic models to describe the development of objects using *stages* and the *evolution, fission,* and *fusion* among stages. A stage represents a distinguishable development status of an object, and a transition between stages represents a significant change in the entropy or growth status of the evolutionary object. Evolution, fusion, and fission are the three possible types of transitions among the evolutionary stages (Figure 6-7).

1. Evolution: The characteristics of an object may evolve with time. For example, a micro-lesion evolves into a macro-lesion over a period of time, as shown in Figure 6-8.

2. Fusion: An object may fuse with other objects to form a new object with different characteristics than either of the constituent objects.

3. Fission: An object may split into two or more independent objects.

The clinical manifestations of a lesion depend on its position with respect to its surrounding brain structures. As an example, a brain lesion is modeled with the temporal, evolutionary, and spatial object constructs as shown in Figure 6-8. Micro-lesions develop **separately** from (modeled in Figure 6-4) the lateral ventricle. Micro-lesions may also **evolve** (modeled in Figure 6-7) into macro-lesions which **invade** (modeled in Figure 6-4) the symmetrical lateral ventricle and make the lateral ventricle become asymmetrical.

Based on the model constructs, we shall present a query language that can express the spatial evolutionary content of the images. The model shown in Figure 6-8 will help formulate the example queries in Section 6.5.

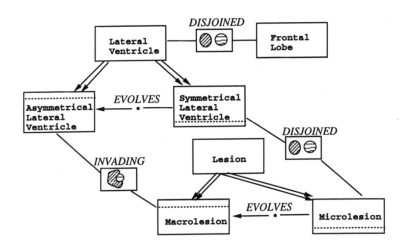

Figure 6-8 The temporal evolutionary and spatial relationships for the growth of a brain lesion.

6.5   The Knowledge-Based Spatial Evolutionary Query Language (KEQL)

Conventional query languages lack the capabilities to query on spatial evolutionary characteristics of medical images [21, 37, 28, 36]. To remedy this, we propose a declarative spatial evolutionary query language, KEQL, which operates on the spatial evolutionary domains of the medical images. In addition to alphanumeric predicates, KEQL contains constructs to specify spatial, temporal, and evolutionary conditions with approximate and conceptual terms.

A KEQL query consists of the following three optional clauses:

```
[SELECT clause]
[WHERE clauses]
[Operations]
```

The SELECT clause selects the desired data items. WHERE clauses describe the selection criteria using alphanumeric predicates, conceptual spatial predicates, predicates describing the evolutionary processes among object types, and predicates for selecting appropriate snapshot(s) of the database. Operations specify the system or user-defined operations such as display, rotate, and superimpose on the selected data.

6.5.1   SELECT and Operations

The SELECT clause identifies the attributes and object types to be retrieved for the query.

The operations in the Operations clauses can either be system-defined or user-defined data, image manipulation, or visualization operations [6], such as movie_loop, display, contour, rotate, and superimpose.

6.5.2   WHERE

WHERE clauses are classified into the following categories.

Symbolic/Semantic Spatial Relationship Predicate

The user can query on the spatial relationship among objects. For example, to retrieve images of the macro-lesion *nearby* the lateral ventricle, the user enters:

```
WHERE Macro-lesion Nearby LateralVentricle
```

To avoid ambiguity in specifying the operators, a pull-down menu is available that displays the available spatial semantic operators, as in the spatial relationship description table (Table 6-2), for the user to select to use in the query.

Spatial Feature Predicate

Spatial feature queries involve the spatial characteristics of the image objects. By inspecting the object classes, the user knows what spatial features are available for querying, and hence, if the user wants to retrieve images of macro-lesions with diameter equal or larger than 25mm, the user enters the following predicate:

```
WHERE Macro-lesion diameter >= 25mm
```

The user may also use the ~= operator to represent *"approximately equal"* in the spatial feature predicate, and the query processor can automatically interpret the predicate to include a suitable value range based on the specific feature and query context. The value range is discovered by the DISC algorithm [9], which provides a different value range for different feature values based on the value distribution of the feature. For example, if the user wants to retrieve the images with micro-lesions of approximately 9mm in diameter, the user writes the following predicate:

```
WHERE Micro-lesion diameter ~= 9mm
```

Based on the result of running DISC on `Micor-lesion.diameter`, 9mm will be relaxed to a suitable value range (such as 8mm to 12mm).

Predicate with Conceptual Terms

Spatial queries may involve conceptual terms, such as *large* and *small*, in the query. For example:

```
WHERE Macro-lesion.size IS 'large'
```

A pull-down menu is also used to display the available conceptual terms for the specified object attribute in the predicate as in the shape feature description table (Table 6-1). The conceptual term is to be interpreted by the knowledge residing in the KL.

Similar-to Operator

Similar-to operators compare the similarity of image objects based on shape or spatial relationship features. The similar-to predicate first selects a target image or object by constraining one of the operand variable to a specific image or object instance (e.g., `Image1.patient.name = "Mary Doe"` in the following example) and then uses the BASED_ON subclause to specify the shape features and/or specific spatial relationships between objects that characterize the target image similarity for the *similar_to operator* [12, 19]. For example:

```
WHERE Image1 SIMILAR_TO Image2
      (Image1.patient.name = "Mary Doe")
      BASED_ON macro-lesion.size and macro-lesion.location
```

If no BASED_ON subclause is presented, then the features supplied in the user model will be used (see next section).

Temporal Relationship Predicates

Temporal relationship predicates select the appropriate snapshot of the data of interest at particular points or periods in time. Temporal relationship predicates include:

- Temporal functions

  Temporal functions manipulate the time points: START_TIME, END_TIME, RECORD_TIME, and EVENT_TIME. They are the operators used in the query language to retrieve the start, end, record, and event times of objects.

- Temporal ordering functions

  Temporal ordering of an object history sorts the object versions in ascending order based on their time stamps, so that retrieval of object versions in a specific order can be identified. These functions include FIRST, LAST, N_th, PRIOR, and NEXT.

- Temporal interval comparison operators

  To specify a more complex temporal condition, the interval specified in the temporal relationship predicates may be subjected to temporal interval comparison operators [37, 28], such as PRECEDES, FOLLOWS, CO-OCCURS, and DURING. These operators specify how the intervals following the temporal relationship predicates are related to some other time intervals. The time point comparison operators such as BEFORE and AFTER are also included.

Evolutionary Predicates

The evolutionary predicate describes various evolutionary processes on a set of evolving object sequences. The evolution of a brain abnormality, such as a lesion, provides a good example of the use of evolutionary operators. The evolution of the lesion can be described as evolving from a micro-lesion to macro-lesion. There are three kinds of evolutionary processes in general: EVOLUTION, FUSION, and FISSION.

The condition "*object_type*₁ EVOLVED_FROM *object_type*₂" selects all evolutionary sequences in which an object instance of *object_type*₂ evolves into an object instance of *object_type*₁. For example, the following evolutionary predicate applies the evolution operator EVOLVED_FROM to retrieve sequences where macro-lesions evolve from micro-lesions:

```
WHERE        macro-lesion EVOLVED_FROM microadenoma
```

All the growing instance sequences of lesion which developed from micro-lesion to macro-lesion will be retrieved.

For a more complete discussion of fusion and fission modeling constructs, the interested reader is referred to [11, 10].

6.5.3   Sample Queries

In this section, we shall present a set of sample queries to illustrate how to use KEQL constructs to express certain clinical queries associated with radiographic findings.

Query 1: "Find patients with similar brain lesions to the patient named 'Mary Doe' based on the lesion size and whose lesion location is NEARBY the lateral ventricle"

```
SELECT   I1
FROM     Image I1, IT
WHERE    I1 SIMILAR_TO IT (IT.patient.name = 'Mary Doe')
             BASED_ON (IT.lesion.size,
                       IT.[lesion,lateral_ventricle].(x_c, y_c, θ_c, d_c))
```

Query 2: *"Find a* large *lesion* NEARBY *the lateral ventricle"*

```
SELECT  Lesion.image
FROM    Lesion, Lateral_Ventricle
WHERE   Lesion Nearby Lateral_ventricle and
        Lesion.size IS 'Large'
```

Query 3: *"Find the lateral ventricle whose upper protrusion is pressed to the right"*

```
SELECT  Lateral_Ventricle.image
FROM    Lateral_Ventricle
WHERE   Lateral_ventricle.left_to_right_symmetry
            IS 'upper_protrusion_pressed_to_the_right'
```

The knowledge representing upper_protrusions_pressed_to_the_right is provided in Color Figure-1.

A brain surgeon wishes to retrieve patients in the database whose brain MR image has similar spatial characteristics to the target MR image. The query is expressed as follows:

Query 4: *"Find images in the database that have similar spatial characteristics as the image shown on the screen"*

```
SELECT   P1, P1.image
FROM     Patient P1, PT
WHERE    P1.image SIMILAR_TO PT.image
                (PT.image SELECTED_ON_THE_SCREEN)
```

SELECTED_ON_THE_SCREEN is a special function to specify the image on the screen as the target image for matching. The intended features and spatial relationships of *Query 4* are derived from the image content in PT.image and the user type (i.e., brain surgeon) according to the knowledge in the knowledge layer. The corresponding query expressed graphically is illustrated in Color Figure-3 (see also Section 6.7).

Query 5: "Retrieve the image frames in which a micro-lesion is nearby the lateral ventricle and approximately 9mm in diameter. The micro-lesion evolves into a macro-lesion with diameter equal or larger than 25mm and invades the lateral ventricle in one year"

This query involves lesion growth and its spatial characteristics with an adjacent object. Based on the object relationship captured in the data model (see Figure 6-8), as well as the object classes and their relationships defined for each object, *Query 5* can be expressed in the following KEQL query by using the AFTER, EVOLVED_FROM, NEARBY, and INVADES operators (the parentheses in the SELECT and DISPLAY clause enforce the pairing of the returned objects):

```
SELECT   (Micro-lesion.Image, Macro-lesion.Image)
FROM     Micro-lesion, Macro-lesion, Lateral_Ventricle LV1 LV2
WHERE    Micro-lesion EVENT_TIME + 1 year AFTER
                      Macro-lesion EVENT_TIME AND
         Macro-lesion EVOLVED_FROM Micro-lesion AND
         LV1 Nearby  Micro-lesion AND
         Micro-lesion diameter ~= 9mm AND
         Macro-lesion Invades LV2 AND
         Macro-lesion diameter >= 25mm AND
         LV1.patient = LV2.patient
DISPLAY SEQUENCES(  (Micro-lesion.Image, Macro-lesion.Image)  )
```

6.6 Knowledge-Level Metadata for Intelligent Interpretation and Access

The knowledge-level metadata consists of the classification of images based on the selected features. The classification is context and user sensitive. The criteria of our image feature clustering algorithm is to minimize the averaged pair-wise Euclidean distance of image feature values in a cluster. Such a measure, known as the *relaxation error* [9], considers both the *frequency* of the value occurrence and the difference between *values*. Based on minimizing the summed *relaxation error* of all the newly partitioned clusters in each iteration, the clustering algorithm, MDISC, recursively partitions the data set to generate a multi-attribute feature type abstraction hierarchy (MTAH). Since both the feature value distribution and the correlation among different attributes of a feature are considered in MDISC, our clustering algorithm provides better image feature classification than if we used standard deviation to represent image similarity [1].

This automatic generation of the knowledge-level metadata based on the selected features of images makes our knowledge-based query answering approach scalable.

6.6.1   Query Interpretation via TAH

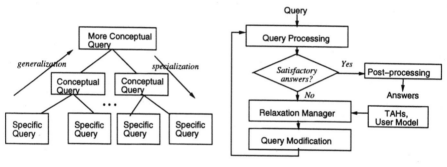

a: Generalization and specialization via TAH   b: The flow diagram of query processing
                                                              with relaxation

Figure 6-9   Knowledge-based query relaxation.

The classification of image features are represented in a hierarchical representation, called *type abstraction hierarchies* [8] for processing *similar-to* and semantic predicates. The concept in the TAH nodes is represented by the feature value ranges (see Color Figure-1 and Color Figure-2). These value ranges can be used to retrieve similar images. As shown in Figure 6-9(a), higher nodes in the TAH represent more generalized concepts (i.e., broader range of feature values) than that of the lower nodes (i.e., narrower range of the feature values). Based on the existing values of the representative spatial relationship features, MDISC can be used to classify image features to represent these semantic spatial relationship operators. The resultant TAH nodes are labeled by domain experts with the conceptual terms (e.g., Nearby, Far_Away, Large, Small, upper_protrusion_pressed_to_the_right) to represent the specific domain concept of the images under the node and the value range is used as the query constraint to retrieve the images satisfying the conceptual predicates[1].

---

[1]The conceptual terms can also be labeled via other approach (e.g., neural networks, vector computation (see Chapter 7), etc.). Our distribution-sensitive clustering algorithm,

These conceptual terms are selected from the *domain dependent descriptive ontologies*. For example, Figure 6-4 is an ontology for various spatial relationships applicable to oncological medical images. A descriptive ontology is a generalization hierarchy for a specific image domain which provides 1) the conceptual terms for labeling the TAH nodes, and 2) the shape, spatial relationship, and/or temporal features for clustering the object instances. These ontologies can be obtained from generic medical terminology (e.g., UMLS [40]) and domain experts. They provide a restricted set of vocabularies for querying image content. Note that the proposed ontology for describing entities (e.g., size, color, distance) are different from the common sense generic ontologies such as Cyc and WordNet [27].

To solve a *similar-to* query whose intended similarity includes the features or spatial relationship classified by the TAH, the lower TAH nodes are attached with more specific value ranges. In solving the *similar-to* query, we shall first locate the TAH node that has a value range closest to that of the target image based on these selected (spatial relationship) features. By traversing up (i.e., generalizing) and down (i.e., specializing) the selected TAH, the feature value range in the matched TAH node can be used for retrieving similar images from the database (Figure 6-9(b)). The traversal along the TAH nodes is controlled by the relaxation policy which is provided either directly from users or from the user model.

There is a *TAH directory* in the system that stores such information as object names, sets of features, spatial relationships, user type of the TAH. Based on this information, the system (or user) selects and retrieves the appropriate TAHs for processing the query. If the retrieved TAH does not match the user's specification, the TAH can be edited to meet the user's requirement.

The time complexity to generate a multi-attribute hierarchy by MDISC is $O(mnlog(n))$, where m is the number of attributes and n is the number of distinct instances used in generating the TAH [9]. Our experiment reveals that generating a MTAH with about one hundred images based on four features takes a fraction of a second's processing time on a Sun Sparc 20 workstation.

---

which is based on the selected features, provides sufficient classification information for the domain experts to label the TAH nodes.

6.6.2   User Model

The user model specifies the user preference for customizing a query so that it is context and user sensitive. The preference of a user under a query context is characterized in a user profile.

In a user profile, the query context to be matched is represented by two different types of objects: *mandatorily matched objects* and *optionally matched objects*. *Mandatorily matched objects* of a user profile specify the objects that must be matched with a given query for the user profile to interpret the query. *Optionally matched objects* provide guidelines for adding additional object feature constraints when the corresponding objects are matched. Optional matching permits a partial matching of user profiles based on the objects appearing in the query and increases the matching occurrences.

The user preference specifies the set of interested features and spatial relationships for a given query context, and the policies for relaxing query conditions when no satisfactory answer is found.

The relaxation policy describes how to relax the selected TAHs when no satisfactory answer is found, since classifying images may involve multiple attributes as well as multiple TAHs to provide more efficient and accurate query answering. Control operators such as the *relaxation order* (e.g., which TAHs should be relaxed first), non-relaxable features, preference list, and *relaxation level* can be used to provide relaxation control.

For example, given MR brain images with lesion(s), the features that are of interest to a typical brain surgeon include the lesion locations and the spatial relationships with other objects in the brain (such as lateral ventricles) as shown in Figure 6-10. The information in the user model can be used for selecting the interested features and the relaxation policy if they are not specified in the query (see *Query 4*). For a given image, different types of users (e.g., radiologists, surgeons, and clinicians) may have different interests which can be specified in the user model.

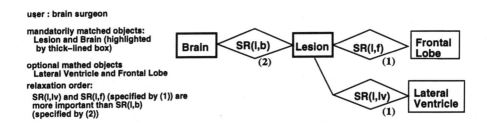

user : brain surgeon

mandatorily matched objects:
  Lesion and Brain (highlighted
    by thick–lined box)

optional mathed objects
  Lateral Ventricle and Frontal Lobe

relaxation order:
  SR(l,lv) and SR(l,f) (specified by (1)) are
  more important than SR(l,b)
  (specified by (2))

Figure 6-10   A user profile for brain surgeons.

6.7   Knowledge-Based Query Processing

The knowledge-based query processing is divided into three phases: *query planning, query execution, and query relaxation* (Figure 6-11) as discussed in the following sections.

6.7.1   Query Planning Phase

A KEQL query is parsed and transformed into a *query execution graph*, a directed acyclic graph (dag) [4] representing the execution plan for the query. The first step is to generate a *sub-parse-tree* for each predicate. Then a query execution graph is formed by linking together the sub-parse-trees by matching their input and output data variables.

There are six types of predicates supported in the KEQL.

- *Type1: alphanumeric predicates*

  Alphanumeric predicates contain arithmetic operators such as $>$, $=$, and $<$ which specify the constraints for the objects. The input of this type of predicate is a set of extracted objects as specified in the predicate. The output is a set of objects satisfying the specified alphanumeric predicates.

- *Type 2: predicate with conceptual terms*

  This type of predicate is similar to the alphanumeric predicate except that the constraints are specified by the conceptual terms (e.g., *large* tumor.size) [19]. The output is the set of objects that satisfy the conceptual terms.

■ *Type 3: semantic spatial relationship predicates*

Semantic spatial relationship predicates are used to specify the spatial relationship constraints for a pair of objects [19]. The input is two sets of spatial object instances which form a set of instance pairs of (spatial) objects for testing against the specified spatial relationship operator. The output is a set of object instance pairs from the two input sets that satisfies

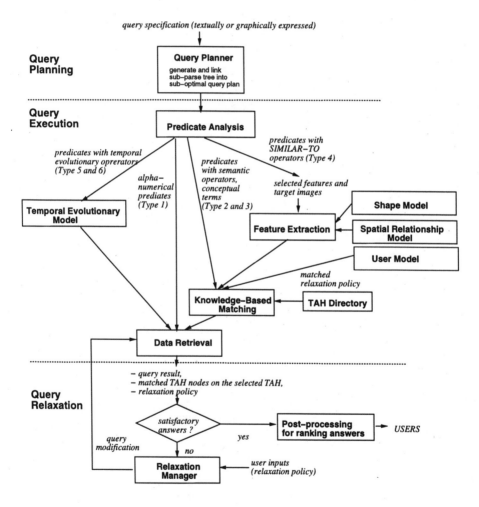

Figure 6-11 Knowledge-based query processing flow diagram for KEQL queries.

the specified spatial relationships. Example sub-parse-tree structures of such predicates are shown in Figure 6-12(a) and (b).

■ *Type 4: similar-to predicates*

In this type of predicate, a set of objects or image instances is compared with a target object or a target image instance [19]. The target image(s) can be derived from the additional predicates in the query (e.g., patient name is *Mary Doe*). The predicate may also specify the features or spatial relationships characterizing the desired similarity of the *similar-to* predicate. The inputs are the target object, the set of objects to be compared, and the *similar-to characteristics specification*. The output is the object instances similar to the target instance. The sub-parse-tree for the *similar-to* predicate is shown in Figure 6-12(c).

■ *Type 5: evolutionary predicates*

Evolutionary constraints are specified in this type of predicate. The input is two or more collections of objects where each collection contains object instances of the same evolutionary stage, and the objects of different stages are linked via the specified evolutionary constructs. The output is a set of evolutionary sequences satisfying the specified evolutionary operator. An example of such sub-parse-tree is illustrated in Figure 6-12(d).

■ *Type 6: temporal relationship predicates*

Temporal relationship predicates specify the temporal relationship of two related objects. The two sets of temporal object inputs are to be evaluated by the temporal relationship operator. The output is a set of temporal object pairs which satisfies the specified temporal relationship operator. An example of such sub-parse-tree is illustrated in Figure 6-12(e).

The individual sub-parse-trees are linked together to form an execution plan based on: 1) the output (variables) of a sub-parse-tree should match the input (variables) of the linked sub-parse-tree, and 2) the derived query execution plan should minimize the execution cost (or a given performance requirement).

Optimizing KEQL query patterns yields the following heuristics: *type 1 predicates are processed first, then type 2 predicates, type 3 predicates, type 4 predicates, type 5 predicates, and lastly the type 6 predicates*. Following this heuristic, the sub-parse-trees are linked together based on this pre-determined order. Figure 6-13 shows the result of linking the sub-parse-trees of *Query 5* (shown in Figure 6-12) together. When more than two separate sub-parse-trees in the lower layer output the same variables and only one sub-parse-tree in the upper

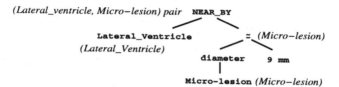

(a) Sub–parse–tree of semantic spatial relationship predicate **(type 3 predicate)**

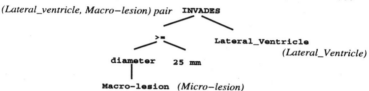

(b) Sub–parse–tree of semantic spatial relationship predicate **(type 3 predicate)**

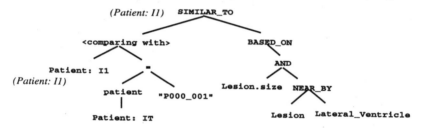

(c) Sub–parse–tree of similar–to predicate **(type 4 predicate)**

(d) Sub–parse–tree of evolutionary predicate **(type 5 predicate)**

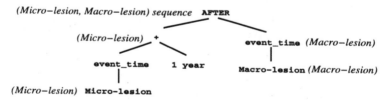

(e) Sub–parse–tree of temporal relationship predicate **(type 6 predicate)**

Figure 6-12 The sub-parse-trees for different types of predicates. (a), (b), (d), and (e) are based on predicates from Query 5 and (c) is based on the predicate from Query 1. The italic strings specify the format of the input and output variables and data type via variable populating for linking the sub-parse-trees together.

layer takes the specified variable as input, depending on the logical operators (i.e., AND and OR) connecting the two corresponding lower-layer predicates, the results from the two sub-parse-trees are either unioned or joined based on their object ID or sequence ID before sending to the upper layer sub-parse-tree.

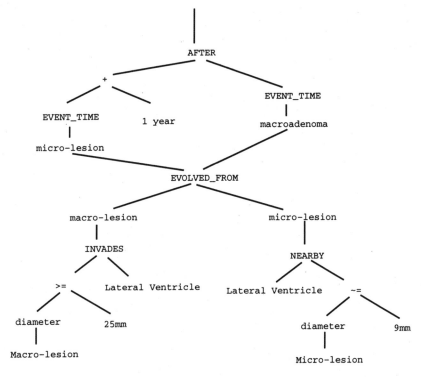

Query Execution Graph

Figure 6-13 Query execution graph for Query 5. The execution is from bottom up.

Optimizing frequently appearing query patterns with the above heuristics is based on the following observations. The semantic spatial relationship predicates and predicates with conceptual terms are converted into value ranges of the corresponding spatial features. Image retrieval using these pre-processed feature values takes less time than processing the evolutionary and temporal predicates, since traditional indexing structures can be easily built to speed up this processing. Therefore, the alphanumeric predicates (Type 1), predicates with conceptual terms (Type 2), and semantic spatial relationship predicates (Type 3) are placed at the bottom of the query plan. Processing the evolutionary and temporal predicates requires comparing the temporal occurrences of the specified objects. Navigating through the links among evolutionary objects usually requires loading the instances into memory to inspect the links. Therefore more processing time is needed. Thus, the temporal and evolutionary predicates are placed above the semantic spatial relationship predicates and predicates with conceptual terms.

Generating the optimal query execution plan depends on many factors. By expressing each type of predicate in an algebraic notation, equivalent query plans can be generated by algebraic permutation. These plans produce the same query result but with different execution cost. The one with the least execution cost can then be selected as the optimal query execution graph.

6.7.2   Query Execution Phase

The query processing can be performed based on the query execution plan. Depending on its type, each predicate is processed accordingly. Since the processing of alphanumeric predicates is well-known [30], we shall present the process of processing our proposed conceptual spatial, temporal, evolutionary predicates.

Processing Predicates with Conceptual Terms, Semantic Spatial Relationship Operators, and Similar-to Operator

Processing predicates with conceptual terms, spatial relationship operators and similar-to operators requires reference to domain knowledge represented in TAHs. Processing such types of predicates requires *predicate analysis and feature selection*, and *knowledge-based content matching*. In the *predicate analysis and feature selection*, based on the target image, query context, and user type, the system analyzes and selects the relevant features and spatial relationships for processing these sub-parse-trees. In the *knowledge-based content matching*, the selected features, spatial relationships, and user types are used to match the TAH(s) that resolve the conceptual terms, semantic spatial relationship operators, and/or similar-to predicates. The system uses the value ranges from the best matched TAH nodes to retrieve images from the image feature database.

To process the predicates with semantic spatial relationship operators and/or conceptual terms, the spatial relationship operators and conceptual terms are used to select the TAH(s) and the TAH node(s) for processing these queries.

The TAH nodes that yield best matching of the semantic operators and/or conceptual terms (which are represented by value ranges) are used as the query conditions to retrieve the images. Their corresponding value ranges are used in the image retrieving.

For the *similar-to* predicate, the features and spatial relationships specified in the BASED_ON subclause are used to match with those of the target image. If no BASED_ON subclause is specified, then the query processor uses the default features and spatial relationships specified in the user model.

The selected features, spatial relationships, and user types are used to choose the TAH(s) for query processing. The selected TAHs are traversed to locate the node(s) whose value range is closest to that of the target image as the best matched TAH node. The set of images contained in that TAH node represents the set of images similar to the target image.

Processing Evolutionary Predicates (Type 5)

There are three types of evolutionary operators, EVOLVE, FUSE, and SPLIT [11, 10]. There is a method defined for each evolutionary operator which takes instances from two or more sets of object collections (EVOLVE_FROM takes two *input collections* and SPLIT_TO and FUSED_FROM take more than two *input collections*) as inputs and returns the set of evolving sequences that satisfy the query conditions. The matched evolving sequences will be returned as a collection of sequences. For more discussion on evolutionary query processing, the interested reader is referred to [11].

Processing Temporal Predicate (Type 6)

During the evaluation of a temporal predicate, if the two input collections are not evolutionary-related, then a cartesian product is applied to the instances of the two collections for constructing all possible object pairs for the evaluation. Every pairing of objects from the two input collections that satisfy the temporal predicate is a meaningful pairing. However, if the two input collections are evolutionary-related (i.e., two different collections of evolutionary instances from one set of evolutionary sequences), then the temporal predicate can be directly evaluated on the input evolutionary sequences embedded inside the two different collections of evolutionary instances. Temporal operators are applied to select the appropriate temporal objects where the temporal relationships of their life span satisfy the required temporal constraints.

For example, in *Query 5*, the event times of the micro-lesion and the macro-lesion are compared to determine whether the evolution took place in less than one year's time. Note only the object pairs appearing in the input evolutionary sequences are evaluated against the temporal predicate AFTER. The result of *Query 5* is shown in Color Figure-3.

6.7.3   Query Relaxation Phase

Within the query relaxation phase, when no answer is returned or the returned answer is not satisfactory, the query conditions are relaxed in accordance with the relaxation specification. For the queries requiring relaxation, an appropriate TAH is selected to relax the query condition. The relaxation is performed by traversing up and down the selected TAH starting from the TAH nodes that best match the current query context. In every relaxation iteration, the query conditions are modified by the value from the TAH nodes. This relaxation process terminates when the answer set satisfies a given user requirement (e.g., number of similar images obtained, relaxation error, etc. [8]). The returned images can be ranked based on a *relaxation error (RE)*, a similarity measure based on the weighted distance of the specified shape and spatial relationship features. Since the relaxation is conducted within a sub-parse-tree, it does not alter the query execution plan.

Figure 6-14 illustrates the query processing for a spatial predicate with *similar-to* operator for the target image as shown in Color Figure-3. The system allows user relaxation control input to overwrite the one provided by the user model. Since neither a relaxation control policy or a BASED_ON subclause is provided by the user in this example, the relaxation control and matching policy specified in the user model are used (details of the matched user model are shown in Figure 6-10). Thus, SR(lesion,lateral_ventricle) is the first candidate TAH to be relaxed. Based on the TAH shown in Color Figure-2, the value ranges for retrieving similar images are:

$(43.91 \leq SR(lesion, lateral\_ventricle).d_c \leq 71.31)$,

$(0.85 \leq SR(lesion, lateral\_ventricle).\theta_c \leq 1.54)$,

$(4.0 \leq SR(lesion, lateral\_ventricle).x_c \leq 49)$,

$(-27 \leq SR(lesion, lateral\_ventricle).y_c \leq 57)$.

These conditions correspond to the value range of the TAH node two levels higher than the matched leaf node (see Color Figure-2). The retrieved images are shown and ranked with the *relaxation error* attached to each retrieved image (see Color Figure-3). There is an *explanation* window which displays the selected features and spatial relationships used for the matching, the relaxation level, and the number of matched images for this TAH node. During the relaxation process, if the relaxation of a TAH reaches a certain *relaxation error threshold*, then the system, according to the relaxation policy, selects another TAH for relaxation. Users can also retrieve images based on complex query conditions by selectively combining the TAHs with logical operations (e.g., AND, OR, etc.).

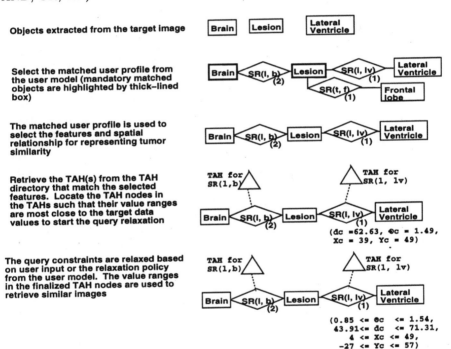

Figure 6-14 Processing steps for Query 4 (the TAH for *lesion* Nearby *lateral ventricle* is shown in Figure 6-4.)

6.8 Implementation

Figure 6-15 illustrates the overall flow and key components of our system. Our raw data set is the images stored in the UCLA Picture Archiving and Communication System [20]. These images are sent through segmentation routines to generate contours of interested objects in the images. Methods of the proposed feature extraction technique (see Section 6.3) compute image features and spatial relationships from the object contours. These features are stored in a *feature database* and mapped with image objects and spatial relationships in the Semantic Layer. The evolutionary constructs are used to describe the temporal characteristics of object development. In addition, the features are classified by the MDISC clustering algorithm to produce the type abstraction hierarchies required for knowledge-based query answering.

A knowledge-based spatial evolutionary query language (KEQL) is developed to express spatial evolutionary queries, which provides direct manipulation of image objects.

The knowledge-based query processor parses the KEQL statement and uses type abstraction hierarchies for the approximate and conceptual matching of image content specified in the KEQL statement. The query result is returned for further presentation and visualization.

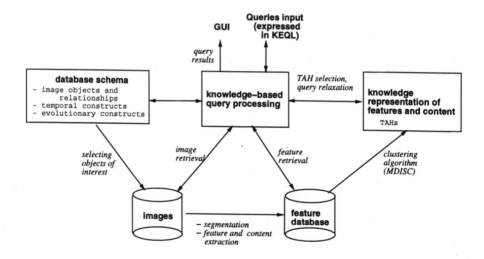

Figure 6-15   Data flow and system architecture.

Using GemStone[2], an object-oriented database, and VisualWorks as the application development tools, a prototype medical image management system [7, 19] has been implemented at UCLA to demonstrate the feasibility of the approach. Currently, the system runs on a Sparc 10 with a RAID of 16 gigabyte disk storage. Using VisualWorks, we have developed a graphical interface, MQuery [14], with pull-down menus and "point-click-drag" features for querying the database. With graphical representation for both objects (e.g., icons) and streams (used for temporal and evolutionary constructs), various KEQL predicates can be directly specified on the objects or streams to formulate a query. Buttons are included in the query window for schema navigation, object display, and query confirmation.

At present, the prototype system has a few hundred hand X-ray and MR brain image studies. Feature extraction for hand X-rays is performed automatically for patients between the ages of 3 and 11 years [32]. A commercially available MR image segmentation and rendering system from ISG Corporation is used to extract features from brain MR images. Contours of objects showing good signal-to-noise ratios can often be automatically acquired using available minimum/maximum thresholding methods. The system also includes a semi-automatic region growing program after specification of an initial seed point. Manual contouring methods are also available. A comprehensive set of tools exists to edit (remove and splice) existing contours.

The time to process a query depends on the complexity of the query and the size of the database involved. The response time ranges from 2 seconds to 15 seconds with an average of 5 seconds. The display of images requires an additional 5 to 30 seconds, depending on the size and number of images.

The response time of a large image system depends on the size of the database and the query optimization technique used. These issues are still under investigation.

6.9   Conclusions

In this chapter, we presented a knowledge-based approach for retrieving images by their features and content. The model supports semantic operators (e.g.,

---

[2]We selected GemStone because it provides richer data types than relational database management systems. This is essential to developing the new modeling constructs proposed in this chapter. Further, GemStone has a gateway to Sybase, which allows us to retrieve the stored patient demographics at the UCLA medical center.

Joined, Disjoined, Nearby, Far_Away), similar-to operators, and conceptual terms (e.g., Large, Small) in the queries.

The image content is captured through three types of metadata: pixel-level metadata; spatial, temporal and evolutionary metadata; and knowledge-level metadata. A three-layered data model is proposed to organize these three types of metadata: the Representation Layer stores the pixel-level metadata; the Semantic Layer stores spatial, temporal and evolutionary metadata; the Knowledge Layer stores knowledge-level metadata. These layers integrate the image representation (i.e., generated image contours in an image) together with the knowledge required to capture and interpret the image content to provide querying by feature and content. The model provides the framework and guidelines for image preprocessing to extract features and relations of objects in the images. Our model also considers shape structure and shape features as well as spatial relationship features. These features can be automatically or semi-automatically extracted from the image contours and stored in a feature database. A new query language, KEQL is developed to express spatial evolutionary queries with conceptual and approximate terms. With semantic information captured in the model, spatial evolutionary queries are answered efficiently. Based on the specified features and spatial relationships, knowledge of the image semantics and image similarity can be generated by our conceptual clustering algorithm automatically. The knowledge is represented in a hierarchical knowledge structure, called a Type Abstraction Hierarchy (TAH). Knowledge-based query processing can be performed by generalization/specialization on the TAHs. The value ranges of the matched TAH node are used to modify the query conditions for retrieving images. A user model is introduced to allow users to customize their specifications in object matching and relaxation policy for query answering. The system also presents the quality of the approximate answers (e.g., measured in *relaxation error*) to the user. Since the feature computation and knowledge acquisition are automated, our proposed technique is scalable.

The Knowledge-based MeDical image system, KMeD, has been implemented at UCLA to demonstrate the feasibility of our approach. The system has been built with a commercial object-oriented database, Gemstone, with ObjectWorks/VisualWorks as the data modeling and user interface development environment. The system runs on a Sun Sparc 10 workstation with a RAID of 16 gigabyte storage capacity. Our preliminary experience reveals that the proposed knowledge-based approach is a feasible and effective way to retrieve images by content for large pictorial databases, and can also be applied to other multimedia applications.

Acknowledgments

This work is supported in part by the National Science Foundation Scientific Database Initiative, Grant IRI9116849, and also in part by DARPA contract F30602-94-C-0207.

The authors would like to thank John David N. Dionisio for implementation of the graphical user interface of the query language, Kuorong Chiang and Timothy Plattner for developing the programs for generating TAHs for images, Christine Chih for her assistance in image segmentation, and Prof. Alfonso Cardenas for his stimulating discussions during the course of writing this chapter.

References

[1] J. R. Bach, S. Paul, and R. Jain. A visual information management system for the interactive retrieval of faces. *IEEE Transaction on Knowledge and Data Engineering*, October 1993.

[2] M. Bart, P. H. Romeny, L. Florack, J. Koenderink, and M. Viergever. Scale space: its natural operators and differential invariants. In *Information Processing in Medical Imaging, Proc. 12th International Conference, IPMI*, 1991.

[3] M. Brummer, A. Van Est, and W. Menhardt. The accuracy of volume measurements from MR imaging data. In *Proc. 8th Ann. Meegint SMRM*, p. 610, Amsterdam, 1989.

[4] C. N. Fischer and R. J. LeBlanc, Jr. *Crafting a Compiler*. The Benjamin/Cummings Publishing Company, Inc., 1988.

[5] S. K. Chang, C. W. Yan, and D. C. Dimitroff. An intelligent image database system. *IEEE Transaction on Software Engineering*, May 1988.

[6] M. Chock, A. F. Cardenas, and A. Klinger. Database structure and manipulation capabilities of a picture database management system (PICDMS). *IEEE Trans. on Pattern Analysis and Machine Intelligence*, PAMI-6(4), July 1984.

[7] W. W. Chu, A. F. Cardenas, and R. K. Taira. A knowledge-based multimedia medical distributed database system — KMeD. *Information Systems*, 20(2):75–96, 1995.

[8] W. W. Chu and Q. Chen. A structured approach for cooperative query answering. *IEEE Transactions on Knowledge and Data Engineering*, 6(5), October 1994.

[9] W. W. Chu, K. Chiang, C. C. Hsu, and H. Yau. An error-based conceptual clustering method for providing approximate query answers. *Communications of ACM, Virtual Extension Edition (URL http://www.acm.org/cacm/extension)*, December 1996.

[10] W. W. Chu, I. T. Ieong, and R. K. Taira. A semantic modeling approach for image retrieval by content. *Journal of VLDB*, 1994.

[11] W. W. Chu, I. T. Ieong, R. K. Taira, and C. M. Breant. A temporal evolutionary object-oriented data model and its query language for medical image management. In *Proceedings of the 18th International Conference on Very Large Databases*, pp. 53–64, Vancouver, Canada, August 1992. Morgan Kaufmann Publishers, Inc.

[12] W. W. Chu, H. Yang, K. Chiang, et al. A scalable and extensible cooperative information system. *Journal of Intelligent Information Systems*, 6(6), 1996.

[13] D. Daneels, D. van Campenhout, et al. Interactive outlineing: An improved approach using active contours. In *Image and Video Storage and Retrieval, SPIE*, 1993.

[14] J. D. N. Dionisio and A. F. Cardenas. Mquery: A visual query language for multimedia, timeline, and simulation data. *Journal of Visual Languages and Computing*, Vol 1, pp: 377–401, 1996. Special issue on *Image and Video Databases: Visual Browsing, Querying, and Retrieval*.

[15] H. Duong, L. Sarazin, P. Bourgouin, and J. L. Vezina. Magnetic resonance imaging of lateral ventricular tumours. *Canadian Association of Radiologists Journal*, 46(6):434–442, Dec 1995.

[16] W. E. L. Grimson. *Object Recognition By Computer: The Role of Geometric Constraints*. MIT Press, 1990.

[17] W. I. Grosky and R. Mehrotra. Index-based object recognition in pictorial data management. *Comput. Vis. Graph. and Image Proc.*, Vol. 52(3): 416–436, 1990.

[18] A. Gupta, T. Weymouth, and R. Jain. Semantic queries with pictures: The VIMSYS model. In G. M. Lohman, A. Sernadas, and R. Camps (eds.), *Proceedings of the 17th International Conference on Very Large Databases*, pp. 69–79, Barcelona, Spain, September 1991. Morgan Kaufman.

[19] C. C. Hsu, W. W. Chu, and R. K. Taira. A knowledge-based approach for retrieving images by content. *IEEE Transaction on Knowledge and Data Engineering*, August 1996.

[20] H. K. Huang, N. J. Mankovich, and R. K. Taira. Picture archiving and communication systems (PACS) for radiological images: State of the art. *CRC Critical Reviews in Diagnostic Imaging*, 28(4), 1988.

[21] W. Kim. A model of queries for object-oriented databases. In *Proc. of the 15th VLDB*, 1989.

[22] W. Kim and H. T. Chou. Versions of schema for object-oriented databases. In *Proc. of the 14th VLDB*, 1988.

[23] M. D. Levine. *Vision in Man and Machine*. McGraw Hill Publishing Co., Inc., 1985.

[24] B. J. Liu, R. K. Taira, J. Shim, and P. Keaton. Automatic segmentation of bones from digital hand radiographs. In *Proceedings of the SPIE: Medical Imaging, Image Processing*, 2434: 659–669, February 1995.

[25] Y. Lu and R. Jain. Reasoning about edges in scale space. *IEEE Transactions on PAMI*, 14(450), 1992.

[26] D. Marr and E. Hildreth. Theory of edge detection. In *Proc.R.Soc.*, p. 187, 1980.

[27] G. Miller. Wordnet: A lexical database for English. *Communications of CACM*, November 1995.

[28] S. B. Navathe and R. Ahmed. A temporal relational model and a query language. *International Journal of Information Science*, 48(2): 57–73, 1989.

[29] W. Niblack, R. Barber, W. Equitz, M. Flickner, E. Glasman, D. Petkovic, P. Yanker, C. Faloutsos, and G. Taubin. The QBIC project: Querying images by content using color, texture, and shape. In *Storage and Retrieval for Images and Video Databases, SPIE*, 1993.

[30] J. Orenstein et al. Query processing in the objectstore database system. In *ACM SIGMOD 1992*, 1992.

[31] J. Orenstein and F. A. Manola. Probe spatial data modeling and query processing in an image database application. *IEEE Transaction on Software Engineering*, May 1988.

[32] E. Pietka, M. McNitt-Gray, M. L. Kuo, and H. K. Huang. Computer assisted phalangeal analysis in skeletal age assessment. *IEEE Trans. on Medical Imaging*, 10(4):616–620, 1991.

[33] D. W. Piraino, S. C. Amartur, B. J. Richmond, J. P. Schils, J. M. Thome, and P. B. Weber. Segmentation of magnetic resonance images using an artificial neural network. In *Proc. Ann. Symp. Comp. Appl. Med. Care*, pp. 470–472, 1991.

[34] F. Rabitti and P. Savino. Image query processing based on multi-level signatures. In *Proceedings of ACM Information Retrieval*, 1991.

[35] F. Rabitti and R. Savino. An information retrieval approach for image databases. In *Proceedings of 18th VLDB Conference*, 1992.

[36] N. Roussopoulos, C. Faloutsos, and T. Sellis. An efficient pictorial database system for PSQL. *IEEE Transaction on Software Engineering*, May 1988.

[37] R. Snodgrass. The temporal query language for TQUEL. *ACM TODS*, pp. 247–298, June 1987.

[38] M. Sonka, V. Hlavac, and R. Boyle. *Image, Processing, Analysis and Machine Vision*, vol. 1. Chapman & Hall Computing, 1993.

[39] R. Taira and H. Huang. A picture archiving and communication system module for radiology. *Computer Methods and Programs in Biomedicine*, 30, 1989.

[40] U.S. Department of Health and Human Services, National Institutes of Health, National Library of Medicine. *UMLS Knowledge Sources*, August 1992.

Chapter

7

A Metadatabase System for Semantic Image Search by a Mathematical Model of Meaning

Yasushi Kiyoki, Takashi Kitagawa*, and Takanari Hayama*

Faculty of Environmental Information
Keio University
Fujisawa, Kanagawa 252, Japan
kiyoki@sfc.keio.ac.jp

*Institute of Information Sciences and Electronics
University of Tsukuba
Tsukuba, Ibaraki 305, Japan
takashi@is.tsukuba.ac.jp, taki@softlab.is.tsukuba.ac.jp

Abstract

In the design of multimedia database systems, one of the most important issues is to extract images dynamically according to the user's impression and the images' contents. In this chapter, we present a metadatabase system which realizes the semantic associative search for images by giving context words representing the user's impression and the images' contents.

This metadatabase system provides several functions for performing the semantic associative search for images by using the metadata representing the features of images. These functions are realized by using our proposed mathematical model of meaning. The mathematical model of meaning is applied to compute specific meanings of context words which are used for retrieving images unambiguously and dynamically. The main feature of this model is that the semantic associative search is performed in the orthogonal semantic space. This space is created for dynamically computing semantic equivalence or similarity between the metadata items of the images and context words.

7.1 Introduction

The design and implementation of metadatabase systems is one of the key issues in the field of multimedia database research. In the design of the metadata for images, the important issues are how to define and represent the metadata items of images and how to extract images dynamically according to the user's impression and the image's contents.

There are many approaches to image retrieval. Two major approaches are direct retrieval using partial pattern matching and indirect retrieval using abstract information of images. We use the latter approach for extracting images.

In this chapter, we present a semantic associative search method for images and its implementation in the metadatabase system for extracting appropriate images according to the user's impression and the image's contents. In this method, the images are selected by using a *mathematical model of meaning* [6, 9] which realizes the semantic associative search. This model was originally applied to support semantic interoperability for multidatabase environments [9]. The realization of semantic interoperability is one of the important issues in the research field of multidatabase systems [17, 18, 16].

The mathematical model of meaning is applied as a fundamental framework for representing the metadata and extracting images. This model realizes the semantic associative search for extracting information by giving its context words. The main feature of this model is that the semantic associative search is performed unambiguously and dynamically in the orthogonal semantic space. This space is created for computing semantic equivalence or similarity between the user's impression and the image's metadata items which represent the characteristics of each image.

We point out that context recognition is essentially needed for multimedia information retrieval. The meaning of information is determined by the relation between contents and the context. The machinery for realizing dynamic context recognition is essentially required for multimedia information acquisition. We have proposed new methodology for realizing the machinery [6, 7, 9].

The advantages and original points of the proposed methodology are as follows:

1. The semantic associative image search based on semantic computation for words is realized by a mathematical approach. This image search method surpasses the search methods which use pattern matching for associative

search. Users can use their own words for representing impression and images' contents for image retrieval, and do not need to know how the images of retrieval candidates are characterized in databases.

2. Dynamic context recognition is created using a mathematical foundation. The context recognition can be used for obtaining multimedia information by giving the user's impression and the contents of the information as a context. A semantic space is created as a space for representing various contexts which correspond to its subspaces. A context is recognized by the computation for selecting a subspace.

The MMM (Mathematical Model of Meaning) consists of:

1. A set of m words is given, and each word is characterized by n features. That is, an m by n matrix is given as the data matrix.

2. The correlation matrix with respect to the n features is constructed. Then, the eigenvalue decomposition of the correlation matrix is computed and the eigenvectors are normalized. The orthogonal semantic space is created as the span of the eigenvectors which correspond to nonzero eigenvalues.

3. Images and context words are characterized by using the specific features (words) and representing them as vectors.

4. The images and context words are mapped into the orthogonal semantic space by computing the Fourier expansion for the vectors.

5. The set of all the projections from the orthogonal semantic space to the invariant subspaces (eigen spaces) is defined. Each subspace represents a phase of meaning, and it corresponds to a context or situation.

6. A subspace of the orthogonal semantic space is selected according to the user's impression or the image's contents, which are given as a context represented by a sequence of words.

7. The most correlated image to the given context is extracted in the selected subspace.

Several information retrieval methods, which use the orthogonal space created by mathematical procedures like SVD (Singular Value Decomposition), have been proposed. Our model is essentially different from those methods using the SVD (e.g., the Latent Semantic Indexing (LSI) method [3]). The essential difference is that our model provides the important function for semantic projections which realizes the dynamic recognition of the context. That is, in our model, the context-dependent interpretation is dynamically performed for computing the distance between words and images by selecting a subspace from the entire orthogonal semantic space. In our model, the number of phases of the contexts is almost infinite (currently 2^{800}, approximately). Other methods do not provide the context dependent interpretation for computing equivalence and similarity in the orthogonal space, that is, the phase of meaning is fixed and static.

In [2], a three-layered data model has been introduced to extract image features and semantics for content-based image retrieval. In this model, a high level semantic retrieval for medial image information is realized. Similarly to our approach, the features of images are obtained from the images themselves, and image contents are extracted with conceptual terms. The image retrieval is realized with the association between the conceptual terms and the image features. Our approach is different from this approach in modeling image contents. In our approach, we realize semantic image search by obtaining impression and object terms of image data by the observation of the entire image. As the medical application is assumed in the approach in [2], spatial and temporal characteristics of objects in images and their spatial relationships are important in image abstraction, and the shape and spatial relationships are described and used in the retrieval.

In this chapter, we present three methods for representing the metadata items for images and the basic functions which extract the appropriate images from the orthogonal semantic space.

7.2   Metadatabase System

7.2.1   The Overview of the Metadatabase System

The metadatabase system selects appropriate images for requests of database users by using metadata items and basic functions. This system consists of the following subsystems (Figure 7-1):

1. Metadata Acquisition Subsystem: This subsystem supports the facilities for acquiring metadata from the database storing the source images.

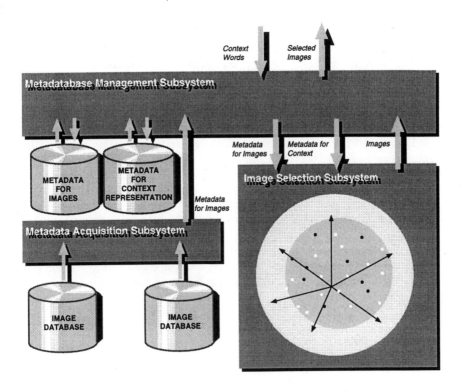

Figure 7-1 The metadatabase system architecture.

2. Metadatabase Management Subsystem: This subsystem supports the facilities for keeping metadata consistent in the orthogonal semantic space. This subsystem also provides the facilities for interpreting users's queries.

3. Image Selection Subsystem: This subsystem supports the facilities for selecting appropriate images by using the MMM. Three methods are provided for representing the metadata items for images. This subsystem maps the metadata items for images into the orthogonal space. By receiving metadata items for context representation, it selects the most correlated image to the context.

7.2.2   Basic Functions and Metadata for Images

The metadatabase system is used to extract image data items corresponding to context words which represent the user's impression and the image's contents. For example, the context words "powerful" and "strong" are given, and the image with the impression corresponding to these context words is extracted. Each metadata item of images is mapped in the orthonogal semantic space. This space is referred to as "orthogonal metadata space" or "metadata space." The MMM is used to create the orthogonal metadata space. By this orthogonalization, we can define an appropriate metric for computing relationships between metadata items for images and context representation. The MMM gives the machinery for extracting the associated information to the context.

Three types of metadata are used.

1. *Metadata for space creation*: These metadata items are used for the creation of the orthogonal metadata space, which is used as a space for semantic image retrieval.

2. *Metadata for images*: These metadata items are the candidates for semantic image retrieval.

3. *Metadata for context representation*: These metadata items are used as context words for representing the user's imagination and the image's contents.

The basic functions and metadata structures are summarized as follows:

1. Creation of metadata space:

   To provide the function of semantic associative search, basic information on m data items ("metadata for space creation") is given in the form of a matrix. Each metadata item is given independently of the other ones. No relationships between the metadata items need to be described. The information of each data item is represented by its features. The m basic metadata items are given in the form of an m by n matrix M where each metadata item is characterized by n features. By using M, the orthogonal space is created as the metadata space $\mathcal{MDS}$. These metadata items are determined as mentioned in the following section.

2. Representation of metadata for images in n-dimensional vectors

   Each metadata item for images is represented in the n-dimensional vector whose elements correspond to n features. The metadata items for images become the candidates for the semantic associative search. Furthermore, each of the context words, which are used to represent the user's impression and the image's contents in semantic image retrieval, is also represented in an n-dimensional vector.

3. Mapping data items into the metadata space $\mathcal{MDS}$

   Metadata items (metadata for space creation, metadata for images and metadata for context representation) which are represented in n-dimensional vectors are mapped into the orthogonal metadata space. Those data items are used as context words and target image data items which are extracted according to users' requests.

4. Semantic associative search

   When a sequence of context words which determine the user's impression and the image's contents is given, the images corresponding to the context are extracted from a set of retrieval candidate images in the metadata space.

7.2.3   A Creation Method of the Metadata Space

We introduce an implementation method for the creation of the $\mathcal{MDS}$.

The procedure for the creation of the $\mathcal{MDS}$ is as follows:

1. To create the data matrix M, we can use "General Basic English Dictionary" [14] in which 850 basic words are used to explain each English definition. Those 850 basic words are used as features, that is, they are used for characterizing metadata as the features corresponding to the columns in the matrix M. The 2000 data items are used as "metadata for space creation." Those metadata items are used as the basic words in the English dictionary "Longman Dictionary of Contemporary English" [20]. Each metadata item for space creation corresponds to a row of the matrix M. In the setting of a row of the matrix M, each column corresponding to the features which appear in the explanation of the data item is set to the value "1". If the feature is used as a negative meaning, the column corresponding to it is set to the value "-1". And, the other columns are

set to the value "0". This process is performed for each of 2000 metadata items. And then, each column of the matrix is normalized by the 2-norm to create the matrix M.

2. By using this matrix M, the $\mathcal{MDS}$ is created as the orthogonal space. The creation method of the orthogonal space is described in Section 7.3.1. This space represents the semantic space for computing contexts and meanings of the metadata items.

To automatically create the data matrix M from the dictionary, several filters are used, which remove unnecessary elements (words), such as articles and pronouns, and transform conjugations and inflections of words to the infinitives. Those elements are removed from the features characterizing each data item. The unnecessary words are not used as features in the data matrix M.

(filter-1) This filter eliminates the unnecessary elements, such as articles and pronouns.

(filter-2) This filter transforms conjugations and inflections to the infinitives.

(filter-3) This filter transforms the large characters to the small ones.

(filter-4) This filter transforms clipped form words to the corresponding original words.

(filter-5) The rows of the matrix M are created for each data item by using the filtered features which characterize the data item.

Each metadata item (metadata item for images, metadata item for context representation) is mapped into the metadata space, by computing the Fourier expansion for the n-dimensional vector representing the metadata item itself. These metadata items are defined as metadata by using the n features. These metadata items are used as context words and metadata items for retrieval candidate images.

7.2.4 Creation Methods of Metadata for Images

We present three methods for creating metadata for images.

In [5], Kashyap et al. have clearly identified and classified various metadata for digital media into three basic categories: *content-dependent metadata, content-descriptive metadata* and *content-independent metadata*. The metadata for images which is used in our semantic associative search is categorized in the content-descriptive metadata, because the metadata is associated with the original image without being extracted directly from the image contents themselves. Furthermore, in [5], the content-descriptive metadata is classified into two categories: *domain-dependent metadata* and *domain-independent metadata*.

In the following Method-1 and Method-2, the metadata for images is categorized into *domain-dependent* because the metadata is extracted from domain-specific concepts, which are used as a basis for the determination of the metadata itself. That is, the metadata type used in these methods is categorized as the *content-descriptive domain-dependent metadata*.

In Method-3, metadata for images is extracted from their color components which are used to characterize image features in an experimental psychology model of correlating colors and their impression words. This type of metadata is categorized as the *content-descriptive domain-independent metadata*.

Method-1

Each image is explained by using the n features which are used in the creation of the data matrix M. In this explanation, the impression or the content of the image is represented by using these features as the metadata for the image. As the result, each image is represented as n-dimensional vector in which a nonzero value is assigned to the corresponding elements of the vector of these features.

An image P is explained and defined by using some of the words which are used in the n features. Then, the image is represented as an n-dimensional vector.

$$P = (w_1, w_2, \ldots, w_n).$$

Each metadata item is mapped into the metadata space by computing the Fourier expansion for the vector corresponding to the image data item itself.

Method-2

An image P is represented in t impression words $o_1, o_2, \ldots, o_t$, where each impression word is defined as an n-dimensional vector:

$$o_i = (o_{i1}, o_{i2}, \ldots, o_{in}),$$

which is characterized by n specific features.

Namely, we define the image P as the collection of t impression words which represent the image.

$$P = \{o_1, o_2, \ldots, o_t\}.$$

Moreover, we define the operator union $\bigoplus$ of impression words $o_1, o_2, \ldots, o_t$ to represent the metadata for the image P as a vector as follows:

$$\bigoplus_{i=1}^{t} o_i \equiv (\text{sign}(o_{\ell_1 1}) \max_{1 \leq i \leq t} |o_{i1}|, \text{sign}(o_{\ell_2 2}) \max_{1 \leq i \leq t} |o_{i2}|,$$

$$\ldots, \text{sign}(o_{\ell_n t}) \max_{1 \leq i \leq t} |o_{in}|)$$

where $\text{sign}(a)$ represents the sign (plus or minus) of "a" and $\ell_k, k = 1, \ldots, n$ represents the index which gives the maximum, that is:

$$\max_{1 \leq i \leq t} |o_{ik}| = |o_{\ell_k k}|.$$

Method-3

In this method, the metadata for images is automatically and indirectly extracted from image data items themselves. Color is known as the dominant factor which affects the impression of images [1]. We use color to derive impressions of images.

The basic idea of this method is to describe both images and impression words in the notion of *color* and compute correlations between images and words. Color used in this method is represented in the Munsell color system as it is more familiar to the human perception. Additionally, the color names defined by ISCC (Inter-Society Color Council) and NIST (National Institute of Standards and Technology) are used to describe both images and impression words in the notion of color. By taking the correlations between images and impression words, we can obtain the suitable words which describe the impressions of images. The metadata for images is computed from the obtained impression words by the previously defined union operator $\oplus$. The details of this method are described in Section 7.7.

7.3 Creation of a Metadata Space and Basic Functions

In this section, we introduce a creation method of the metadata space $\mathcal{MDS}$ for systematically storing metadata and for implementing the semantic associative search for images.

7.3.1 Creation of a Metadata Space

The semantic associative search for images is created by using our mathematical model of meaning [6, 9]. For the metadata items for space creation, a data matrix M is created. When m data items for space creation are given, each data item is characterized by n features $(f_1, f_2, \ldots, f_n)$. For given $\mathbf{d}_i (i = 1, \ldots, m)$, the data matrix M is defined as the $m \times n$ matrix whose i-th row is $\mathbf{d}_i$. Then, each column of the matrix is normalized by the 2-norm in order to create the matrix M.

Figure 7-2 shows the matrix M. That is $M = (\mathbf{d}_1, \mathbf{d}_2, \mathbf{d}_3, \ldots, \mathbf{d}_n)^T$.

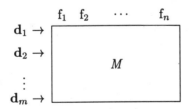

Figure 7-2 Representation of metadata items by matrix M.

1. The correlation matrix $M^T M$ of M is computed, where M^T represents the transpose of M.

2. The eigenvalue decomposition of $M^T M$ is computed.

$$M^T M = Q \begin{pmatrix} \lambda_1 & & & \\ & \ddots & & \\ & & \lambda_\nu & \\ & & & 0 \cdot \cdot \cdot 0 \end{pmatrix} Q^T,$$

$0 \leq \nu \leq n$.
The orthogonal matrix Q is defined by

$$Q = (\mathbf{q}_1, \mathbf{q}_2, \ldots, \mathbf{q}_n)^T,$$

where $\mathbf{q}_i$'s are the normalized eigenvectors of $M^T M$. We call the eigenvectors "semantic elements" hereafter. Here, all the eigenvalues are real and all the eigenvectors are mutually orthogonal because the matrix $M^T M$ is symmetric.

3. Defining the metadata space $\mathcal{MDS}$,

$$\mathcal{MDS} := span(\mathbf{q}_1, \mathbf{q}_2, \ldots, \mathbf{q}_\nu),$$

which is a linear space generated by linear combinations of $\{\mathbf{q}_1, \ldots, \mathbf{q}_\nu\}$. We note that $\{\mathbf{q}_1, \ldots, \mathbf{q}_\nu\}$ is an orthonormal basis of $\mathcal{MDS}$.

7.3.2 The Set of the Semantic Projections Π_ν

The projection P_{λ_i} is defined as follows:
$P_{\lambda_i} \xleftrightarrow{\text{d}}$ Projection to the eigenspace corresponding to the eigenvalue λ_i,
i.e., $P_{\lambda_i} : \mathcal{MDS} \to span(\mathbf{q}_i)$.
The set of the semantic projections Π_ν is defined as follows:

$$\begin{aligned} \Pi_\nu \; := \; & \{ \, 0 \, , \, P_{\lambda_1}, P_{\lambda_2}, \ldots, P_{\lambda_\nu}, \\ & P_{\lambda_1} + P_{\lambda_2}, P_{\lambda_1} + P_{\lambda_3}, \ldots, P_{\lambda_{\nu-1}} + P_{\lambda_\nu}, \\ & \vdots \\ & P_{\lambda_1} + P_{\lambda_2} + \cdots + P_{\lambda_\nu} \}. \end{aligned}$$

The number of the elements of Π_ν is 2^ν, and accordingly it implies that 2^ν different contexts can be expressed by this formulation.

7.3.3 Semantic Operator

The correlations between each context word and each semantic element are computed by this process. The context word is used to represent the user's impression and the image's contents for images to be extracted. A sequence

$$s_\ell = (\mathbf{u}_1, \mathbf{u}_2, \ldots, \mathbf{u}_\ell)$$

of ℓ context words and a positive real number $0 < \varepsilon_s < 1$ are given, the semantic operator S_p constitutes a semantic projection $P_{\varepsilon_s}(s_\ell)$, according to the context. That is,

$$S_p : T_\ell \longmapsto \Pi_\nu$$

where T_ℓ is the set of sequences of ℓ words and $T_\ell \ni s_\ell$, $\Pi_\nu \ni P_{\varepsilon_s}(s_\ell)$. Note that the set $\{\mathbf{u}_1, \mathbf{u}_2, \ldots, \mathbf{u}_\ell\}$ must be a subset of the words defined in the matrix M.

The constitution of the operator S_p consists of the following processes:

1. Fourier expansion of $\mathbf{u}_i (i = 1, 2, \ldots, \ell)$ is computed as the inner product of $\mathbf{u}_i$ and $\mathbf{q}_j$ u_{ij}, i.e.,

$$u_{ij} := (\mathbf{u}_i, \mathbf{q}_j) \ , \ for \ j = 1, 2, \ldots, \nu.$$

$\widehat{\mathbf{u}}_i \in \mathcal{I}$ is defined as
$$\widehat{\mathbf{u}}_i := (u_{i1}, u_{i2}, \ldots, u_{i\nu}).$$

This is the mapping of the context word $\mathbf{u}_i$ to the $\mathcal{MDS}$.

2. The semantic center $\mathbf{G}^+(s_\ell)$ of the sequence s_ℓ is computed as

$$\mathbf{G}^+(s_\ell) := \frac{\left(\sum_{i=1}^\ell u_{i1}, \ldots, \sum_{i=1}^\ell u_{i\nu} \right)}{\| \left(\sum_{i=1}^\ell u_{i1}, \ldots, \sum_{i=1}^\ell u_{i\nu} \right) \|_\infty},$$

where $\| \cdot \|_\infty$ denotes infinity norm.

3. The semantic projection $P_{\varepsilon_s}(s_\ell)$ is determined as

$$P_{\varepsilon_s}(s_\ell) := \sum_{i \in \Lambda_{\varepsilon_s}} P_{\lambda_i} \ \in \Pi_\nu,$$

where $\Lambda_{\varepsilon_s} := \{ \ i \ | \ | (\mathbf{G}^+(s_\ell))_i \ | \ > \varepsilon_s \}$.

7.3.4 Function for Semantic Image Search

We introduce a function to measure the similarity between images and context words. The function measures the quantity of association or correlation between context words and the candidate images. We also introduce a dynamic metric depending on the context between two images.

Function to Measure the Association

The function measures the association between context words and the candidate images. Suppose a sequence of associate context words is given to search an image, e.g., { dynamic, powerful }. We can regard the context words as the words forming the context s_ℓ. We can specify some subspace by using the semantic operator with weights c_j's which are given by

$$c_j(s_\ell) := \frac{\sum_{i=1}^{\ell} u_{ij}}{\left\| \left(\sum_{i=1}^{\ell} u_{i1}, \ldots, \sum_{i=1}^{\ell} u_{i\nu} \right) \right\|_\infty}, \quad j \in \Lambda_{\varepsilon_s}.$$

Since the norm of the image, which can be calculated from the metadata of the image, reflects the correlation between the image and the semantic elements included in the selected subspace, we may use it as a measure for the association between the context words and the image data.

We introduce a function for computing the norm of the image. The function $\bar{\eta}_0(\mathbf{x}; s_\ell)$ is defined as follows:

$$\bar{\eta}_0(\mathbf{x}; s_\ell) = \frac{\sqrt{\sum_{j \in \Lambda_{\varepsilon_s} \cap \mathcal{S}} \{c_j(s_\ell) x_j\}^2}}{\|\mathbf{x}\|_2},$$

where the set $\mathcal{S}$ is defined by $\mathcal{S} = \{i | sign(c_i(s_\ell)) = sign(x_i)\}$.

In this function, we eliminate the effect of the negative correlation. We note that the sum in the numerator of this function is sought over the selected semantic subspace from the context s_ℓ, while the norm in the denominator is sought over the whole metadata space $\mathcal{MDS}$.

Dynamic Metric

We introduce a dynamic metric between the image data items according to a context. Since each image data item can be represented as a vector via the union operator $\oplus$ defined in Section 7.2.4, we can utilize the metric, which we defined for two distinct words in [6, 7, 9], to compute the similarity between metadata items of images. The dynamic metric $\rho(\mathbf{x}, \mathbf{y}; s_\ell)$ for $\mathbf{x}, \mathbf{y} \in \mathcal{MDS}$ is introduced to compute the similarity between metadata items for images.

The metric $\rho(\mathbf{x}, \mathbf{y}; s_\ell)$ to compute the similarity between metadata items $\mathbf{x}, \mathbf{y}$ of two images in the given context s_ℓ is defined as follows:

$$\rho(\mathbf{x}, \mathbf{y}; s_\ell) = \sqrt{\sum_{j \in \Lambda_{\varepsilon_s}} \{c_j(s_\ell)(x_j - y_j)\}^2},$$

This metric, because of the presence of dynamic weights c_j, can faithfully reflect the change of the context.

7.4   Semantic Associative Search for Metadata for Images

The proposed system realizes the semantic associative search for metadata items for images.

The basic function of the semantic associative search is provided for context-dependent interpretation. This function performs the selection of the semantic subspace from the metadata space. When a sequence s_ℓ of context words for determining a context is given to the system, the selection of the semantic subspace is performed. This selection corresponds to the recognition of the context, which is defined by the given context words. The selected semantic subspace corresponds to a given context. The metadata item for the most correlated image to the context in the selected semantic subspace is extracted from the specified image data item set $\mathcal{W}$. By using the function defined in Section 7.3.4, the semantic associative search is performed by the following procedure:

1. When a sequence s_ℓ of the context words for determining a context (the user's impression and the image's contents) is given, the Fourier expansion is computed for each context word, and the Fourier coefficients of these words with respect to each semantic element are obtained. This corresponds to seeking the correlation between each context word and each semantic element.

2. The values of the Fourier coefficients for each semantic element are summed up to find the correlation between the given context words and each semantic element.

3. If the sum obtained in step 2 in terms of each semantic element is greater than a given threshold ε_s, the semantic element is employed to form the semantic subspace $P_{\varepsilon_s}(s_\ell)\mathcal{MDS}$. This corresponds to recognizing the context which is determined by the given context words.

4. By using the function $\bar{\eta}_0(\mathbf{x}; s_\ell)$, the metadata item for the image with the maximum norm is selected among the candidate metadata items for images in $\mathcal{W}$ in the selected semantic subspace. This corresponds to finding the image with the greatest association to the given context words from $\mathcal{W}$.

7.5 Examples of Creating Metadata

7.5.1 Method-1

To create the metadata as vectors for images by using the 850 basic words of "General Basic English Dictionary," the designer of metadata looks at an image and checks features that correspond to the image. If the feature corresponds to the image, the value 1.0 is put for that feature; if it does not correspond to the feature, the value 0.0 is put; and if it negates the image, the value -1.0 is put. Although the cost is very high, the simplest way is to check for 850 features one by one for each image. A vector is created for each image, and mapped into the $\mathcal{MDS}$.

7.5.2 Method-2

As the previous method, the same features from "General Basic English Dictionary" are used. This method creates metadata by giving impressions of the original image or referring to objects composing it. The impression words or

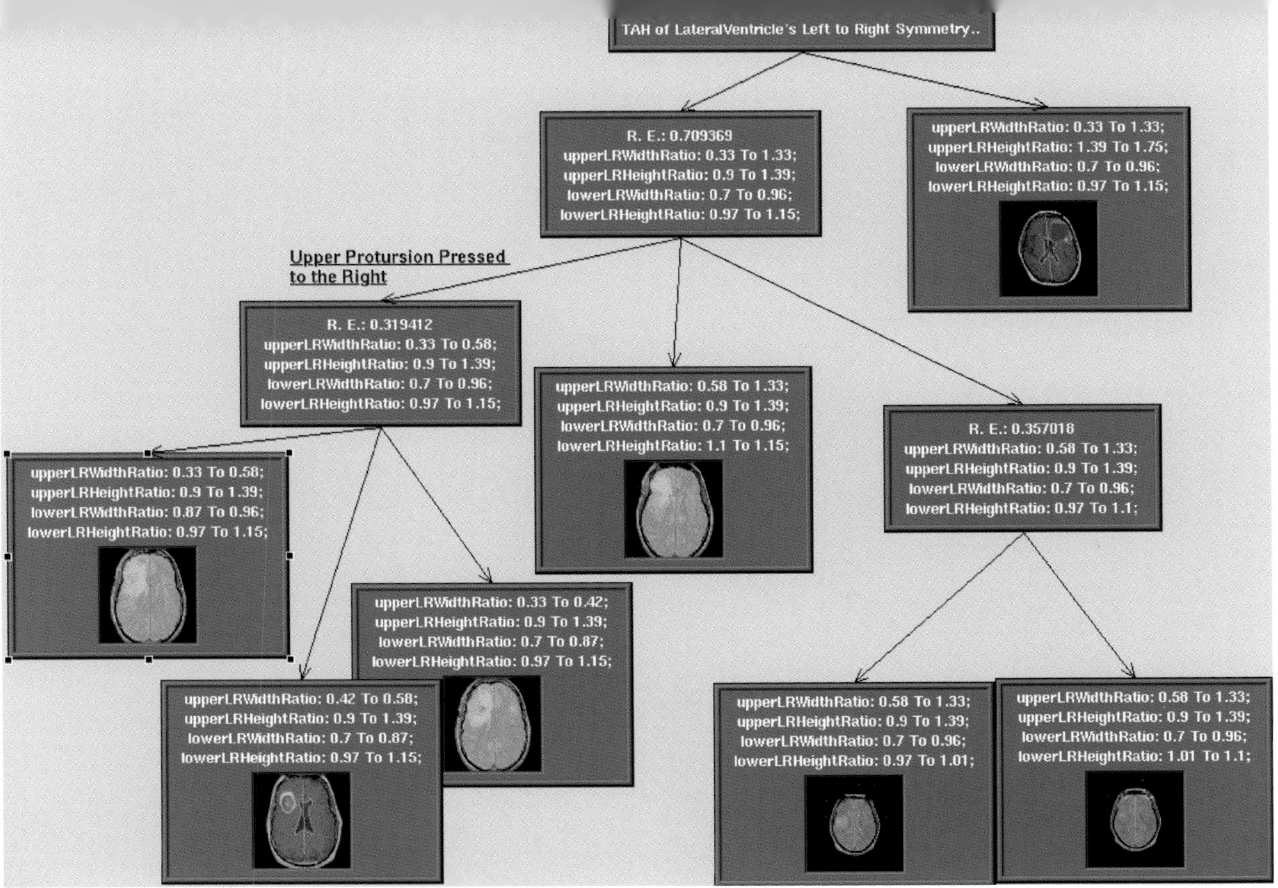

Color Figure-1 Multi-attribute type abstraction hierarchy (generated by MDISC based on the decomposed four protrusions) representing the left to right symmetry of the lateral ventricles.

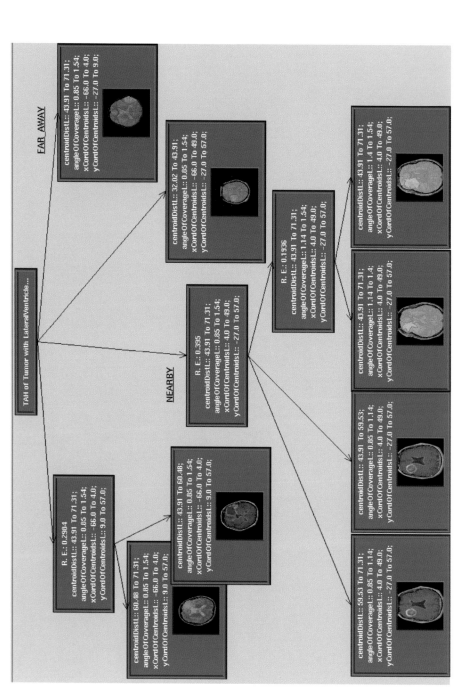

Color Figure-2 The MDISC-generated TAH (based on d_c, θ_c, x_c, and y_c) ... ... spatial relationship between tumor and lateral ventricle.

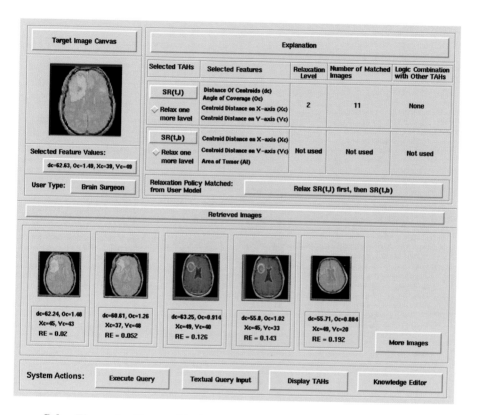

Color Figure-3 The graphical user interface (GUI) of the knowledge-based query answering showing the retrieved images that are most similar to the given target image.

Bouquet 1
(The Birth of Love)

Bouquet 2
(Marbled Flowers)

Bouquet 3
(Bouquet of Remembrance)

Bouquet 4
(The Extraordinary Bouquet)

Bouquet 5
(The Resting Butterfly)

Bouquet 6
(Outburst of Happiness)

Bouquet 7
(The Closeness of
Your Bouquet)

Bouquet 8
(The Radiant Bouquet)

Color Figure-4 Image data items.

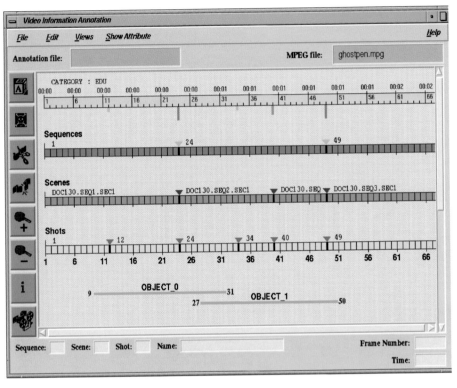

Color Figure-5 Vane: Video annotation engine.

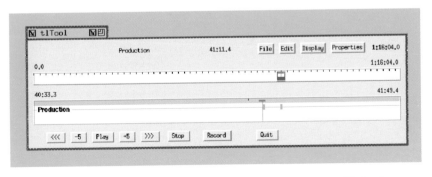

Color Figure-6 Audio browser with keyword 'production' highlighted.

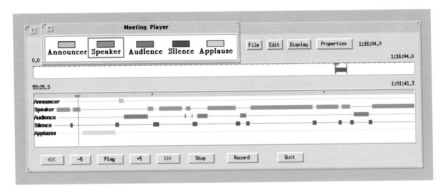

Color Figure-7   Audio browser with speaker segmentation.

Hybrid-electric drives

- The wheels are driven wholly or mostly electrically by up to 4 ?hub-integrated switched reluctance motors (a British technology that is inherently smaller, lighter, cheaper, stronger, faster, quieter, and more efficient, rugged, fault-tolerant, and controllable than asynchronous or permanent-magnet motors). Braking is electronic and regenerative.
- Electricity is made onboard as needed in a tiny IC or EC engine, gas turbine, thermophotovoltaics, or fuel cell, *e.g.* an Otto (probably Orbital-derivative 2-stroke) $\eta = 0{,}3$ engine or $\eta = 0{,}5$ semiadiabatic Diesel.
- A few batteries (or a C-fibre superflywheel or ultracapacitor) store braking energy for hill-climbing and acceleration—*not* for range, since lead-acid batteries have ~1% as much energy per kg as fuel. Only ~0.5 kWh is needed; 2.5 kWh & 40 kW of hybrid-optimized NiMH weigh ~50 kg.
- Later, ideally a modular fuel cell (?monolithic solid-oxide, self-reforming and reversible, thereby eliminating the buffer storage too).
- Dramatically lower accessory loads and parasitic mechanical drag.
- Extremely light but crashworthy (advanced polymer composites); max. payload/mass; designed like an airplane, not a tank; 'fly-by-light/power-by-wire', smart active suspension, and powerful integrative software.

DOC SEGMENT 4

However, a hypercar isn't an ordinary electric car, running on batteries that are recharged by being plugged into utility power. Despite impressive recent progress, such cars still can't carry very much or go very far without needing heavy batteries that suffer from relatively high cost and short life. Since gasoline and other liquid fuels store a hundred times as much useful energy per pound as batteries do, a long driving range is best achieved by carrying energy in the form of fuel, not batteries, and then burning that fuel as needed in a tiny onboard engine to make the electricity to run the wheel motors. A few batteries (or, soon, a carbon-fiber "superflywheel") can temporarily store the braking energy recovered from those wheel motors and reuse at least 70 percent of it for hill climbing and acceleration. With its power so augmented, the engine needs to handle only the average load, not the peak load, so it can shrink to about a tenth the current normal size. It will run at or very near its optimal point, doubling efficiency, and turn off whenever it's not needed.

This arrangement is called a "hybrid-electric drive," because it uses electric wheel motors but makes the electricity onboard from fuel. Such a propulsion system weighs only about a fourth as much as that of a battery-electric car, which must haul a half ton of batteries down to the store to buy a six-pack. Hybrids thus offer the

Color Figure-8 Result of search for the keywords "battery" and "batteries" in different media. The audio browser shows speaker segmentation and keyword locations. For the slides, the single search term "batter*" was used; the identified keywords in the slide are highlighted. A portion of one Text-Tile containing the keywork is shown.

object names which are extracted from the image are referred to from "General Basic English Dictionary," and the explanatory words for each impression word or object name are checked as features, and the value for each feature in the vector corresponding to the impression word or object name is set. Then, the vector corresponding to the image is created from the vectors corresponding to the impression words or object names by the union operator defined in Section 7.2.4.

7.5.3   Method-3

In this method, metadata for an image is created by referring to color components. Digital images, which are usually represented in the RGB color system, are transformed to color vectors in the Munsell color space by using the MTM (Mathematical Transformation to Munsell) [12]. The MTM is described in Section 7.7. Scaler values of color vectors for corresponding color are defined in the range from 0.0 to 1.0 according to given rules. One of the rules which we have used defines each value by referring to occupancy of colors in images.

The difficulty of this method is defining the association between the colors and impression words; that is, creating the descriptive metadata for context words. To solve this difficulty, we referred to the results from the field of the experimental psychology. Many word association tests have been done to make clear the relation between colors and psychological effects.

7.6   Experiments

7.6.1   Metadata Items in the Experiment

In this experiment, we use 30 images and the corresponding metadata items representing the impressions of those images. Those metadata items are represented in the impression words shown in Table 7-1. Each impression word is explained by using several features from the 850 basic words of "General Basic English Dictionary." Method-2 is used for creating the metadata items for each image.

As the metadata items which are given as context words, we use several vocabulary entries shown in Table 7-2. These metadata items are used to express

image data name	impression
chagalla1	vivid,quiet,substance
chagallb1	grief,sombre,terrible
chagallc1	sober,dynamic,motion
chagalld1	shine,tender,calm
corota1	beautiful,calm,grand
corotb1	beautiful,delicate,calm
corotc1	grief,sombre,sober
corotd1	shine,beautiful,calm
gogha1	delight,shine,merry
goghb1	grief,sombre,terrible
hokusaia1	dynamic,motion,strong
hokusaib1	fight,motion,calm
hokusaic1	delicate,calm,quiet
hokusaid1	vivid,motion,speed
loiranda1	shine,grand,calm
loirandb1	delight,shine,calm
loirandc1	delight,grand,calm
loirandd1	quiet,substance,material
nelsona1	grand,dynamic,motion
nelsonb1	twilight,calm,quiet
renoira1	dim,tender,quiet
renoirb1	delight,dim,calm
renoirc1	loud,bustle,crowd
renoird1	fine,strong,quiet
sarthoua1	dynamic,motion,speed
hiroa1	twilight,grand,quiet
hirob1	cheer,dim,quiet
hiroc1	beautiful,quiet,calm
hirod1	fine,beautiful,shine
hiroe1	fine,beautiful,calm

Table 7-1 Image data and their definitions (impression words).

the user's impression. Each vocabulary entry is defined by using several explanation words listed in Table 7-2.

7.6.2 Experimental Results

The experimental results are shown in Tables 7-3, 7-4, and 7-5. In each experiment, 30 image data names are listed in the order of the selected images in each context. The function $\bar{\eta}_0\left(\mathbf{x}; s_\ell\right)$ is used for computing the norm of each image.

vocabulary entry	explanation (features)
brave	ready to go into danger, having self-control in danger or pain
clear	able to be seen through
cloud	(a mass of) mist high in the sky
dark	with little or no light
depress	make sad, unhappy
dynamic	of physical power, forces producing motion
excite	get (person, condition) worked up
glad	pleased, happy
grace	quality of being beautiful, sp. harmony of structure or motion
happy	full of pleasure, pleased
interesting	causing feeling of interest
light	that which makes things able to be seen
merry	laughing, happy, bright
might	great power, force
natural	of, forming a part of, in agreement with, nature or one's nature
pale	(sp. of face) having little color
power	quality of being strong enough, able, to do something, sp., physical force
sad	unhappy
simple	of one substance, unmixed, without division into parts
stir	put or become in motion, make or become awake
strong	having, using, marked by, great, sp., physical, force

Table 7-2 Vocabulary entries used as context words.

The value of correlation in each image represents the norm of the vector in the selected subspace. The norm of the vector is normalized as shown in Section 7.3.4. The values of correlation have only comparative significance for a given computation $\bar{\eta}_0(\mathbf{x}; s_\ell)$.

1. Experiment using context "power, strong" (see Table 7-3)

   As shown in the experimental result, the image data named "hokusaia1" is in the first ranking (rank 1). This result reflects the recognition of the context "power, strong" to this image.

2. Experiment using context "light, strong" (see Table 7-4)

   The image data named "renoird1" is in the first ranking (rank 1). This result reflects the recognition of the context "light, strong" to this image.

3. Experiment using context "happy, glad" (see Table 7-5)

   The image data named "gogha1" is in the first ranking (rank 1). This result reflects the recognition of the context "happy, glad" to this image.

Context: power, strong		
rank	image data	correlation*
1	hokusaia1	0.377136
2	renoird1	0.345938
3	nelsona1	0.306403
4	sarthoua1	0.303013
5	hokusaib1	0.262247
6	renoirc1	0.261547
7	loirandd1	0.221684
8	loirandc1	0.219976
9	hokusaid1	0.208567
10	corota1	0.206876
11	chagalla1	0.202815
12	loiranda1	0.202088
13	gogha1	0.201686
14	renoirb1	0.199490
15	loirandb1	0.195207
16	goghb1	0.193655
17	chagallb1	0.193655
18	corotc1	0.188142
19	hiroa1	0.176600
20	hiroc1	0.176152
21	chagalld1	0.175089
22	corotd1	0.172304
23	hirod1	0.167228
24	renoira1	0.156583
25	hirob1	0.156354
26	hiroe1	0.155545
27	nelsonb1	0.147163
28	chagallc1	0.139549
29	hokusaic1	0.136931
30	corotb1	0.130039

Table 7-3 The order of selected images in the context (power, strong).

7.7   Automatic Creation of Image Metadata

In the semantic associative image search, each image is characterized in an n-dimensional vector as the metadata item in Methods 1 and 2. Currently, it is assumed that the designer of metadata checks each image data item, one by one, and defines n-dimensional vectors which represent image data items subjectively. As each image data item is defined subjectively, it causes individual variations. When several designers define metadata for each image data item, we need some sort of guideline.

Context: light, strong	
image data	correlation*
renoird1	0.313255
hokusaia1	0.272313
sarthoua1	0.191604
chagalla1	0.187024
gogha1	0.186192
nelsona1	0.184015
hokusaib1	0.183724
loirandd1	0.180893
loirandb1	0.177737
hokusaid1	0.175774
hiroa1	0.172693
loirandc1	0.168848
loiranda1	0.166349
renoirc1	0.163451
corota1	0.154491
chagallb1	0.150202
goghb1	0.150202
nelsonb1	0.149441
hiroc1	0.147595
renoirb1	0.146058
hirod1	0.145653
corotd1	0.144162
chagalld1	0.138508
hirob1	0.136352
renoira1	0.127080
hiroe1	0.123317
corotc1	0.117761
hokusaic1	0.114034
chagallc1	0.106145
corotb1	0.090652

Table 7-4 The order of selected images in the context (light, strong).

In this section, we show a simple and effective method for generating metadata items for image data. In the algorithm shown in this section, impression words of each image data item are derived via the color space. Impression words of image data are not derived directly from the image data themselves. We use colors as intermediates to derive impressions of images. First, we discuss how an image is transformed to its color representation. Then, we discuss how impression words are derived from the color representations of images. Finally, we present the method to derive impression words from image data items with its example.

Context: happy, glad	
image data	correlation*
gogha1	0.270147
hirob1	0.267835
hokusaic1	0.220439
loirandc1	0.213378
renoira1	0.209098
loirandb1	0.200794
corotb1	0.198720
hiroc1	0.197461
renoirb1	0.196746
renoirc1	0.194097
loirandd1	0.188176
chagalla1	0.187586
loiranda1	0.179469
chagalld1	0.179020
corota1	0.178073
nelsona1	0.170461
nelsonb1	0.168503
hokusaid1	0.167831
corotd1	0.165786
renoird1	0.165509
hiroa1	0.161292
sarthoua1	0.155030
hokusaia1	0.152708
hiroe1	0.152525
hokusaib1	0.146644
hirod1	0.142228
chagallc1	0.135303
goghb1	0.103767
chagallb1	0.103767
corotc1	0.088858

Table 7-5   The order of selected images in the context (happy, glad).

7.7.1   Creation of Metadata

The procedure to extract impression words of an image is as follows:

1. **Color Transformation:** Transform color representation of an image I from the RGB color space to the Munsell color space by the MTM.

2. **Clustering:** Cluster each color component of the image into p clusters of colors. As the result, the image is represented in the form of image vector P.

3. **Derivation of Impression Words:** Derive impression words from the image by calculating correlations between the image vector and impression word vectors.

4. **Creation of Metadata for Image:** The derived impression words are used to create metadata for the image I by Method-2 defined in Section 7.5.2. The impression words for the image I are represented as the metadata item of the image by the operator union $\oplus$.

The remainder of the chapter describes each of the steps in detail.

7.7.2   Impressions of Images and Colors

The impressions of images are derived from several factors. It is known that the color component of images is one of the dominant factors which affect the impressions of images strongly. That is, we can approximate the impressions of images from the color components. Concerning the color components of an image, we must consider the following points:

1. Colors appearing in the image

2. Ratio of the area size of each color to the whole image

3. Allocation of colors in the image

In our current method, only the first two points are considered to define impressions of the images. It is assumed that the impression of an image roughly depends on colors appearing in the images, and it is fixed by complex combinations of various impressions derived from each color component. Allocation of each color appearing in an image is also important. In this method, we do not consider the structural information of an image. Therefore, the image I which consists of q color components is defined as follows:

$$I = \{c_1, c_2, ..., c_q\}.$$

Where c_i is the size of the area which the color component i occupies. It is defined as follows:

$$c_i = \frac{\text{Total area size of the color component } i}{\text{Total area size of the image } P}, \quad \text{where } i = 1, 2, ..., q.$$

To derive the impressions of images from color components, colors of images should be represented in psychological color [13]. Next, we discuss how the physical colors of the images are transformed to the psychological colors.

Psychological Color

Normally, colors of image data items are expressed in the RGB color system. Each color in this color system is expressed as a mixture of three basic colors, red, green, and blue.

Although it is a convenient color system to handle colors, there is a gap between the color representation in the RGB color system and the psychological color representation. To deal with colors and their impressions, the psychological color, such as the well-known Munsell color system, is used. The Munsell color system identifies each color in three dimensions, (H, V, C) where H is the color, V is the lightness or darkness of the color, and C is the dullness or purity of the color [13]. This three-dimensional space has psychologically linear scales.

The transformation between the RGB color representation and the Munsell color representation can be performed mathematically by the MTM (Mathematical Transformation to Munsell) [12]. The MTM uses the Adams color space[1] to mediate the transformation between two color systems as $L^*a^*b^*$ of CIE. In our algorithm, color components of image data are transformed to the Munsell color data by the MTM.

Clustering of Colors

Many colors are usually used in a single image, and they produce various impressions. To clarify these impressions, colors should be grouped into several meaningful clusters of colors.

---

[1]It is also known as ULCS (Uniform Lightness-Chromaticness Scale).

To cluster the color components it is necessary to calculate the difference between any two colors. In the Munsell color system, the color-difference between two Munsell colors (H_j, V_j, C_j) and (H_k, V_k, C_k) is calculated with the following Godlove color-difference formula [4]:

$$\Delta E = \sqrt{2 C_j C_k \{1 - \cos(\frac{2\pi \Delta H}{100})\} + (\Delta C)^2 + (4\Delta V)^2},$$

where ΔH, ΔV and ΔC are expressed as follows:

$$\begin{aligned}
\Delta H &= |H_j - H_k|, \\
\Delta V &= |V_j - V_k|, \\
\Delta C &= |C_j - C_k|.
\end{aligned}$$

First, cluster centers are selected for each color component. By calculating the color-difference between these cluster centers and each color component, the cluster which the color component belongs to is fixed. Each color component belongs to the closest cluster, that is, the one with the smallest ΔE.

Then, the image I is defined as a p-dimensional vector, where p is a number of clusters. The p-dimensional vector is image vector P and defined as follows:

$$P = (v_1, v_2, ..., v_p),$$

where v_i is a summation of c_j of color components in the cluster i. The impressions of the image I are derived from this vector P.

7.7.3   Color and Impression

In the field of experimental psychology many word association tests have been done on colors [1, 15, 11, 19]. For instance, to derive the association between colors and words, some experiments have been done by showing a single color to numbers of testees and asking them the impression words.

The results of such experiments show that there are associations between words and colors. For instance, the color 'strong orange' (e.g., 5YR7/14 in the Munsell color system) is likely to be selected as the associated color to the word 'warm' [1]. To describe the impression words in the notion of colors, the results of these psychological experiments can be used effectively.

Additionally, those psychological experiments have shown that there are two types of associations. One type of association depends on individual mental background such as a culture. The other type of association is extracted by using a universally common background. In image databases as the shared data resources, an image must be explained in the common impressions. By defining universally common impressions in terms of colors, the impressions can be acceptable.

As we use words to describe these impressions in our model, we call the words which describe impressions *impression words*. Assume that there are s impression words to describe the impressions of colors. The impression word W_j can be represented as a p-dimensional vector as follows:

$$W_j = (u_1, u_2, ..., u_p) \qquad \text{where } j = 1, 2, ..., s,$$

where p is the number of clusters as described in Section 7.7.2, u_i is a correlation coefficient between the cluster center (the color) of the cluster i and the impression word W_j, and s is the number of impression words for representing images.

7.7.4   Correlation Between Image Vectors and Impression Word Vectors

Impressions of the images are derived by finding impression words which correspond to the images. We have discussed how images and impression words are represented in the form of p-dimensional vectors. Correlation between images and impression words are calculated with these vectors.

Correlation is calculated by the inner product of each impression word vector W_j and the image vector P:

$$C_j = (W_j, P) \qquad \text{where } j = 1, 2, ..., s.$$

The impression word vectors which have a high correlation with the image vector P are selected, and the impression words corresponding to the selected vectors are extracted as the impressions of the images.

7.7.5   Examples

Table 7-6 and Table 7-7 are definitions of the impression word vectors and the image vectors, respectively. Table 7-6 is created based on psychological experiments [1]. Each impression word corresponds to an emotional property of colors. Two impression words are selected for each emotional property of colors to describe the opposite meanings. We selected seven colors, red, yellow, green, blue, purple, white, and black, as the primitive colors which we have set for describing impressions. Selected cluster centers, therefore, are 5R/14 (red), 5Y8/12 (yellow), 7.5G5/8 (green), 10B4/8 (blue), 10P4/8 (purple), N9 (white) and N1 (black). As an example, we use eight images painted by Marcestel [10]. The images are shown in Color Figure-4. Although the images have the same motif of a bouquet, each image is different in color components. Table 7-7 shows the definition of the image vectors. These image vectors are obtained by the method described in Section 7.7.2.

By computing correlations between the image vectors and the impression word vectors, the impression words shown in Table 7-8 are obtained for each image data item. The correlation coefficients in this table are the results of the inner product between impression word vectors and image vectors. Bouquet1, for instance, has a blue color as its basic background color. The obtained impression words are satisfactory words to describe the color's impressions.

The metadata items for images are created with the obtained impression words by the union operator of Method-2.

7.8   Conclusion

In this chapter, we have introduced new methodology for retrieving image data according to the user's impression and the image's contents. We have presented functions and metadata for performing semantic associative search for images. The functions are realized on the basis of mathematical model of meaning.

Impression Words	Red	Yellow	Green	Blue	Purple	White	Black
showy	1.892	1.752	0.775	-0.508	-0.879	0.188	-1.083
sober	-1.892	-1.752	-0.775	0.508	0.879	-0.188	1.083
natural	0.000	0.318	1.807	0.339	-1.319	1.032	0.083
artificial	-0.000	-0.318	-1.807	-0.339	1.319	-1.032	-0.083
warm	1.558	1.035	-0.258	-2.202	-1.026	-0.375	0.083
cold	-1.558	-1.035	0.258	2.202	1.026	0.375	-0.083
bright	1.224	1.752	1.549	-1.016	-1.319	1.314	-1.833
dark	-1.224	-1.752	-1.549	1.016	1.319	-1.314	1.833
intellectual	-1.558	-0.637	1.033	1.016	-0.147	1.032	0.583
emotional	1.558	0.637	-1.033	-1.016	0.147	-1.032	-0.583
soft	0.000	0.717	0.516	-1.186	-0.879	0.657	-1.333
hard	-0.000	-0.717	-0.516	1.186	0.879	-0.657	1.333
light	0.000	1.274	0.775	-0.678	-1.759	1.032	-1.583
grave	-0.000	-1.274	-0.775	0.678	1.759	-1.032	1.583
plain	-0.891	0.239	-0.516	-0.508	-1.319	1.595	-0.333
insistent	0.891	-0.239	0.516	0.508	1.319	-1.595	0.333
strong	1.670	1.433	1.549	1.863	0.733	-0.282	1.333
feeble	-1.670	-1.433	-1.549	-1.863	-0.733	0.282	-1.333
favorite	0.445	0.478	0.775	0.339	-0.879	1.314	0.917
disliked	-0.445	-0.478	-0.775	-0.339	0.879	-1.314	-0.917
static	-1.336	-1.035	-0.516	1.016	0.586	1.032	0.750
dynamic	1.336	1.035	0.516	-1.016	-0.586	-1.032	-0.750
cheerful	1.224	1.274	-0.258	-1.016	-1.319	0.375	-1.083
gloomy	-1.224	-1.274	0.258	1.016	1.319	-0.375	1.083
beautiful	0.557	0.478	1.033	0.169	-0.440	1.314	0.333
ugly	-0.557	-0.478	-1.033	-0.169	0.440	-1.314	-0.333
manly	-0.891	-0.239	1.033	1.355	-1.026	-0.469	2.000
womanly	0.891	0.239	-1.033	-1.355	1.026	0.469	-2.000
vivid	0.891	1.354	1.807	1.016	-0.293	0.845	1.000
vague	-0.891	-1.354	-1.807	-1.016	0.293	-0.845	-1.000
clear	0.111	0.955	1.033	0.508	-0.879	1.408	-0.083
muddy	-0.111	-0.955	-1.033	-0.508	0.879	-1.408	0.083
simple	0.223	0.955	1.033	0.508	-1.319	1.314	-0.250
complicated	-0.223	-0.955	-1.033	-0.508	1.319	-1.314	0.250
graceful	-0.223	0.159	0.258	0.678	0.000	1.408	0.750
vulgar	0.223	-0.159	-0.258	-0.678	-0.000	-1.408	-0.750
new	0.445	0.717	0.516	0.169	-0.879	0.751	-0.250
old	-0.445	-0.717	-0.516	-0.169	0.879	-0.751	0.250
excited	0.891	0.796	-0.516	-1.016	-1.026	0.000	-0.750
melancholy	-0.891	-0.796	0.516	1.016	1.026	-0.000	0.750

Table 7-6 Impression words and their vectors.

For the creation of the metadata for images, we have introduced three methods (Method-1, Method-2, and Method-3). The metadata created by those

Image Data (Title of the Image)	Red	Yellow	Green	Blue	Purple	White	Black
Bouquet1 (The Birth of Love)	0.0363	0.1611	0.0087	0.4494	0.0798	0.2262	0.0385
Bouquet2 (Marbled Flowers)	0.2279	0.4124	0.0037	0.0004	0.0039	0.3446	0.0071
Bouquet3 (Bouquet of Remembrance)	0.0034	0.6351	0.2100	0.0008	0.0016	0.1489	0.0003
Bouquet4 (The Extraordinary Bouquet)	0.3888	0.1161	0.0038	0.0182	0.1073	0.3289	0.0370
Bouquet5 (The Resting Butterfly)	0.0011	0.0268	0.0065	0.0003	0.0023	0.5854	0.3777
Bouquet6 (Outburst of Happiness)	0.0605	0.3885	0.0060	0.0129	0.2416	0.2744	0.0163
Bouquet7 (The Closeness of Your Bouquet)	0.0840	0.2443	0.4436	0.0003	0.0483	0.1783	0.0013
Bouquet8 (The Radiant Bouquet)	0.3769	0.0233	0.0019	0.0005	0.00100	0.2521	0.3444

Table 7-7 Image vectors.

methods is categorized in the type of *content-descriptive metadata* according to the metadata classification for digital media presented in [5]. Furthermore, the metadata created by the first two methods, Method-1 and Method-2, is categorized into the content-descriptive domain-dependent metadata, and the metadata by the third method is classified as the type of content-descriptive domain-independent metadata.

We have implemented the semantic associative search system to clarify its feasibility and effectiveness. Currently, we are designing a learning mechanism to adapt metadata for context representation and images according to the individual variation. The learning is a significant mechanism for semantic associative search, because the judgment of accuracy for the retrieval results might be dependent on individuals. In the learning, if an inappropriate retrieval result for a request is extracted, appropriate image data which must be the retrieval results is specified as suggestions. Then, the learning mechanism is applied to the semantic associative search system for adapting the metadata for context representation and images. The learning mechanism can be used to create individual semantic search environments by adjusting individual metadata for context representation to the semantic space.

Images	Order	Impression Words	Correlation Coefficient
Bouquet1	1	strong	1.189
	2	cold	0.932
	3	vivid	0.929
	4	graceful	0.672
	5	clear	0.640
Bouquet2	1	bright	1.441
	2	showy	1.210
	3	vivid	1.065
	4	cheerful	0.920
	5	strong	0.893
Bouquet3	1	bright	1.634
	2	vivid	1.368
	3	showy	1.307
	4	strong	1.202
	5	light	1.122
Bouquet4	1	strong	0.891
	2	bright	0.890
	3	showy	0.860
	4	vivid	0.812
	5	beautiful	0.676
Bouquet5	1	favorite	1.132
	2	graceful	1.113
	3	vivid	0.921
	4	beautiful	0.914
	5	static	0.857
Bouquet6	1	strong	0.812
	2	vivid	0.781
	3	bright	0.762
	4	showy	0.614
	5	beautiful	0.487
Bouquet7	1	bright	1.386
	2	vivid	1.345
	3	strong	1.165
	4	natural	1.000
	5	showy	0.920
Bouquet8	1	strong	1.055
	2	vivid	0.928
	3	favorite	0.826
	4	beautiful	0.668
	5	warm	0.543

Table 7-8 Impression words derived automatically from the images.

We will use this system for realizing a multimedia metadatabase environment. As our future work, we will extend this system to support multimedia data retrieval for video and audio data. This system will be integrated in a distributed multimedia database environment [8, 9].

Acknowledgments

Special thanks to Amit Sheth and Wolfgang Klas for their constructive and valuable comments and suggestions on this work. We would like to thank W. W. Chu for his valuable comments. We would also like to thank Marcestel who kindly gave us the opportunity for using his images in the experiments.

References

[1] H. Chijiiwa, *"Color Science"*, Fukumura Printing Co., 1983.

[2] W. W. Chu, C. C. Hsu, I. T. Ieong, and R. K. Taira, *"Content-Based Image Retrieval Using Metadata and Relaxation Techniques,"* Managing Multimedia Data, Chapter 6, W. Klas, A. Sheth (eds.), McGraw-Hill, 1997.

[3] S. Deerwester, S. T. Dumais, T. K. Landauer, G. W. Furnas, and R. A. Harshman, *"Indexing by Latent Semantic Analysis,"* Journal of the American Society for Information Science, Vol.41, No.6, pp. 391–407, 1990.

[4] I. H. Godlove, *"Improved Color-Difference Formula with Applications to the Perceptibility and Acceptability of Fadings,"* Journal of the Optical Society of America, Vol.41, No.11, pp. 760–772, July 1951.

[5] V. Kashyap, K. Shah, and A. Sheth, *"Metadata for Building the Multimedia Patch Quilt,"* V. S. Subrahamanian, S. Jajodia (eds.), Multimedia Database Systems, pp. 297–319, 1996.

[6] T. Kitagawa and Y. Kiyoki, *"A Mathematical Model of Meaning and its Application to Multidatabase Systems,"* Proc. 3rd IEEE International Workshop on Research Issues on Data Engineering: Interoperability in Multidatabase Systems, pp. 130–135, April 1993.

[7] Y. Kiyoki, T. Kitagawa, and T. Hayama, *"A Metadatabase System for Semantic Image Search by a Mathematical Model of Meaning,"* ACM SIGMOD Record (Special issue on metadata for digital media), W. Klas, A. Sheth (eds.), Vol.23, No. 4, pp. 34–41, December 1994.

[8] Y. Kiyoki and T. Hayama, *"The Design and Implementation of a Distributed System Architecture for Multimedia Databases,"* Proc. 47th Conference of International Federation for Information and Documentation, pp. 374–379, October 1994.

[9] Y. Kiyoki, T. Kitagawa, and Y. Hitomi, *"A Fundamental Framework for Realizing Semantic Interoperability in a Multidatabase Environment,"* Journal of Integrated Computer-Aided Engineering, Vol.2, No.1 (Special Issue on Multidatabase and Interoperable Systems), pp. 3–20, John Wiley & Sons, January 1995.

[10] Marcestel, *"Marcestel,"* Kyoto Shoin Co., 1993.

[11] A. Mehrabian, *"Measures of Individual Differences in Temperament,"* Educational and Psychological Measurement, Vol.38, pp. 1105–1117, 1978.

[12] M. Miyahara and Y. Yoshida, *"Mathematical Transformation of (R,G,B) Color Data to Munsell (H,V,C) Color Data,"* SPIE's Visual Communications and Image Processing '88, Vol.1001, No.118, pp. 650–657, November 1988.

[13] S. M. Newhall, D. Nickerson, and D. B. Judd, *"Final Report of the O.S.A Subcommittee on the Spacing of the Munsell Colors",* Journal of the Optical Society of America, Vol.33, No.7, pp. 485–418 July 1943.

[14] C. K. Ogden, *"The General Basic English Dictionary,"* Evans Brothers Limited, 1940.

[15] J. A. Russel and A. Mehrabian, *"Evidence for a Three-Factor Theory of Emotions,"* Journal of Research in Personality, Vol.11, pp. 273–294, 1977.

[16] H. Shimizu, Y. Kiyoki, A. Sekijima, and N. Kamibayashi, *"A Decision Making Support System for Selecting Appropriate Online Databases,"* Proc. 1st IEEE International Workshop on Interoperability in Multidatabase Systems, pp. 322–329, April 1991.

[17] A. Sheth and J. A. Larson, *"Federated Database Systems for Managing Distributed, Heterogeneous, and Autonomous Databases,"* ACM Computing Surveys, Vol.22, No.3, pp. 183–236, 1990.

[18] A. Sheth, *"Semantic Issues in Multidatabase Systems,"* ACM SIGMOD Record, Vol.20, No.4, pp. 5–9, 1991.

[19] P. Valdez and A. Mehrabian, *"Effects of Color on Emotions,"* Journal of Experimental Psychology: General, Vol.123, No.4, pp. 394–409, 1994.

[20] *"Longman Dictionary of Contemporary English,"* Longman, 1987.

Metadata for Content-based Retrieval of Speech Recordings

Martin Wechsler and Peter Schäuble

Swiss Federal Institute of Technology (ETH)
Information Systems, ETH Zentrum
CH-8092 Zürich, Switzerland
{wechsler,schauble}@inf.ethz.ch

Abstract

We present an information retrieval system that allows a search for audio recordings containing spoken text. The retrieval system accepts vague textual queries and performs a best-match search to find those documents that are relevant to the query. The output of the retrieval system is a list of ranked documents where the documents on the top of the list satisfy best the user's information need. The relevance of the documents is estimated by means of metadata (document description vectors). The metadata are *automatically* generated by indexing methods, and they are organized such that queries can be processed efficiently. The indexing methods, which are based on phoneme recognition output, are able to compensate the large number of occurring speech recognition errors. Further, they are suitable for a language where many word inflections and compounds may occur (e.g., German). We have evaluated the retrieval effectiveness of two indexing methods on a test collection of 1289 documents and 26 queries. The best results are achieved using an approximative term matching method that takes into account characteristics of the speech recognition system. We also present theoretical work about the influence of recognition errors on the retrieval effectiveness.

8.1   Introduction

A system for *content-based retrieval of speech recordings* accepts vague queries and it performs a *best-match* search to find speech recordings that are likely to be relevant to the queries. Content-based speech retrieval is based on metadata that contain clues about the content of the speech recordings. These metadata are generated by an *automatic* indexing process. To achieve reasonable response times of less than one or two seconds, the metadata have to be organized in suitable data structures.

The speech recordings – subsequently called *speech documents* – are only available in digital format, e.g., sampled at 16 kHz with 16 bit resolution. Queries are entered as text, e.g., *"I am interested in radio news about the earthquake in Japan."* The retrieval system estimates the probability for every speech document that the information need of the user is satisfied by this document, and it then presents a ranked list of the documents to the user in decreasing order of these probabilities. The probabilities or equivalent scores are called *Retrieval Status Values* (RSV).

Figure 8-1 shows a screen dump of our prototype retrieval system. Accepting queries typed as natural language text, it provides access to four hours of Swiss radio news spoken in German. The ranked list contains broadcast passages of 20-second duration denoted by date, time, and a passage number (each date's broadcast was segmented into 20-second passages). The user may select a rank to listen to a specific passage.

The process of generating *metadata* for content-based retrieval is called *indexing*. In this chapter, we focus on *automatic* indexing which is based on speech recognition. Automatic indexing of speech documents is a difficult task for several reasons. One main reason is the limited size of vocabulary of speech recognition systems, which are at least one order of magnitude smaller than the indexing vocabularies of text retrieval systems. Another main problem is the deterioration of the retrieval effectiveness due to speech recognition errors that invariably occur when speech documents are converted into sequences of language units (e.g., words or phonemes). This raises the question of how to automatically index speech documents such that the impact of recognition errors can be overcome. Another important question is how to organize the metadata for efficient query evaluation.

This chapter is structured as follows. We first give a brief insight into speech recognition (Section 8.2). We also elaborate on our recognition strategy with respect to the retrieval problem. In Sections 8.3 and 8.4 we present possible ways to automatically generate metadata from the speech documents. Section 8.5 outlines how the metadata can be organized for efficient query evaluation. In Section 8.6 we investigate the impact of recognition errors on the retrieval effectiveness. Section 8.7 reports on our retrieval experiments and the corresponding results. Some final conclusions are drawn in Section 8.8.

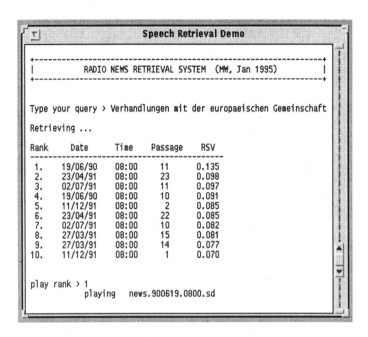

Figure 8-1 Speech retrieval system prototype. The query means: *Negotiations with the European Community.* The system is playing the top ranked document.

We observe quite a few research activities in speech retrieval. In the Informedia project at Carnegie Mellon University, a news video retrieval system is being developed [6]. In Cambridge, researchers work on a video mail retrieval system that currently accepts 35 query words [18]. Similar work was also done by [9], who experimented on retrieval of *English* radio news. English speech retrieval is less difficult than German speech retrieval because there are fewer word inflections and in particular there exists a large amount of training data for English speech [4, 12, 13]. The main difference of our contribution is that we perform retrieval on *German* data. Recognition of German speech is challenging because much less training data is available. Also, the German language encompasses a large number of different word inflections and compounds, which makes the retrieval task more difficult. For example, a very large number of German words have completely different pronunciations for their various appearances: singular and plural in nouns, e.g., *Haus, Häuser* (house); declinations of irregular verbs, e.g., *nehme, nimmst, nimmt, nehmen, nehmt* (take), etc. The German language also allows the composition of nouns as in *Tageszeitungsleserbriefzeile*, which corresponds to *daily-newspaper-readers'-letter's-line.* This

variety has to be taken into account when analyzing German query text as well
as when searching German speech recordings.

8.2   Speech Recognition

This section gives a very general overview of speech recognition. This topic is
discussed extensively in various books [3, 10, 17]. A speech recognition system
consists of a signal processing and a pattern matching component. In the signal
processing component a speech signal is analyzed to yield a sequence of features
or feature vectors that characterize the uttered sounds. The basic technique applied is time-dependent spectral analysis; e.g., Mel-Frequency-Cepstrum analysis [3]. The output of the signal processing stage is passed to a pattern matching
machine which determines what *logical units* fit best to the feature sequence.
Possible logical units are, e.g., words, subwords, or phones. To each instance
of a logical unit a model has to be defined and trained. In speech recognition
the application of *Hidden Markov Models (HMMs)* became the predominant
approach for this purpose. A Hidden Markov Model is a stochastic finite state
automaton used to model a logical unit of speech [3]. With respect to speech
recognition, HMMs have the following advantages: First, their stochastic nature addresses the problem of speech variability. Second, a training algorithm
exists which adapts the parameters of HMMs to their aimed logical units as
soon as *training data* is available. Finally, HMMs are easily scalable, i.e., larger
models such as sentences or even languages can be constructed by simply concatenating HMMs. More information about HMMs can be found in [8].

For the application of speech retrieval it is useful to define Hidden Markov
Models on a phone level. In this case, the output of the speech recognition stage
to a given speech document is a *sequence of phones.* Phones are the basic sound
units of speech. Table 8-1 shows the alphabet of phones we use for our German
documents. This phone set is a slight modification of the so-called SAMPA[1]
phone alphabet. Two pseudo phones [Q] and [#p:] denote short and long
silences which have to be modeled as well. A piece of read text together with
the corresponding phonetic transcription is given in Figure 8-2. To outline the
presence of recognition errors, the recognition output is shown as well. Many
phones have been substituted, inserted, or deleted by the recognition system.

---

[1]The SAMPA alphabet evolved from the European SAM project, which develops methodologies, tools, and databases for the assessment of multilingual speech recognition systems.

```
Text:                Im  Norden       am  Vormittag        sonnig
Phones:        [       i m n O r d @  n a m f o: r m i t a: g s O n i g ]
Rec. Phones:   [ #p: d i   n O r t 6  n a m f o    m i t a: k s u n i r ]
Phonemes:      /       i m n O r d @  n a m f o r m i t a g s O n i g /
Rec. Phonemes: / sil d i   n O r t er n a m f o    m i t a  k s u n i r /
```

Figure 8-2 Sample utterance, phonetic, and phonemic transcriptions with corresponding speech recognition output.

Phone	Example	Phone	Example	Phone	Example
[a:]	Kahn	[y:]	Hüte	[s]	Saat
[a]	kann	[y]	kyrillisch	[z]	lesen
[e:]	Beet	[Y]	Hütte	[t]	Tau
[e]	Meteor	[9]	Hölle	[v]	wann
[E:]	Käse	[2]	Ökonom	[C]	ich
[E]	Bett	[2:]	Höhle	[x]	Dach
[@]	lesen	[b]	Ball	[S]	Schwan
[6]	Leser	[d]	Dach	[Z]	Loge
[i:]	riet	[f]	Fall	[OY]	neun
[i]	Politik	[g]	gut	[aU]	Bauch
[j]	ja	[h]	Hast	[aI]	zwei
[I]	ritt	[k]	Kahn	[E~]	Teint
[o:]	bog	[l]	Luft	[O~]	Saison
[o]	Motto	[m]	Maus	[a~]	Restaurant
[O]	Bock	[n]	Neu	[Q]	*Glottal Stop*
[u:]	Mus	[N]	Rang	[#p:]	*pause*
[u]	Kulisse	[p]	Pult		
[U]	muss	[r]	Rand		

Table 8-1 Phone Alphabet.

When analyzing the types of recognition errors we observed that many substitutions arose due to the fact that some phones in our set are very similar, e.g., [s] and [z]. Additionally, the set differentiates between short and long vowels. However, most speakers are not aware of uttering the same words with large phonetic and temporal variation. In other words, this phone level tends to be too specific for comparing a dictionary-based transcription to a speech recogni-

Phoneme	Phone(s)	Phoneme	Phone(s)	Phoneme	Phone(s)
/a/	[a:] [a]	/b/	[b]	/r/	[r]
/e/	[e:] [e]	/d/	[d]	/s/	[s] [z]
/E/	[E:] [E] [E~]	/f/	[f]	/t/	[t]
/@/	[@] [9]	/g/	[g]	/v/	[v]
/er/	[6]	/h/	[h]	/ch/	[x] [C]
/i/	[i:] [i] [j] [I]	/k/	[k]	/sch/	[S] [Z]
/o/	[o:] [o]	/l/	[l]	/eu/	[OY]
/O/	[O] [a~] [O~]	/m/	[m]	/au/	[aU]
/u/	[u:] [u] [U]	/n/	[n]	/ei/	[aI]
/ue/	[y:] [y] [Y]	/N/	[N]	/sil/	[Q] [#p:]
/oe/	[2:] [2]	/p/	[p]		

Table 8-2   Phoneme Alphabet.

tion output. For this reason, we introduce a slightly more general level of detail by clustering some of the most similar phones into phone classes. We call those classes *phonemes*, although the term phoneme has a slightly different meaning in phonology[2]. Table 8-2 shows our current phoneme set with the underlying phones. The last two lines in Figure 8-2 show the phonemic transcriptions to our example.

Another difficult problem in speech recognition is the detection of word boundaries, because when speaking, one does not separate words acoustically. For retrieval, this increases the effort of matching a query to the documents, since a query word may occur at any phoneme position in a speech document. We will show in Section 8.5 how we can achieve fast query processing.

The reader might ask why we do not use *words* as Hidden Markov Models in speech recognition. In this way, a speech document could be transcribed into full text, and standard text retrieval methods could be applied. We believe that for the application of speech retrieval, words are not appropriate units. First, state of the art word recognition systems have a limited recognition vocabulary (currently about 64,000 word forms). This bound is too low for information retrieval. As an example, the TREC collection [5] contains more than 500,000 different word stems. This limitation is even more dramatic in German due to the high number of word inflections and compounds. Second,

---

[2]In phonology, a phoneme is a minimal unit differentiating between meanings. However, in the context of speech recognition, the term phoneme is used as in this chapter.

for information retrieval, words like proper names, company names, countries, etc. should be recognized. However, for such words there are usually too few training utterances to determine robust parameters for the corresponding Hidden Markov Models. Additionally, selecting a recognition vocabulary is critical, because it is not known in advance which words are going to be present in the speech documents.

Using phones as recognition units is simpler from the recognition perspective. There are only between 30 and 50 different phones to be trained, and any speech document can be used to train the Hidden Markov Models, as long as both the corresponding text and a phonetic dictionary are available. Analogously, from the information retrieval perspective we will see that phone recognition is advantageous because it does not pose any restrictions to the metadata generation process. Starting at the phone level it is possible to define various indexing methods, particularly subword-level based methods, which are important concerning languages with many word inflections and compounds.

8.3   Indexing and Retrieval by N-Grams

In the following, we describe how metadata can be automatically derived from a given phonemic transcription of a speech document. Before dealing with N-grams, we give a general description of an indexing and retrieval method based on the vector space model. Let D be a collection of speech documents and q be a user query. An *indexing method* is a function that assigns a document $d_j \in D$ or a query q to a document description vector $\vec{d_j}$ or a query description vector $\vec{q}$. The dimension of $\vec{d_j}$ and of $\vec{q}$ is equal to the cardinality of the set of *indexing features* $\Phi = \{\varphi_0, \ldots, \varphi_{m-1}\}$. These description vectors are defined as

$$\vec{d_j} \quad := \quad (a_{0j}, \ldots, a_{m-1j})^T \tag{8.1}$$

$$\vec{q} \quad := \quad (b_0, \ldots, b_{m-1})^T \tag{8.2}$$

with *weights* a_{ij} and b_i that represent the relevance of the indexing feature φ_i in the document d_j and in the query q.

To come up with a ranked list of documents to a query q, the system computes the Retrieval Status Value (RSV) between q and every document d_j using a retrieval function, e.g., the cosine measure [20]. This measure corresponds to the cosine of the angle between d_j and q:

$$RSV(q, d_j) \quad = \quad \frac{\vec{q}^T \vec{d_j}}{|\vec{q}| \, |\vec{d_j}|}.$$

The indexing method described in this section is based on indexing features that are *phoneme N-grams* for a given N. The technique of using N-grams for indexing is well known in searching tasks, e.g., letter-based N-grams in text retrieval [19]. The phonemic transcription of a speech document d_j is simply decomposed into overlapping phoneme N-grams. The example in Figure 8-2 would yield the indexing features *sil_d_i*, *d_i_n*, ... for $N = 3$. The weight a_{ij} of the feature φ_i in a document description vector d_j in (8.1) is usually a function of the following two sources:

- The *feature frequency* $\text{ff}(\varphi_i, d_j)$ denotes the number of occurrences of φ_i in d_j. It represents the relevance of an indexing feature relative to the document.

- The *inverse document frequency* $\text{idf}(\varphi_i)$, which is a function of the document frequency $\text{df}(\varphi_i)$, that is the number of documents containing φ_i. The inverse document frequency is defined as

$$\text{idf}(\varphi_i) \quad := \log\left(\frac{1+|D|}{1+\text{df}(\varphi_i)}\right).$$

  It represents the relevance of an indexing feature relative to the whole *collection*.

The weights a_{ij} are determined by a simple multiplication of ff and idf:

$$a_{ij} \quad := \quad \text{ff}(\varphi_i, d_j)\,\text{idf}(\varphi_i). \tag{8.3}$$

A user query q is indexed as follows. The query is entered as natural language text. This text is then transcribed into a phonemic transcription using a pronunciation dictionary. Thereafter, it is also decomposed into N-grams, and $\vec{q}$ is derived according to (8.2), using the weights

$$b_i \quad := \quad \text{ff}(\varphi_i, q)\,\text{idf}(\varphi_i). \tag{8.4}$$

An important property of this indexing method is its *data drivenness*: The indexing features can be derived directly from the stored data, i.e., from the documents. Thus, it is possible to precalculate the document descriptions off-line, i.e., before the user formulates the query. This method is suitable for indexing *speech* documents for the following reasons. First, it accounts for different word inflections and compounds that are very frequent in German. Although the query and the document may contain different inflections of the same word, it is likely that there are matching N-grams corresponding to common parts of the word. Second, this method is tolerant to recognition errors if N is not too large. Any sequence of N correctly recognized phonemes yields a correct N-gram. In Section 8.7, we will report on retrieval experiments using different values for N.

8.4   Indexing and Retrieval by Word Matching

In this section, we describe an indexing method that is based on a fuzzy matching between the query words and the speech documents. Again, phonemic transcriptions of the query words and the speech documents form the common base for the matching procedure. This method was originally applied in [15] where retrieval is performed on scanned images containing text.

Let φ_i be a query word (indexing feature). One source of evidence for the relevance of a document d_j to the query word φ_i is its feature frequency $\mathrm{ff}(\varphi_i, d_j)$. It is impossible to determine the exact ff-value because of recognition errors; however, we are able to calculate an estimate for $\mathrm{ff}(\varphi_i, d_j)$ using a probabilistic approach as described in the following.

Let $w = (w[1] \ldots w[I])$ be a phonemic transcription of a query word φ_i and $t = (t[1] \ldots t[R])$ be a phonemic transcription of a document d_j. Assume we knew a set of subsequences $\{s_0, \ldots, s_{r-1}\}$ of t that are similar to the query transcription w. Further, assume that we know the probability p_k that s_k corresponds to the spoken word φ_i. We will explain the estimation of p_k later in this section. Then, we can estimate the *expected feature frequency* of φ_i in d_j as

$$\mathrm{eff}(\varphi_i, d_j) \quad = \quad \sum_{k=0}^{r-1} p_k. \tag{8.5}$$

The estimation of occurrence probabilities p_k is mainly based on an *edit distance* computed between the phonemic transcription w and a subsequence s, where the statistical distribution of recognition errors is taken into account. The edit distance $d(w, s)$ is a measure for the dissimilarity of w and s. It is defined recursively in the usual way.

$$
\begin{aligned}
d(w, s) &:= \delta(I, J) \\
\delta(i, j) &:= \infty \quad (i < 0) \vee (j < 0) \\
\delta(0, 0) &:= 0 \\
\delta(i, j) &:= \min \begin{cases} \delta(i - 1, j) + C_{\text{Del}}(w[i]) \\ \delta(i, j - 1) + C_{\text{Ins}}(s[j]) \\ \delta(i - 1, j - 1) + C_{\text{Sub}}(w[i], s[j]) \end{cases} \quad \text{otherwise} \quad (8.6)
\end{aligned}
$$

The different cases in (8.6) refer to the different types of errors occurring in phoneme recognition. $C_{\text{Ins}}(ph)$, $C_{\text{Del}}(ph)$, and $C_{\text{Sub}}(ph, ph')$ are cost functions representing penalties in the case of phoneme insertion, deletion, or substitution. We defined those cost functions by analyzing the errors of our phoneme recognizer on the training speech.

For the estimation of the occurrence probabilities, we also used other parameters than the edit distance, namely, the length of w (denoted by I), and the number of equal phonemes in w and s (denoted by e). Those three sources have to be combined suitably to give a reliable estimation of the occurrence probabilities. A common technique hereby is the application of logistic regression [7], which is a method to fit a function according to a set of training samples. Our function to fit is the occurrence probability function

$$
p(I, e, d(w, s)) \quad := \quad \frac{e^{\alpha_0 + \alpha_1 I + \alpha_2 e + \alpha_3 d(w,s)}}{1 + e^{\alpha_0 + \alpha_1 I + \alpha_2 e + \alpha_3 d(w,s)}}. \tag{8.7}
$$

The parameters $\alpha_0, \ldots, \alpha_3$ have to be determined using training data. Given several words w and phoneme sequences s, our training samples are quadruples (I,e,d(w,s),p), where the label p represents the occurrence probability and is set to either one or zero according to whether s corresponds to an utterance of w or not. We computed I, e and $d(w, s)$ for a set of 355 words and several substrings s on a small training set. The p values were determined by manual checking. Using approximately 11,000 quadruples, we applied logistic regression to estimate the coefficients $\alpha_0, \ldots, \alpha_3$.

We have to determine a set of candidate subsequences $\{s_0, \ldots, s_{r-1}\}$ that possibly match the query word w. In this implementation, we simply consider *all* subsequences in t that have length $J \in [I - \Delta, I + \Delta]$. The parameter $\Delta > 0$ is necessary because of phoneme insertion and deletion errors. Using definition (8.7), we select those r subsequences with maximal occurrence probability, such that the subsequences do not overlap.

The query words are obtained as follows. Given a query q, the stop words are first removed. For the remaining words, the sets of candidate subsequences are determined, and the expected feature frequencies are calculated according to (8.5). Finally, the following weights are used in the description vectors (8.1) and (8.2).

$$a_{ij} := \mathrm{eff}(\varphi_i, d_j)\, \mathrm{idf}(\varphi_i) \tag{8.8}$$

$$b_i := \mathrm{ff}(\varphi_i, q)\, \mathrm{idf}(\varphi_i). \tag{8.9}$$

Note that we do not calculate the expected idf-values in this approach. We use approximative idf-values that were derived from a text collection of a similar domain.

In contrast to the N-gram method presented in Section 8.3 the word matching method is *query driven*. The set of indexing features is given by the query words. Note that it is not feasible to generate the metadata in advance, unless all potential query words would be matched against all documents. However, the strength of this method is that the characteristics of the recognition system concerning recognition errors can be directly incorporated into the indexing process. This is done using a phoneme confusion matrix as a parameter in the edit distance calculation. Furthermore, logistic regression guarantees an optimal estimation of the occurrence probabilities. In Section 8.7, we will compare both indexing methods in terms of retrieval effectiveness.

8.5 Metadata Organization and Query Processing

The problem of evaluating best-match queries is the following. Given are the query description vector $\vec{q}$, the document description vectors $\vec{d_0}, \ldots, \vec{d}_{n-1}$, the retrieval function ρ, and a number k; find those k documents d_j having the highest function values $\rho(\vec{q}, \vec{d_j})$. Because the response time should be less than one second, a naive comparison of the query description with every document description is inadequate when the document collection contains a few thousands of documents or more. The standard approach to the evaluation of best-match queries takes advantage of:

1. the fact that most documents have no indexing features in common with any query,

2. the fact that the retrieval status value $RSV(q, d_j)$ is minimum if the query q and the document d_j do not have any features in common, and

3. possibly certain stopping conditions considering the maximum similarity that the query can have with documents not yet examined.

In the simplest form, the metadata are organized as an *inverted file*. An inverted file is a data structure where each indexing feature φ_i – as the key of the structure – directs to a set of postings

$$\{(j, a_{ij}) \mid a_{ij} \neq 0\},$$

i.e., to those documents that contain this feature. Given such an inverted file, the algorithm for fast query processing looks as follows.

> Determine the set of query features;
> FOR EACH query feature φ_i DO
>> Compute b_i;
>> Lookup the corresponding list of postings;
>> FOR EACH posting (j, a_{ij}) DO
>>> Increment $RSV(q, d_j)$ by $a_{ij} b_i$;
>> END;
> END;
> Divide positive $RSV(q, d_j)$'s by $\sqrt{\vec{q}^T \vec{q} . \vec{d_j}^T \vec{d_j}}$;
> Sort the RSVs and return the top k documents;

In addition to this basic query evaluation algorithm, various acceleration methods are available to achieve short response times even for very large document collections [1, 11, 16]. In [2] and [11], more sophisticated methods are presented for the case of dynamic document collections.

8.6 Recognition Errors and Retrieval Effectiveness

In this section, we present a surprising result concerning how the retrieval effectiveness is affected by recognition errors. There are two types of recognition errors that can occur. The speech recognition component may not detect a logical unit (e.g., a word or a subword unit) or it may locate a logical unit at a position where it is not present. The former is called a *miss* and the latter is called a *false alarm*. Our intuition would be that the higher the miss and false alarm probabilities the more the retrieval effectiveness is deteriorated. In what follows, we show that this intuition is not always correct. In particular, we will show that the effects of recognition errors are *vanishing* for long documents when

$$\text{RSV}(q, d_j) \quad := \quad \frac{1}{l_j} \sum_{\varphi_i \text{in} q} \text{ff}(\varphi_i, q) \text{ff}(\varphi_i, d_j), \qquad (8.10)$$

is used where l_j denotes the length of the document d_j measured in number of tokens (i.e., occurrences of indexing features).

The data corruption that is introduced by a recognition process can be described by a random experiment which generates for a given collection of *perfect documents* $d_0, \ldots, d_{n-1}$ the collection of *noisy documents* $X(d_0), \ldots, X(d_{n-1})$; in our case, sequences of phonemes. For a given document the probability space consists of all sets of possible corrupted documents which could be produced by the recognition process. Characteristic values of the recognition process, such as detection probabilities of characters or features or confusion matrices, are often used to get hints about the probability distribution on this space.

Important random variables on this probability space are the *noisy weights*, i.e., the weights assigned to features in corrupted documents. They are usually based on the *noisy feature frequency*

$$\text{nff}(\varphi_i, d_j) \quad := \quad \text{ff}(\varphi_i, X(d_j)).$$

We derive from these noisy frequencies the random variable *noisy retrieval status value*,

$$\begin{aligned} \text{nRSV}(d_j, q) \quad &:= \quad \text{RSV}(X(d_j), q) \\ &= \quad \frac{1}{l_j} \sum_{\varphi_i \text{in} q} \text{ff}(\varphi_i, q) \text{nff}(\varphi_i, d_j). \end{aligned}$$

As defined earlier, l_j denotes the number of occurrences of an indexing feature (i.e., the number of tokens) in the perfect document d_j. We assume that the length of $X(d_j)$ is also l_j. This is obviously not true in general but for our model it is supposed to be a reasonable assumption. Thus, we can speak of l_j slots in d_j. The k-th slot, $0 \le k < l_j$, of d_j contains exactly one occurrence of the feature φ_i, which is mapped by the recognition process to the feature $x(\varphi_i)$ in the k-th slot of the document $X(d_j)$. As the notation $x(\varphi_i)$ already suggests, it is assumed that the recognition process does not depend on the slot in which the feature occurs or on the document, but only on the feature itself.

For a fixed slot k in d_j and a given feature φ_i we are interested in the feature that occurs in the slot k of $X(d_j)$. We distinguish two conditional probability distributions over the set of all possible features: first for those slots of the perfect document which contain the feature φ_i, second for those slots of the perfect document which do not contain φ_i.

For slot k and the feature φ_i we define the following random variables: If the slot contains φ_i

$$Y_k \quad := \quad \begin{cases} 1 & \text{if } x(\varphi_i) = \varphi_i \\ 0 & \text{else.} \end{cases}$$

If the slot contains an arbitrary $\varphi_h \neq \varphi_i$

$$Z_k \quad := \quad \begin{cases} 1 & \text{if } x(\varphi_h) = \varphi_i \\ 0 & \text{else.} \end{cases}$$

The detection probability $p_d(\varphi_i)$ of a feature φ_i is the probability that φ_i is recognized as φ_i or more formally

$$p_d(\varphi_i) \quad := \quad P\{Y_k = 1\}.$$

Not only can unrecognized features, i.e., *misses*, destroy the feature frequencies, falsely recognized features, i.e., *false alarms*, are also disturbing. We assume independence of the specific feature $\varphi_h \neq \varphi_i$ and again we assume independence of slot and the particular perfect document and define

$$p_f(\varphi_i) \quad := \quad P\{Z_k = 1\}.$$

The noisy feature frequency now can be expressed as a sum of Bernoulli variables:

$$\text{nff}(\varphi_i, d_j) \quad = \quad \sum_{\substack{\text{slots } k \text{ of } d_j \\ \text{containing } \varphi_i}} Y_k + \sum_{\substack{\text{slots } k \text{ of } d_j \\ \text{not containing } \varphi_i}} Z_k.$$

This leads to a formula for the expectation of the noisy feature frequency:

$$\begin{aligned}
\text{E}(\text{nff}(\varphi_i, d_j)) &= \sum_{\substack{\text{slots } k \text{ of } d_j \\ \text{containing } \varphi_i}} \text{E}(Y_k) + \sum_{\substack{\text{slots } k \text{ of } d_j \\ \text{not containing } \varphi_i}} \text{E}(Z_k) \\
&= \text{ff}(\varphi_i, d_j) p_d(\varphi_i) + (l_j - \text{ff}(\varphi_i, d_j)) p_f(\varphi_i) \\
&= (p_d(\varphi_i) - p_f(\varphi_i)) \text{ff}(\varphi_i, d_j) + l_j p_f(\varphi_i).
\end{aligned}$$

There is also a simple description of the variance of the nff since in our model we assume pairwise stochastic independence of Y_k and Z_k. Then

$$\text{Var}(\text{nff}(\varphi_i, d_j))$$
$$= \sum_{\substack{\text{slots } k \text{ of } d_j \\ \text{containing } \varphi_i}} \text{Var}(Y_k) + \sum_{\substack{\text{slots } k \text{ of } d_j \\ \text{not containing } \varphi_i}} \text{Var}(Z_k)$$
$$= \text{ff}(\varphi_i, d_j)p_d(\varphi_i)(1 - p_d(\varphi_i)) + (l_j - \text{ff}(\varphi_i, d_j))p_f(\varphi_i)(1 - p_f(\varphi_i))$$
$$= (p_d(\varphi_i)(1 - p_d(\varphi_i)) - p_f(\varphi_i)(1 - p_f(\varphi_i)))\text{ff}(\varphi_i, d_j) + l_j p_f(\varphi_i).$$

The following conclusions interpret the above formulas:

- As the detection probability approaches one and the false alarm probability approaches zero, we expect nff to approach ff.

- If the false alarm probability is neglectable, the nff can be expected to be proportional to the ff.

- The closer the detection probability gets to one and the closer the false alarm probability gets to zero the smaller is the variance.

- If p_f is not neglectable, the length of the document has a linear influence on the degree of the variation.

- The variance grows only linearly in terms of ff and l_j.

Given the RSV-function (8.10), the corresponding random variable is

$$\text{nRSV}(q, d_j) \quad = \quad \frac{1}{l_j} \sum_{\varphi_i \text{in} q} \text{ff}(\varphi_i, q)\text{nff}(\varphi_i, d_j).$$

The following proposition specifies an upper bound for the probability that the ranking order of two documents is changed because of recognition errors.

Proposition 1 *Let d_j be a document that is ranked before the document d_k according to the correct retrieval status values, i.e., $\text{RSV}(q, d_j) > \text{RSV}(q, d_k)$. If*

$$E(\text{nRSV}(q, d_j)) \quad > \quad E(\text{nRSV}(q, d_k)).$$

then

$$P(\text{nRSV}(d_k, q) > \text{nRSV}(d_j, q))$$
$$\leq \quad \frac{1}{(\Delta_{jk}(q))^2} \sum_{\varphi_i \text{in} q} \text{ff}^2(\varphi_i, q) \left(\frac{\text{Var}(\text{nff}(\varphi_i, d_j))}{l_j^2} + \frac{\text{Var}(\text{nff}(\varphi_i, d_k))}{l_k^2} \right),$$

where $\Delta_{jk}(q) := E(\text{nRSV}(d_j, q)) - E(\text{nRSV}(d_k, q))$.

Thus, the upper bound for the probability of changing the order of two documents is vanishing for increasing document lengths. This result is proven in detail in [14].

We would like to emphasize that the conclusions drawn from the preceding analysis also hold for weighting schemes depending linearly on ff (e.g., an inverse document frequency weighting with document frequencies determined on a non-corrupted training collection) or for normalization schemes depending on l_j^α, for $\alpha > 0$.

8.7   Experiments

In this section, we report on retrieval experiments performed on our prototype system in order to determine the retrieval effectiveness. We built an information retrieval test collection consisting of 1289 speech documents and 26 text queries that are message titles gathered from the Swiss News Agency. Each query contains eight words on average. An example of such a query is: *"Kroaten stimmten über Unabhängigkeit ab"*[3]. By listening to all the documents we determined which documents are relevant to a corresponding query.

In the first retrieval experiment we applied the N-gram indexing method described in Section 8.3. The goal was to compare N-gram indexing for various values for N. The results are presented as *recall-precision graphs* in Figure 8-3.

---

[3]The Croats took a vote on independence.

A recall-precision graph shows the characteristics of a ranked list of documents to a typical query. In the top ranks the ratio of relevant to non-relevant documents is high (precision). The more documents that are examined the more that contain non-relevant information, i.e., precision drops. On the other hand, recall increases with every new relevant document found. An ideal retrieval system retrieves all relevant documents on top of the ranked list, i.e., precision = 1. Evidently, the trigram and tetragram methods perform much better com-

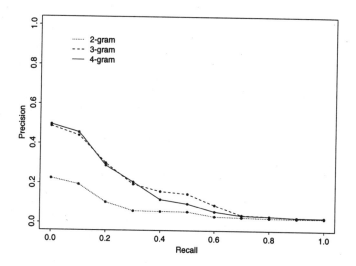

Figure 8-3   Recall-precision graphs for N-gram indexing methods.

pared to bigrams. Using the trigram method, a 225% improvement of average precision can be observed. Bigrams are too short and too common units for indexing purposes. They are not able to discriminate the documents sufficiently because they occur in many different documents.

On the other hand, tetragrams would contain much evidence about the underlying text. However, a 3% degradation of average precision compared to trigrams indicates that in the context of speech retrieval, too long units are not useful. This is due to phoneme recognition errors that prevent a document feature from being matched to a query feature. Apparently, trigrams seem to be a suitable compromise between indexing power and recognition errors.

The second retrieval experiment contains a comparison between the word matching and the trigram method. For the word matching method, we assume that

a query word does not occur more than three times in a document ($r = 3$).
This is a reasonable assumption for documents 20 seconds long. The graph

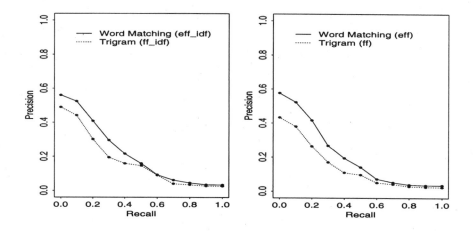

Figure 8-4   Recall-precision graphs for trigram and word matching method
for weighting schemes with and without inverse document frequency.

on the left of Figure 8-4 shows the results using weighting schemes as defined
in Section 8.3. The word matching method achieves an average precision of
0.2008, that is a 32% improvement over the trigram method (average precision:
0.1515).

In the graph on the right of Figure 8-4, the experiment was repeated without
using idf-weights in (8.3),(8.4),(8.8), and (8.9), respectively. In this case, the
word matching method achieves an average precision of 0.1878, which is a 43%
improvement compared to trigram indexing (average precision: 0.1314). The
comparison of both graphs confirms that the idf-weights help to improve the
retrieval effectiveness. The improvements in average precision are 7% (word
matching) and 15% (trigram), respectively. The more significant performance
gain in the trigram method can be explained by the presence of stop words. In
N-gram indexing, we did not remove stop words with the intention that phrases
(e.g., *in Italien*) might produce additional matches. N-grams occurring in stop
words tend to have a low idf-value. Thus, incorporating idf into weighting
naturally degrades the relevance of stop word N-grams.

A clear advantage of the word matching method is that it considers more of
the context in the phonemic transcriptions when matching a word. A trigram

bears much less context, and no information about neighbouring trigrams is used, because the retrieval is based on the vector space model.

On the other hand, the word matching method is computationally more expensive due to the calculation of the expected feature frequencies. However, a phoneme trigram index could be used to restrict the search space significantly when looking for a set of possible subsequences. Additionally, the calculation of expected feature frequencies has to be done only for previously unseen query words, because the eff-values can be retained.

8.8 Conclusions

Recent experiments clearly show that speech retrieval is feasible in the case of radio news recorded in a studio and in similar cases. In other cases, for instance short interviews with background noise, speech retrieval is still problematic because of a poor recognition performance and because recognition errors do not cancel out as they would in the case of very long documents.

Finally, it should be mentioned that improving the recognition performance of a few but not all indexing features may deteriorate the retrieval effectiveness as shown in [14].

References

[1] C. Buckley and A. F. Lewit. Optimization of Inverted Vector Searches. In *ACM SIGIR Conference on R&D in Information Retrieval*, pp. 97–110, 1985.

[2] D. Cutting and J. Pedersen. Optimization for Dynamic Index Maintenance. In *ACM SIGIR Conference on R&D in Information Retrieval*, pp. 405–411, 1990.

[3] J. R. Deller, J. G. Proakis, and J. H. L. Hansen. *Discrete-Time Processing of Speech Signals*. Macmillan Publishing Company, New York, 1993.

[4] J. S. Garofolo, L. F. Lamel, and W. M. Fisher. *DARPA TIMIT Acoustic-Phonetic Continuous Speech Corpus CD-ROM*. U.S. Department of Commerce, Gaithersburg, MD 20899, 1990.

[5] D. Harman. Overview of the Fourth Text Retrieval Conference (TREC-4). In *TREC-4 Proceedings*, 1996.

[6] A. G. Hauptmann, M. J. Witbrock, A. I. Rudnicky, and S. Reed. Speech for Multimedia Information Retrieval. In *User Interface Software Technology Conference*, 1995. Pittsburgh, November; see also URL http://www.informedia.cs.cmu.edu/.

[7] D. W. Hosmer and S. Lemeshow. *Applied Logistic Regression*. John Wiley & Sons, New York, 1989.

[8] X. D. Huang, Y. Ariki, and M. A. Jack. *Hidden Markov Models for Speech Recognition*. Edinburgh University Press, Edinburgh, 1990.

[9] D. James. *The Application of Classical Information Retrieval to Techniques to Spoken Documents*. PhD thesis, University of Cambridge, UK, 1995.

[10] E. Keller. *Fundamentals of Speech Synthesis and Speech Recognition*. John Wiley and Sons, Chichester, England, 1994.

[11] D. Knaus and P. Schäuble. Effective and Efficient Retrieval from Large and Dynamic Document Collections. In *TREC-2 Proceedings*, pp. 163–170, 1993.

[12] L. F. Lamel, R. H. Kassel, and S. Seneff. Speech Database Development: Design and Analysis of the Acoustic-Phonetic Corpus. In *DARPA Speech Recognition Workshop*, pp. 100–109, February, 1986.

[13] LDC, 1992. Linguistic Data Consortium, Williams Hall, University of Pennsylvania, Philadelphia, USA, ldc@unagi.cis.upenn.edu.

[14] E. Mittendorf and P. Schäuble. Measuring the Effects of Data Corruption on Information Retrieval. In *Symposium on Document Analysis and Information Retrieval*, 1996.

[15] E. Mittendorf, P. Schäuble, and P. Sheridan. Applying Probabilistic Term Weighting to OCR Text in the Case of a Large Alphabetic Library Catalogue. In *ACM SIGIR Conference on R&D in Information Retrieval*, pp. 328–335, 1995.

[16] M. Persin. Document Filtering for Fast Ranking. In *ACM SIGIR Conference on R&D in Information Retrieval*, pp. 339–348, 1994.

[17] J. Rabiner. *Fundamentals of Speech Recognition*. Prentice-Hall, 1993.

[18] K. Sparck-Jones, J. T. Foote, G. J. F. Jones, and S. J. Young. Spoken Document Retrieval - A Multimedia Tool. In *Symposium on Document Analysis and Information Retrieval*, pp. 1–10, Las Vegas, 1995.

[19] B. Teufel. *Informationsspuren zum numerischen und graphischen Vergleich von reduzierten natürlichsprachlichen Texten*. PhD thesis, Swiss Federal Institute of Technology, 1989. VdF-Verlag, Zürich.

[20] C. J. van Rijsbergen. *Information Retrieval*. Butterworths, London, second edition, 1979.

Chapter

9

Video Data Management Systems: Metadata and Architecture

Arun Hampapur and Ramesh Jain*

IBM TJ Watson Research Center, H1-D47
30 Saw Mill River Road, Hawthorne
NY 10532, USA
arunh@watson.ibm.com

* Virage Inc
177 Bovet Road, Suite 520
San Mateo CA 94403, USA
jain@virage.com

Abstract

Most video management approaches either treat video as textual information, based on the assumption that video has been annotated, or as a raw image sequence signal to which signal processing techniques are applied. The fact that video is a audiovisual media that is produced with a specific intent demands a radically different approach to video management. This work recognizes the special characteristics of video as a media and uses it in proposing an architecture for a video data management system. The chapter also analyzes the data modeling requirements for video and proposes a generic data model for video retrieval.

9.1 Introduction

Computer and Communication Technology has made producing and sharing information a very open and common process. Technical advancements in the field of digital media are changing the nature of information that is generated. Textual information is being augmented with increasing amounts of non-textual information like images, video and audio. Technological advancements are also creating new information sources which produce purely non-textual information like videos of medical procedures, videos produced by cameras mounted in police cars, etc. Technology has played an important role in increasing the amount of information created by the traditional information sources like movie studios and television stations. This trend of making more affordable and useable cameras, camcoders, and multimedia computer systems combined with the growth of the web as a common media for information exchange is creating an explosion in the total quantity of non-textual and unstructured information that is available. This explosion of information and its changing nature toward multimedia is sure to grow in the future. The value of this huge information base can be realized only by effective reuse. Technology development in the areas of non-textual information management is still in its infancy; there are several technologies which need to mature before effective solutions can be applied to manage the growing quantum of multimedia information.

Video (the term is used to refer to audiovisual temporal data) is by far one of the most powerful and expressive non-textual media because it is a streaming media (temporally extended) with high resolution and multiple channels. These properties of video make it a popular media for capturing and presenting information. At the same time these very properties of video along with its massive storage requirements present *technical challenges* from the data management perspective. The challenges include *storage of video on computer systems, real-time synchronized delivery of video*, and *content based retrieval*. The video data management system discussed in this chapter primarily addresses the content based retrieval task.

Content based retrieval of video entails several tasks like *data modeling, automatic extraction of data models, query and retrieval mechanisms*, etc. Existing database technology uses well developed techniques for data modeling, query processing and retrieval of structured data. However, the data models needed for video are significantly different from those used for structured data, and additionally the task of extracting the data model from video (commonly referred to as *video annotation*) is extremely tedious and demands the development of automatic techniques. This need for automatic processing of video combined with the special nature of video makes the task of data model design challenging. There have been several research projects which have addressed the automatic processing aspects of video data management [1, 5, 7, 11, 28], but very few attempts have been made to design a data model for video which accommodates the multimodal temporal nature of video and the automatic processing requirements. The data model presented here accounts for both.

Developing data models for video requires a good understanding of video as a media, the typical applications of video and the types of queries that will be encountered in different applications. Since the data models must be used in the insertion and retrieval process, having the overall vision of a video data management system is essential. The goal of this chapter is to present two perspectives of a video data management system, the *user's* and the *designer's*.

We begin the chapter with the presentation of an example usage scenario for an ideal video data management system. This is followed by a discussion (Section 9.3) which compares and contrasts the nature of video data against traditional alphanumeric data. Designing a video data management system requires a good knowledge of how video is used. We have presented several example applications of video and the related queries in Section 9.4. The challenges of integrating video into a database are discussed in Section 9.5. This discussion leads to a set of requirements for a video data model. A data model for video called **ViMod** is presented in Section 9.6. Finally we present an architecture which supports the special requirements of video in Section 9.7. A summary of the chapter is presented in Section 9.8.

9.2 Video Data Management System (VDMS)

Any data management system allows the storage and retrieval of data. The queries for retrieving data have to be based on the data model that is being used. A video data management provides the same facilities for video. Given the temporal nature of video, the data management system will have to support temporal queries. And since video is a non-alphanumeric media, the database will also need to support special similarity queries and a user interface that allows the user to specify queries in terms of media specific properties like motion, image and audio features. This section presents an example scenario of a video data management system. The scenario is designed to highlight all the types of queries which should be supported by VDMS.

9.2.1 Example Scenario: Sporting Event Video Data Management System

The video data management system discussed here manages sporting event videos for a football team. The main purpose of the video database is to help in the postgame analysis of the team's performance, to support the planning of strategies for future games, to analyze game strategies of opposing teams, to analyze the performance of players, etc. The video data in this database is mainly taken from commercial network broadcast of the games. The following is a transcript of the usage of the database during a typical coaching session. The presentation uses the following format:

Question: A verbal description of the query.

Query: The typical formulation of the question into a query.

Response: A description of the response by the video data management system.

1. **Question:** ......remember the OSU game from last fall?

   Query: *Retrieve* < Game=Football> < School = OSU-UM> < Year= 1994 >

   Response: The video is cued to the beginning of the OSU-UM game of 1994.

2. **Question:** ...didn't OSU score a field goal in the third quarter of the game?

   Query: *Locate* < Quarter = 3> < Play =field-goal> < Team =OSU>

   Response: The retrieved video is marked with the time points of all field goal attempts.

3. **Question:** ......can we see a close up shot of this kick?

   Query: *Retrieve* < Play =field-goal> <Shot = Close up >

   Response: The database is searched for a close up shot and the video is cued if the search is successful.

4. **Question:** ....let's look at the track of the kicker's foot.

   Query: *Tracking Mode.* Using the interface, a bounding box is placed around the kicker's foot to indicate the object to be tracked.

   Response: The system tracks the kicker's foot through the shot, and displays a track of the foot.

5. **Question:** ....let's see other kickers with similar kicks in last years NCAA football.

    Query: *Similarity Search* < Year = 1993> < Game=NCAA-football> < Play =Field Goal > < Match-Criteria = Intra video object location based matching>

    Response: The system searches through the NCAA games of 1993 for field goal attempts, and compares the kickers' tracks for these attempts. A ranked set of video icons is displayed. Each icon represents videos of similar kicks and the ranking is based on the similarity.

A system which supports such an interaction with a collection of video data is a video data management system. A state of the art video data management system will allow the retrieval video based on various audio-visual properties like color, texture, voice similarity, tunes, sound effects, etc. Video access based on content description like topic of video, persons in a scene, actions being performed in a scene, and several combinations of spatio-temporal properties of the objects in the video will also be part of the data management system.

Definition: A **Video Data Management System** is a software system which provides content based access to a collection of digital video data. The access is based both on the audiovisual content of video and the semantic content of video. The system provides the following facilities:

1. All the facilities provided by a standard DBMS (insertion, deletion, schema definition, etc).

2. A user interface for smooth interaction between the user and the video data collection.

3. A predefined set of query classes and an associated query interface.

4. A set of tools for navigating and manipulation video data.

9.3   Nature of Video Data

The first part of this section addresses the issue of video content and classifies it into two types. This classification is used to distinguish between different types of video queries. The second part compares video (non-alpha-numeric data) to alphanumeric data in order to understand differences between the two types. This comparison provides insights into the differences between managing video and traditional alphanumeric data.

9.3.1   Content of Video

The focus of this discussion is to answer the question *What is in video?* Video is an audiovisual media of information presentation. Figure 9-1 shows a high level view of video content which has been grouped into two types:

Semantic Content: This is the message or information conveyed by the video. For example, after watching a news story about a crime, the viewer has *acquired information* from the video about several aspects of the crime, like what was the crime, where did it occur, who were the victims, etc. This information was conveyed to the viewer via the audiovisual media of video.

Audiovisual Content: Audiovisual content of video includes the video clips and audio signals. For example, in the the news story on crime, the viewer sees the location of the crime and hears the associated sound track. Depending on how the video was produced, the same semantic content can be presented through infinitely many different audiovisual presentations.

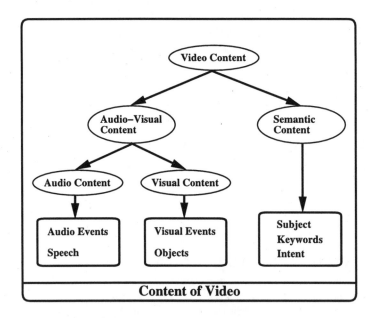

Figure 9-1   Content of video.

The key distinction between the *information content* and *audiovisual content* is the amount of contextual information and knowledge required to extract each of these contents. The process of extracting the *semantic content* from a video requires a significant amount of background knowledge. This task is very complex and cannot be performed automatically. The *audiovisual content* is primarily oriented toward the aural and visual senses and does not require an understanding of the information. The audiovisual content can be extracted from video based on the capabilities like audio, speech and image understanding.

The management of video from a *semantic content* perspective has similarities to managing textual information. This task has been addressed by the library and information sciences community. They address the issues at a very coarse grain. For example, in conventional libraries the unit of information is a book, and the access patterns are by the *title, author, subject*, etc. In the case of video data access is envisioned at a much finer grain. For example, some of the queries listed in Section 9.4 access video by content at the granularity of scenes and shots. This granularity of access corresponds to accessing books at the level of chapters and sections. Thus managing video from a *semantic content* perspective has some degree of overlap with the traditional information management task.

The *audiovisual content* of video either visualizes a script or logs audiovisual activity. For example, in the case of feature films, the audiovisual content is created explicitly with the purpose of visualizing the script, whereas the security video from a shopping mall is just a log of the audiovisual activity within the field of view of the camera. Many different types of audiovisual events can be extracted from video. The visual medium can be used for recognizing objects, tracking objects over time, recognizing temporal events, etc. The audio track can be used to recognize words and sentences, unusual sound events, etc. The task of managing video based on its audiovisual content is a largely unaddressed research task. The type of video management envisioned in this chapter allows the access of video based on fine grained visual properties such as camera and object motion within a video, color properties in a video, texture and audio properties like loudness, pitch, etc., in addition to user annotations.

In summary, a video can be considered as an audiovisual representation of information. The information may be generated for the purpose of making the presentation or may be generated as a part of some other process (Section 9.4.1). The audiovisual content is directly extractable from the video with minimal external knowledge and lends itself to automatic extraction, whereas the semantic content requires the use of significant amount of contextual knowledge and typically requires user interaction.

9.3.2   Unique Characteristics of Video

This section addresses the question *How is video different from other classes of data?* This question is answered by classifying data into two categories, alphanumeric data and non-alphanumeric data, and comparing them. The definition of the classes and a list of comparison criteria are also presented.

Alphanumeric Data: The data in this class is generated from a finite set of symbols. The symbols may be drawn from some given finite set of languages. For example, the data in a telephone directory is composed of a finite set of symbols. The symbols are drawn from the *valid set of telephone numbers in a city*, the possible set of names, and the *valid set of addresses* in the city. There are several other examples of alphanumeric data, like *free text data, computer programs, product data,* etc.,

Non-Alphanumeric Data: This data is not derived from a finite set of symbols. Typical examples in this class include signal level data like images, speech signals, ECG Data, MRI Data, Video Data, Weather Data, etc. The key difference between symbolic and non symbolic data is that *the former is essentially generated by human agency whereas the later is generated by an instrument or sensor.*

The following are the criteria used for comparing the two types of data.

Resolution: The resolution of a particular media is the detail that the media provides. For example, a textual description of a scene is more abstract, whereas an image or a video of the scene provides a very detailed view. Typically, a non-alpha-numeric media provides much higher detail than the alphanumeric media.

Production Process: The spectrum of different classes of data ranges from a structured record at one end to video sequence at the other. A structured record is generated from a *finite symbolic alphabet* and a video sequence is a bit stream generated from a very large symbol set. Alphanumeric media originates through direct human agency, i.e, it originates from a human being. Non-alphanumeric data originates from sensors, such as a camera, a microphone, a MRI imager, etc.

Ambiguity of Interpretation: This criteria is a measure of the number of interpretations derivable from the data. The number of interpretations for video is much larger compared to a structured data record. The interpretation process depends on the interpreting agent. For example, on viewing the video clip, one person may register the color properties of the video, while another may take note of the aural properties. But given a structured record of information the ambiguity is limited.

Interpretation Effort: This is a measure of the computational effort required to interpret a given unit of information. The effort required to interpret a structured record is much smaller than that required to interpret an image or a video.

Data Volume: In terms of digital storage, the volume of video is about seven orders of magnitude larger than a structured data record.

Similarity: The idea of similarity between two units of information is well defined in the case of structured alphanumeric data. As the resolution of the media increases, the concept of similarity is less well defined.

Criteria	Alpha Numeric Data	Non Alpha Numeric Data
Resolution	Low	High
Production Process	Finite Symbol Set	Infinite Symbol Set
Interpretation Ambiguity	Low	High
Interpretation Effort	Low	High
Data Volume	Low	High
Similarity	Well Defined	Ill Defined

Table 9-1 Comparison between alphanumeric and non-alphanumeric data.

Table 9-1 summarizes the comparison between alphanumeric and non alphanumeric data. The voluminous nature of video data, its higher degree of interpretation ambiguity, interpretation effort and ill defined concept of similarity pose the most significant challenges in managing video. The greatest advantage of video is its resolution, multimodality and temporal nature, which make video a challenging media for automatic management.

9.4 Applications of Video

This section presents a detailed study of different usages of video. The goal is to identify the nature of queries which are used to drive the design of the video data models. Each of the applications is analyzed from several perspectives like *video intent, video content, video production,* and *video usage.* The analysis of each application is followed by a list of users and queries. The section concludes with a classification of queries in a video data management system.

The example applications used are *feature films, news videos, sporting event videos, biomechanical analysis of sports* and *building security videos.* These video applications are examined from the following perspectives:

Video Intent: *What was the purpose of making the video?* This questions the purpose of producing the video. The answer to this question provides clues into the structure of video, content of the video and the organization.

Video Content: *What is the typical content?* This question probes the issue of video content for the particular class of videos. Depending on the domain of the video the predictability of the content varies.

Video Production: *How was the video made?* This addresses the issue of the nature of the production process. The answer to this question provides information about the syntactic structure, and the audio-visual properties of the video data. The video production process is very complex. It involves a number of parameters; the degree of control that the video producer has on these parameters directly affects the content of the video. Typically, videos with a high degree of production control have a higher degree of structure which can be effectively used in the automatic analysis of the video data [12].

Script Control: Some videos are visualizations of a certain script or an audiovisual log. Script control is a measure of the degree of visualization control. For example, a feature film can have multiple takes of the same scene, whereas a sporting event video must capture the event as it occurs.

Filming Control: The key process in making a video is the step which captures images onto the media. This involves an environment in which the video is made, the subject and the video filming parameters. Filming control is a measure of the degree of control exercised by the filmmaker on these parameters.

Composition Control: A video can be the result of composing many individual pieces of film footage into a temporal composition. Using this as a criteria for classifying videos provides a broad classification of videos.

Channel Control: Since video is an audiovisual media, the relative semantic content in the two channels can be used as a criteria to classify videos. This provides clues into the best techniques for indexing a class of videos.

Video Usage: The way a video is used dictates the queries that arise in the database context. A video archivist is typically interested in accessing footage at a much different granularity from a video editor.

The discussion presented above listed the perspectives from which video information can be viewed. This set of perspectives will be used to evaluate the example applications.

9.4.1   Example Video Applications

The word video commonly refers to feature films and home video. A more careful study reveals a much larger set of video applications. In this section, we present a list of videos applications and a short discussion of each application. The list is by no means exhaustive but covers most of the usage categories.

Example 1: Feature Films

Video Intent: The purpose here is to provide entertainment. The director of the film has a message to convey to the audience. Video is used as a communication channel to communicate this message.

Video Content: The content of a movie spans a wide range of subjects and each subject or story can be filmed in many different ways. A standard classification scheme is used for classifying movies, and each class is referred to as a *genre*. Extensive studies on the classification of films based on content can be found in literature [20]. *Western Movies* and *War Movies* are examples of classes of movies. Given a particular class of movies, the content is predictable. For example, in the case of *war movies*, a number of things are known; the subject of the movie is a war and typically it would contain a number of battle scenes.

Video Production: The production of feature films is a planned and controlled process.

Script Control: The degree of control that the filmmaker has on the exact message to be conveyed is very high. The script can be altered and hence the nature of the video produced is very structured.

Filming Control: The degree of control that the filmmaker has on the filming process is very high. All aspects of filming, the location, the action, and the cinematography are planned and controlled.

Composition Control: A significant portion of film production is done through the use of editing, which plays a very important role. The degree of control on the editing process is very high.

Channel Control: This parameter is completely under the control of the filmmaker. Some films have a strong visual orientation while others tend to be dominated by aural information.

Video Usage: Feature films have many different groups of users and each group will require a distinct access pattern to the movie data. The following is a list of users and the typical queries expected from them. The list is not exhaustive but does cover the major categories of users.

Film Viewer: This is a set of users who use feature films just for the purpose of entertainment. They are typically interested in a particular type of film, their queries are related to choosing feature films.

List films with *Title = X, Actors = Y, Directors =Z, Producers =A,*
....

Film Critic and Analysts: This set of users views films with the purpose of evaluating the films from many different perspective such as general appeal, artistic appeal, director evaluation, actor evaluation, cinematographic evaluation, special effect evaluation, etc. In addition to being able to locate films, this group of users will require finer grain access to the films. Typical queries here would include

Find scene where *Actor =X & Emotion= Crying.*

Find shot with *Camera = Stationary, Lens Action= Zoom In.*

Find scene with *Special Effect = Morphing.*

Film Database Managers: These are the group of people who own and operate movie rental organizations. The primary types of questions that are of interest are statistical in nature. For example,

What is the number of rentals for Title = X, Actor = Y?

Average number of movies per customer per week = ?

Example 2: News Video

News video here stands for a regular television news bulletin. A typical example would be the NBC Nightly News.

Video Intent: The purpose of a news video is to convey the news to its audience. The news here is defined as the events that occurred over a given duration of time as observed by a certain team of people. A news video reports the events along with the necessary background information to provide a self-contained and understandable presentation.

Video Content: The content of a news video is unrestricted, but has a definite presentation structure. For example, newscasts begin with the main points and have segments dedicated to *politics, sports, social stories, science,* etc. All the news segments are presented to the viewer by the anchor person, and each individual segment has a structuring of its own, with a reporter anchoring the individual segment. A discussion of the structuring of television news can be found in [21, 25].

Video Production: The production of television news is less controlled than a feature film.

Script Control: The degree of control is limited to the structure of the news. Specifically, the stories that are reported on a news bulletin are controlled; however, the exact content of the stories and their presentation are less controlled. With the use of satellites, news bulletins incorporate *live news reports* in which the degree of control on the content is very limited. Thus, as compared to a feature film, the degree of control exerted on the actual message conveyed by a news bulletin is smaller.

Filming Control: The environments typically involved in a news bulletin include the studio environment which tends to be well controlled and the *news location* environment which tends to be less controlled. The cinematographic aspects of news bulletins again have two distinct portions the studio segments which incorporate standard cinematographic practices, while the actual news reports in many cases do not adhere to standard practices. Thus the overall degree of control that can be exercised on the filming aspects of news bulletins is less than that of feature films.

Composition Control: News bulletins are composed videos. The degree of control exercised on recorded reports is higher than that exercised on live reports or on transitions between live segments and recorded segments. As compared to feature films the degree of composition control tends to be smaller.

Channel Control: The information in news tends to be more in the audio channel; the visuals are used mainly as an enhancing mechanism for the audio report. The degree of control exercised on the distribution again tends to be smaller as compared to feature films.

Video Usage: The following is a list of news video users and the expected queries.

News Browser: This set of users is interested in news only from the perspective of viewing news. The queries here are typically at the granularity of news reports. Typical examples would be retrieve hockey events that occurred between certain dates, retrieve results of 1992 elections, etc.

News Producers and Reporters These users reuse news for news report production. They are interested in researching facts related to a particular story. For example, the nomination of a new presidential candidate will typically result in a report with highlights in the person's life beginning from birth.

Example 3: Sporting Event Videos

These are videos of team sporting events like football and basketball. The videos are typically taken from commercial telecasts of the games.

Video Intent: Sporting event videos are made with two purposes in mind: as a log of the sporting event, and also for the purpose of providing entertainment to the viewers. In the case of small non professional sporting events like high school football games and local sporting event the purpose is to catalog the event. In the case of professional, national and international games the intent of making the video is both as a record and for entertainment.

Video Content: Sporting events are highly structured. This structure in the game translates to structure in the video. For example, a basketball game has four quarters, hence the game video also has four distinct segments each corresponding to one quarter. Thus in game videos, the large scale temporal structure of the video is predictable given the actual sporting event; however, the more detailed structure of the video in terms of actual game events like plays, passes, etc., in the case of football, are not known.

Video Production: The production control exercised on sporting event videos is comparable to that of news videos.

Script Control: The sporting event occurs independently of the the video production. In a feature film the event is staged for the purpose of making the video; in a sporting event the maker of the video has no control of the actual event.

Filming Control: The *environment* in the case of sporting events is specifically set up to accommodate the requirements of the game. Hence the environment *cannot be modified* for the purpose of making the video. The *subject of the video* is the progress of the sporting event, and the actual progress of the event *cannot be controlled* for the purpose of the video. The *cinematography* of the video *can be controlled* to a large extent, as the nature of the sporting event is known a priori.

Composition Control: Videos of sporting events are composed of several segments. The composition of sports videos is controlled. The degree of control is less than feature films and is comparable to live news reports.

Channel Control: The maker exercises almost complete control of the information distribution between the audio and video channels. These videos are, however, mainly visually oriented with audio being used as a supporting media.

Video Usage: The typical users of sporting event videos and the queries are listed.

Casual Viewer: These users are primarily interested in the event from an entertainment perspective. Queries are targeted toward locating game videos. The nature of these queries is similar to those of a film viewer.

Sports Coaches, Trainers These users use the video for purposes of coaching teams, analyzing player performance, game strategies, etc.

Example 4: Biomechanical Analysis Videos

Scientific applications are increasingly exploiting video for recording the results of procedures and experiments. There are several applications such as video microscopy, video surveying (location tagged video), educational videos and biomechanical analysis which are extensively using video. Here we discuss biomechanical analysis as a typical example of video in scientific applications.

Biomechanics is the study of human motion while performing various physical actions and is used to study and analyze the performance of athletes and sportsenthusiasts. One of the techniques used in biomechanical analyses of sports is called Cinematographic Analyses [23]. This is the study of human motion performance through the use of videos or motion picture.

Video Intent: Athletes perform a number of different types of ballistic motions, like motion of legs while running, arm motions while passing the ball, etc. The human eye can perceive these motions; however, it is incapable of performing a detailed analysis of the motion. Videos of athletic performances are made in order to have a permanent record of the sporting event and to study the component parts of different motions. Using video allows an objective analysis of different types of motions.

Video Content: The domain of biomechanical analysis videos is a much more constrained domain than feature films or news videos. Here the videos will necessarily incorporate the motion of athletes involved in some particular sporting event. The exact nature of the content is dependent on the sport. As opposed to feature films, news videos and sporting events, the biomechanical analysis videos do not have a very well defined large scale temporal structure. This is because the *video intent* is not to convey a message but rather to capture visual information for analysis. The content here is dominated by segments of athletic motion.

Video Production: The production control in biomechanical analysis videos lies in between feature films and news videos.

  Script Control: There are two possibilities for making such analysis videos. The first is where the film is made during an ongoing sporting event (real event videos), the second is where the event is staged for the purpose of making the video (staged videos). In the first case the maker has no script control, while in the second the video maker has complete control of the occurrence of the event. In the following discussions only staged videos are considered. Real event videos have the same properties as the sporting event videos discussed in the previous example.

  Filming Control: In the case of staged biomechanical analysis videos, the *environment* in which the video is made *can be controlled*. The *subject* in this case is typically the athlete performing the sporting motion. The video maker has *complete control* of the occurrence of the event; however, the video maker has very little control of the detailed motion performed by the athlete. The *cinematography* of the video can be controlled.

Composition Control: These are typically uncomposed videos, as their main purpose is analysis and data recording as opposed to communication.

Channel Control: The video maker exercises complete control over the information distribution between the audio and visual channels. However, these videos tend to be primarily visually oriented videos.

Video Usage: The main users of these types of videos are *sports coaches* and *athletes*. The goal of using such videos is typically to spot mistakes in the motion patterns of athletes while performing different types of athletic motions.

Example 5: Building Security Videos

These are videos generated by security cameras mounted at strategic locations within public buildings.

Video Intent: The intent of the building security videos is to maintain a video log of all the events that occur within the field of view of the camera. The purpose of the video log is to be able to get information about events like crimes, fires, etc. Typically, this information is used to solve the crimes, determine the cause of accidents, etc.

Video Content: The domain of security videos again is much better constrained than feature films and news. Typically, these videos do not have a large scale temporal structure and the content of the videos is fairly well defined given the location of the security cameras. For example, for the camera near the checkout register, the typical content would be different people approaching the checkout counter, paying the cashier and leaving the checkout counter.

Video Production: The type of video production involved here is different from typical video production in the case of feature films, tv shows, etc. Here the video production is much more passive. Here production involves the choice of camera locations within a building, choice of exact camera positioning to set its field of view and the subjects of the video are not controlled.

Script Control: Since the video intent in this case is to log data, the issue of script control is not applicable in this case.

Filming Control: The *environment* of the video *is controllable* through the initial choice of locations for cameras within a building. The other factors in the environment like lighting can be controlled for the benefit of proper data logging. The subjects of the video are uncontrolled. The *cinematography* reduces to the initial positioning of the video camera which determines the field of view of the camera.

Composition Control: These are video logs, and hence do not have any composition.

Channel Control: Since the intent of the video is data logging, there is no control of the information distribution between the audio and video channels.

Video Usage: The purpose of making a building security video is to maintain a visual log of the activities within strategic areas in the building. The users of these videos are typically *security analysts, police personnel*, etc. The typical types of queries include cueing into video based on time, cueing into video based on events, cueing to unusual events in the video, etc.

9.4.2   Classification of Video Queries

This section proposes a classification scheme for video queries which is based on the analysis of examples in Section 9.4.1. Figure 9-2 shows the classification scheme used for video queries.

Content Type: This criteria groups queries based on the nature of the video content required to satisfy the query.

Semantic Query: IQ These are queries which require high level semantic recognition and interpretation of the content of the video. The information needed to satisfy such a query will typically be derived from *user annotation* of the video. For example, in the feature film application, *Find scene with Actor = X & Emotion = Crying* is a semantic query.

Audiovisual Query: AVQ These queries depend only on the audiovisual information in the video and require a minimal degree of interpretation of the audiovisual signal in the video. The information needed to satisfy such queries can be derived by automatic or semi-automatic processing of the video data. An example query of this type is *Find shot with Camera=Stationary, Lens Action = Zoom In.*

Matching Required: User queries to the database are initially processed by the query processor, optimized and reduced to atomic query operations by the query optimizer. The atomic queries are used to extract matching objects from the database. There are two different types of matching that can be performed, exact and similarity based.

Exact Match Queries: EMQ Here it is possible to obtain an exact match between query and the data. For example, *Find scene with Actor = X* can be exactly matched up to scenes which contain actor X.

Similarity Based Queries: SBQ Here the nature of the query does not allow exact matching. For example, in the biomechanical analysis example, *Find all triple axles by female skaters with similar launching patterns* is a similarity based query.

Function: Given that video is a temporal medium, there are two main types of functions that queries perform.

Location Queries: LQ These queries locate video information within the database. For example, *Find scene with Actor = X* will result in pointers to the beginning of scenes with the video which contain actor X.

Tracking Queries: TQ These queries deal with tracking visual quantities within the video. For example, *Track the ball through this shot* results in the location of the ball in each of the frames in the shot.

Temporal Unit Type: This criteria pertains to the granularity of the video required to satisfy a particular query.

Unit Query: UQ These are queries which deal with complete units of video. For example, *Find Films with Actor =X.*

Subunit Query: SUQ These queries deal with subunits of video. The actual size of the subunit may vary. For example *Find scenes with Actor = X* is a subunit query where the sub unit is a scene.

In addition to these classes of queries there are several other types like *Statistical Queries* which provide information about the entire database. This study of video queries is used in Section 9.6 as the basis for choosing video features.

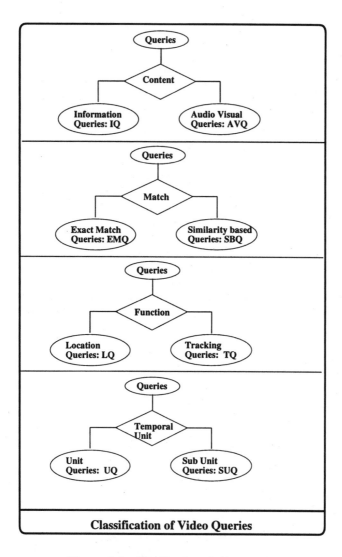

Figure 9-2 Classification of video queries.

9.5 Challenges in Video Data Management

This section addresses the issues in the management of video data. The discussion begins by examining the issues in traditional databases. The same set of issues is then examined in the context of video databases. The issues in traditional databases are designing a *data model* to represent the data, the *data insertion task*, the *data organization* task and the *data retrieval task* [4, 18]. The meaning of each of these tasks is as follows:

Data Modeling: Data modeling deals with the issue of designing application specific data representations which support a certain set of queries. The role of data modeling in databases is very critical and its importance cannot be overemphasized. The choice of the proper data model can simplify the database management problem and by the same measure, an inappropriate data model can result in an unusable data management system.

Data Insertion: This deals with the issue of introducing new data items into an existing collection. It includes the process of extracting the necessary information for instantiating a data model. For example, if a new employee is being added to an employee database, the data insertion process would involve the gathering of information necessary to instantiate the data model from the employee and the physical process of entering the data. In the case of video, insertion would typically include some degree of automatic processing to extract low-level temporal indices like *scene transitions*. Automatic video processing may also be used to extract less certain indices like object and visual events, which can be used in an user assisted interactive process to annotate the video. The data insertion process may also include the task of digitizing and compressing video.

Data Organization: This deals with the arrangement of data items with reference to each other in the collection. This task is commonly referred to as data indexing. The process of indexing involves the choice of fields or features to be used for data indexing and the choice of data structures for indexing the database. There exists a significant body of work on indexing as applied to image and temporal databases [27]. However, the indexing problem for video data is a largely unexplored area of research.

Data Retrieval: This deals with extracting data items from the collection. This process involves the formulation and processing of queries in order to get access to the video data that satisfies the queries.

Each of the key issues listed above takes on a different form depending on the exact nature of the data being stored and the nature of the application queries. Inserting *news videos* would require both audio and video indexing while *aerial survielance videos* would require only video indexing.

9.5.1   Managing Video Data

The goal of this section is to examine how the key issues of data management translate to the case of video data. The four basic issues of data management are discussed. One of the specific goals of this section is to arrive at a *requirements summary* for a data model which can support video. The requirements identified here are used to drive the design of the data model in Section 9.6.

Data Model: The video data model is the central component of a content based video retrieval system. Designing a suitable data model is key to the useability of a database. In this section, we present a derivation of the requirements of a video data model based on the analysis of example queries from a set of example applications (Section 9.4.1).

Film Viewer Queries: The queries that are generated by a film viewer interacting with the feature film database are typically limited to queries which locate feature films (Example 1, Section 9.4.1). Thus a data model for supporting these types of queries requires *a high level description* of the video, which include details of the makers of the video, the topic of the video, the classification, etc.

Film Critic & Producer Queries: Typical queries that can be expected from this class of users are listed in Example 1 of Section 9.4.1. These are queries which require access to the video data at a granularity which is finer than locating feature films. These queries require access to parts of a film like scene and shot. Thus a data model for video should be able to support *a segmented representation for video.* Associated with these segments the model should have *qualitative descriptions* like shots names, scene labels, etc.

Biomechanical Analysis Queries: Example queries of this type are listed in Example 4 of Section 9.4.1. The queries require the partitioning of the video based on different portions of an object track. The queries in this application also require comparison of object tracks between two videos. Thus the data model used for video should be able to support representation of raw data features like locations of objects over a period of time.

Data Insertion: Video is a temporal medium. The effort required to insert a video unit into a database is directly related to the granularity at which the video will be accessed in the database. For example, consider a feature film database that supports only queries by a *film viewer* (Section 9.4.1, Example 1). In this case, inserting a film is reduced to *manually entering* in the data record with fields like *Title, Actors, Directors, Genre, Studios*. However, if the database also supports queries by *Film Critics and Analysts* (Section 9.4.1, Example 1), then the insertion task would be much more complex. The steps needed for insertion in such a case are:

1. Segment the video data based on the suitable criteria.

2. View each segment to extract the necessary details about the segment.

3. Annotation and logging of the video segment.

Given that a typical feature film lasts for about 2 hours, the effort required to perform such manual insertions becomes unacceptable as the volume of the data to be inserted begins to grow. For fine grain access to video, the task of inserting video into a database requires some form of automation [10, 12].

Data Organization: The task of organizing video data is very dependent on the exact nature of the data model used. For example, in a feature film database supporting *film viewer* queries, the database can be organized by indexing records using *titles, actors, directors*, etc., as search keys. The title of the feature film can be the primary index. On the other hand, if the data model included descriptions like paths of objects over a segment of video, the organization in this case would require a way of measuring the distance between two paths, and organizing a set of such paths based on their similarity. A detailed study of various similarity metrics for image data has been presented in [15]. Similarity measurement for video data and video features is a largely unexplored research area.

Data Retrieval: One of the key issues in data retrieval for video is the design of a user interface for presenting video data. Since video data is a temporal media there are several interesting problems when it has to be presented spatially. The second equally interesting issue is the one of query specification for audiovisual queries. There are several issues related to specifying queries based on object paths over time, colors, and other visual properties which are unaddressed problems. Given the temporal nature of video, one of the most important query types is the properties of video over a finite time interval and the relationship of such video units to other time intervals. Snodgrass et al. have addressed the problem of temporal querying from the perspective of temporal databases [24]. Temporal query processing and indexing of video data are relatively unexplored areas of research.

Requirements Summary for Video Data Model In order to build a video data mangement system which can support queries discussed above and in the example scenario of Section 9.2 the video data model must have the following properties. The design of such a data model is presented in Section 9.6.

- A notion of time.
- A segmented representation for time intervals.
- A relationship between time intervals.
- A set of descriptions associated with each time interval.

9.6   ViMod: The Video Data Model

The video data model is the most critical component of a video data management system. All the functionality available in the system relies on the video data model to access data. Thus the design of the video data model takes on a very significant role. The requirements summary for a video data model were derived in the previous section. This was based on a study of different types of applications of video data and the typical queries that arise in these applications. This section addresses the design of the video data model based on the requirements summary. A preliminary version of this model has been presented in [13].

Let $\mathcal{V}$ be the video being modeled. The structure of the model is shown in Equation 9.1.

$$
\begin{array}{rl}
\mathcal{V} \quad : & \text{Video Interval: } [t_b, t_e] \\
: & \text{Temporal Relations: } \mathcal{R} \\
: & \text{Feature Count: } n \\
: & \text{Feature Type: } (\omega_0, \omega_1, \ldots, \omega_n) \in \Omega \\
: & \text{Features: } (\mathcal{F}_1, \mathcal{F}_2, \mathcal{F}_3, \ldots \mathcal{F}_n)
\end{array}
\tag{9.1}
$$

Video Interval: t_b, t_e represent the beginning and end of the video respectively. All the other elements of the video model refer to this time interval.

Temporal Relations: $\mathcal{R} = ((r_1, \mathcal{V}_1), (r_2, \mathcal{V}_2), \ldots (r_k, \mathcal{V}_k))$ is a set of k temporal relationships. r_i is one of the thirteen possible relationships between time intervals listed in [2]. Thus every video segment can maintain temporal relationships to k other video segments.

Feature Count: n is the number of features used to describe the video segment. This corresponds to the number of strata used to describe a video [5].

Feature Type: ω_i is the feature type for feature $\mathcal{F}_i$. The different possible types of features are discussed in Section 9.6.2.

Features: $(\mathcal{F}_1, \mathcal{F}_2, \mathcal{F}_3, \ldots \mathcal{F}_n)$ is the feature set used to model the video data. The actual structure of the features is discussed in Section 9.6.2. The number and type of features used in a video depend on the exact nature of the application.

9.6.1 Video Intervals

The ViMod data model presented in Equation 9.1 uses a temporal interval as the basic unit of video. The rest of the model describes the video in the specified interval from the perspective of the application. One of the important questions that needs to be addressed while building a video database for a particular application is the nature of this time interval. In other words, *"What are the criteria for choosing the video interval"*? The problem of choosing a video time interval based on a certain criteria is termed *video segmentation* [12, 10]. The criteria used for segmentation is often referred to as the *segmentation criteria* [14]. This section specifically addresses the problems of *"What are the different segmentation criteria"* and *"How do different video intervals relate to each other"*.

Segmentation Criteria

Given a video, the basis on which a particular interval of the video can be chosen is called the segmentation criteria. The process of choosing a time interval is called segmentation. This subsection presents several different examples of video segments chosen from different application domains. Based on the properties of these segments, segmentation criteria are grouped into different types. Table 9-2 is a list of video segments chosen from a set of representative applications. The table presents the application domain, video segment name and its meaning. The list of applications and video segments is not intended to be complete but is meant to illustrate the different types of segmentation criteria.

Application Domain	Segmentation Criteria	Meaning
Feature Films	Scene	A single story event
	Shot	A single camera operation
	Segment	An arbitrary segment
News Video	Shot	A single camera operation
	Anchor Person segment	Segment with anchor person
	Reporter Segment	Segment with reporter
	Story Footage	News Story Segment
Sports Video (Football)	Shot	Single camera operation
	Quarter Number	Segment with one quarter
	Plays	Segments with plays
	Time Outs	Segment with timeout
Security	Day Segment	Time based segmentation
	Noon Segment	Time based segmentation
	Still Segment	No movement in FOV
	Motion Segment	Movement within FOV
	Low Activity Segment	Small motion segment
	High Activity Segment	Large motion segment

Table 9-2 Video segmentation criteria: examples.

In Table 9-2 FOV stands for field of view. On observing the entries in Table 9-2 the following grouping of criteria is evident:

Syntactic Segmentation Criteria: In feature films, news videos and sports videos one of the common criteria is a shot. This refers to an *image sequence generated by a single operation of the camera.* Such domain independent segmentation criteria are termed as *syntactic segmentation criteria.*

Semantic Segmentation Criteria: In each of the application domains there are segments which are specific to that domain. These segmentation criteria are very specific to that type of video and need a high level interpretation of the video. For example, Anchor-Person Segment, News-Reporter Segment, etc., are specific to the news video domain. Such domain specific segmentation criteria are termed *semantic segmentation criteria.*

Interval Relationships

Given a video, it can be segmented based on several different segmentation criteria (see Table 9-2). The resulting segments bear a temporal relationship to each other. The temporal relationships between different segments is very important from the perspective of a *user navigating through a video*. In order to describe the *qualitative relationships* between time intervals, a system like the one presented by Allen [2] can be used. These relationships are part of the video model presented in Equation 9.1.

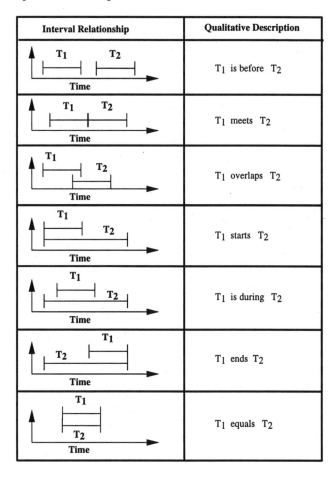

Figure 9-3 Relationships between temporal intervals.

Figure 9-3 presents all the possible relationships between two intervals of time and the qualitative descriptions associated with each relationship. Given two time intervals T_1 and T_2, the relationships can be described by terms like T_1 is before T_2, T_1 overlaps T_2, etc. Maintaining such relationships betweens different segments of video data will allow the user to navigate through a video. The user can use qualitative queries like *Proceed to the next Clip*. Such a qualitative representation can also be used to compose more complex temporal relationships.

9.6.2 Video Features and Video Feature Types

The video model presented in Equation 9.1 associates with each temporal interval of video a set of n features, fid_1, fid_2, fid_3, ..., fid_n. Each of these features is of a particular type. In this section, the term feature is defined and the different types of video features are listed. The features are classified into five types based on a set of criteria. The set of criteria proposed for metadata classification have been derived based on a bottom up view of video as a digital medium. Kashyap et al. [16] have proposed other criteria which are based on a top down database perspective of digital media. Depending on the applications context, the video database administrator may choose to use a subset of the following features.

Definition: Feature *A feature provides information about a video interval. A feature fid has associated with it a feature type ω. Given a feature associated with a video data model, it can be classified based on the following criteria.*

Content Dependence: A feature is said to be content independent if the feature is not directly available from the video data. For example, *the budget of a video* is not normally available in the contents of a video, whereas *the story* can always be understood by viewing the video. Content dependent features are called *data features* and content independent features are called *meta features.*

Temporal Extent: Certain aspects of video can be specified based on viewing a single frame in a temporal interval (e.g., the dominant color in the video, spatial locations of objects, object labels, etc.), whereas other features like motion can be specified only based on a time interval (like feature track, type of action, etc.). Temporally extended features are called *video features*; others are referred to as *image features*. A spatial representation like the VIMSYS model [9] can be used to represent image features.

Labeling: The changes that occur in video can be tracked (e.g., the track of a basketball in game footage) over the extent of a time interval. Domain models are used to assign a *qualitative label* to the feature (in the case of a basketball, labels like, *pass, dribble, dunk,* etc.). Domain model based labels of video are referred to as *qualitative features (Q-Features)*. Features which rely on low level domain independent models like object trajectories are called *raw features (R-Features)*.

Thus the different possible types of features are shown in Table 9-3. Figure 9-4 shows the hierarchical organization of feature properties which leads to the different types of features.

Symbol	Feature Type	Example
ω_1	Meta	Table 9-4
ω_2	Data, Video, Qualitative	Table 9-5
ω_3	Data, Video, Raw	Table 9-6
ω_4	Data, Image, Qualitative	Table 9-7
ω_5	Data, Image, Raw	Table 9-8

Table 9-3 Types of video features.

Meta Features ω_1: These are content independent features of video. They in general apply to a complete video and rarely to smaller time intervals. Such features are referred to as *meta features* (Table 9-4). For example, consider a feature film, in which the different scenes are filmed out of order and on different dates. The dates on which particular scenes in a feature film were made constitute a valid feature of video. However, this information cannot be extracted from viewing the feature film itself, thus it is a *meta feature* of video. However, the feature of video like its *genre* [20], (action, comedy, tragedy, etc.) can be derived by viewing the video; hence the genre would be a *data feature* of the video.

Video Q-Features ω_2: These are content dependent, temporally extended, labeled features of video (Table 9-5). A qualitative feature essential has a value which belongs to a finite set of labels. The typical feature could be some low level property (referred to as content dependent metadata in [16]) of video like its cinematographic properties [17] or higher level properties like time frame, point of view (referred to as content descriptive properties in [16]).

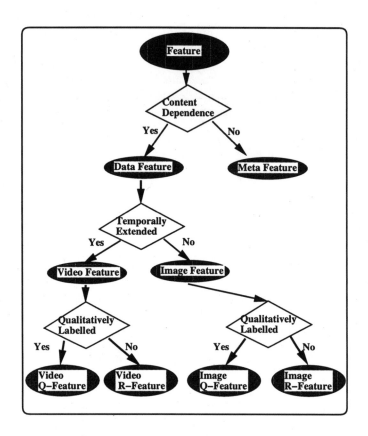

Figure 9-4   Feature type classification in ViMod.

Feature	Typical Value
Producer Info	Name
Date of Production	Date
Length	Number of Frames
Original Medium	Film, video

Table 9-4   Meta features of video

Feature	Typical Value
Shot Distance	Long, Medium, Close up
Shot Angle	Low, Eye Level, High
Shot Motion	Tracking, Dolly, Pan
Shot Objects	One Shot, Two Shot
Audio Labels	Dialogue, Music
Shot Properties	Color, Texture, lighting
Time Frame	What point in history
Video Class	News, Sports
Video Type	Has objects, no objects
Point of View	Whose point of view
Subjective Properties	Intentions, Emotions
Object Properties	People, Trees

Table 9-5   Video Q-features of a time interval.

Video R-Features ω_3: These are content dependent, temporally extended, raw data values (Table 9-6). It is important to note that the values the feature takes is a set which is indexed by time. Such features are typically entities like tracks of object motions within a video shot, variations in lighting over time, variations in audio level over time, etc.

Feature	Typical Value
Object Track	Set of image positions
Camera Pan	Camera Pan in degrees
Camera Tilt	Camera Tilt in degrees
Camera Height	Camera Height in meters
Audio Levels	Dialogue dB levels
Lighting levels	Average Lux

Table 9-6   Video R-features of a time interval.

Image Q-Features ω_4: These are content dependent, single frame, labeled features of video (Table 9-7). A qualitative image feature takes on labels from a finite set. Here the feature refers to a single instant of time in the video shot. These features are typically used to describe properties of a video that do not change over the time interval of the video. For example, consider a video shot of the White House; based on a single frame it is possible to recognize the building. Such a feature is an image Q-feature of video. Lower level features like audiovisual properties of images can also be given labels, like texture type = (Random, Regular, Oriented). Such features are also classified as image-Q-features.

Feature	Typical Value
Image Brightness	Indoor, Outdoor, Cloudy
Texture Type	Random, Regular, Oriented
Ambient Lighting	Blue, Red
Spatial Activity	Clustered, Uniform
Audio Properties	Pitch, Loudness, Timbre
Object Name	Tree, Car
Object Color	Green, Cyan
Object Location	Center, Left, Right
Object Structure	Shape and Size
Audio Keywords	Begin, End

Table 9-7   Image Q-features of a time interval.

Image R-Features ω_5: These are content dependent, single frame, raw feature values of images (Table 9-8). These features tend to be raw image measurements made from frames in the video sequence. Typically these features measure low level properties of images and do not directly provide information about the video. However, given a specific context, these features can be used as indicators of certain high level entities of interest. Example image raw features include properties like histograms, gradient maps, etc.

9.6.3   Summary of Video Data Modeling

This section discussed the various aspects of designing video data models. A segmented representation for modeling video has been proposed. The representation was chosen based on a study of video applications and the typical queries that arise in these applications. Each segment of video has associated with it a number of descriptions called features. A classification of video features has

Feature	Typical Value
Histograms	Float Arrays
Gradient Maps	Image
Edge Maps	Image
Feature Maps	Image
Audio FFT Maps	Float Arrays

Table 9-8   Image features of a time interval.

been presented and a number of typical features have been listed for each class of video features. Given a specific application, the video data model used will include some of the features presented in this section, along with some which are application specific.

9.7   Architecture for a Video Data Management System

This section proposes an architecture for a video data management system. The architecture called *V-1* is designed to provide a management system for video data as envisioned in this chapter. Figure 9-5 shows the block level architecture of a video data management system. The function of each of these blocks is described below.

Video Server This is the physical store for the video data. The video data is in a compressed digital form. The video server manages the low-level storage issues and ensures the proper delivery of video data. The server software has to address the problems of streaming video to a client, synchronizing the video and audio data, etc. There is a significant body of research on the issues of space efficient video storage and video delivery [19].

Database Interface This module provides the interface between the video processing and video query software and a database management system. The interface is responsible for storing the metadata generated by the interactive video processor into the metadata store. The interface also translates the video queries formulated by the user into appropriate queries to retrieve the metadata information from the store.

Metadata Store This module is the database which stores the video meta data. Each unit of video in the database is represented by an instance of the video data model. The exact nature of the data model depends on the type of application and the nature of the queries supported by the video data management system (Section 9.6). The indexing of the video in the metadata store depends on the type of video. For example, in a biomechanical analysis database, a set of video clips may be indexed based on the motion profiles of objects, whereas in a sporting event video the index may be built on the important events for each video segment.

Query Processor: The basic function of the query processor is to allow the user to formulate queries for retrieving video data. It performs the transformation between the queries formulated by the user into a data model representation which can be used to locate the data using the metadata store. The user queries will be specified in a variety of different languages. For example, queries dealing with relationships of video intervals can be specified in a temporal query language like *tquel* [24]. Many of the queries dealing with visual properties can be specified using an *iterative query by example mechanism*. Other high level informational queries can be formulated in terms of regular expressions. There has also been significant research in the field of information filtering (see Chapter 10) based on user preferences and profiles which can be used in the design of very sophisticated video retrieval mechanisms.

Insertion Module: The insertion module is one of the most important modules in a video data management system. This module deals with the raw video data as it is being inserted into the video database. Due to the voluminous nature of video, the insertion module takes on a very critical role. The primary function of the insertion module is to facilitate the extraction of the data model from the video data. This goal can be achieved by various means, from a completely manual approach to a completely automated approach. A more detailed discussion of the insertion module can be found in Section 9.7.1

User Interface: The user interface in a video data management system plays a critical role in the overall usability of the system. Given the spatio temporal nature of video data, there are several interesting issues on the representation of such data on a 2D computer interface [22, 26]. The user interface also allows the specification of queries to the database. The ease with which the query can be formulated and the mechanisms for formulating visual and spatio temporal queries are issues of vital importance in the design of user interfaces for video data management systems.

Block Interactions: The typical interaction of the blocks in the *V-1* architecture while performing the insertion and retrieval operations are presented below:

Data Insertion Operation: The data insertion operation primarily involves the Database Interface, Metadata Store and the insertion module and the user interface. Depending on the data model used in the video data management system, the interactive video processor parses the video into segments. The parsed video may be manually annotated. The data models generated by the segmentation and indexing process are the input to the database system. The database system updates the index structures.

Data Retrieval Operation: The data retrieval operation involves the query processor, the user interface, the database interface and metadata store. The user formulates a query using the facilities provided by the user interface. The query is typically specified using a temporal query language, a spatio-temporal query language, examples, or regular expressions of search keys. These queries are transformed into a data model representation by the query processor. This data model is used to derive the actual location of the physical data by the database system. Once the physical location of the data that satisfies the query is available, the data is retrieved from the video database and is output onto the user interface in a suitable format.

9.7.1   Insertion Module

The goal of the insertion module is to instantiate a video data model (Equation 9.6) for each new video unit that is inserted into the database. This goal is achieved through the appropriate combination of operator input and video processing algorithms. Figure 9-6 shows the major components in the insertion module. Each of the blocks in the insertion module is specialized toward extracting a certain type of video feature (Section 9.6.2). The function of each of these blocks is discussed below.

Video Segmentor: The video data model proposed uses a segmented representation (Equation 9.6), i.e., the basic unit of video is a temporal interval.

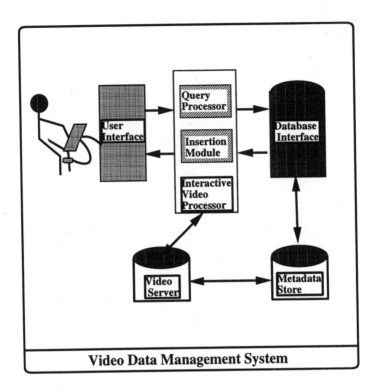

Figure 9-5   The video data management system: architecture.

The function of the video segmentor is to extract from the video data the beginning and end of this temporal interval. The video interval identified depends on the type of segmentation criteria used (Table 9-2). The extraction process may be either completely automatic or interactive, depending on the segmentation criteria being used; thus *the video segmentor identifies the basic unit of video on which the rest of the blocks operate.*

Video Feature Extractor: This unit interactively extracts video features from the video data. The features could be either *video Q-features* which include labels like *car chase segment, emotional segment, gun battle*, etc., or much lower level raw features, such as *object tracks, variations of image properties over time*, etc. In a typical design, the extraction of the *video Q-features* is mainly manual, while the extraction of the *video R-features* is semi-automatic or automatic. The indexing techniques presented in [10] can be used as a part of this block.

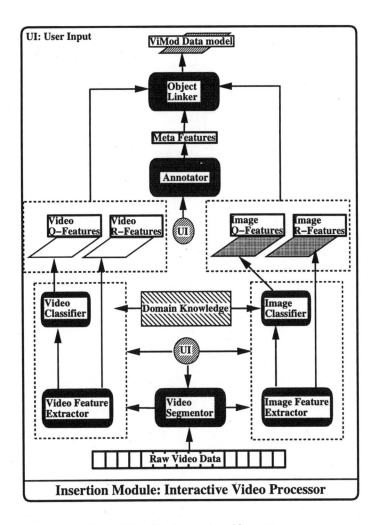

Figure 9-6 The interactive video processor.

Video Classifier: This block deals with the *video R-features* extracted by the feature extractor. The output of this block is a set of labels which are assigned to the raw feature vectors which are used along with a set of domain models to generate qualitatively labeled features. The domain information is typically incorporated in terms of filter constants and threshold values, and discriminant functions which combine features to arrive at a set of classes.

Image Feature Extractor: This module is mainly concerned with the extraction of image properties in a video. Typical *image-Q-properties* that are extracted include, 'this is the *white house*', 'the *weather is sunny*', etc. The *image-Q-features* are typically interactively extracted and use a significant amount of user input. The types of functions used to extract image-Q-features include object recognition, spatial structure extraction, etc. This block also performs the extraction of low level image features like lines and regions, referred to as *Image-R-features*. The features extracted here are used to build an image based representation which is typically used when a key frame is used to represent a video interval and video operations are done based on key frames [3].

Image Classifier: The *image-R-features* extracted in the image feature extraction block are labeled qualitatively based on some set of domain models. Typically the classification operations performed in this block result in qualitative labels for low level image features like random texture, periodic texture, dominant color labels, shape labels, etc. The labeling is done using automatic labeling algorithms.

Annotator: This is one of the key modules in the insertion unit. Most of the high level or semantic content of video has to be extracted manually by a human operator who views the video. The annotator is the unit which facilitates this operation of annotation. The design of this unit can critically affect the performance of the video data management system. The main function of the annotator is to help the user pick the correct annotation to describe the video segment under consideration. There are several issues in the design of an annotation system for video. Some of these issues have been addressed by Davis [7, 6].

Object Linker: Video is a temporal medium. The events in a video are placed apart in time. However, many of these temporal events bear a relationship to each other. The object linker provides the functionality of specifying and maintaining temporal interval relationships in a video data management system. Specifically, it maintains the temporal relationship $\mathcal{R}$ between different video intervals (Equation 9.6). The relationships can be maintained using the qualitative representation proposed in Section 9-2.

The architecture presented above (Figure 9-5) shows all the blocks necessary to building a video data management system. Most of the blocks are part of any traditional database system. The *interactive video processor* and the *video server* are the blocks which are special to a video data management system. The interactive video processor is the module which handles the video data at the time of insertion and extracts the data model for each video object that is inserted into the database system. This block encompasses all the techniques necessary for making video a standard and useable datatype.

In the case of video data the voluminous nature of the data and the real-time streaming requirements demand that the storage of the physical data be distinct from the storage of the metadata that is used for content based retrieval of video. The video server is a storage management device that is optimized to manage the large volume of video data while ensuring the quality of service for video delivery (like real-time streaming, channels synchronization).

9.8 Conclusions

This chapter has presented an overview of a video data management system. The chapter began describing a typical usage scenario for a video data management system. This description then lead to discussion about the nature of video data and how it differed significantly from alphanumeric data. The difference between video and other types of data was further enunciated by considering the applications of video data and a discussion of several example. A classification of video queries based on the study of applications was presented. The apparent differences in the nature of video and the way it is used as a media demand specialized data models and architectures for managing video data. A video data model for representing video was proposed. Finally an architecture which could support the specialized requirements of video was discussed.

Development of such integrated video management systems is in progress both in the industry [8] and in academic circles. As such systems become commercially available and deployed many more research issues relating to the integration of video into databases will be exposed. Feedback from real users of such systems will provide the direction for further development.

References

[1] A. Akutsu and Y. Tonomura. Video tomography: An efficient method for camerawork extraction and motion analysis. In *Prooceedings Second Annual ACM MultiMedia Conference*. Association of Computing Machinery, October 1994.

[2] J. F. Allen. Maintaining knowledge about temporal intervals. *Communications of the ACM*, 26(11):832–843, November 1983.

[3] F. Arman, R. Depommier, A. Hsu, and M. Y. Chiu. Content-based browsing of video. In *Prooceedings Second Annual ACM MultiMedia Conference*. Association of Computing Machinery, October 1994.

[4] C. J. Date. *An Introduction to Database Systems*. The Systems Programming Series. Addison-Wesley Publishing Company, 1975.

[5] G. Davenport, T. A. Smith, and N. Pincever. Cinematic primitives for multimedia. *IEEE Computer Graphics & Applications*, pp. 67–74, July 1991.

[6] M. Davis. Media streams: An iconic visual language for video annotation. In *IEEE Symposium on Visual Languages*, pp. 196–202. IEEE Computer Society, 1993.

[7] M. Davis. Knowledge representation for video. In *Working Notes: Workshop on Indexing and Reuse in Multimedia Systems*, pp. 19–28. American Association of Artificial Intelligence, August 1994.

[8] A. Hampapur et al. The virage video engine. In *Storage and Retrieval for Still Image and Video Databases V*. SPIE - The International Society of Optical Engineering, February 1997.

[9] A. Gupta, T. Weymouth, and R. Jain. Semantic queries with pictures: the VIMSYS model. In *Proceedings of the 17th International Conference on Very Large Data Bases*, September 1991.

[10] A. Hampapur. *Designing Video Data Management Systems*. Ph.D. thesis, The University of Michigan, 1994.

[11] A. Hampapur, R. Jain, and T. Weymouth. Digital video segmentation. In *Prooceedings of the ACM Conference on MultiMedia*. Association of Computing Machinery, October 1994.

[12] A. Hampapur, R. Jain, and T. Weymouth. Production model based digital video segmentation. *Journal of Multimedia Tools and Applications*, 1, March 1995.

[13] R. Jain and A. Hampapur. Metadata in video databases. In *Sigmod Record: Special Issue On Metadata For Digital Media*. ACM: SIGMOD, December 1994.

[14] R. Jain, R. Kasturi, and B. G. Schunck. *Introduction to Machine Vision*. McGraw Hill, 1995.

[15] R. Jain, J. Murthy, P. L.-J. Chen, and S. Chaterjee. Similarity measures in image databases. Technical report, University of California, San Diego, 1994.

[16] V. Kashyap, K. Shah, and A. Sheth. Metadata for building the multi-media patch quilt. In *Multimedia Database Systems: Issues and Research Directions*. Springer-Verlag, 1995.

[17] I. Konigsberg. *The Complete Film Dictionary*. Penguin Books, 1989.

[18] H. F. Korth and A. Silberschatz. *Database System Concepts*. McGraw Hill Book Company, 1986.

[19] T. D. C. Little, G. Ahanger, R. J. Folz, J. F. Gibbon, F. W. Reeve, D. H. Schelleng, and D. Venkatesh. A Digital Video-on-Demand Service Supporting Content-Based Querries. In *ACM MultiMedia93*, August 1993.

[20] F. Manchel. *Film Study: An Analytical Bibliography*. Associated University Presses Inc, 1990.

[21] G. Millerson. *The Technique of Television Production*. Hastings House Publishers, 1975.

[22] M. Mills, J. Cohen, and Y. Y. Wong. A magnifier tool for video data. In *Proceedings of ACM Computer Human Interface*, May 3-7 1992.

[23] J. W. Northrip, G. A. Logan, and W. C. McKinney. *Introduction to Biomechanic Analysis of Sport*. WM.C. Brown Company, 1974.

[24] R. T. Snodgrass. The temporal query language tquel. *ACM Transactions on Database Systems*, 12:299–321, June 1987.

[25] D. Swanberg, C.-F. Shu, and R. Jain. Architecture of a multimedia information system for content-based retrieval. In *Audio Video Workshop*, San Diego, California, November 1992.

[26] Y. Tonomura, A. Akutsu, Y. Taniguchi, and G. Suzuki. Structured video computing. *IEEE Multimedia*, 1(3):34–43, Fall 1994.

[27] D. White and R. Jain. Similarity indexing: Algorithms and performance. In *Storage and Retrieval for Still Image and Video Databases V*. SPIE - The International Society of Optical Engineering, February 1996.

[28] H. J. Zhang, A. Kankanhalli, and S. W. Smoliar. Automatic partitioning of video. *Multimedia Systems*, 1(1):10–28, 1993.

Chapter

10

The Use of Metadata for the Rendering of Personalized Video Delivery

William Klippgen[1], Thomas D. C. Little, Gulrukh Ahanger, and Dinesh Venkatesh[2]

Multimedia Communications Laboratory
Department of Electrical and Computer Engineering
Boston University, Boston, Massachusetts 02215, USA
tdcl@bu.edu

[1] Currently with Excite, Inc. of Mountain View, California
[2] Currently with EMC Corporation of Hopkinton, Massachusetts

Abstract

Information personalization is increasingly viewed as an essential component of any front-end to a large information space. Personalization can achieve customization of the presentation of information by tailoring of the content.

In this chapter, we investigate techniques for personalizing information delivery based on metadata associated with diverse information units including video. We begin with a survey of approaches to information personalization and the requirements for this task. Subsequently, we present a characterization of the use of metadata to facilitate video information personalization.

10.1 Introduction

The need for some form of information personalization is clear: it is unreasonable for individuals to traverse the vast amount of information currently available via electronic means. Efforts to deliver information in a broadcast mode consume enormous bandwidths with no guarantee of interest by the end recipient. Personalization attempts to bridge the gap between the users and the providers of information in a variety of application contexts.

The act of personalization can yield a variety of results. In a simple case, it can bring a region of interest to a user (e.g., a listing of football scores from last night's games) either by passive means (i.e., filtering) or active means. In a more complex scenario it might create a coherent composition of information that can be delivered to the user (e.g., a five minute synopsis of the nightly news).

Historically, most work on personalized content delivery has been done in the text domain. Personalization for text-based information is commonly achieved through the use of keywords or text vector space analysis to compare a set of documents with a set of user profiles. Audio and video data have characteristics without parallels in text, most significantly in the way video sequences can be combined to create new meaning and by the ability of these media to directly represent real-world objects.

Consider a scenario for news video delivery consisting of an archive of thousands of hours of news broadcasts (e.g., the archive at Vanderbilt University). If suitably annotated (i.e., metadata have been collected identifying the contents of the news items and their location), then it is feasible to use existing personalization techniques of the text domain to deliver personalized video-based news. Content can be indexed, segmented, and ultimately retrieved in a recorded sequence based on a viewer's needs. Figure 10-1 illustrates such a scenario in which the viewer initiates the composition of a variety of news items into a video stream.

Supporting such scenarios requires the ability to create indices, match user characteristics with content, and locate video objects (news items). A similar scenario exists for the delivery of instructional video based on student needs.

Creation of video objects can be achieved by extracting video segments from live broadcasts, or archives of live broadcasts and edited video can be created and edited specifically for this format. In the former, tools are necessary to facilitate rapid conversion from live broadcasts to recorded and indexed topics, and the linking of related static materials (e.g., references to sources or text-based information). These same tools must also allow the elimination of outtakes, or other errors that the editor deems unacceptable.

Once the video data are indexed, there is a data management and access problem. For example, if the news items of Figure 10-1 consist of complex multimedia objects, satisfying a user request requires location of components, assembly, and timely delivery. Because video data are best served by a storage system supporting continuous media, it is desirable to separate the data searching and

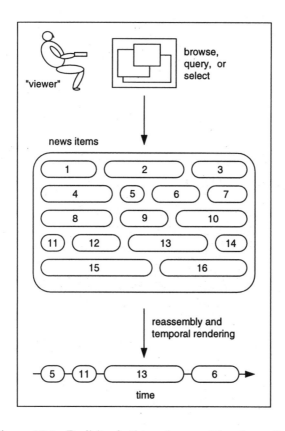

Figure 10-1   Explicit selection and composition of news items.

location functions from the raw storage functions. For these reasons a distinct metadata management scheme is appropriate for multimedia content. Appropriate search tools and engines are also needed and they can be conventional text-based engines. More sophisticated image-based or motion-based tools for content searching can be used, but their utility in this application domain is not clear at this time.

In the remainder of this chapter, we consider personalization of video content for both filtering and composition. In Section 10.2, we consider existing text-based personalization schemes. Section 10.3 explores the unique characteristics of audio and video data. In Section 10.4, we discuss the metadata required to support personalization. Section 10.5 presents a video annotation tool for collecting video metadata necessary for personalization. In Section 10.6 we propose a personalized video environment based on the news domain. Section 10.7 concludes the chapter.

10.2   Personalization of Content Delivery

Personalization deals with the tailoring of an application instance to the needs of individual users. For content delivery purposes, this personalization can affect the selection, scheduling, and presentation of a set of documents. In this section, we focus on how a set of user preferences can be applied to select and sort a collection of documents.

Typically, the current preferences can be expected to correlate with past and present user contexts. Context includes factors such as user knowledge, the tasks being performed, the problems being solved, and the user's system resources [20]. We define personalization as the process of adapting the selection, sequential sorting and presentation of the set of available documents to the user context. The aim of the adaption is to let the user complete a task in the shortest amount of time using the least amount of resources.

This selection, sorting, and presentation is represented as a sequence of operations performed on the combined attribute space of users and document profiles. A set of parameters is associated with each operation. Figure 10-2 illustrates an example where metadata describing the user context combined with metadata describing the documents are used to generate a sorted view of the information space.

Traditional information retrieval techniques aim to find data in a large collection of documents through a sequence of independent queries and query results. Information filtering can be defined as a reverse process of information retrieval where queries are stable and specific, reflecting long-term user interests.

A document now takes the role of a traditional query, while the stable collection of queries can be seen as documents representing user profiles. The time persistence of user profiles makes adaptation toward true user preferences possible via *learning*. Learning can be defined as updating the queries describing estimated user needs by minimizing the differences between predicted and observed user preferences. The user interaction with a set of documents must be mapped to

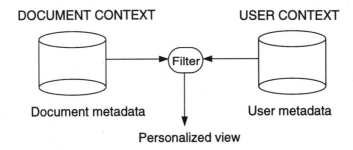

DOCUMENT CONTEXT   USER CONTEXT

Document metadata   User metadata

Personalized view

Figure 10-2 Personalization as the filtering of documents based on the current user and document context using both document and user metadata.

the user query based on explicit and/or implicit preferences extracted from this interaction.

User profiles or metadata must be represented in a way that allows a proper mapping between the user and a universe of documents. The two main classes of user models are *canonical* and *descriptive*. The canonical model requires a formal encoding of a cognitive (semantic) user model as in the BGP-MS user modeling system [12]. The models are hard to acquire and their complexity hides the represented semantics from the user [20]. Descriptive user models can be automatically created by observing user behavior. Their content is a mapping from previous document accesses and does not require any semantic processing. A large number of observations is needed to be able to draw high quality conclusions.

Recently, *agents* have been used to implement information filtering functionality along with other aspects related to the collection, selection and presentation of documents [17, 29, 30]. An agent is an autonomous program that has a set of goals it tries to fulfill in a given dynamic environment. The agents can operate individually or cooperate by sharing knowledge and work [15]. One important aspect of agents is their ability to travel across networks.

10.2.1   Information Filtering

Present strategies in information filtering are classified as *cognitive, social*, and *economic* [18, 30]. We also include *pattern-based* filtering techniques, generalized from work in the field of *software agents*, and adaptive hypermedia. We will discuss each of these approaches in the remainder of this section and how they can relate to the personalization of video delivery.

Cognitive Filtering

Cognitive filtering is a technique in which the description of a document is matched against a user profile where descriptions relate to static autonomous properties. The document profile consists of descriptors associated with the actual contents (e.g., concept keywords or structural annotations) and with content creation (e.g., document author, creation date, or creation location). The user profile typically follows the structure of the document profile, but can contain other parameters describing the user.

Cognitive filtering draws on traditional textual information retrieval techniques that can be divided into *statistical, semantic* and *contextual/structural* [19]. While semantic and contextual/structural techniques try to extract meaning through natural language processing, the relatively simplistic statistical approach has been the most popular. In particular, the vector space model by Salton [27] introduces a *document vector* to represent documents and queries. The document vectors span an n-dimensional space consisting of a set of keywords or concepts extracted from the document set. There exist various methods to scale each component as well as to compute the similarity between two vectors. One method of comparison is simply to compute the vector angle. A smaller angle indicates higher similarity.

We briefly summarize Salton's ideas:

The document vector can simply be comprised of the terms as they appear in the text itself, or can be processed through one or more of the following three steps:

- Words that appear in a designated list of stop words that carry little or no meaning are removed from the text.

- A stemming function reduces words to their stems by using a list of common suffixes and prefixes or general stemming rules.

- A dictionary of synonyms maps each word stem to a concept class term reducing the dimensions of the space while improving the vector quality.

For a binary vector representation W, the presence of a term i gives a binary weight $w_i = 1$; the absence gives $w_i = 0$. Salton's more expensive weighted document vector representation is described in the following. The occurrence of each term i is counted to form a term frequency TF_i. By doing lookups in a larger collection of N documents, the document frequency, DF_i, is found for each term i (i.e., the number of documents in which the term appears). We can now calculate the inverse document frequency, IDF_i, often defined as:

$$IDF_i = log_2(\frac{N}{DF_i}). \tag{10.1}$$

Each vector component can be calculated as:

$$w_i = \frac{TF_i \times IDF_i}{\sqrt{\sum_{j=0}^{N} TF_j^2 \times IDF_j^2}} \tag{10.2}$$

This scheme weights rare terms more heavily, while frequent terms are weighted near zero. Finally, each vector is normalized to length 1 to make comparison scores uniform across documents.

To improve retrieval, content creation metadata about a document are often available. For example, a document represented in SGML can have portions tagged to describe titles, authors, structural labels (sections headings), abstracts, etc. On-line news articles frequently possess such fields. These fields can have variable importance when filtering documents for different users [16, 30]. Here, correlation of past documents that were chosen by the user has been used to assign weights to each field. The weights are used to scale the scoring of similarity between the user profile and each of the document fields. The user metadata contain corresponding sections to organize the user preferences as illustrated in Figure 10-3. In this example, the news article *source* field is demonstrated to be more than four times more significant than the *location* field of the reported story.

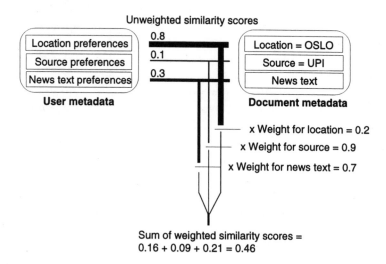

Figure 10-3   Different fields of a news message may have different importance to different users.

Social Filtering

Cognitive filtering requires semantic descriptors to be attached to documents. Except for interpretation of closed-captioned text, cut-detection, and extraction of basic camera operations like zoom, pan, and tilt [1], automatic extraction of descriptors is difficult for video data. Even when automatic extraction is possible, cognitive filtering does not take assessment of quality, timeliness, composition, or correctness into account when scoring documents [28]. To overcome these limitations and personalize delivery even when content descriptors are erroneous or missing, *collaborative* or *social filtering* has been applied in various formats [16, 18, 24, 26, 28].

Social filtering is based on the aggregate filtering of documents by a community of users. Documents are recommended to the user based on previous accesses by the community. For each access, the system estimates how a user liked the document, either implicitly or by letting the users explicitly rate the document. Based on the similarity measure between a user and individuals or subsets of the community, previous ratings by the community of a given document are mapped to a prediction of how the user will rate the same document. The Tapestry system [9] requires explicit specification of similarities by the user.

The GroupLens system [26] uses previous ratings of USENET news articles to form similarity values between users of the system. GroupLens requires users to pass a threshold of similarity before using their ratings as advice for each other.

A problem with social filtering is the need for a large community. A document in general must be exposed to a high number of users before reliable advice can be given. This suggests that cognitive or economic filtering techniques be used in conjunction or that other methods ensure unfiltered access to documents until a level of confidence in the system prediction has been reached.

We expect social filtering for video to prove an interesting research area as the infrastructure for interactive video delivery improves.

Economic Filtering

Economic filtering techniques base their selection and ordering on the costs and benefits associated with production and consumption of a document [18]. This type of filtering can be applied to both the document provider and receiver. In the video arena, the content provider wants to sell a video "stream" for the highest price while minimizing costs (e.g., bandwidth), while the receiver would like to minimize the price and maximize the quality.

For this video delivery perspective, cost factors can include the cost of the intellectual property (movie licensing), bandwidth, transmission time, image resolution, required screen size, required buffer space, and playback time including client processing time.

A video news story can be priced according to its age from the time of creation. An economic filtering approach might attempt to find the most recent story with the lowest price. Using additional cognitive filtering techniques, the user's willingness to pay can be made a function of expected interest in the news topic.

Pattern-Based Filtering

Pattern-based filtering can be defined as the selection and sorting of documents based on non-cognitive analysis of previous access patterns.

Supposing that merely updating a set of user preferences is insufficient, work by Cypher demonstrates how repeated patterns of document accesses can be generalized [5]. These generalized patterns can be used by the system to present documents during subsequent accesses to the same documents. We view this as a filtering of the set of possible sequences.

As indicated by Orwant [24], sequences of user actions can be modeled as discrete Markov chains. For example, it is possible to use higher order Markov models to capture World Wide Web access patterns and to group users based on similarities in this access using clustering.

For use in personalized content delivery systems, pattern-based filtering extends previous methods by considering the sequence of document access. In a hypermedia network or in a temporal medium such as video, the sequence of access is significant and pattern-based filtering can select and order a personalized sequence chosen from a set of valid sequences. In a hypermedia presentation, hyperlinks can be automatically generated based on previous access patterns. The pattern-based approach presented by Yan et al. [31] also makes use of social filtering to let users with similar access patterns share information.

10.2.2   Content, Format, and User-Driven Presentation

Previous work in multivariant movies by Davenport and Murtaugh [6] and Evans [8] has focused on automated sequencing of story elements using mainly visual story telling techniques.

As the video granules are played back, objects in the video stream appear and disappear, concepts are introduced, treated in more detail, and replaced. By using metadata associated with each scene, we can model the current sequence context by mapping the metadata attributes to a movie context model [6]. We can use this movie context model with the composition conventions to generate a pure *movie-driven* composition. Instead, we could keep a static or slowly changing user context model when choosing granules, making it a fully *user-driven* composition.

As previously shown, such a model requires the use of metadata for both the past and present user actions. While present session metadata can be constructed by implicit or explicit expression of user preferences during playback, the past session metadata can represent a summarized and processed version of a past session's user interaction. The present user metadata can consist of two parts: A user query to establish the overall objective and format of the presentation and mapping from a user's subsequent interactions as the sequence is constructed and played back.

Format-driven composition is guided by a representation of cinematographic knowledge trying to preserve rules such as continuity and the use of an establishing shot when changing topics in the presentation. Appropriate metadata are required as input for the rules. Later, we will identify classes of these metadata necessary to obtain different properties for personalization.

We believe that a system for presenting news video should be driven by a combination of the three composition strategies. User preferences, available content, and cinematographic rules form a set of constraints that in combination make it possible to automatically choose a satisfactory sequence (composition) at any given time. We call this personalization of temporal composition *sequential information filtering*.

10.2.3 Existing Systems

A number of systems for personalized delivery of information exist today. Most process information available via the Internet such as electronic mail, USENET articles, and World Wide Web content. A few commercial services offer access to more general news material from wire services and other commercial news providers. The only video delivery system that can be said to be partly personalized is the ConText system [6].

ConText demonstrates how cognitive annotations of video material can be used to individualize a viewing session by creating an entirely new version through context-driven concatenation. This dynamic reconstruction can include video material made in a totally different context, thus performing a *repurposing* of the material. The system requires a uniform set of metadata which poses a challenge to metadata normalization when repurposing a distributed population of video material.

Evans defines a framework in which a limited set of metadata are assigned to a collection of shots using an application called *Log Boy* [8]. This video database supports a companion access application called *Filter Girl* that relies on a hierarchy of filters to generate queries to the database. The queries produce a sequence from a subset of the available shots in the database as output.

MovieSelect from Paramount Interactive Inc. uses a variation of social filtering also proposed by Shardanand and Maes [28]. By measuring similarity between documents instead of users, new documents are suggested by evaluating the previous ratings of other documents weighted by the estimated similarity between the rated and unrated document. Other video-on-demand systems surveyed only consider delivery of entire linear movies, that is, any content-based selection yields large fragments of the original video.

By observing user actions while using a USENET news reader and a mail application, agent software developed by Maes gradually learns user preferences [16]. This work also introduces the concept of *trust* in agent decisions. The agents are reluctant to perform operations when the amount of past observations in similar situations is small. Each action taken by the user is associated with the current situation into so-called *situation-action pairs* and is used to find patterns. This system makes use of both cognitive and social filtering and is interesting for a wide range of applications since it presents a generalized method of personalization using pattern-based filtering.

10.3   Characteristics of the Video Medium

Computer technology has finally evolved to a point where Nelson's browsable, vari-sequenced hyperfilm [23] is a practical reality. Until now, access to the video medium, even via computer, has been accomplished only using edited linear sequences. Computer assisted access to the video medium provides opportunities for at least four conceptually different methods of navigating video sequences [11] with potential for supporting personalization:

- Navigation in the representation of the original storage medium, (e.g., by moving back and forth along the original linear time line or between various tracks).

- Navigation in the three-dimensional reality represented in the recording (e.g., a virtual environment).

- Navigation in a *semantic space* derived from the video contents. The semantic space can be defined as the sum of meaning decoded from the visual and aural contents of the video stream.

Personalization of video delivery can adopt aspects of all of these methods. We focus on the semantic space. In the remainder of this section, we describe the characteristics of the video medium that are relevant to video personalization. This includes an overview of basic techniques for a visual narration, a description of relevant metadata, and a synopsis of the television news format.

10.3.1   Structures of Video Narration

The language of film consists of conventions for spatial and temporal composition [21]. We choose to consider personalization a function of only the temporal composition and treat spatial composition as fixed. Since our focus is on techniques for the personalization of navigation in the semantic space, we want to look at how the information is conveyed to the user (i.e., how the story is told). Existing story structures for providing non-linear video access can be divided into the following categories [8]:

- **Hypermedia networks using hardwired links:** The links have simple rules based on previous access patterns.

- **World models:** As in the Oz project [2], viewers are immersed in a simulated world and become characters. The video presentation depends on how the user interacts with objects and other characters in this world.

- **Description-based structures:** These structures focus on filters that use content description and user preferences to create a customized version of the contents.

As pointed out by Evans [8] and Davenport [6], description-based structures are suitable for automated presentation of content without constant user interaction. This achieves a level of user immersion in the story that is lost by traditional browsing in hypermedia networks. Most interactive movies have a looser conversational user control in which the user chooses among several options at specific points in the story line to create a personalized story. The ConText system described earlier [6] provides the user with the option to interfere with the selection of video sequences, making it a promising hybrid method where the user interacts only when dissatisfied with the current presentation.

10.3.2   Video Metadata

We classify video metadata as describing structure or content. Video structure includes media-specific attributes such as recording rate, compression format, and resolution, and cinematographic structure such as frames, shots, sequences, and the spatio-temporal characterization of represented objects.

Video content metadata deal with the remaining universe of semantic information. We further decompose this universe into the set of tangible objects and the set of conceptual entities including events, actions, abstract objects, and concepts appearing in or resulting from the media stream. This classification of video content metadata is not intended to yield disjoint sets.

In the following, we concentrate on metadata for news video; however, these aspects can be generalized to other video domains.

Structure Metadata

A personalized presentation of video will typically range from small modifications on a composed linear sequence to complete recomposition of a set of individual linear units as illustrated in Figure 10-4.

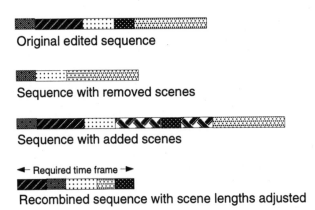

Original edited sequence

Sequence with removed scenes

Sequence with added scenes

◀— Required time frame —▶

Recombined sequence with scene lengths adjusted

Figure 10-4   Personalization ranging from simple filtering of a linear sequence to re-composition using one or more shots.

Video structure includes media-specific attributes such as recording rate, compression format, and resolution, and cinematographic structure such as frames, shots, sequences, and the spatio-temporal characterization of represented objects. In summary, video structural metadata include the following:

- **Media-specific metadata:** Describe implementation-specific information (e.g., video compression format, playout rate, resolution).

- **Cinematographic structure metadata:** Describe creation-specific information (e.g., title, date recorded, camera motion, lighting conditions, weather; shots, scenes, sequences; object spatio-temporal information).

Structural annotations represent linear video sequences as a hierarchy of frames [7]. Frames recorded continuously in time are called *shots* and represent the smallest structural unit. A set of shots presented continuously along a time line combine to form a higher level structural granule called a *scene*. *Sequences* are again made up of scenes. Thus, a hierarchy of frames, shots, scenes, and sequences constitutes the simplest video structural model.

Content Metadata

Video content metadata are concerned with objects and meaning in the video stream that appear within or across structural elements. Content metadata are further decomposed as:

- **Tangible objects:** Describe objects that appear as physical entities in the media stream (e.g., a dog, a disc).

- **Conceptual entities:** Describe events, actions, abstract objects, context, and concepts appearing in or resulting from the media stream (e.g., running, catching, tired, master).

Both content and structure metadata are required for personalization. Structure metadata (e.g., shots) can sometimes be automatically extracted from raw video data. Content metadata, necessary for personalization, usually must be obtained manually. Closed-captioned text contains both structural (time offsets) and content (text) information.

10.3.3 Characteristics of News Video

Most television news is composed of aural story telling techniques delivered by an anchor person, reporter, or people being interviewed. The common news story formats are differentiated by how the anchor or reporter interacts with the visual and aural-based footage. Often a television news item consists of an introduction by the studio anchor followed by field footage or images and graphics illustrating the story. A reporter usually mediates the material either on location or as voice-over. The anchor person contributes to the credibility of the presentation. In a personalized multi-source presentation an anchor person can have an even more important role, but instead of hosting a broadcast, the anchor would host individual segments.

We can classify news stories by the following five distinct story styles [22]:

- **Spot news or actuality:** A breaking news story that is covered live or quickly after it has happened. Scenes follow each other in a linear fashion and voice-over from the studio and live sound including commentaries from the scene are used.

- **Stand-upper:** This second most common format is prepared by a reporter gathering information, e.g., footage recorded to match the story, interviews either taken right on the site of the story or prearranged, or comments of the people at the site of the story. The reporter is reading the story into the camera. Often, the reporter is seen at the end of the story for the last lines including the sign-off.

- **Wraparound:** The wraparound consists of two parts, the opening and closing sequences and the middle sequence. Typically, the opening and closing might be done by the anchor and the reporter will do a stand-upper middle part intermixed with interviews or other on-location footage.

- **Voice-over:** A less important story is made by the anchor or reporter reading the whole story while footage matching the text is shown either as motion pictures or as stills.

In addition to these styles, Musburger [22] identifies two more extensive categories of *feature story* and *sports story*.

10.4   Metadata for System Resource Management

Ultimately, the task of delivering personalized information to the user is the burden of the host computer, storage, and network distribution system in cooperation with client computers. Collectively, this system must achieve the goals of personalization. Because personalization introduces diversification (e.g., narrowcasting) rather than generalization (e.g., broadcasting), it increases the burden on all aspects of the system's resources. In this section, we describe the trade-offs in personalization versus generalization and the metadata required for both.

Personalization, from a system's viewpoint can be approached from two perspectives:

- From a system performance standpoint, where the aggregate behavior of a user population is used to predict usage patterns and optimize resource usage.

- From a user performance viewpoint, where the attributes specific to a user's preference (e.g., content preferences, interface requirements, reneging behavior, connectivity, cost) are used to customize the presentation of information to a user.

Unfortunately, these objectives are orthogonal to one another. Aggregating users (e.g., broadcasting) reduces the ability to personalize information delivery while personalization increases the cost of providing the service. It is clear that a balance must be achieved for optimal system performance and user acceptance.

Aggregated user behavior can be used by the system in prefetching of data on a client or server-initiated basis. In client-initiated personalization, metadata that are processed remotely by the server are made available to the client, which subsequently decides whether or not to retrieve the information. In server-initiated personalization, the metadata are processed at the server, which then aggressively uses this information to push the data to its client population.

Metadata are commonly cited for use in indexing data to simplify the search process that a user must undertake in extracting relevant information from a data set. As a result, the metadata typically contain key attributes extracted from the data and organized in a form optimized to minimize database search times. This view is consistent with traditional text-only databases where searches typically involve searching for keywords in a document set.

For these systems, there is little need to embed additional information about the "documents" into their metadata. Accesses to these databases are characterized by· repetitive requests for a small subset of the entire data space and traditional cache management techniques suffice to improve the performance of the system.

Multimedia databases change this requirement. Multimedia data types such as audio and video also have the additional attributes of playout times and required bandwidth associated with them. It thus becomes necessary for the system to be aware of the timing and bandwidth characterizations of a multimedia object when requested, so that appropriate resources can be reserved to ensure the timely delivery of data. The use of metadata to support database browsing or personalization functions is significant due to the potential bandwidth used in video delivery. By using a metadata scheme, the data delivery process can be decoupled from the database management functions.

Personalization of information delivery adds a new dimension to this perspective. Data must now not only be characterized by their physical attributes, but in addition, a correlation between the data and their users must be established. Once such a relationship has been established it must be used effectively to enhance the performance of the system at a maximum benefit to the end-user. We therefore see that the previously mentioned constraints must also include system performance constraints when finding an optimal playout sequence.

The following scenario illustrates the use of metadata in resource management for the system:

- A user initiates a session. The user is presented with a menu based on predicted user preferences. As the user navigates through the sessions, user preferences are mapped onto existing usage patterns to tailor information presented (aggregate metadata plus user metadata).

- The metadata about the actual data are combined with the user preferences to ensure that appropriate resources are reserved ahead of time (e.g., bandwidth for live video playback).

Tailoring individual delivery to a large number of users is extremely expensive without some form of simplification or aggregation of behaviors. In the extreme case, all information about an individual can be recorded and maintained by the system. For each user a database and database analysis would be required to understand each user's behavior and personalization requirements. Such analysis, if based on text vector-space techniques, is computationally expensive with current processing and storage technologies. Therefore, we seek techniques that simplify the data set characterizing individuals and permit a simpler representation of the same information.

User Clustering

One method of behavior aggregation is by clustering of users and assigning user profiles. Clustering can be achieved by observing interface usage behavioral patterns [24, 25] or by analyzing accesses to the set of documents previously visited by the user. The result is a set of profiles characterizing the user population, but pre-presented by a subset of the original data describing the great detail about individual users.

Of interest here as with any clustering technique is the effectiveness in reducing the amount of information and information processing required to achieve the personalization goals. To this end, we introduce the concept of *preference entropy* to measure the relative success of a set of parameters in characterizing a personal profile. Essentially, we can quantify the relationships among the metadata categories, the user behavior, and the deviation from the ideal case with this concept.

A preference entropy close to zero indicates that the user has no particular preference among the options, while a large entropy indicates that the preferences are non-uniform.

Once we have established a need for a particular metadata component for a single user, it must be considered with respect to the user population. The individual's set of option preferences might coincide with the average option preferences in a user population, it might coincide with the average option preferences in a subset of the population, or it might be clearly distinct from any other user. To decide whether the population can be divided into clusters of users with similar preferences we can use the simple technique of finding the covariance of the difference between a user's option preferences and the average preferences in the population at large. Or we can apply more advanced calculations on the set of users for the same goal.

By only allowing a subset of the available parameters to be personalized for any given user or for a given user cluster, we can reduce computation while minimizing loss of adaptation by choosing parameters with minimum entropy.

10.5   Collection of Metadata for Video: Vane

As one might imagine, the ability to provide personalization on video metadata
depends on the quality and quantity of information extractable from the video
data. Here, we overview a system designed to capture metadata from video
content to support video personalization.

10.5.1   An Overview of Vane

Vane is a video annotation tool (see Color Figure-5) developed at the Multimedia Communications Laboratory at Boston University [4]. Video annotation with the tool involves automatic segmentation of video data followed
by manual content annotation (Figure 10-5). The tool automatically detects
camera breaks and displays the detected shots along a time line (structural
metadata). The information model is defined by SGML document type definitions (DTD) for the desired video domain. After annotations (structural and
content metadata) have been collected as SGML files, they can be converted
to any database format suitable for personalization functions (we currently
use a relational DBMS). Specifics of the Vane tool's construction for metadata
collection are described next.

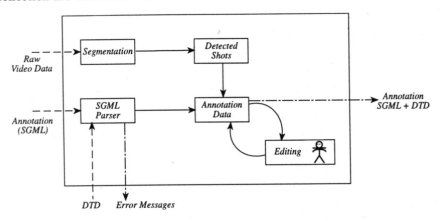

Figure 10-5   Data flow for Vane.

10.5.2   The DTD and the Dynamic Annotation Interface

Vane, at load-time, reads in the domain DTD and brings up appropriate fields to record metadata. Metadata are stored in SGML files according to the format specified in the DTD. If an existing annotation file is loaded into Vane, it first checks the file format for errors with respect to the DTD. One of the advantages of having an information model defined by a DTD is its adaptability. One needs only to change the DTD rather than the tool to accommodate a new video domain. With a new DTD, the interface gets automatically updated.

Scenes and sequences are identified manually. Metadata about each shot, scene, sequence, and complete document are captured in the forms indicated by the DTD. Metadata are stored at various levels of granularity, e.g., keywords, headlines, abstract, transcripts, etc., to cater to different requirements of the application domain. Links are provided within text (abstracts and transcript), linking text to images, text, or video segments. Shots, scenes, and sequences can also be linked to images, text, and video segments, creating information paths for user traversal and information presentation.

The ability of SGML to nest several elements inside one another allows Vane to easily define a structured view of the video content. For example, a shot description can be nested inside a scene description. We applied these concepts in the creation of a baseline DTD with the following syntax:

```
<!ELEMENT FULLDOC   - - (ABSTRACT?, CATEGORY?, REF*, SEQUENCE*, OBJECT*)>
<!ELEMENT SEQUENCE  - - (ABSTRACT?, REF*, SCENE*)                       >
<!ELEMENT SCENE     - - (ABSTRACT?, REF*, SHOT*)                        >
<!ELEMENT SHOT      - - (ABSTRACT?, REF*, TRANSCR?)                     >
<!ELEMENT OBJECT    - - (OBJECT*)                                       >
<!ELEMENT ABSTRACT  - - (#PCDATA & REF*)*                               >
<!ELEMENT TRANSCR   - - (#PCDATA)                                       >
<!ELEMENT REF       - - O EMPTY                                         >
<!ELEMENT CATEGORY  - - (EDU | NEWS | MOVIE | DOC | SPORT)              >
```

The salient features of this description are the ability to characterize video structure and content attributes as metadata, the ability to extend the DTD (and interface) at run-time, nesting of concepts and objects, and the automatic generation of cross-references. Details of the tool and its construction can be found in [4].

10.5.3   Translation to Alternative Representations

Once the metadata are collected, it is desirable to analyze, condense, and re-format collected metadata into a representation suitable for serving the user population. This includes generation of indices to information, cross-references, and organization of data for fast access and delivery.

In Figure 10-6, we provide an example of a metadata representation constructed for simple access to news video. Here a single news broadcast is considered as a document. The structure of this news document comprises elements from different categories (sports, politics) where each category consists of multiple news items. We collect cinematic metadata such as the source, time, date, and location for a complete document. We can then extract the content information from each news item such as keywords, transcript, representative still image, and objects. Objects can belong to different categories such as people, location, field footage, shots, events, texture, color, etc. An object can be composed of multiple objects. We can also store metadata about the associations between the objects, (e.g., a dog playing with a disc).

In this example, a relational database model is used; however, any suitable representation can be applied.

10.6   A Framework for Composing
Personalized Video

In the previous sections, we investigated a variety of techniques for filtering, collecting, and describing metadata for personalized video delivery. In this section, we focus on a scenario in the news video domain and present techniques for composing news "documents" with sequential elements, as illustrated in Figure 10-1. Here, our objective is to achieve a methodology for creating cohesive, time-constrained, and personalized video delivery when content originates from many sources while preserving a format close to present television news stories. The characteristics of our personalized news delivery service are:

- A composition of multiple sources makes up each news item and priority is given to sections deemed relevant to both the flow of the story and the user.

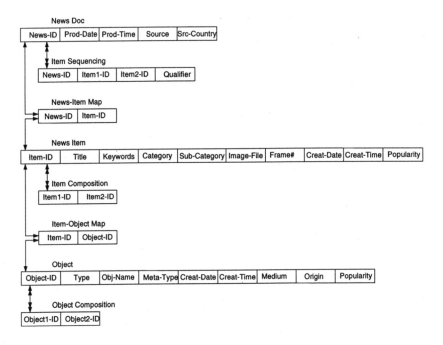

Figure 10-6 Newscast schema.

- Duplication from multiple sources producing almost equivalent accounts of news events must be suppressed.

- The duration and order of each news story sequence reflects its estimated interest to the user. High interest items should be played out early and be given more time than less interesting items.

- The presentation accepts but does not rely on interactive participation by the user. Hyperlinks providing more information on individual news stories are one way of giving control to the user.

- Learning user preferences for content, structure, and presentation is achieved through implicit and explicit feedback.

- Notification of major news events is provided.

The remainder of this section describes an approach to achieving this vision.

10.6.1   Metadata for a Personalized News Service

To be able to filter the news segments using user preferences, we have to require identification of attributes that must be present in the news segment and user metadata.

News Segment Metadata

Table 10-1 shows the news segment metadata used in our trials. For the personalization scheme to function, we require acquisition of structural and content metadata describing the news segments. In our trials, this is captured by reading the closed-captioned text or by the use of Vane. A more suitable approach of obtaining this metadata is directly from the news providers.

User Metadata

Since we use cognitive filtering, our user profile corresponds closely to metadata available for each news segment (i.e., user metadata are nearly identical to content metadata). We thereby choose a descriptive user profile constructed by observing user manipulations of previously constructed news story sequences.

Not all fields represented in Table 10-1 are of interest for representing long-term user preferences. Time of recording and fields specifying what track is the most important for the segment semantics are parameters anticipated to be of little value for expressing long-term user preferences.

Mapping Content to User Metadata

Using Salton's techniques [27], mapping content metadata to user metadata can be achieved with field vectors. The user metadata can be stored in vector format and the news segment metadata must be converted to vector format, either at the news provider or locally on the client. Since some parameters needed for calculating vector entries are only available at the provider side, we suggest that the news provider construct the vectors.

By using binary vectors for the subset of fields (labeled 'B' in the table) and weighted vectors for another subset of fields (labeled 'D' in the table), we now have a representation that leads to simple relevance comparison between

Field	Description	Sample Entry	Vector
.time	Time of broadcast	96062518 66.38	
.source	News source	CBS	B
.semantics	Audio, video or audio-video	A	
.tracks	Audio, video or audio-video	AV	
.origtime	Time of content recording	n/a	
.question	Commentator question		D
.duration	Duration of recording	32.40	
.structure	Structure of composition	Anchor	
.synchronous	True or false (audio)	True	
.concept country	Country under consideration	Saudi Arabia	B
.concept state	State under consideration		B
.concept city	City under consideration	Dhahran	B
.country	Country of origin	USA	B
.state	State of origin	DC	B
.city	City of origin	Washington	B
.building	Building of origin	White House	B
.concept person	Person under consideration	Clinton, Bill	B
.freetext	Free-form text	In Saudi Arabia...	D

Table 10-1 Metadata fields for user profiles with sample data from an evening news segment.

segments or between segments and user profiles. The vectors span spaces made up of all terms encountered in the available collection of similar fields.

To find the anticipated user preference for a new news story, we calculate the similarity between the user profile and the corresponding metadata fields associated with the news story, both represented as vectors. The similarity measure can be estimated by computing the vector angle. We expect varying user interest in matches between different field pairs as well as varying weight distributions among news subjects. The distribution is likely to be a function of both the field values and the field type; however, we currently pursue the one-profile-per-user simplification.

10.6.2   Composing News Video On-the-Fly

To generate a personalized news presentation, a typical client system would first process all metadata for a given day's news from a number of sources. Queries to find additional material could also be issued at this time. The material necessary for presentation would be downloaded from the various sources, stored in a cache, and eventually played back to the user. Personalized presentations could be provided on-demand or scheduled for particular times to meet system resource constraints. They could also be triggered by the availability of user-defined material or by breaking news exceeding a certain interest threshold defined by the user.

In the remainder of this section, we will concentrate on the composition of a single news story sequence from a number of sources.

News Segments

News is a narrative with a combination of voice and images. News is rarely conveyed with images only, but often is represented with voice and a picture of the speaker. Sometimes it is rendered with the speaker plus supporting images and original sound is of little importance. Here, the speaker interprets the images and forms a view. Thus, current newscasting norms indicate correlation of spoken words and images.

News stories comprise fragmented pieces of events, commentaries, and interviews that are well suited for automated concatenation. Today, the editor and narrator ensure that a news item is coherent. In our personalized system we want this to be automated.

To personalize the presentation of an individual's news story, each segment of audio and video must be given a relevance score as a *member* of a set of related content and as a *part* of a particular composition.

We define a *news segment* as our basic structural unit. It is a sequence of related shots that are available from a given provider. The segment is expected to have a meaningful linear structure and it may include shots of varying lengths and quality. Available news segments about a particular news story are expected to be ordered in a meaningful way even if this is not essential for our purposes.

Attributes within a segment can be relevant to the beginning, the middle, the end, or any combination. The sample entries of Table 10-1 give an example of a news segment and associated attributes about a truck bombing in Saudi Arabia from a CBS newscast.

To simplify the discussion, a valid sequence of news segments consists of a path of non-overlapping segments. To further refine the presentation, we want to fill in missing audio or video with data from other segments, but we defer this task. We also note that many news segments suffer from lack of moving images due to the absence of live or recent feeds. We therefore greatly improve the quality of the composition by allowing alternative video segments (e.g., live footage) to augment concatenations.

We expect metadata for each news segment to be available for retrieval, independent from the access to the aural and visual data (e.g., as collected by the Vane tool). The metadata for a segment must indicate whether the audio, the video, or both audio and video are necessary to convey the content. (It becomes important to distinguish audio and video as separate media.)

Inter- and Intra-story Clustering of News Segments

Our initial task to group related news segments into sets of material addressing a particular news story is pre-supposed. While related segments from the same source will carry a common thread identifier, we cannot expect a uniform identifier across all sources. Simple clustering methods like the Leader algorithm can be used [3, 10] to divide the segments into dissimilar groups.

The semantics of a segment group are represented by creating a *super segment vector* set. This super vector set is a set of vector sums created by adding the vectors in each metadata field and normalizing them. Our observation of closed-caption data for news stories indicates that relevance decreases with time. Using clustering techniques, one can also find clusters within each news story cluster. In this way, duplicate news items are grouped to optimize for spread when picking and scheduling representative segments later.

Assigning Durations to News Story Clusters

After the clustering step, we expect all available news story material to belong
to distinct news story groups. Comparing all super segments with the relevant
user profile, we end up with a set of normalized relevance scores for each cluster.

Unlike traditional approaches, we also include the production time and amount
of available material (cluster size) in the relevance judgment. This facilitates
playout time constraints (e.g., a news synopsis in 10 minutes). Borrowing from
concepts used for automated layout in the Krakatoa Chronicle [13], we can use
density as a measure for how many news stories a user wants to see per unit of
relevance, and *sensitivity*, as a measure for how much the news item duration is
allowed to vary as a function of its perceived interest. A high sensitivity would
let a news item capture almost the entire time of the personalized newscast if
it had a much better match with the user profile than any other item.

Scheduling a Sequential News Presentation

To perform set and sequential filtering on a particular cluster of news segments
we use a set of filters that each are associated with a weight that is a function
of playout time within the news story. This approach is an application of
Evans' ideas but with support for a time-dependent filter hierarchy. We call
this *timed-based filtering*. The following filters would be applied:

- **Relevance to user profile:** This filter generates the relevance between
  a segment and the appropriate user profile.

- **Relevance to center of story:** This filter generates the relevance between a news segment vector set and the super segment vector set for the
  segment cluster.

- **Relevance to the introduction, middle, and end of the story:**
  These filters are based on the values in the *structure* field that let news
  providers define where the segment will be appropriate (e.g., introduction,
  background, or coverage of the current event). The middle of the story
  might be about the current event while the end of the story might contain
  background coverage.

- **Timeliness:** This filter returns a normalized value that reflects the relative
  age of an input news segment.

- **Continuity:** This filter ensures continuity. One possible continuity filter uses a division of the freetext field into two equal parts, each represented by a document vector. This filter returns the expected normalized relevance between the second part of the present segment and the first part of the next segment in the composition.

- **Spread of representative segments:** This filter prevents related segments originating from the same cluster from appearing in the same composition. Clusters contributing segments to a composition will be given lower scores than unvisited clusters.

We propose to make these filters operate in parallel except for the repetition filter that makes sure no segment is scheduled for playback twice. Scheduling of segments will continue until the allowed time slot for the news story has been filled and scheduling of the next news story will begin. Thus, the operation of the filters on the metadata from the segments and from the user yields personalized delivery of video content.

10.7   Summary and Conclusion

The existence of solutions for information personalization using text-based methods affirms the viability of creating personalized video delivery using metadata. In this chapter, we have described techniques to facilitate this personalization, overviewed the unique characteristics of the video medium, and proposed a framework for personalized delivery of video information in the news domain.

Although unrealized, our proposal is based upon the application and integration of existing techniques of video content and structure modeling, metadata collection, vector space analysis, personalization and filtering, metadata management, and video and audio composition. The core of the concept is the use of a set of vector-based and time-dependent filters for audio and video segment selection to generate formatted video-based compositions on-the-fly. We focused primarily on the news domain, but we expect the concepts to be appropriate for other areas of information composition using motion video.

References

[1] G. Ahanger, D. Benson, and T.D.C. Little, "Video Query Formulation," *Proc. IS&T/SPIE Conf. on Storage and Retrieval for Image and Video Databases*, Vol. 2420, February 1995, pp. 280–291.

[2] J. Bates, "The Nature of Character in Interactive Worlds and The Oz Project," in *Virtual Realities: Anthology of Industry and Culture*, C.E. Loeffler (ed.), 1993.

[3] J. Bezdek and S. Pal, *Fuzzy Models for Pattern Recognition*, IEEE Press, 1992.

[4] M. Carrer, L. Ligresti, G. Ahanger, and T. D. C. Little, "An Annotation Engine for Supporting Video Database Population," *Journal of Multimedia Tools and Applications*, Vol. 5, No. 3, November 1997.

[5] A. Cypher (ed.), *Watch What I Do: Programming by Demonstration*, MIT Press, Cambridge MA, 1993.

[6] G. Davenport and M. Murtaugh, "ConText Towards the Evolving documentary," *Proc. ACM Multimedia '95*, San Francisco, November 1995.

[7] G. Davenport, T. G. Aguierre Smith, and N. Pincever, "Cinematic Primitives for Multimedia," *IEEE Computer Graphics & Applications*, July 1991, pp. 67–74.

[8] R. Evans, "Log Boy Meets Filter Girl: A Tool Kit for Personalizable Movies," *M.S. Thesis*, MIT, Cambridge MA, 1994.

[9] D. Goldberg, D. Nicholas, B. M. Oki, and D. Terry, "Using Collaborative Filtering To Weave an Information Tapestry," *Communications of the ACM*, Vol. 35, No. 12, December 1992, pp. 61–70.

[10] J. Hartigan, *Clustering Algorithms*, John Wiley, 1975.

[11] W. Klippgen, "Navigation in Digital Video Archives," (in Norwegian), *Diploma Thesis*, Norwegian Institute of Technology, March, 1995.

[12] A. Kobsa and W. Pohl, "The User Modeling Shell System BGP-MS," *User Modeling and User-Adapted Interaction*, Vol. 4, No. 2, 1995, pp. 59–106.

[13] T. Kamba, K. Bharat, and M. C. Albers, "An Interactive, Personalized, Newspaper on the WWW," *Proc. 4th Intl. World Wide Web Conf.*, 1995.

[14] T. D. C. Little, G. Ahanger, H.-J. Chen, R. J. Folz, J. F. Gibbon, A. Krishnamurthy, P. Lumba, M. Ramanathan, and D. Venkatesh, "Selection and Dissemination of Digital Video via the Virtual Video Browser", *Journal of Multimedia Tools and Applications*, Vol. 1, No. 2, June, 1995, pp. 149–172.

[15] P. Maes, "How to do the Right Thing, " AI-Laboratory, Vrije Universiteit Brussel and AI-Laboratory, MIT, Cambridge MA, 1989.

[16] P. Maes, "Agents that Reduce Work and Information Overload," *Communications of the ACM*, Vol. 37, No. 7, July 1994, pp. 31–40.

[17] P. Maes and U. Shardanand, "Social Information Filtering: Algorithms for Automating 'Word of Mouth'," *Proc. ACM CHI '95*, Denver CO, May 1995.

[18] T. W. Malone, K. R. Grant, F. A. Turbak, S. A. Brobst, and M. D. Cohen, "Intelligent Information Sharing Systems," *Communications of the ACM*, Vol. 30, No. 5, May 1987, pp. 390–402.

[19] R. S. Marcus, "Computer and Human Understanding in Intelligent Retrieval Assistance," *Proc. 54th American Society for Information Science Meeting*, Vol. 28, October 1991, pp. 49–59.

[20] N. Mathe and J. Chen, "A User-Centered Approach to Adaptive Hypertext based on an Information Relevance Model," *Proc. 4th Intl. Conf. on User Modeling (UM'94)*, Hyannis MA, August 1994, pp. 107–114.

[21] J. Monaco, *How to Read a Film. The Art, Technology, Language, History and Theory of Film and Media*, Oxford University Press, New York, 1981.

[22] R. B. Musburger, *Electronic News Gathering*, Focal Press, Boston, 1991.

[23] T. Holm Nelson, "A File Structure for the Complex, the Changing and the Indeterminate," *Proc. 20th National ACM Conf.*, New York, 1965, pp. 84–100.

[24] J. Orwant, "Heterogeneous Learning in the Doppelgänger user Modeling System," *Journal of User Modeling and User-Adapted Interaction*, 1995.

[25] A. Perrig and A. Ballim, "The Design of a User Classification System," Project of 8th Semester LITH, EPFL Lausanne, Switzerland, 1996.

[26] P. Resnick, N. Iacovou, M. Suchak, P. Bergstrom, and J. Riedl, "GroupLens: An Open Architecture for Collaborative Filtering of Netnews," *Proc. CSCW '94*, Chapel Hill, NC, October 1994.

[27] G. Salton, *Automatic Text Processing – The Transformation, Analysis and Retrieval of Information by Computer*, Addison-Wesley, 1989.

[28] U. Upendra Shardanand and P. Maes, "Social Information Filtering: Algorithms for Automating Word of Mouth," *Proc. ACM CHI '95*, 1995.

[29] B. Sheth and P. Maes, "Evolving Agents for Personalized Information Filtering," *Proc. 9th IEEE Conf. on Artificial Intelligence for Applications*, 1993.

[30] B. D. Sheth, "A Learning Approach to Personalized Information Filtering," *Master's Thesis*, MIT, Cambridge MA, February 1994.

[31] T. W. Yan, H. Jacobsen, H. Garcia-Molina, and U. Dayal, "From User Access Patterns to Dynamic Hypertext Linking," *Proc. 5th Intl. World Wide Web Conf.*, May 1996, Paris, France.

[32] M. M. Yeung, B.-L. Yeo, W. Wolf, and B. Liu, "Video Browsing using Clustering and Scene Transitions on Compressed Sequences," *Proc. Multimedia Computing and Networking*, Vol. 1005, SPIE, San Jose California, February 1995.

Chapter

11

Metadata for Mixed-Media Access

Francine Chen, Marti Hearst, Don Kimber, Julian Kupiec, Jan Pedersen*, and Lynn Wilcox**

Xerox Palo Alto Research Center
3333 Coyote Hill Road
Palo Alto, CA 94304, USA
{fchen,kimber,kupiec}@parc.xerox.com
hearst@sims.berkeley.edu

*Verity Inc.
894 Ross Dr.
Sunnyvale, CA 94089
jpederse@verity.com

**FX Palo Alto Laboratory
3400 Hillview Ave. Bldg 4
Palo Alto, CA 94304, USA
wilcox@pal.xerox.com

Abstract

In this chapter, we discuss *mixed-media access*, an information access paradigm for multimedia data in which the media type of a query may differ from that of the data. This allows a single query to be used to retrieve information from data consisting of multiple types of media. In addition, multiple queries formulated in different media types can be used to more accurately specify the data to be retrieved. The types of media considered in this chapter are speech, images of text, and full-length text. Some examples of metadata for mixed-media access are locations of keywords in speech and images, identification of speakers, locations of emphasized regions in speech, and locations of topic boundaries in text. Algorithms for automatically generating this metadata are described, including word spotting, speaker segmentation, emphatic speech detection, and subtopic boundary location. We illustrate the use of mixed-media access with an example of information access from multimedia data surrounding a formal presentation.

11.1   Introduction

Modern document databases contain information in a variety of media; audio, video, and image data are becoming increasingly common companions to plain text. Access to this rich and variegated information is typically accomplished in standard systems through queries over manually supplied topic keywords or descriptive text. Recent work suggests that fully automatic methods operating directly on the data can offer comparable characterizations. Moreover, analyses tuned to particular media can expose structure that can refine and augment queries based on simple keyword information.

We are exploring these issues through a paradigm we call *mixed-media access*, which encourages the user to query in a variety of media, regardless of the media type of the data. This encompasses, for example, spoken access to textual databases, as well as queries that combine cues across the media types present in a complex document.

Special metadata considerations arise within such a paradigm. For our purposes, mixed-media metadata is defined as derived properties of the media which are useful for information access or retrieval. These properties can be derived either in advance or "on the fly". Our focus is on automatically derived metadata for speech, scanned text images, and full-length text.

In a purely textual database, metadata for information access typically consists of indices on word tokens. The state-of-the-art in speech and image recognition is such that we cannot reliably create a word-level transcription for arbitrary speech documents [21] or text images [5]. Therefore, in a multimedia database prepared for mixed-media access it is unrealistic to suppose that a full transcription is available in advance as metadata. We can, however, robustly recognize particular keywords, a process known as *word spotting* [30]. Word spotting produces metadata in the form of time indices of keywords in audio [31], or locations of keywords in a text image [3].

In addition, we can enrich this word-level metadata with information that captures some of the context implicit in particular media. For example, in speech data one important aspect is the identity of the speakers. We can automatically detect speaker changes in audio, in a process which we refer to as *speaker segmentation* [32]. This produces metadata in the form of time indices of the audio segments corresponding to the different speakers. When the speakers are known, each segment can be annotated with the identity of the speaker, a process known as *speaker identification*. This information helps characterize the data, and can be stored as metadata and used for indexing.

Another source of information in speech not present in plain text is prosodic information. Prosodic information includes changes in pitch, amplitude, and timing, and is used by a speaker to signal regions of speech that are important. We can automatically detect regions of emphatic speech [4] and note the time indices of the audio segments in which emphatic speech occurs. These regions are another form of metadata and can be used as a method of indexing into a conversation.

A full-text document can often be characterized as consisting of one or more main topics or themes, as well as a sequence of subtopical discussions that take place in the context of the main topic themes. Thus, another source of information for metadata which can be applied to both spoken and written text is that of subtopic extent. We can determine when the discussion within a text changes from one subtopic to the next [10], and then generate indices that indicate which paragraphs or which regions correspond to each subtopic segment. A separate, but related, text analysis task is the assignment of category information to the full text and its subtopical segments [11]. The contrast between discovery of subtopic boundaries and discovery of subtopic categories bears an analogical resemblance to the contrast between discovery of speaker change boundaries and discovery of speaker identity.

In order to illustrate how mixed-media access can be used to retrieve information from multimedia data, we provide an example based on a presentation on Hypercars[1]. The data consists of an audio recording of the talk, scanned images of the slides used in the talk, and text from a paper on Hypercars. Queries can be posed as spoken keywords, text keywords, or natural language text. Spoken keywords can be used to retrieve information from text and audio data, while text keywords and natural language queries can be used to retrieve data from slide images and text. In addition, structure in the audio imposed by different speakers, and structure in the text imposed by topic boundaries, can be used to refine these queries.

---

[1]According to [19], Hypercars are very lightweight passenger cars, constructed of carbon-fiber material, driven by hybrid-electric drives meant to achieve very high gas mileage. The authors write "Far from sacrificing other attributes for efficiency, ultralight hybrids could be more safe, peppy, clean, durable, reliable, quiet, comfortable, and beautiful than existing cars, yet be priced about the same or less."

In the remainder of this chapter, we first provide more detail about the three media types and their corresponding metadata. We then describe how this metadata can be derived automatically, and finally present an example of the use of such metadata in mixed-media access.

11.2 Characteristics of the Media and the Derived Metadata

Digitized speech and scanned images of text are not easily searched for content. However, they contain information which can be organized to provide easier access. Wechsler and Schäuble [28] show how to use phone sequences[2] to index audio recordings. In this chapter, we restrict our attention to metadata at the word level. Metadata providing indices to speech includes keyword locations, segmentation of a conversation by speaker, and regions which a speaker highlighted by speaking more emphatically. In text images, keywords, and layout may be identified.

Queries may consist of a Boolean expression, which requires searching for a small number of keywords or phrases, or for a particular speaker. In information retrieval, a trade-off has been observed between searching using only fixed categories and allowing the user access to unlimited vocabulary. The evidence suggests that when category information is combined with free text search, results are improved over allowing either alone [20, 17]. If the set of keywords is fixed, metadata based on keyword locations can be precomputed and stored for later indexing. This is efficient, in that keyword spotting can be done off-line, but restrictive, in that the available query terms are limited to a predefined set of keywords. Currently, it is not possible to reliably generate precomputed word-level metadata that supports unrestricted vocabulary searching over image or audio data. However, it is possible to support this search style by spotting for keywords "on the fly".

11.2.1 Speech

Audio is by nature a time-sequential media. Portions of audio data can be accessed by specifying starting and ending times for a desired segment. However, indexing solely by time interval is restrictive; the development of sophisticated

---

[2]Phones are the basic sound units of speech, somewhat similar to the alphabet for text.

speech analysis techniques allows for attribute-based interval specification, such as locating the portion of an audio stream in which a comment was made by a particular speaker.

Speech can be analyzed in different ways. One is in terms of the presence of specific keywords in the speech [30]. Another is in terms of the identity of the speakers in the audio [32]. A third is in terms of prosodic information [4], which can be used by a speaker to draw attention to a phrase or sentence, or to alter the word meaning. This information can be exploited to obtain metadata for access to audio.

Metadata describing keywords consists of the keyword and its starting and ending time in the audio. Because the process of spoken keyword identification is not perfectly accurate, a confidence score is also a part of the metadata representation.

Metadata describing the identity of the speakers consists of the name of the speaker, and a list of the time intervals during which the speaker talks. Speaker-independent indices are also maintained by taking note of when one speaker finishes talking and either silence or another speaker follows. In this case, starting and ending times for each of the different speakers in the audio are recorded, but only symbolic names are attached to the speakers, for example, speaker A, speaker B, etc. This allows for retrieval of logical speaker units even when the identity of the speakers is not known. Additionally, silence and non-speech sounds can be identified and stored as metadata.

Metadata describing emphasized regions of speech consists of the time indices of the intervals where the speech was emphatic, as well as a measure of certainty that the particular region did indeed contain speech which the speaker intended to emphasize.

11.2.2   Text Images

Text image data can be characterized in terms of the layout structure of the document, e.g., columns and paragraphs [12], the semantic information contained in the document [8], and by the words in the document [25]. However, a reliable word-level transcription of arbitrary pages containing text is not yet possible. Therefore, rather than use a word-level transcription, we characterize image data by the location and identity of keywords, which can be stored as metadata. As in the audio example, the representation may also include a score indicating the degree of confidence in the identification of the keyword.

11.2.3 Full-Length Text

Full-length texts are natural language expressions of sufficient length to exhibit topical substructure. For example, a magazine article will be composed of numerous sections each illuminating aspects of the overall topic. Often these sections will be demarked by author provided typographical annotations, perhaps in a markup language such as SGML [26]. However, author provided subtopic markup is neither always available nor always reliable.

Full-length text shares the same basic representation as shorter text forms, such as titles and abstracts: words. Therefore standard mechanisms for text indexing, such as inverted indices [24], can act as metadata. For retrieval based on spoken multi-word queries, index mechanisms which support search with proximity constraints are also useful. In addition, current work in computational linguistics allows for the assignment of additional information at the word token level, e.g., part-of-speech tags [6] and morphological derivation [7].

Full-length texts can also be segmented at topic and subtopic boundaries. Algorithms that detect subtopic structure can either partition the text or allow overlap among multi-paragraph units. In both cases, the metadata consists of indices indicating which paragraphs or which regions of tokens correspond to each subtopic segment. Additionally, information that characterizes the content of the subtopics and the main topics can serve as useful metadata [11]. Automated determination of main topic content is an active area of research [18].

11.3 Extraction and Use of Metadata

This section describes implemented techniques for the automated extraction of the kinds metadata described in Section 11.2.

Reducing drag coefficient, C_D

1970: norm ~0,5–0,6
1992: U.S. average 0,33, best sedan 0,29, best productionized 2-seat 0,18
1992: best worldwide production platform (Adam Opel) 0,255
1921: Rumpler 7-seat Tropfenwagen (midengine prototype) 0,28
1985: Ford Probe V concept car 0,137 (<F-15's C_D!)
1987: Renault Vesta II 4-seat concept car 0,186
1991: GM Ultralite 4-seat concept car 0,192
1990s: likely practical limit w/ passive boundary-layer control ~0,08–0,10

Reducing frontal area, A (m^2)

1992: average U.S. 4/5-seat production platform ~2,3; 2-seat Honda DX 1,8
1987: Renault Vesta II 4-seat concept car 1,64
1991: GM 4-seat Ultralite concept car 1,71

So today's typical 0,33 × 2,3 m^2 C_DA = 0,76 m^2; GM's Ultralite, 0,33 m^2; the best parameters separately shown for 4-seaters, 0,137 × 1,64 = 0,22 m^2 (30% of today's); and edge-of-envelope, ~0,08 × 1,5 m^2 = 0,12 m^2 (16% of today's). We assume C_DA = 0,27 near-term, 0,17 later, ~0,13 edge-of-envelope.

Figure 11-1   Result of spotting for "production*".

11.3.1   Word-Image Spotting

Word-image spotting refers to the task of detecting and locating user-specified keywords and phrases in images of text. Several systems for spotting whole words in scanned images of text have been developed. In noisy document images, where optical character recognition systems perform poorly [14, 15], these systems have been found to locate keywords more accurately than the option of performing optical character recognition (OCR) and then searching for keywords as text strings. However, the image-based word-spotting systems require as input an image that has been correctly segmented into words.

A word-image spotting system developed at Xerox PARC detects words in a variety of fonts within lines of imaged text. The user-specified keywords and phrases can be partially specified, similar to a simple "grep", but over images of text [3]. For each word identified as a keyword by the word-image spotter, the location of the word in the image can be stored as metadata. Figure 11-1 shows the result of spotting for "production*", where "*" represents a wildcard, in one of the digitized overhead transparencies used in a formal presentation on Hypercars. Note that the alternate word forms "productionized" and "production" were detected. The spotted characters composing "production" are highlighted. Although the search is for a partially specified keyphrase, the location of the entire word could be highlighted by configuring the word-image spotter to identify interword space.

The PARC word-image spotter is based on the use of multi-resolution image morphology [1] to identify bounding boxes of text lines, and hidden Markov modeling to identify specific words within a text line. Each text line bounding box is normalized to a standard height, and the width of the bounding box is scaled proportionally, producing a gray-scale image. This scaling permits recognition of words in a variety of fonts in a range of sizes. A feature vector characterizing a scaled bounding box is derived from the columns of pixel values within that bounding box.

A prespecified set of keywords, as is commonly used in word spotting systems, is not required. Instead, for each keyword or keyphrase specified by the user in a query, a hidden Markov model (HMM) is created "on the fly" from pretrained character models. Another pretrained HMM is used to model the data which are not part of a keyword or phrase. The non-keyphrase model coarsely represents the columns of pixels in a bounding box. A non-keyphrase model composed of all characters and symbols connected in parallel could be used instead, but would be much more computationally expensive.

The models are trained on data labeled with the characters appearing in each line of text and with the location of each line of text, but not the location of each character. Baum-Welch training [23] is used to estimate the parameter values of the models. To detect keywords or phrases, the keyphrase models and non-keyphrase model are connected in parallel to create a spotting network. Keyphrases within a bounding box are identified using Viterbi decoding [23] on the spotting network. The detected keywords and phrases and their locations in a text image can then be used as metadata. A fixed set of keywords can be spotted and stored as metadata in a preprocessing step. As users specify additional keyword and phrase searches during access, indices to these search terms can be added to the metadata. In this approach the lexicon is not limited, in contrast to the approach of performing OCR followed by indexing, which is susceptible to errors caused by words being "out of vocabulary."

11.3.2 Audio Word Spotting

Audio word spotting is the ability to locate keywords or phrases in previously recorded speech. It differs from isolated word recognition, in which words to be recognized must be spoken in isolation, and continuous speech recognition, in which each word in a continuous stream must be recognized. Word spotting generates metadata in the form of time indices for the beginning and ending of keywords. This provides indexing by keywords into long audio files, thus allowing retrieval of specific information without the need to listen to the entire recording.

Certain word spotting systems assume there is a fixed set of keywords to be spotted in continuous speech from many different speakers. An example is the operator assisted telephone call task in [34], where spotting for only five keywords is required. Such systems are based on whole word models, and require training data for each of the keywords from a large database of speakers. They are thus appropriate in tasks for which a small number of fixed keywords suffice. Other speaker-independent keyword spotting systems are based on large-vocabulary continuous speech recognition. For example, the system proposed by SRI [29] uses the $Decipher^{TM}$ large-vocabulary speech recognition system to transcribe the speech, and any keywords that occur in the transcription are hypothesized. A drawback of this approach is that certain keywords, for example, proper names, are unlikely to be included in the vocabulary of the recognizer.

An alternative to the above speaker-independent word spotting systems is the interactive system developed at Xerox PARC [31]. The system is speaker-dependent, so that the audio is restricted to speech from a single speaker. When word spotting is to be performed, the speaker simply speaks the keyword or phrase to be located. Alternatively, a keyword can be manually excised from a recording. There are no linguistic assumptions, so that the word spotting system is multi-lingual. In addition, spotting can be performed for non-speech sounds such as music or laughter.

The PARC word spotting system uses a hidden Markov model (HMM) to model arbitrary, user-defined keywords in the context of continuous speech [30]. Training the HMM consists of two stages: an initial, static stage in which statistics for a given speaker are learned and a model for the non-keyword speech is obtained, and a second, dynamic stage in which the keyword model is trained as the system is in use. Data for the static training stage consists of an arbitrary segment of the speaker's speech. The dynamic training stage is novel in that it requires only a single repetition of a keyword; thus, there is no distinction between keyword training and word spotting.

The search technique for locating instances of a keyword in continuous speech is a "forward-backward" search which uses peaks in the *a posteriori*, or forward [23], probability of the keyword end state to detect potential keyword endpoints. State probabilities are then recursively computed backward to find a peak in the keyword start state. In this way, a score for the keyword is obtained in addition to the starting and ending times, which helps to prevent false alarms. This search is efficient, in that backtracking is only required when a keyword is hypothesized.

Color Figure-6 shows a display of the audio portion of the formal presentation on Hypercars. The user specified an audio query for the keyword "production" by locating an instance of the word in an initial portion of the audio. The keyword search was performed to locate all other instances of this keyword. The intervals corresponding to the times when the keyword "production" was spotted are highlighted. By listening to the audio in the vicinity of these intervals, information on the production of hypercars can be obtained.

11.3.3   Text Access via Spoken Queries

In Section 11.3.2 we described how spoken utterances can be used as input to a search of audio media. Spoken utterances can also be used as input to text search. This allows a user to utter spoken words and be presented with portions of text containing those words. This mode of input could be especially natural in settings where the user is also providing speech input for audio access. The relevant metadata for text retrieval given speech input is an inverted index structure capable of supporting proximity constraint searches.

Text access via spoken query necessarily involves large vocabulary speech recognition. Typically this requires a language model which constrains the recognition task by disallowing or assigning very low probability to most word sequences [13]. This language model is often constructed from statistical analysis of a large amount of training text taken from the application domain. An alternative approach, however, is to use word proximity information as metadata which provides an implicit language model.

In the simplest form, the access is achieved by performing standard large vocabulary word recognition and using the recognized words as input to a text search engine. Recognition errors, however, may cause the search to fail to locate correct regions of text. To address this problem, the speech recognizer can be configured to output multiple hypothesis for each spoken word. For example, if the single word "president" was spoken, the recognizer output might be the list ("precedent", "prescient", "president", ...) rank ordered by the estimated likelihood that each of the words had been spoken. The text can then be searched for regions containing a word from this list. This increases the chance of locating the desired text, but of course at the expense of locating undesired regions. However, when the spoken query contains multiple words from a phrase occurring within the text data, very often the only regions of text containing one word from each hypothesized wordlist are those in which the actual spoken words occur. For example, if the spoken phrase contains the words "president" and "Kennedy", resulting say in hypothesized wordlists ("precedent", "prescient", "president", ...) and ("kennerty", "Kennedy", "kemeny, ...), then with very high probability the only regions of text containing words from each list, within close proximity, will in fact contain "president Kennedy." The reason is simply that other combinations of the words do not commonly co-occur.

In general we have observed that the intended words of a spoken query tend to co-occur in text documents in close proximity whereas word combinations that are the result of recognition errors are usually not semantically correlated and thus do not appear together. We refer to this as *semantic co-occurrence filtering*. Note that in exploiting this principle, the text proximity metadata can be interpreted as providing an implicit language model used with the recognizer.

At Xerox PARC, we have implemented a text retrieval system using semantic co-occurrence filtering [16]. Our system is based on speaker-dependent, isolated word phonetic recognizer, although this is not an inherent requirement.

11.3.4   Speaker Segmentation

In speaker segmentation, the audio is partitioned into intervals, with each interval containing speech from a single speaker. The metadata derived from this consists of starting and ending times for each speaker, as well as the identity of the speaker. Pauses, or silence intervals, as well as non-speech sounds such as music or applause, can also be identified for use in indexing. A speaker index provides the capability to access portions of the audio corresponding to a particular speaker of interest, or to browse the audio by skipping to subsequent speakers.

The basic framework for segmentation of the audio is an HMM network consisting of a sub-network for each speaker and interconnections between speaker sub-networks [32]. Speaker segmentation is performed using the Viterbi algorithm [23] to find the most likely sequence of states and noting those times when the optimal state sequence changes between speaker sub-networks. The speaker sub-networks used here are multi-state HMMs with Gaussian output distributions. In addition to modeling speakers, sub-networks are also used to model silence and non-speech sounds such as a musical·theme.

In applications where the speakers are known *a priori*, and where it is possible to obtain sample data from their speech, segmentation of the audio into regions corresponding to the known speakers can be performed in real time, as the speech is being recorded. This is done by pretraining the speaker sub-networks using the sample data, and then using the Viterbi algorithm with continuous traceback for segmentation. Real-time speaker segmentation is useful, for example, in video annotation systems where annotations are made during the recording process [27].

When no prior knowledge of the speakers is available, unsupervised speaker segmentation is possible using a non-real-time, iterative algorithm. Speaker sub-networks are first initialized, and segmentation is achieved by iteratively using the Viterbi algorithm to compute a segmentation, and then retraining the speaker sub-networks based on the computed segmentation. It is necessary for the iterative segmentation algorithm to have good initial estimates for the speaker sub-networks. One way of obtaining the initial estimates is by hand-labeling a portion of the audio for each of the speakers. Experiments indicate that 30 to 60 seconds of data per speaker is sufficient [32]. However, hand-labeling by speaker can be difficult, particularly when the number and identity of the speakers are unknown.

Another method for initializing speaker clusters is agglomerative clustering. The data is first divided uniformly into 3 second intervals. The distance between each pair of intervals is computed, and the closest pair of intervals is merged. This process is repeated until a desired number of clusters is obtained, or until the merge distance exceeds a fixed threshold. This provides a course segmentation of the data, accurate only to the length of the original 3 second intervals. However, the iterative resegmentation algorithm can be performed using this as the initial clustering to obtain more accurate segmentation.

Color Figure-7 shows the audio portion of the presentation on Hypercars segmented according to speaker. The segmentation was obtained by first using the unsupervised clustering to obtain an initial set of five clusters. These clusters were hand-labeled as "Announcer", "Speaker", "Audience", "Applause", and "Silence". We refined this initial segmentation by using it as training data for the iterative resegmentation algorithm. Each of the resulting clusters is displayed on a different track. In addition to the usual play, fast forward and reverse options, the audio browser provides skip buttons to skip forward to the next speaker, or backward to the previous speaker. Speaker buttons provide the capability to play audio corresponding to the individual speakers.

11.3.5   Emphatic Speech Detection

By modifying the pitch, volume, and timing, that is, the prosodics of speech, a talker can convey syntactic and semantic information, in addition to the spoken words. Prosodics can be used to alter the meaning of words, to signal whether a sentence is a statement or question, or to indicate a phrase boundary. Butzberger et al. [2] used prosodic information to classify isolated words as a statement, question, command, calling, or continuation. Wightman et al. [33] combined the use of prosodic information and word recognition information to identify intonational features in speech. Based on prosodic information, metadata can be created identifying when a question was asked, and identifying phrase boundaries for use as endpoints for presentation.

Prosody is also used in natural, conversational speech to give more emphasis to some words and phrases. When making a point, the spoken words are given greater and more frequent emphasis. This prosodic information can be exploited to serve as indices to regions of possible interest.

Emphatic speech has been found to be characterized by prominences in pitch and volume. To estimate pitch, the fundamental frequency (F0) of the glottal source is computed. To locally estimate speaking volume, energy in a short duration of the speech signal is computed [22]. In our work at PARC, emphatic speech is identified by matching the set of prosodic features computed from a speech signal against an HMM network designed to model different prosodic patterns [4]. Prosodic features were selected which contain information to capture emphatic prominences; these features include F0, energy, change in F0, change in energy, and voicing to indicate vocalic regions.

To identify emphasized speech, syllable-based HMMs are created to model different patterns of emphatic speech. Separate models are created for unemphasized speech, which has a relatively flat prosodic pattern, for background noise, and for pauses.

A network modeling variations in emphasis is created by connecting the models of emphasized speech, unemphasized speech, and background noise in parallel. An optional pause is allowed between each of the models. Viterbi decoding [23] is, used to find the best path through the network. When the best path passes through an emphatic speech model, the time indices are recorded as an emphatic region.

Regions with a high density of emphatic speech are more likely to contain parts of a conversation which a speaker wished to highlight. The time indices of these regions are stored as metadata indicating regions of possible interest for browsing.

11.3.6   Subtopic Boundary Location

Both automatically identified and author-identified structural information are important for locating information in full-text documents. The structure of expository texts can be characterized as a sequence of subtopical discussions that occur in the context of one or a few main topic discussions. Subtopic structure is sometimes marked by the author in technical texts in the form of headings and subheadings. When author-identified structure is available, indices corresponding to SGML markup can be easily generated; therefore this discussion focuses only on automatically generated structural information.

For the cases in which texts consist of long sequences of paragraphs with very little structural demarcation, we have developed an algorithm, called TextTiling, that partitions these texts into multi-paragraph segments that reflect their subtopic structure [10]. This algorithm detects subtopic boundaries by analyzing the term repetition patterns within the text. The main idea is that terms that describe a subtopic will co-occur locally, and a switch to a new subtopic will be signaled by the ending of co-occurrence of one set of terms and the beginning of the co-occurrence of a different set of terms. In texts in which this assumption is valid, the central problem is determining where one set of terms ends and the next begins. Figures 11-2 and 11-3 show the results of TextTiling the Hypercars article. The larger peaks in the graph represent a relatively large amount of lexical cohesion [9] among the words within the sentences within the peak. The valleys represent breaks in lexical cohesion between adjacent text blocks. The algorithm's success is determined by the extent to which these simple cues actually reflect the subtopic structure of the text.

The core algorithm has three main parts: tokenization, similarity determination, and boundary identification. Tokenization refers to the division of the input text into individual lexical units. The text is also grouped into 20-word adjacent token-sequences, ignoring sentence boundaries in order to avoid length

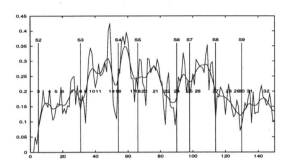

Figure 11-2 Result of TextTiling on the Hypercars article, first 150 token-sequences. The x-axis represents sentence numbers, the y-axis represents a measure of similarity between adjacent text blocks, and internal numbers indicate the locations of paragraph boundaries within the text. The vertical lines indicate topic boundaries marked by the algorithm.

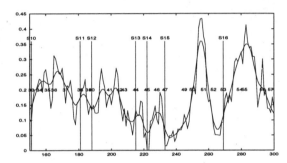

Figure 11-3 Result of TextTiling on the Hypercars article, second 150 token-sequences.

normalization concerns. A record of the locations of paragraph boundaries is maintained.

After tokenization, adjacent pairs of blocks of token-sequences are compared for overall lexical similarity. Token-sequences are grouped together into blocks to be compared against an adjacent block of token-sequences. Actual paragraphs are not used because their lengths can be highly irregular, leading to unbalanced comparisons.

Similarity values for adjacent blocks are computed for every token-sequence gap number. Boundaries are determined by changes in the sequence of similarity scores. The token-sequence gap numbers are ordered according to depth scores, that is, the sum of the heights of the plot on either side of the token-sequence gap. Segment boundaries are assigned to the token-sequence gaps with the largest corresponding depth scores, adjusted as necessary to correspond to true paragraph breaks. The cutoff for boundary assignment is a function of the average and standard deviations of the depth scores for the text under analysis. A boundary is drawn only if the depth score exceeds a threshold, and this threshold is a function of the properties of the graph, and so scales with the size of the document.

The TextTiling procedure when run on the Hypercars article *Reinventing the Wheels* produces 17 TextTiles, or subtopic segments, the contents of which can be glossed as:[3]

S1 Title, Table-of-Contents, and Abstract
S2 The Movement Towards Alternative Automobiles
S3 Ultralight Material is the Solution to Steel
S4 How Hypercars Differ from Electric Cars
S5 The New Idea: Combining Hybrid Fuel with Lightweight Material
S6 Lightweight Material Leads to Cheaper Accessories
S7 Lightweight Material Leads to Large Savings
S8 GM's 1991 Prototype
S9 The Role of Alternative Fuels
S10 Why Composites are Better than Steel
S11 Continuation of Theme S10
S12 Changes in Competitive Strategies
S13 Most Automakers Cannot Accept these Changes
S14 Continuation of Theme S13
S15 The Role of Oil in American Politics
S16 Gas Taxes and Related Issues
S17 Innovative Public Policy Ideas

The paper has 60 paragraphs and 6 sections explicitly marked with section headings. Although the algorithm is not instructed to take note of the section headings, it nevertheless placed boundaries at four of them (tiles S3, S5, S10, and S16). The algorithm missed one section heading by one short paragraph (after tile 11), and missed the last heading by one long paragraph (after tile S15). In two cases (tiles S11 and S14), the breaks suggested by the algorithm are probably extraneous, since in both cases the subject matter continues from the previous section.

---

[3]The settings used were: token-sequence size set to 20, 2 rounds of smoothing with a smoothing width equal to 3, blocksize set to 6. The gloss is provided for illustrative purposes and is not done automatically.

11.3.7 Summary of Metadata

In this chapter, we have discussed how metadata can be derived from various types of media. Table 11-1 summarizes the types of metadata discussed in this chapter and the media which they serve to index. The column labeled "Media" gives the media type of the document, the column labeled "Metadata" describes the metadata used to index the media, and the column labeled "Extraction" shows the method for obtaining the metadata.

Media	Metadata	Extraction
Image	Keyword	Word-image spotting [3]
Audio	Keyword	Word spotting [30]
	Speaker ID	Speaker Segmentation [32]
	Emphasis	Emphasis Detection [4]
Text	Subtopic Boundary	TextTiling [10]
	Inverted Index	Co-occurrence Filtering [16]

Table 11-1 Types of media indexed, metadata used for indexing, and how metadata is extracted.

11.4   Use of Metadata in Mixed-Media Access

Word-oriented information is present in full-length text, text image, and speech data; hence the user may expect to approach such data with a degree of uniformity. In particular, this may include accessing the media via queries in the same media type, for example, keyword spotting in speech using a spoken keyword. It also includes situations in which the media type of the query is different from that of the data, for example, a text query to an image database. The metadata used must be flexible enough to accommodate each useful combination. This section discusses an example of mixed-media access.

11.4.1   Hypercar Forum

The multimedia data considered in this example is based on a formal presentation on Hypercars, and includes recorded audio, scanned slides, and online text for an article on Hypercars [19]. In order to make full use of this material, we need to be able to retrieve information from each of these media. Using mixed-media access, this retrieval can be done simultaneously.

Metadata for the audio in the form of speaker segmentation is pre-computed. As discussed previously, the speakers in the audio are defined as "Announcer", "Speaker", "Audience", "Silence", and "Applause". "Announcer" is the person who introduces the speaker prior to the talk. "Speaker" is the person giving the talk. "Audience" is not actually a single speaker, but all members of the audience who asked questions. Thus queries involving the speaker can specify whether information from the speaker, announcer, or audience is desired. In addition, a search can be made for a non-speech sound, in this case applause. This is useful for locating likely highlights of the talk, as well as finding its beginning and end.

Metadata for the online text, namely, the TextTile segmentation of the text into topic regions, is also precomputed. This allows the relevant passages of text to be retrieved in response to a keyword query. All other metadata used in this example is computed "on the fly".

Color Figure-8 illustrates the response to a mixed media query consisting of the textual query for the keywords "battery" or "batteries", to be searched for in the online text and slide image data, an audio query for the keyword "battery", to be searched for in the audio data, and a specification that the keyword be spoken by "Speaker". Since the mixed-media query was over three types of media, relevant portions of each of these media are displayed.

The audio browser displays a timeline of the audio portion of the meeting, with different speakers corresponding to different tracks on the timelime. There is also a track for the specified keyword "battery"[4]. Since the query specified the keyword "battery" spoken by "Speaker", the cursor is positioned to the first occurrence of "battery" by "Speaker". The user can listen to the portion of the audio in the region where the speaker mentioned the word battery.

The image data query for "battery" or "batteries" was expressed as a search for "batter*", where "*" is a wildcard. The response to this query is to display the slide containing the specified character sequence "batter*". In this case, the slide is titled "Hybrid-electric drives". Finally, the query for "batteries" in the online text produces a window view into the full-length text, displaying one of the TextTiles (subtopical segments of text) containing the specified keyword.

---

[4]In addition, there is a track for the keyword "production" which was specified in a previous query.

In this case, the fourth segment is displayed, in which hypercars are contrasted to electric cars running on batteries.

11.5 Summary

Multimedia databases are typically accessed through text queries, often referring to manually assigned keywords. Recently developed methods provide ways to automatically generate metadata for audio, images, and text that enable more natural access modes such as mixed-media access.

Acknowledgments

We would like to thank Jeanette Figueroa for her enthusiasm and administrative support.

References

[1] D. S. Bloomberg, "Multiresolution Morphological Approach to Document Image Analysis," In Proc. of the International Conference on Document Analysis and Recognition, Saint-Malo, France, September 1991.

[2] J. W. Butzberger Jr., M. Ostendorf, P. J. Price, and S. Shattuck-Hufnagel. "Isolated Word Intonation Recognition Using Hidden Markov Models." In Proc. International Conference on Acoustics, Speech, and Signal Processing, Albuquerque, New Mexico, April 1990.

[3] F. R. Chen, D. S. Bloomberg, and L. D. Wilcox. "Detection and Location of Multicharacter Sequences in Lines of Imaged Text." Journal of Electronic Imaging, 5(1):37-49, 1996.

[4] F. R. Chen and M. M. Withgott. "The Use of Emphasis to Automatically Summarize a Spoken Discourse." In Proc. International Conference on Acoustics, Speech and Signal Processing, San Francisco, California, March 1982.

[5] S. Chen, S. Subramaniam, R. M. Haralick, and I. T. Phillips. "Performance Evaluation of Two OCR Systems." In Proc. Symposium on Document Analysis and Information Retrieval, Las Vegas, Nevada, April 1994.

[6] D. Cutting, J. Kupiec, J. Pedersen, and P. Sibun, "A Practical Part-of-Speech Tagger," The 3rd Conference on Applied Natural Language Processing, Trento, Italy, 1991.

[7] M. Dalrymple (ed.), *Tools for Morphological Analysis*, Center for the Study of Language and Information, Stanford, California, 1987.

[8] A. Dengal. "The Role of Document Analysis and Understanding in Multimedia Information Systems." In Proc. International Conference on Document Analysis and Recognition, Tsukuba Science City, Japan, October 1993.

[9] M. A. K. Halliday and R. Hasan, *Cohesion in English*, Longman, London, 1976.

[10] M. A. Hearst. "Multi-paragraph Segmentation of Expository Text." In Proc. 32nd Annual Meeting of the Association for Computational Linguistics, Las Cruces, New Mexico, 1994.

[11] M. A. Hearst. "Using Categories to Provide Context for Full-Text Retrieval Results." In Proc. RIAO 94, Intelligent Multimedia Information Retrieval Systems and Management, Rockefeller, New York, 1994.

[12] D. J. Ittner and H. S. Baird. "Language-Free Layout Analysis." In Proc. International Conference on Document Analysis and Recognition, Tsukuba Science City, Japan, October 1993.

[13] F. Jelinek. "Self-Organized Language Modeling for Speech Recognition". In *Readings in Speech Recognition*, A. Waibel and K. F. Lee, eds. Morgan Kaufmann, San Mateo, California, 1990.

[14] S. Khoubyari and J. J. Hull. "Keyword Location in Noisy Document Images." In Proc. Symposium on Document Analysis and Information Retrieval, Las Vegas, Nevada, April 1993.

[15] S. Kuo and O. E. Agazzi. "Machine Vision for Keyword Spotting Using Pseudo 2d Hidden Markov Models." In Proc. International Conference on Acoustics, Speech and Signal Processing. Minneapolis, Minnesota, April 1993.

[16] J. Kupiec, D. Kimber, and V. Balasubramanian. "Speech-Based Retrieval Using Semantic Co-occurrence Filtering." In Proc. ARPA Human Language Technology Workshop, Plainsboro New Jersey, March 1994.

[17] F. Lancaster, "Vocabulary Control for Information Retrieval, Second Edition," *Information Resources,* Arlington, VA, 1986.

[18] D. D. Lewis and P. J. Hayes, *ACM Transactions of Office Information Systems,* Special Issue on Text Categorization, 12(3), 1994.

[19] A. Lovins and L. Lovins, "Reinventing the Wheels", *Atlantic Monthly,* January 1995.

[20] K. Markey, P. Atherton, and C. Newton, "An Analysis of Controlled Vocabulary and Free Text Search Statements in Online Searches," *Online Review* 4: 225–236, 1982.

[21] R. D. Peacocke and D. H. Graf. "An Introduction to Speech and Speaker Recognition". Computer, 23(8), August, 1990.

[22] L. R. Rabiner, R. W. Schafer. *Digital Processing of Speech Signals.* Prentice-Hall Inc., Englewood Cliffs, New Jersey, 1978.

[23] L. R. Rabiner. "A Tutorial on Hidden Markov Models and Selected Application". Proc. IEEE, Vol. 77, No. 2, February 1989.

[24] G. Salton, *Automatic Text Processing: The Transformation, Analysis, and Retrieval of Information by Computer,* Addison-Wesley, Reading, Massachusetts, 1988.

[25] J. Schürmann, N. Bartneck, T. Bayer, J. Franke, E. Mandler, and M. Oberländer. "Document Analysis–From Pixels to Contents." In Proceedings of the IEEE, 90(7), July 1992.

[26] International Organization for Standardization. "Information Processing, Text and Office systems, Standard Generalized Markup Language (SGML), International Standard; 8879", 1986.

[27] K. Weber and A. Poon. "Marquee: A Tool for Real-Time Video Logging". Proc. CHI '94, ACM SIGCHI, April 1994.

[28] M. Wechsler and P. Schauble. "Metadata for Content Based Retrieval of Speech Recordings". Chapter 8 in this book.

[29] M. Weintraub. "Keyword-Spotting Using SRI's *Decipher*^{TM} Large-Vocabulary Speech-Recognition System". Proc. International Conference on Acoustics, Speech and Signal Processing, Minneapolis, Minnesota, April 1993.

[30] L. D. Wilcox and M. A. Bush. "Training and Search Algorithms for an Interactive Wordspotting System." Proc. International Conference on Acoustics, Speech and Signal Processing, San Francisco, California, March 1992.

[31] L. D. Wilcox, I. Smith, and M. A. Bush. "Wordspotting for Voice Editing and Audio Indexing." Proc. CHI '92, ACM SIGCHI, Monterey, California, May, 1992.

[32] L. D. Wilcox, F. R. Chen, D. Kimber, and V. Balasubramanian. "Segmentation of Speech Using Speaker Identification." Proc. International Conference on Acoustics, Speech and Signal Processing, Adelaide, Australia, April 1994.

[33] C. W. Wightman and M. Ostendorf. "Automatic Recognition of Intonational Features." Proc. International Conference on Acoustics, Speech and Signal Processing, San Francisco, California, March 1992.

[34] J. G. Wilpon, L. R. Rabiner, C. H. Lee, and E. R. Goldman. "Automatic Recognition of Keywords in Unconstrained Speech Using Hidden Markov Models". IEEE Transactions on Acoustics, Speech and Signal Processing, 38(11), November 1990.

A Framework for Meta-Information in Digital Libraries

Kate Beard and Terence R. Smith*

National Center for Geographic Information and Analysis and
Department of Spatial Information Science and Engineering
University of Maine
Orono, ME 04469-5711, USA
beard@spatial.maine.edu

*Department of Computer Science and Department of Geography
University of California at Santa Barbara
Santa Barbara, CA 93106, USA
smithtr@cs.ucsb.edu

Abstract

Typical tasks of users in a library are to search for information, retrieve it, evaluate it for appropriateness and obtain it for use if it is found to be suitable. Traditional libraries have been structured to support these tasks. Collectively the components of a library, the catalog, the stacks, documents, operations, and librarians, contribute to the effectiveness of these tasks. These same tasks need to be supported in a digital library but the traditional mechanisms for their support are now removed. Meta-information as we refer to it in this chapter provides a basis for supporting these tasks in the digital library.

This chapter discusses the challenges of developing meta-information for digital libraries and outlines the contents of meta-information needed to support search, retrieval, evaluation and transfer functions. The chapter presents a framework for modeling meta-information in a digital library catalog. The framework takes the form of a four-component model of a catalog: an information object modeling component, a query modeling component, a query matching component, and a catalog interoperability component (see Figure 12-1). Meta-information is modeled in the catalog as relations between nominal representations of information objects and their properties and sets of relations between properties. Multiple languages are used to express these relations both within and across catalog components. Various possibilities for the languages include natural languages, subsets of natural languages, graphic languages, and formal languages. This catalog framework has advantages of more expressive modeling and query functionality but the disadvantages of more complex intra- and interoperability issues. The Alexandria Digital Library (ADL) provides specific examples of this framework.

12.1   Introduction

Libraries have been described as controlled collections of information. Their structure and operations were designed to support efficient access to information. In a traditional library, multiple sources of information provide access, such as librarians, catalogs, and the manner in which the collections are organized physically. Digital libraries (DLs) are libraries in which the collections are in digital form and access to the information in the collections is based almost entirely on digital technology [27]. This chapter presents a framework for the design of the meta-information environments for DLs that takes advantage of digital technology and compensates for the loss of direct physical object and person to person interactions available in a traditional library. The framework supports the modeling of information bearing objects (IBOs) and user queries in terms of meta-information, without imposing undue restrictions on the content, representation, or exchange of such models.

We begin with a functional characterization of meta-information for digital libraries. The functional characterization looks at the tasks that the meta-information is intended to support.

12.1.1   Functional Characterization of Meta-Information

The six digital libraries funded by NSF, NASA and ARPA under the Digital Library Initiative (DLI) offer a wide range of services and collections. Their metadata efforts are strongly influenced by their particular choice of service focus and collection characteristics. Many of the libraries have directed their metadata efforts to descriptions of their collections which range from full text to spatially referenced data sets [2, 32] to video [30]. The Stanford DL, on a different tack, has focused on an infrastructure for disparate services which can interoperate. Their metadata efforts have thus been more directed to service descriptions [5]. The Alexandria Digital Library has chosen to embrace the traditional library paradigm and actively employs many of the traditional forms of library metadata including thesauri, subject headings and gazetteers.

All of the six digital library projects support a basic set of library functions that include: (1) search, (2) retrieval, (3) evaluation, and (4) transfer. Characterization of meta-information along these functions allows us to focus on commonalties across the libraries rather than their differences which stem from their different collections. This functional characterization is also useful in that it helps to distinguish meta-information associated with libraries from meta-information created and managed by information producers or information users.

With respect to the search function, meta-information assists the user to discover if the information of interest exists within the available collections. At a minimum the meta-information represents the context of information objects, such as author, publisher, and lineage but also the content (topics, focus, methodologies) and relationships (similar, synonymous, part of) of one IBO to another. In a two-pronged approach, meta-information for search can be associated with users (preferences, past search requests) as well as with IBOs. Meta-information for search should be sufficiently broad based to support search along various spatial, thematic, and temporal dimensions. Meta-information for search can be content-independent, content-dependent, content-descriptive, domain-dependent or domain-independent [20]. It is more likely to be media-independent. Meta-information to support search need only reside in a catalog. It can be hidden from users and it need not travel with the information when it is retrieved.

To support the retrieval function, meta-information should provide the information for users to acquire the information of interest. The library analogy for this is the procedure for checking out a book. The retrieval component of meta-information may be as simple as providing a URL identifying the location of an electronic data set, to as complex as covering security issues or arranging a financial transaction to access the information. It may include information on the off-line location of the data, the contact person, media, formats, restrictions on access to the data such as licensing agreements and information on pricing. Meta-information for retrieval will generally be content-independent.

Meta-information to support transfer should provide the necessary information for users to use retrieved information in their particular work environments. This component includes information on the size of the data set (and its meta-information), the logical and physical structure of the information and meta-information, and such information as encoding and compression methods. This category overlaps with Böhm and Rakow's [7] category "metadata for the representation of media types". Meta-information for transfer will generally be content-independent and media-dependent.

The evaluation function of meta-information is the most complex. Meta-information to support evaluation can consist of any information which assists users in determining if data will be useful in a particular application context. Meta-information for evaluation can include browsable images of the information, information on data collection procedures, and data quality information. Meta-information for evaluation overlaps the other meta-information categories. In some cases a very small set of properties is sufficient for evaluation (e.g., author or publisher). In general the more rigorous the application, the greater will be the requirement for meta-information that supports evaluation. Unlike search where the meta-information can be hidden from users, for evaluation it should be directly available and comprehensible for users. Some evaluation of IBOs should be possible prior to retrieval particularly if there are fees for use of the IBOs. In addition some meta-information will need to travel with retrieved IBOs so that evaluation can occur or continue subsequent to retrieval. Meta-information for evaluation can be content-independent, content-dependent, or content-descriptive.

12.1.2   Challenges in Developing Meta-Information for Digital Libraries

The design and implementation of schemes for meta-information to support digital library functions is challenging. Among the challenges are: (1) the characteristics of digital IBOs, (2) characteristics of a digital library itself, and (3) the expanding demands of users in a digital environment.

Characteristics of IBOs

A traditional library contains physical information objects (books, maps, journals). Levy [22] notes that traditional cataloging carves up the bibliographic universe into relatively discrete, stable, and long-lived units. In a digital library the IBO is a logical unit. Any number of logical units can be defined which do not need to correspond to the traditional set of discrete physical units [27]. In particular the granularity of the digital IBO changes [13, 17]. For example, a book in digital form becomes a composite of text, illustrations, table of contents, index, etc. Text based documents are decomposable to individual words or letters. Similarly digital maps may be decomposed to individual line segments, polygons, or symbol types, and video to individual frames or video paragraphs [10]. Böhm and Rakow [7] present this as a multimedia problem. A digital environment allows this decomposition to be managed logically rather than physically so original context is maintained.

Digital IBOs have the potential to become more complex objects that combine content and functionality. Phelps and Wilensky [24] have developed multivalent documents – complex documents comprised of multiple layers of content bundled with behaviors which bind the disparate layers together. A multivalent document is presented to a user as a single unified conceptual document.

Digital IBOs are also more fluid. Lines within a map or text within a paragraph may be updated frequently. Thus the concept of editions changes. This has direct bearing on temporal search since a single publication date will be too coarse. In summary the primary challenges in modeling digital IBOs are accommodating a much more varied, complex and dynamic sets of objects which are not always well defined. The advantage is that modeling is more flexible with logical IBOs than physical IBOs.

Characteristics of Digital Libraries

Traditional libraries are seen as controlled collections. In the world of digital libraries there is a continuum from widely distributed and uncontrolled to fully "controlled". The World Wide Web (WWW) is an example of the uncontrolled extreme. Levy and Marshall [23] refer to this as an example of a broadly construed library. These "libraries" are independent of traditional institutions and as widely distributed as the ownership of personnel computers. Theoretically anyone can submit personal data to uncontrolled libraries. The Alexandria Digital Library (ADL) and many of the other digital libraries funded under the Digital Library Initiative fall closer to the "controlled" library.

Digital collections can also be independent of traditional library protocols and unconstrained by recognized library standards. The problem is not solely managing collections that lack standards but integrating many possible domain specific standards. For example, there may be submissions which are compliant with US MARC or TEI, others which use the FGDC metadata content standard [11], yet others which use the Dublin core [31] or other possibilities. Under this altered structure, challenges for meta-information modeling are to:

- create methods for simple, extensible cataloging procedures so anyone can easily document and contribute their collection, and

■   support interoperability between collections and their representations (cat-
    alogs).

As argued later, various cataloging methods and structured formats are seen
as languages which need to interoperate.

Digital library locations are not static. Collections can easily change their
locations over time as well as their formats and other characteristics. Collection maintenance is thus a critical limitation of the broadly construed digital
library [1].

Traditional libraries organize physical IBOs by attributes such as subject matter and author. The organization of stacks by the Library of Congress Classification (LCC) or Dewey Decimal Classification (DDC) system allows information of similar content to be stored in close physical proximity. This structure,
when known to users, supports ad hoc searching. If one did not find a particular document from an organized search of the catalog one could often locate
the relevant topic and search the stacks. New digital library search mechanisms
based on similarity metrics for IBO properties could replace this ad hoc search
method. The concept of similarity can easily extend beyond similar subject
headings. While the physical ordering based on subject is lost, the DL opens
the possibilities for multiple logical organizations of IBOs.

Loss of access to the physical documents in the DL limits some search and
browse functions, but more critically it affects the evaluation function. Intrinsic
properties of IBOs discovered by having the object in hand, such as intellectual
content and physical form, need to be replaced in the DL. The challenge lies in
capturing and modeling meta-information to encode the intrinsic properties of
IBOs.

Other significant changes occur in the meta-information environment of a digital library. In terms of advantages, having the IBOs in digital form permits
the use of digital technology in extracting information from the IBOs. The extracted information may satisfy a user's ultimate need for information or it may
be employed by "digital librarians" in characterizing the IBOs in the collection.
In the latter case, this meta-information may be employed in providing access
to the information encoded in the IBOs. In terms of disadvantages, important
interactions between librarians and users that occur in the meta-information
environments of traditional libraries may be lost with the near-automation of
information access in DLs.

User Characteristics

The WWW and other technologies are fueling user awareness and demand for more sophisticated information services. Just as the granularity of IBOs has increased by converting them to digital form, users' units of search can increase in granularity in a DL. For example, users may no longer be satisfied with searching for a book, but desire information on specific contents or characteristics of a book such as a typeface. The basic user task has been transformed from retrieving IBOs per se to answering queries [32]. The answer to a query does not necessarily reside in a single IBO or in textual form. User expectations are thus shifting the focus from context (author, title) and structure based access to content based access. Users also have growing expectations of being able to process and use IBOs directly in their own applications.

The digital library will not be successful from the users' perspective unless their requests can be easily and intuitively expressed. The particular challenges in modeling users' queries are that their expectations are greater and they are situation-dependent. Requests are personal, context-dependent and time-dependent. In the near term, we cannot reasonably expect DL catalogs to provide complete descriptions of IBOs. This is particularly true of multimedia IBOs [14]. One solution is for meta-information to remain implicit until needed.

With the functional characterization and challenges as background the next section presents a set of requirements for meta-information in digital libraries.

Requirements for Meta-Information

A key requirement for meta-information is that it provide a representation of all aspects of digital collections that are relevant in supporting access to appropriate information. From the challenges described above we can extract a number of specific requirements for meta-information which we try to address within the proposed framework. These (only in the order in which they relate to the challenges above) include:

- robust yet simple IBO modeling independent of a librarian/expert

- standards/language/catalog interoperability

- support for hierarchical structuring of IBOs

- flexibility and extensibility in IBO modeling

- content as well as context and structure based search

- support for expression and searching on similarity among IBOs

- support for intuitive user request languages

- dynamic creation of meta-information in response to different user views

In the next section, we present a framework for constructing models of IBOs and user queries. In this case we restrict the scope to meta-information which is stored in the catalog of a DL. The main ideas in the framework are illustrated with examples from the Alexandria Digital Library for spatially referenced information [2] and other digital libraries [5].

12.2   A Model of the Digital Library Catalog

A traditional library catalog consists of a set of entries, each of which represents an item in the collection and which describes certain characteristics of the item, such as author, title, publisher, and so on. Cataloging as noted by Levy [22] is a form of order-making, which puts a library's collections in order and provides access through a set of systematically organized surrogates. The traditional catalog models intrinsic characteristics of IBOs through descriptive cataloging and minimal content through subject cataloging. In a digital environment, models of IBOs can cover the continuum from the IBO itself to the most abstract model, which is the IBO ID. In response to the broad modeling requirements for digital library meta-information, the DL catalog (see Figure 12-1) is seen to consist of:

1. an IBO modeling component through which models of the library's holdings are constructed and maintained;

2. a query modeling component in which the system interacts with the user to construct a model of the user's query;

3. a query matching component in which the system interactively matches its model of the user's query with models of IBOs and selects appropriate information to return to the user;

4. a catalog interoperability component in which the system transforms library requests to other ("alien") catalogs and interprets requests from alien catalogs.

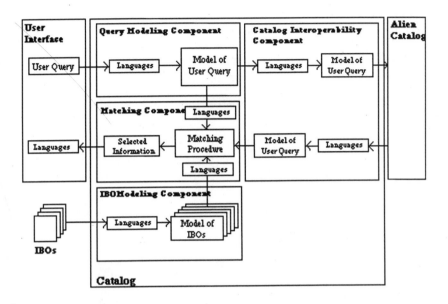

Figure 12-1   Four component model of a DL catalog.

12.2.1   Meta-Information as Relations

Meta-information within the catalog is modeled using a set of relations. Sheth and Kashyap [25] use a similar approach to modeling metadata with attribute value pairs. We first describe these relations and then discuss how this aspect of the framework addresses some of the meta-information requirements outlined above.

We employ two classes of relations in modeling digital library meta-information. First, we employ relations between nominal representations of IBOs and various properties of the IBOs of the form

$$R = \{[information\_object\_id, [property, value]]\} \qquad (12.1)$$

where $\{\}$ indicates a set of elements. Second, we employ relations between representations of the various properties of IBOs

$$R = \{[[property\_1, value\_1], [property\_2, value\_2]]\} \qquad (12.2)$$

Relations of type (1) given in (12.1) are critical for supporting user access, since the inverse relations

$$R^{-1} = \{[[property, value], information\_object\_id\} \qquad (12.3)$$

may be used to find the appropriate IBOs given user-specified properties and values. To build the meta-infomation, an initial set of relations of type (1) are constructed in the IBO modeling component of the catalog. Relations of type (1) and of type (2) given in (12.2) may occur in the remaining three components of the catalog.

A hierarchical structure is easily imposed through relations of type (1) and by assuming an information object id is just another property. In this case we may have an IS_PART_OF relation (e.g., a document is part of a collection, or a chapter is part of a book). The hierarchical relation does not need to be created unless it is desirable to do so. For example, a map may be treated as a discrete IBO (all properties apply uniformly to the document) until there is need or desire to decompose it to a relevant set of constituent objects (points, lines or polygons).

Relations of type (2) provide the basis to determine a metric of similarity among a set of IBOs. Similarity is expressed as a metric on property value pairs or within the value domain of a single property. Equivalence is established if all explicit properties for IBOs being compared have identical values. For example, assuming the complete set of properties are author and publisher, R1 and R2 are equivalent if $R1 = \{[[Author, Clark, R.J.], [Publisher, Wiley]]\}$ and $R2 = \{[[Author, Clark, R.J.], [Publisher, Wiley]]\}$. Using the thirteen Dublin Core [31] elements as the set of properties, two IBOs are equivalent if they have identical values for each of the thirteen elements. Using a simple metric of similarity on property value pairs, two objects can have a similarity value of 1 if one property value pair deviates in value, a value of 2 if two property value pairs deviate, and so on. Another metric of similarity can be established across a value domain for a specific property. For the subject property, the Library of Congress Classification (LCC) system provides such a metric. Bruns and Egenhofer [8] provide a metric for similarity of spatial footprints. The inverse of relations of type (1) modified to support a value range

$$R^{-1} = \{[[property, value\_range], [information\_object\_id]]\} \qquad (12.4)$$

mapped against relations of type (2) can support user requests to the catalog for similar IBOs within a single property value domain.

One advantage to viewing meta-information in terms of the two sets of relations is that it emphasizes in a natural manner (inverse relations) that the primary purpose of meta-information is to access IBOs on the basis of their properties. The second advantage is that meta-information does not have to be represented in explicit form (e.g., as a set of tables in an RDBMS), but may be represented implicitly until the time of query evaluation. Meta-information may be represented in terms of implicit values that are made explicit by the application of some procedure and by the appropriate composition of relations of type (1) and type (2). A third advantage is extensibility, since one may specify an extension to a meta-information scheme by simply adding new relations. The model of catalog meta-information as a set of relations thus clearly supports the requirements for a hierarchical structure, similarity metrics, dynamic creation of meta-information and extensibility.

12.2.2   Meta-Information Management Using Multiple Languages

Many of the tools that librarians typically employ in constructing catalogs and in supporting catalog operations may be viewed as definitions of languages whose expressions denote the properties of IBOs. In traditional libraries such tools include subject heading lists, thesauri, and gazetteers. These tools support the construction of meta-information in which IBO properties are typically expressed in either natural language (as in the representation of titles, author names, and abstracts) or in highly constrained subsets of natural language (as in the representation of subject headings). This view extends easily to the counterparts and generalizations of such tools in digital libraries, with the difference that formal languages may also be used. Several examples from the literature [18, 26] point to the use of language applied to meta-information management. Baldonado et al. [5] indicate languages used within the Stanford DL.

Traditional catalogs have involved a multiplicity of languages with distinct semantics and digital catalogs will likely employ an even larger number of languages. The use of multiple languages offers several benefits, these primarily being more expressive power for specific functions. The obvious disadvantages are the problems created for semantic intra- and interoperability. Intraoperability issues are present since a single catalog may involve one or more languages within its components.

Smith et al. [28] point out that languages employed in DL catalogs can be specified at conceptual, logical and physical levels. The conceptual level involves relatively informal specifications of the language, typically in terms of natural language, and an informal specification in terms of the cognitive processing of the reader. In particular, expressions in the language are interpreted in terms of the cognitive representation of "concepts". The logical level involves a more formal approach in which the semantics of expressions may be defined in terms of the expressions of another (declarative) language. Many of the languages employed in library catalogs, for example, may be specified in terms of a language of the first order predicate calculus (FOPC). In this case, a simple truth value semantics may be appropriate in providing meaning to the expressions of the language. Finally, the physical level involves digital representations of the languages in some computational device, and whose semantics are specified in terms of machine operations.

Cataloging Tools and Associated Languages

We illustrate the important roles of languages in the construction and use of catalogs in terms of two examples, the first being traditional thesauri and their generalizations for digital libraries and the second being the Federal Geographic Data Committee (FGDC) metadata content standard for digitized documents of spatially indexed information [11].

Traditional thesauri (see [3]) specify simple languages whose terms have denotations in limited domains of application. As we note below, however, a thesaurus may also define a metalanguage. This fact has implications for the role of a thesaurus in the four-component catalog model. The specification document for a thesaurus may be viewed as specification at the conceptual level. It is typically impossible to eradicate all ambiguity in relation to the denotations of the terms, which are ultimately provided by the informal interpretations of the cognitive processing of the reader.

Specification of a thesaurus at the logical level reveals more clearly the nature of the language being defined at the conceptual level. For a typical thesaurus, recasting at the logical level leads to a specification in terms of a set of constant symbols that denote either classes of entities (such as "igneous rock") or instances of entity classes (such as "gabbro"), and a set of relation symbols that denote relations between the entities denoted by the constant symbols. Examples of the standard relation symbols include "narrow-term", "broad-term".

Furthermore, the definitions of narrow and broad terms can be recast as a set of axioms associated with the language. For example, the fact that "gabbro" is a narrow term with respect to "igneous rock" may be expressed in terms of the syntax of FOPC as:

$$\forall \chi ISA\ (\chi, gabbro) \Rightarrow ISA\ (\chi, igneous\_rock) \tag{12.5}$$

The linguistic complexity of thesauri appears in the synonymy relationship that is typically an important aspect of thesauri. One may view it as part of a metalanguage that defines aspects of the semantics of the thesaurus. In this sense, the synonymy relation between constant symbols for two synonymous terms $t1$, $t2$ is "$SYNONYMOUS\ (t1,\ t2)$". An alternative, and perhaps more useful view, is that of an inference rule of the form:

$$SYNONYMOUS\ (t1, t2)/EXP\ (t1) \equiv EXP(t2) \tag{12.6}$$

in which EXP is some expression and $\equiv$ is semantic equivalence. This inference rule indicates that one may substitute $t1$ for $t2$ in the same expression without changing its meaning.

A thesaurus may be used in different ways in different components of a catalog. The basic language for a thesaurus, for example, may be used in the IBO modeling component (e.g., indexing of IBOs using "canonical" terms of the thesaurus) and the query modeling component (e.g., query formulation using "canonical" terms of the thesaurus and reformulation of queries using broad-term/narrow-term relations). The metalanguage component of a thesaurus is used mainly in the query modeling component, where expressions employed by users may be replaced using the inference rule (6).

One may perform a similar analysis on the FGDC metadata content standard for digital spatially referenced information. This standard has been adopted and implemented as a language in both the IBO modeling and the query modeling component of ADL. One may again represent this language as a special case of a FOPC language. The content standard is modeled in ADL in terms of the relational data model. This is in turn implemented in terms of RDBMS. Therefore one may view the relational schema as specifying a FOPC language in which the properties of IBOs are represented. The elements of the relations represented in the language may be viewed as a set of axioms associated with the language, as may constraints that are part of the language specification. Also the relational algebra used to manipulate the relations may be viewed as an inference mechanism.

Multiple Languages of the Catalog Components

To maintain generality in the catalog framework there are no constraints on the languages that may be used. Various possibilities for the languages include natural languages, subsets of natural languages, graphic or cartographic languages [6], and formal languages. The multiple languages help to support a large range of IBO properties that must be represented in the meta-information of a catalog. Since the content of an IBO may relate to any phenomenon representable in symbolic or iconic form, linguistic expressiveness is essential. This is particularly true of DLs whose collections include many complex IBOs such as multimedia or spatial representations such as GIS databases.

Different languages have different degrees of "natural" expressiveness with respect to the phenomena that they are able to represent, and correspondingly different costs of usage, particularly in computational environments. While natural language is highly expressive, and is useful for human to human communication and machine to human communication, it is too complex (i.e., costly to use) and too ambiguous in its full generality for human to machine and machine to machine communication.

A common strategy, therefore, is to use constrained subsets of natural language (controlled languages) or formal languages that have a relatively simple syntax and whose expressions have relatively unambiguous interpretations in terms of limited sets of phenomena. The first approach typically involves the use of specialized thesauri developed for limited domains of application.

The use of a variety of relatively simple languages represents a "divide-and-conquer" approach to the problem of modeling a diverse array of IBO properties in the catalog. As an example, the catalog component of ADL involves multiple languages. The IBO modeling component of ADL currently employs two languages for specifying the relations between IBOs and their properties.

These are languages based on the USMARC specification of meta-information and on the FGDC content standard for digital spatial information. Development plans for ADL involve the use of additional languages, including subject heading languages and various thesauri. These languages are still controlled languages understood best by cataloging professionals. To meet the requirement of robust yet simple IBO modeling an additional language is needed. One option is the Dublin Core [31] developed by the library community to fill the niche between automatically generated records which contain too little information (web indexes) and MARC or FGDC records created by professional information providers. Examples of similar but less standardized efforts are appearing in the literature [19].

The current query modeling component of ADL not only employs the languages of the IBO modeling component (i.e., FGDC and USMARC), but also a language based on gazetteers and a graphical language. A gazetteer creates a mapping between named features on and near the surface of the Earth and representations of the "spatial projection" or footprint of the feature on the surface of the Earth. The language of a gazetteer supports queries in which the user specifies a named feature to be contained in any retrieved map. The footprint of the feature is then "matched" with footprints of maps modeled in the meta-information of the IBO modeling component. The graphical language in the query interface allows users to sketch a region of interest on a map. The graphic sketch of a region establishes a relation between a sequence of coordinate pairs and a footprint. This footprint is then, in a manner similar to the gazetteer result, "matched" with footprints of maps modeled in the IBO modeling component. The multiplicity of languages in the query modeling component gives users more options and intuitive choices for phrasing requests. Development plans call for the use of languages based on subject headings and thesauri, on "extended thesauri" containing information on the co-occurrence of expressions in various languages, as well as more complex graphic or cartographic expressions.

The catalog interoperability component of ADL involves languages based on components of the Z39.50 protocol [4], such as BIB-1 and the proposed GEO-1. Research on algorithmic generation of language translations [9], languages for interoperability [16], and the semantics of expressions in other languages [21] is relevant to development of languages in this component. The match component currently involves no languages of its own.

12.2.3   The Distribution of Meta-Information Among Components of a Catalog

An important property of the catalog framework is that meta-information is not restricted to the IBO modeling component. It is distributed over the four components of the catalog. This is done for reasons of efficiency. While one could construct meta-information models of digitized maps that contained all named examples of Earth features occurring in gazetteers, the costs associated with the construction, storage, and searching of these "records" would be relatively high. By placing the gazetteer feature-footprint relation in the query modeling component, however, the user can choose the named features to be represented in the maps of interest. Retrieval of the appropriate maps can then be computed "on the fly".

Similarly, meta-information constructed by the graphical language overcomes inefficiencies in the gazetteer. A gazetteer has limitations since it cannot possibly encode all possible spatial partitions of the globe desired by users. Through a sketch at query time the user in effect adds a run time entry to the gazetteer.

Another reason for distributing meta-information over catalog components relates to differences in their functionality. Languages for modeling objects in the IBO modeling component may be chosen for their efficient representation of object characteristics or because they are part of some standard. From a user's perspective, however, other characteristics may be more important for accessing information. If such characteristics can be expressed in a language employed in the query modeling component and if its expressions can be related semantically to those of the meta-information in the IBO modeling component, then multiple languages are beneficial.

In general languages in the query modeling component are "richer" from a user's viewpoint than the languages in the IBO modeling component. As a simple example, a thesaurus may be used to translate a relatively broad array of user terms into synonymous "canonical" terms. A less trivial example involves generalizations of thesauri in which co-occurrences of terms are derived from empirical analyses of documents. The richer set of terms in the model of the user's query may then be interpreted statistically using the more limited terms of the IBO models.

12.2.4 The Four Components as Knowledge Representation Systems

The preceding discussion of catalog tools, such as thesauri and the FGDC metadata content standard, indicated how such tools could be viewed in terms of languages. It also showed, by example, how they could be viewed as possessing associated sets of axioms and inference mechanisms. We also noted that a multiplicity of languages requires an ability to interpret the expressions of one language in the terms of some other language.

If we regard the linguistic expressions of meta-information relations as a subset of the associated set of axioms, we may view the components of the catalog in terms of various knowledge representation systems. The components of these systems include a body of knowledge K, which covers the concept domain, objects described, expressions used to name objects, and relations among objects; a language L, a set of inference rules F, and semantics, S, for interpreting between languages. The languages may include natural languages, declarative formal languages, graphic languages and programming languages.

The interpretations of languages play an important role in multilanguage catalogs. In the matching component, for example, queries expressed partly in one language must be interpreted in terms of another language in order to carry out a semantically meaningful match. In the catalog interoperability component, queries from alien catalogs that employ different languages must be interpreted in terms of the languages employed in constructing the IBO models.

Reasons for analyzing the components of a catalog in terms of a knowledge representation system are that, first, it provides a basis for the analysis of the expressive power of the meta-information and of the computational complexities associated with processing queries in such systems. Second, it provides a framework for designing and extending catalog systems in a modular and systematic manner.

In order to make this view of catalog components clear, we present an example showing how the representation of a gazetteer in the query modeling component of ADL may be viewed in a knowledge representation structure. At the logical level, the constant symbols of the language, L, include symbols that are employed to denote feature classes, feature instances, and aspects of the footprints of the feature instances, such as points, lines, and polygons. The function symbols of the language include symbols that denote a spatial projection operator and the usual binary set operators (intersection, union,...).

The relation symbols include the same set of relation symbols as thesauri, including "PART_OF". The body of knowledge K includes relations "ISA" and "PART_OF" of a thesaurus and relations between named feature instances and their footprints, such as:

$$Equals(\Pi(OhioRiver, [p1, \ldots, pn])) \qquad (12.7)$$

in which the second term in the relation represents a polygon defined in terms of n points. The inference rules F may be viewed as the standard inference rules of FOPC. Both the construction and manipulation of meta-information may be viewed as involving the use of these inference rules. The semantics S may include rules for mapping from the expressions of L into the expressions of the language associated with the FGDC standard.

12.3   Issues Raised by the Framework

The catalog framework provides a natural means of analyzing and resolving two basic issues that arise from the multiplicity of languages employed. Catalog intraoperability concerns the trade-off of designing and implementing efficient yet expressive catalog systems. The trade-off involves the advantages of a divide-and-conquer approach in which IBOs and queries are modeled in terms of a set of relatively simple and specialized languages, and the disadvantages of constructing and applying interpretations to ensure semantic compatibility in a multilanguage environment. If the choice of languages in the components is determined, then the problem becomes one of making the interactions between the different languages semantically compatible in the most efficient manner. We term this the "weak version" of the catalog intraoperability issue.

Catalog interoperability concerns the goal of making different catalog systems semantically interoperable in as efficient a manner as possible. Since the reason for using different languages in this case is not to construct an "optimal" catalog, but rather to provide an efficient solution in the face of uncontrollable language heterogeneity, the problem is to apply multiple interpretations as efficiently as possible.

The weak version of the catalog intraoperability problem is clearly almost identical to the catalog interoperability problem, so it follows that the strategy for solving these problems should be similar. Two distinct strategies include

(1) making direct translations between any pair of languages that interact (e.g., through the match component); (2) translating from each language to some intermediary language. Clearly we may combine these strategies in different ways.

We examine the issues of intraoperability and interoperability, and discuss some of the approaches that have been taken in ADL with respect to these two sets of issues. If a problem involves N languages, we term the first strategy the "N^2 strategy" since in general one must construct of the order of N^2 translations of the languages. We term the second strategy the "N" strategy, since one must construct of the order of N translations.

12.3.1 Catalog Intraoperability

Specific issues that arise in the catalog intraoperability problem include (1) deciding which languages to use in each of the components of the catalog, particularly in the IBO modeling and the query modeling components and (2) deciding how to solve the language translation problem in cases of multiple languages. Choices in the latter problem include adopting the N or the N^2 strategy or performing the appropriate translations prior to performing the match operations or embedding the translation process in the match procedure itself.

A particularly simple solution involves using a single language for modeling both IBOs and queries. A prototype version of ADL employed this approach by using FGDC as the main language in both components. In this common denominator solution, one loses expressiveness if the language is too restrictive, while one pays a heavy computational price if the language is too general (e.g., natural language).

In relation to the choice of language translation strategy, the advantages of embedding the translation process in the match procedure include computational efficiencies if the translation is procedurally part of the match. Disadvantages include the lack of modularity and hence of flexibility if it is necessary to modify either the match procedure or the interpretations. The trade-offs in choosing between the N and N^2 strategies are relatively self-evident, and involve the issue of finding a single appropriate language and the cost of making the translations.

Since such problems are difficult to analyze in the general case, we provide some specific examples of the intraoperability problem. In particular, we briefly discuss two problems that arose during the construction of the ADL catalog. The first problem, alluded to above, involved the decision of whether to construct IBO models for maps containing meta-information about the features represented in them or whether to embed meta-information relations from the gazetteer in the query modeling component. The latter solution was adopted on the grounds of the amount of processing that is required to construct the meta-information models of the maps and the size of the models that would result.

The second problem concerned the construction of the gazetteer in the query modeling component. The basic issue was that two distinct gazetteers were available, namely, the Geographic Name Information System (GNIS) from the USGS and the Board of Geographic Names (BGN) from the DMA. Both of these gazetteers contain a list of features, a classification of the features and the spatial projections of the features. The basic problem was that the underlying languages of the two gazetteers, while similar, were sufficiently different to require non-trivial interpretations between their corresponding terms. Hence the issue of semantic compatibility arose.

For example, the GNIS classifies its features into 65 feature types. It also has an implicit concept of "generics", which is a subclassification of features. The generics, however, are not proper subsets of the feature types, so a pure hierarchy is difficult to construct. The BGN contains nine feature classes as the highest level of a hierarchy. It also stores an explicit sub-level of the hierarchy in the form of 638 feature types. Unlike the GNIS hierarchy, which is informal, the BGN feature types are proper subsets of the feature classes forming a formal hierarchy. Because the classification schemes for features in the two gazetteers depend on the cognitive categories applied to real world objects (i.e., they are specified at the conceptual level), it is difficult to combine them and maintain this hierarchy. To the extent that the ADL gazetteer uses a hierarchy to facilitate queries, this mismatch between GNIS and BGN was problematic.

One possible solution to the gazetteer language problem was to use both gazetteers as distinct languages. The difficulty with this approach is that their domains of application overlap. Hence significant inefficiencies would result from this approach. An alternative approach was to translate both of them to a common language (i.e., construct a merged gazetteer). The latter solution was adopted with the most difficult issue relating to the integration of the feature types/classes. The resulting gazetteer is a superset of the two gazetteers and involves a more general classification scheme.

12.3.2   Catalog Interoperability

The key catalog interoperability issue is to efficiently interpret the languages of one catalog into the expressions of the languages in another catalog. While the N^2 and N strategies provide basic approaches to this problem, there is a large space of possibilities to explore. In adopting the N strategy, for example, there are many candidates for the intermediary language, including the language components of Z39.50, various knowledge representation languages such as KIF [12], ONTOLINGUA [15], and Representational Structures [29]. Furthermore, within Z39.50, it is possible to exchange expressions in other languages, with an indication of the language that is being used for any specific set of expressions. Since the resolution of such issues requires a great deal of further investigation, we limit our discussion to describing three limited investigations involving the N^2 and N strategies. These experiments were intended to determine the relative costs of the two approaches.

Catalog Interoperability Experiment I: An N^2 Solution

An interoperability experiment was performed by ADL and the digital library being developed at the University of California at Berkeley (UCB). The goal of the experiment was to match models of queries from the UCB catalog with models of documents from the ADL catalog. For the experiment, both DLs limited their query models and their IBO models to those based on the FGDC language. Furthermore, both DLs represented the FGDC language in terms of the relational data model and implemented it in terms of the Illustra extended relational DBMS. The main difference was that the two DLs independently constructed different schema for their data models. As part of the experiment, a direct mapping was established between the two schemas, as part of an N^2 approach. Interconnection was provided via Illustra's client-server architecture.

While the experiment led to good performance in terms of interoperability, the costs of employing this strategy were significant. It took an expert database programmer over 6 person-weeks to create the schema mapping. Given a realistic DL environment with a large number of catalogs using multiple languages, one must conclude that if these costs are typical, then the approach would scale poorly.

Catalog Interoperability Experiment II: An N Solution

An interoperability experiment between ADL and the Stanford DLI project was established to investigate the N (or intermediary-language) approach. The two DLs implemented their catalogs in different languages, and used different DBMSs in the IBO modeling components.

Z39.50-BIB-1 was chosen as the intermediary language, for translating between the internal languages of each library. As in the case of the experiment with UCB, mapping decisions were still made manually. More significantly, the intermediary language had a limited set of attributes (over 50 in Z39.50 BIB-1 compared with over 300 in ADL's internal language). This restricted both the expressiveness of the intermediary language and the information that could be shared. In contrast, the approach allows libraries to share any information that both of their internal languages can represent. This shortcoming, however, is inherent in the specific intermediary language chosen, and not in the N approach itself.

The implementation in this experiment took 2 person-days, and good performance with respect to interoperability was achieved. An advantage of the N strategy is that no further time investment is required, on the part of either ADL or Stanford, should other libraries decide to participate.

12.4   Summary

The transition from physical to digital libraries opens opportunities and creates constraints to information access. Meta-information is an essential ingredient which makes information exchange possible in a digital library. The framework presented in this chapter provides a rational basis for modeling meta-information in DL catalogs. Several requirements for meta-information identified in a discussion of challenges are addressed by the framework. The representation of meta-information through a set of relations provides a flexible and direct approach. Through two straightforward relations and their inverses we manage the evolving granularity of IBOs, semantic content of IBOs expressed through properties, and a basis for expressing similarity among IBOs. The representation is easily extended and supports implicitly as well as explicitly held meta-information. The use of multiple languages for catalog management and query support provides efficient and expressive access to information. The trade-offs to the benefits from multiple languages are catalog intraoperability and interoperability issues. A number of solutions to intraoperability and interoperability are possible such that we argue the benefits of multiple languages outweigh the costs.

Acknowledgments

This work is partially supported by NSF under IRI94-11330 and SBE-8810917. This support is gratefully acknowledged.

References

[1] M. S. Ackerman and R. T. Fielding. Collection maintenance in the digital library. In *Proceedings Digital Libraries*, Austin TX, 1995. URL http://csdl.tamu.edu/DL95/.

[2] D. Andresen, L. Carver, R. Dolin, C. Fischer, J. Frew, M. Goodchild, O. Ibarra, R. Kothuri, M. Larsgaard, B. Manjunath, D. Nebert, J. Simpson, T. Smith, T. Yang, and Q. Zheng. The WWW prototype of the Alexandria Digital Library. In *Proceedings of the International Symposium on Digital Libraries*, Tsukuba, Japan, 1995.

[3] ANSI/NISO. Guidelines for the construction, format, and management of monolingual thesauri, 1993. ANSI/NISO Z39.19.

[4] ANSI/NISO. Information retrieval: Application service definition and protocol specification, 1995. ANSI/NISO Z39.50 Draft.

[5] M. Baldonado, C.-C. K. Chang, L. Gravano, and A. Paepcke. The Stanford digital library metadata architecture. *International Journal of Digital Libraries*, 2, 1997.

[6] J. Bertin. *Graphical semiology*. University of Wisconsin Press, Madison, WI, 1985.

[7] K. Böhm and T. C. Rakow. Metadata for multimedia documents. *SIGMOD Record*, 23:21–26, 1994.

[8] H. T. Bruns and M. J. Egenhofer. Similarity of spatial scenes. In M.-J. Kraak and M. Molenaar, editors, *Seventh International Symposium on Spatial Data Handling (SDH '96)*, Delft, The Netherlands, 1996. Taylor & Francis.

[9] H. Chen, T. Yim, D. Fye, and B. R. Schatz. Automatic thesaurus generation for an electronic community system. *Journal of the American Society for Information Science*, 46:175–193, 1995.

[10] M. Christel. Addressing the contents of video in a digital library. In *Electronic Proceedings of the ACM Workshop on Effective Abstractions in Multimedia*, San Francisco, CA, 1995.

[11] Federal Geographic Data Committee. Content standards for digital geospatial metadata, 1994.

[12] M. R. Genesereth et al. *Knowledge Interchange Format Version 3.0. Reference Manual.*

[13] M. Goodchild. Report on a workshop on metadata. Technical report, National Center for Geographic Information and Anaylsis, Santa Barbara, CA, 1996.

[14] J. Griffioen, R. Yavatkar, and R. Adams. Automatic and dynamic identification of metadata in multimedia. In *Proceedings First IEEE Conference On Metadata*, Silver Springs, MD, 1996. URL http://www.computer.org/conferen/meta96/adams/paper.html.

[15] T. R. Gruber. Ontolingua: A mechanism to support portable ontologies.

[16] M. Haines, P. Mehrotra, and J. Van Rosendale. Smartfiles: An OO approach to data file interoperability. In *OOPSLA*, 1995.

[17] R. Jain and A. Hampapur. Metadata in video databases. *SIGMOD Record*, 23:27–33, 1994.

[18] M. Jarke et al. Conceptbase – A deductive object base for meta data management. *Journal of Intelligent Information Systems*, 3:167–192, 1995.

[19] C. Kacmar, D. Jue, D. Stage, and C. Koontz. Automatic creation and maintenance of an organizational spatial metadata document digital library. In *Digital Libraries 95*, 1995. URL http://csdl.tamu.edu/DL95/.

[20] V. Kashyap, K. Shah, and A. Sheth. Metadata for building the multimedia patch quilt. In S. Jajodia and V. Subrahmanian, editors, *Multimedia Database Systems: Issues and Research Directions*. Springer-Verlag, 1995.

[21] V. Kashyap and A. Sheth. Semantics based information brokering. In *Proceedings of the 3rd International Conference on Information and Knowledge Management (CIKM)*, Gaithersburg, MD, 1994.

[22] D. M. Levy. Cataloging in the digital order. In *Digital Libraries '95*, 1995. URL http://csdl.tamu.edu/DL95/.

[23] D. M. Levy and C. C. Marshall. Going digital: A look at assumptions underlying digital libraries. *Communications of the ACM*, 38:77–84, 1995.

[24] T. Phelps and R. Wilensky. Toward active extensible, networked documents: Multivalent architecture and applications. In *Proceedings of ACM Digital Libraries '96*, Bethesda, MD, 1996.

[25] A. Sheth and V. Kashyap. Media-independent correlation of information: What? How? In *Proceeding First IEEE Conference on Metadata*, Silver Springs, MD, 1996.
URL http://www.computer.org/conferen/meta96/sheth/index.html.

[26] L. Shiklar, K. Shah, and C. Basu. Putting legacy data on the web: A repository definition language. *Computer Networks and ISDN Systems*, 27:939–951, 1995.

[27] T. Smith. The meta-information environment of digital libraries. *D-Lib Magazine*, 4, 1996.

[28] T. Smith, S. Geffner, and J. Gottsegen. A general framework for the meta-information and catalogs in digital libraries. In *Proceedings 1st IEEE Conference on Metadata*, Silver Springs, MD, 1996.
URL http://www.computer.org/conferen/meta96/smith/ieee.html.

[29] T. Smith, J. Su, A. El Abbadi, D. Agrawal, G. Alonso, and A. Saran. Computational modeling systems. *Information Systems*, 20:127–153, 1995.

[30] H. Wactlar, T. Kanade, M. Smith, and S. Stevens. Intelligent access to digital video: Informedia project. *Computer*, 5, 1996.

[31] S. Weibel, J. Godby, and E. Miller. OCLC/NASA metadata workshop report. Technical report, OCLC/NCSA, 1995. URL http://www.oclc.org:5046/conferences/metadata/dublin_core_report.html.

[32] R. Wilensky. Toward work-centered digital information services. *IEEE Computer Special Issue on Digital Libraries*, May, 1996.

Biographies

Gulrukh Ahanger is a Ph.D. candidate in the Department of Electrical and Computer Engineering at Boston University. She is currently a research assistant in the Multimedia Communications Laboratory. Her research interests include multimedia databases and visual query systems for video. Ms. Ahanger received her BE degree in Electronics and Communications Engineering from the Regional Engineering College, Srinagar, India in 1988 and the MS degree in Systems Engineering from Boston University in 1993. She consulted as a software engineer for Siemens Medical Electronics, Danvers, Massachusetts from May 1992 to January 1993. She also interned at Siemens Corporate Research Inc. during the summer of 1993 where she developed a prototype video query system. Currently she is involved in a project for fast access to multimedia information for applications in distance learning and customized-news-service delivery.

Dr. Kate Beard is chair of the Department of Spatial Information Science Engineering at the University of Maine and research faculty with the National Center for Geographic Information and Analysis (NCGIA). She holds a M.S. (1984) and Ph.D. (1988) from the Institute for Environmental Studies, Land Resources Program, University of Wisconsin-Madison where she specialized in geographic information systems. Dr. Beard's research interests cover digital libraries, metadata and spatial data quality, visualization of spatial data uncertainty, and multiple representations of spatial data at different resolutions. She is a collaborator on the NSF, NASA, DARPA funded Alexandria Digital Library project and is developing a digital library for the Gulf of Maine. Work on data quality covers metadata representation, management and tracking of errors in spatial databases, and various methods for visualizing and communicating spatial data uncertainty. Work in the area of multiple representations includes development of generalization operations and designs for user interaction in generalization. Under NCGIA she served as co-leader of the initiative "Visualization of the Quality of Spatial Information" and co-leader on the initiative "Roles for GIS in US Global Change". Dr. Beard sits on the editorial board of the URISA Journal and is a member of the Association of

Computing Machinery (ACM), American Association of Geographers, American Congress on Surveying and Mapping (ACSM), Automated Mapping and Facilities AM/FM International, and Urban and Regional Information Systems Association (URISA).

Klemens Böhm is a researcher in the division for open adaptive information systems at GMD-IPSI in Darmstadt, Germany. His work mainly deals with structured document storage, and he is also interested in query optimization and applications of object-relational database technology. In 1997, he finished his Ph.D. and in 1993 he earned a diploma degree in information science from the Technical University of Darmstadt, Germany.

Susanne Boll is a research assistant in the division for Database and Information Systems (DBIS) at the University of Ulm, Germany. Her research interest lies in the area of multimedia database systems and she works on the integration of flexible presentation services into multimedia database technology. In 1996 she began her Ph.D. at the Integrated Publication and Information Systems Institute (IPSI) of the German National Research Center for Computer Science (GMD), which she is now continuing at the University of Ulm as a doctoral student of Wolfgang Klas. She obtained her diploma degree in computer science at the Technical University of Darmstadt, Germany, in 1996.

Francine Chen received the B.S.E. degree from the University of Michigan and the M.S. and Ph.D. degrees in electrical engineering from the Massachusetts Institute of Technology. After completing her Ph.D. in 1985, she joined Hewlett-Packard Laboratories where she worked on speech recognition. In 1986 she joined Xerox PARC and is currently manager of the Quantative Content Analysis Area. At PARC she has worked on projects in speech, images and text, including phrase spotting in imaged text, speech recognition, speaker segmentation, and summarization of text, imaged text, and conversations. Her research interests include information access, image and speech analysis, and pattern recognition.

Wesley W. Chu is a professor of Computer Science and was the past chairman (1988-1991) of the Computer Science Department at the University of California, Los Angeles. He received his B.S.E. (EE) and M.S.E. (EE) from the University of Michigan. He received his Ph.D. (EE) from Stanford University. From 1964 to 1966, he worked on the design of large-scale computers at IBM, Menlo Park and San Jose, California. From 1966 to 1969, he researched computer communications and distributed databases at Bell Laboratories, Holmdel, New Jersey. He joined the University of California, Los

Angeles in 1969. He is also a consultant to government agencies and private industries. He has authored and co-authored more than 100 articles on information processing systems and has edited four textbooks. His current research interests are in the areas of Distributed Processing, Intelligent Databases, and Knowledge-Based Multimedia Medical Information Systesm. He received a meritorious award for his service as an associate editor for the IEEE Transactions on Computers (1978-1982). He also received a Certificate of Appreciation award for his significant service to the IEEE First International Workshop on Systems Management (1993). He is currently a member of the Editorial Board of the Journal of Very Large Databases and an Associate Editor for the Journal of Data and Knowledge Engineering. Dr. Chu is a Fellow and member of the Golden Core Society of IEEE.

Pamela Drew is currently manager of the Information and Document Management Group in the Applied Research and Technology Division of the Boeing Company. The charter of this group is to assess, apply, and extend, when necessary, advanced information and collaborative technologies to the Boeing environment. Previously, Dr. Drew was an assistant professor in the Computer Science Department at Hong Kong University of Science and Technology, and a member of technical staff in the research laboratory of U S WEST Advanced Technologies. Concurrent to her work at U S WEST, she completed her Ph.D. in Computer Science at the University of Colorado, Boulder. She is author of over twenty-four papers and book chapters on the topics such as advanced transaction managment and heterogeneous databases. She has also served as program committee member and reviewer on numerous database conferences and journals, and actively serves in professional capacities organizing workshop and conference events.

Dr. Farshad Fotouhi is an Associate Professor of Computer Science at Wayne State University in Detroit, Michigan. He received his B.S. in 1981 and M.S. in 1982, both from Western Michigan University and Ph.D. in computer science from Michigan State University in 1988. He is a member of the Advisory Board, Journal of Database Management and has been member of various database-related conferences. Dr. Fotouhi's current research interests include: Multimedia/Hypermedia information systems, object-oriented databases, data warehouses, and user interfaces. Dr. Fotouhi is a member of ACM and IEEE Computer Society.

Dr. William I. Grosky is currently professor and chair of the Computer Science Department at Wayne State University in Detroit, Michigan. His current research interests are in multimedia information systems, hypermedia, and web technology. Dr. Grosky received his B.S. in mathematics from MIT in 1965, his M.S. in Applied Mathematics from Brown University in 1968, and his Ph.D. in Engineering and Applied Science from Yale University in 1971. He is currently on the editorial boards of IEEE Multimedia, Pattern Recognition, and the Journal of Database Management. In January 1998, he will be the new editor-in-chief of IEEE Multimedia.

Oliver Günther received his Diplom in Industrial Engineering from the University of Karlsruhe in 1984, and M.S. and Ph.D. degrees in Computer Science from the University of California at Berkeley in 1985 and 1987, respectively. After a postdoc at the International Computer Science Institute in Berkeley, he was an Assistant Professor of Computer Science at the University of California at Santa Barbara during the academic year 1988/89. From 1989 until 1993, he was Director of the Environmental Information Systems Division at FAW, a computer science research laboratory in Ulm, Germany. Since 1993, he has been Professor and Director of the Institute of Information Systems at Humboldt University in Berlin. Since 1996, he has also been Chair of the Berlin-Brandenburg Graduate Program in Distributed Information Systems. Professor Günther has conducted research projects in the areas of database management, knowledge-based systems, geographic and environmental information systems, as well as distributed information management. He published nine books and more than 70 papers on related topics, and he was one of the founders of the SSD symposium series on spatial databases. Oliver Günther held visiting professorships at the University of Cape Town, the University of California at Berkeley, and the École Nationale Superieure des Télécommunications in Paris. He serves as a consultant to various government agencies and industrial companies on issues relating to environmental data management.

Arun Hampapur got his Ph.D. in Computer Science and Engineering from the University of Michigan in Ann Arbor in May 1995. His dissertation research was titled "Designing Video Data Management Systems". He worked for Virage Inc, a pioneering company providing media management solutions from June 1995 to June 1997. He joined the IBM TJ Watson Research Center as a Member of Research Staff in the Exploratory Computer Vision Group in July 97. He is currently working on issues of media management in the context of HDTV Studios. His research interests include cross media based video indexing, event recognition in video data and media management system design.

Takanari Hayama received his BS, MS degrees in information science from University of Tsukuba in 1993 and 1995, respectively. He is a Ph.D. student in information science at University of Tsukuba. His research interests include distributed processing systems for multiple continuous media and multimedia systems.

Marti Hearst is an assistant professor at the University of California Berkeley in the School of Information Management and Systems (SIMS). From 1994-1997 she was a Member of the Research Staff at Xerox PARC. She received her BA, MS, and Ph.D. degrees in computer science from the University of California at Berkeley. Prof. Hearst's research focuses on user interfaces and robust language analysis for information access systems, and on furthering the understanding of how people use and understand such systems. Her research projects to date include multi-paragraph discourse segmentation (TextTiling), corpus-based word sense disambiguation, a graphical interface for showing the relationship between query term hits and retrieved documents (TileBars), an investigation of the use of document clustering for understanding search results (Scatter/Gather on retrieval results) and the use of very large category hierarchies to improve information search and browsing (Cat-a-Cone).

Chih-Cheng Hsu is a Ph.D. candidate in UCLA Computer Science Department. He received his B.S. degree from National Taiwan University in 1988 and his M.S. degree from State University of New York at Stony Brook in 1991 both in Computer Science. Currently he is working on UCLA KMeD project. His research interests include multimedia data modeling, knowledge-based query language and query processing for multimedia data, and knowledge discovery on spatial and temporal data.

Ion T. Ieong received his B.S. degree from Hua Chiao University in China in 1985. He received his M.S. degree from the University of Connecticut in 1987. He received his Ph.D. degree in Computer Science from UCLA in 1993. Currently, he is a senior software engineer at NCR Corporation at El Segundo, CA. His research interests include modeling and analysis of computer systems, distributed processing, multimedia and distributed database systems.

Ramesh Jain is currently a Professor of Electrical and Computer Engineering, and Computer Science and Engineering at University of California at San Diego. Before joining UCSD, he was a Professor of Electrical Engineering and Computer Science, and the founding Director of the Artificial Intelligence Laboratory at the University of Michigan, Ann Arbor. His current research interests are in multimedia information systems, interactive video, image databases, machine vision, and intelligent systems. He was the founder and the Chairman of Imageware Inc and is the founding chairman of Virage. Currently he is the President and CEO of Praja Inc., a company to commercialize MPI

Video technology. Ramesh is a Fellow of IEEE, AAAI, and Society of Photo-Optical Instrumentation Engineers, and member of ACM, Pattern Recognition Society, Cognitive Science Society, Optical Society of America, and Society of Manufacturing Engineers. He has been involved in organization of several professional conferences and workshops, and served on editorial boards of many journals. Currently, he is the Editor-in-Chief of IEEE Multimedia, and is on the editorial boards of Machine Vision and Applications, Pattern Recognition, ACM/Springer Journal of Multimedia Systems, Multimedia Tools and Applications Journal, Journal of Digital Libraries, and Image and Vision Computing. He received his Ph.D. from IIT, Kharagpur in 1975 and his B.E. from Nagpur University in 1969.

Zhaowei Jiang is an assistant professor and engineer chief in the Neurological Surgery Department at Wayne State University, Detroit, Michigan. His specialties include virtual environment databases and computer assisted surgery (CAS) which covers computer assisted neurosurgery and computer assisted orthopedic surgery. Over past several years, he developed a novel image-guided surgery system, and performed numerous research projects in related fields. His research interests include multimedia information systems, virtual reality information systems, and medical intelligence systems. Recent published papers mainly focus on intraoperative image guided surgery. Jiang received his Bachelor of Engineer degree in electronic computer engineering from Tsinghua University, Beijing, China, in 1988, and his Master of Science degree in computer science from Wayne State University, in 1991. He obtained his Ph.D. degree in computer science at Wayne State University in July 1996. Now he is member of IEEE, SPIE and ACM.

Dr. Wolfgang Klas is currently Professor at the Computer Science Department of the University of Ulm, Germany. Until 1996 he was head of the Distributed Multimedia Systems Research Division (DIMSYS) at the Integrated Publication and Information Systems Institute (IPSI) of the German National Research Center for Computer Science (GMD) and directed many research projects and industrial collaborations in the fields of object-oriented database technology, multimedia information systems, interoperable database systems, and cooperative systems. In 1993 he was a visiting professor at the Johannes-Kepler-University of Linz, Austria, and in 1991/1992 Dr. Klas was a visiting fellow at the International Computer Science Institute (ICSI) at the University of California at Berkeley. His research interests are currently in multimedia information systems and Internet-based applications of database systems. Dr. Klas serves currently on the editorial board of the VLDB Journal and he has been a member and chair of program committees of many conferences.

William Klippgen is a member of the International Engineering team of Excite, Inc. of Mountain View, California. Prior to joining Excite, Mr. Klippgen studied Multimedia Computing at Boston University under a Fulbright Fellowship where he developed a Java-based personalization system for the delivery of on-line news. In his native Norway, Mr. Klippgen was employed with Mogul Media of Oslo, in 1995, where he was involved in multimedia authoring and production; and Norwegian Telecom, as a C++ application developer. Mr. Klippgen received the Sivilingenioer degree in Computer Science and Engineering Cybernetics from the Norwegian Institute of Technology 1995 and the MS degree in Computer Engineering from Boston University in 1996. His technical interests include automated video summary generation, personalization, user navigation tracking, and learning by observation. He plans to participate in a Norwegian Internet start-up company that will focus on smart information and advertising distribution.

Don Kimber received his B.E.E.E. from Stevens Institute of Technology in 1980, and worked as a software engineer before returning to school and receiving an M.S. in Computer and Information Science from University of California, Santa Cruz in 1988. His masters thesis was on the inference of stochastic automata (e.g. hidden Markov models) using algorithms which extend simulated annealing to infinite state spaces. He then worked as a research intern at Xerox PARC while pursuing a Ph.D. at Stanford University. He completed his Ph.D. in 1995 with a thesis on geometric methods for modeling the configuration spaces of dynamical systems, with application to speech recognition. Mr. Kimber has been a full time research member of the Collaborative Systems area at PARC since 1995. His work at PARC has included the development of a stochastic modeling toolkit, which has supported a variety of research projects and applications, including real time speech recognition, word spotting and speaker recognition/segmentation. He also worked on the design and implementation of a system for multimedia recording and playback of meetings and presentations. His current research interests are in technology support of collaborative work, and in a systems approach to organizational processes.

Takashi Kitagawa was born 1956 in Gifu, Japan. He received his Ph.D. from Nagoya University, Doctoral course in Computer Science. He was a visiting scholar at Dept. of Computer Science, Stanford University, 1980-81, Assistant Professor at Dept. of Mathematics, Ehime University, 1982-89. He is currently an Associate Professor at Inst. of Information Sciences and Electronics, University of Tsukuba. He is engaged in inverse problems, numerical analysis, multimedia information systems.

Yasushi Kiyoki received his BS, MS and Ph.D. degrees in electrical engineering from Keio University in 1978, 1980 and 1983, respectively. He is currently an associate professor of Department of Environmental Information at Keio University. During 1990 and 1991, he was a visiting researcher at University of California at Irvine and University of Texas at Austin. His research addresses multidatabase systems, semantic associative processing, and multimedia database systems.

Julian Kupiec is a member of the research staff at Xerox Palo Alto Research Center. His research interests include stochastic methods for modeling speech and natural language, and their use in applications for information access. He has worked at the Centre for Speech Technology Research (1986-1987) at Edinburgh University, Scotland. From 1981 to 1986 he worked on computer controls for nuclear accelerators at CERN, Geneva and at SLAC in Stanford, California. He obtained his B.Sc. and Ph.D. degrees from Heriot-Watt University, Edinburgh. His doctoral thesis was on simulation techniques and graphical design methods for various systems modeled as networks.

Thomas D.C. Little is an associate professor in the Department of Electrical and Computer Engineering at Boston University. He is director of the Multimedia Communications Lab at Boston University where he is involved in the development of enabling technologies and applications for interactive multimedia systems. Dr. Little received the BS degree in biomedical engineering from Rensselaer Polytechnic Institute in 1983, and the MS degree in electrical engineering and Ph.D. degree in computer engineering from Syracuse University in 1989 and 1991. He is a member of the IEEE Computer and Communications Societies and the Association for Computing Machinery. He serves on the editorial boards of IEEE Multimedia and ACM/Springer Multimedia Systems and on various program committees for the ACM and IEEE.

Jan Pedersen is currently manager of the Advanced Technology Group at Verity Inc., a leading vendor of text retrieval products. Previously, Jan worked for ten years at Xerox PARC, where he was the Area Manager of the Quantitative Content Analysis Group. In that capacity, he led a technical team responsible for a number of inventions in information retrieval. These include the origination of the Scatter-Gather, cluster-based, document browsing paradigm, statistical approaches to text categorization and natural language processing, and object-oriented design of text retrieval systems. Jan has an undergraduate degree in Statistics is from Princeton University; he earned a doctorate in the same subject from Stanford University.

Peter Schäuble leads a research group at the Swiss Federal Institute of Technology (ETH) Zürich. Current research projects focus on various aspects of information retrieval such as automatic speech indexing and cross-language retrieval. Peter Schäuble has a M.S. (Dipl. Math. ETH) in mathematics and a Ph.D. (Dr. Sc. Techn.) in Computer Science both from ETH. He has been a technical staff member of the European Space Agency (ESA) and a visiting scientist at Hewlett-Packard Laboratories in Palo Alto. He is currently an assistant professor at the Computer Science department, ETH Zürich. Peter Schäuble is an Associate Editor of ACM TOIS and served as program chair of the SIGIR Conference in Zurich in 1996. He recently published a book on Multimedia Information Retrieval (Kluwer). In 1995, Peter Schäuble founded the spin-off company Eurospider Information Technology AG, which offers a commercial version of the retrieval system Eurospider.

Dr. Amit Sheth directs the Large Scale Distributed Information Systems (LSDIS) Lab and is an Associate Professor of Computer Science at the University of Georgia. Earlier he worked for nine years in the R&D labs at Bellcore, Unisys, and Honeywell. He has lead projects on heterogeneous DDBMS, factory information system, integration of AI-database systems (BrAID), federated database tools (BERDI and TAILOR), multidatabase consistency, and data quality (Q-Data). Current research at the LSDIS is in the area of (a) work coordination and collaboration system (projects METEOR and CaTCH) and (b) integration of and information brokering involving heterogeneous digital media using metadata, logical correlations, contexts, and ontologies (projects VisualHarness and InfoQuilt). Prof. Sheth has over 100 publications, given over 90 invited talks including conference keynotes and many tutorials, participated in 19 panels, and has lead four international conferences and workshops as general/program chair or co-chair. He has also served twice as an ACM Lecturer, has been on about forty program and organization committees, and is on the editorial board of five journals. Prof. Sheth's work has lead to commercial products and successful technology transfer. He is the president of Infocosm, Inc. whose goal is to enable Infocosm in which we will have information any time, any where, and in many form, for effective decision making, better development and utilization for human intellect, and more fun.

Terence R. Smith is Professor of Geography and Professor of Computer Science at UCSB. He received his BA from Cambridge University in 1965 and his PhD from Johns Hopkins University in 1971. He has served as Chair of the Department of Computer Science at UCSB (1986-90); as Associate Director of the National Center for Geographic Information and Analysis (1988-90); and he is currently director of the Alexandria Digital Library Project at UCSB.

His current research interests focus on the design, development and testing of digital libraries for geo-referenced information; computational systems that support the modeling of complex phenomena; and the computational modeling of fluvial phemonena. Dr. Smith is the author of over 100 published research papers and the recipient of numerous research funding awards.

Ricky K. Taira is an Associate Professor of the Radiology Department at the University of Washington and the Children's hospital in Seattle. He received his B.S. in Electrical Engineering from UCLA in 1982 and received his Ph.D. from the same institution in 1988. After receiving his Ph.D., Professor Taira held a postdoctoral position in the Medical Imaging Division at UCLA from 1988 to 1989. In 1989 he became a Visiting Assistant Professor of the Department of Radiological Sciences, an Assistant Professor of the same department later that year, and in 1997 an Associate Professor of the same department. In 1997, he moved to his current position as an an Associate Professor of Radiology at the University of Washington. Professor Taira received the Sylvia Greenfield Award in Medical Physics in 1988 from the UCLA Department of Radiological Sciences. In 1988, he won the Ralph and Marjorie Crump Award from the Crump Institute for Medical Engineers, the James T. Case Award from the UCLA Department of Radiological Sciences, and the first place award in the pre-doctoral student paper competition of the Society of Computer Applications in Medical Care. He is currently a member of the American Association of Physicists in Medicine and the Society of Photo-Optical and Instrumentation Engineers (SPIE).

Dinesh Venkatesh is a Principal Design Engineer in the Network Storage Group at EMC Corporation of Hopkinton Massachusetts, where he designs and implements video storage systems. He is also associated with the Multimedia Communications Laboratory at Boston University. Mr. Venkatesh holds a BE in Electronics Engineering from Bangalore University, an MS in Computer Engineering from Boston University, and received his Ph.D. in Computer Engineering from Boston University in the fall of 1997. Mr. Venkatesh is a member of the ACM.

Agnés Voisard received Master's and Ph.D. degrees in Computer Science from the University of Paris at Orsay and INRIA (French National Computer Science Research Institute) in 1989 and 1992, respectively. During the academic year 1992/93 she was an INRIA Postdoctoral Fellow at the University of Munich. Since 1993 she has been Assistant Professor of Computer Science at the Free University of Berlin. Her areas of expertise include geographic and environmental information systems, object-oriented databases, data modeling, user interfaces, and multimedia applications. She has participated in several program committees and was General Chair of the 5th Symposium on Spatial Databases (SSD'97).

Martin Wechsler is a research assistant and doctoral student in the group of Peter Schäuble at the computer science department of the Swiss Federal Institute of Technology (ETH) Zürich. His research focuses on indexing and retrieval of spoken information. Martin Wechsler has a M.S. (Dipl. Informatik-Ing. ETH) in computer science from ETH. He was also a summer student at the Xerox Palo Alto Research Center (PARC). Martin Wechsler is a co-founder of the spin-off company Eurospider.

Lynn Wilcox received the Ph.D. and M.S. degrees in Mathematical Sciences from Rice University, and a B.S. degree in Mathematics from University of California, Davis. She worked as an engineering specialist at Ford Aerospace before joining Hewlett Packard Labs in 1980, where she developed a speech recognition system for personal computers. She was a Member of the Technical Staff at Xerox PARC from 1986 to 1996, where her research included word spotting in images and audio, and segmentation of audio by speaker. She has been at FX Palo Alto Laboratory since 1996, where she manages the Integrated Media group. Her current research interests are in combining digital ink, audio, and video in personal note-taking devices, and in audio and video indexing and retrieval.

Jerry Ying (M.Phil. Hong Kong University of Science and Technology) is now a Consultant in Unisys China/Hongkong Ltd. responsible for designing a Information Display System for Hong Kong Railway using an object-oriented real-time knowledge base system to enable signal control over different network objects in a distributed environment. Previously, he was a research assistant in the Department of Computer Science in the Hong Kong University of Science and Technology. He specialized in the area of a metadata management facility to enable global information exchange over a heterogeneous distributed database framework. His research interests include multi-databases, metadata management, data mining and database architectures.

Index

About the Editors

Amit Sheth, Ph.D., directs the Large Scale Distributed Information Systems Lab and is an associate professor of computer science at the University of Georgia. He previously worked in R & D at Bellcore, Unisys, and Honeywell.

Wolfgang Klas, Ph.D., is professor of computer science at the University of Ulm, Germany, and the author of numerous articles on information technology. Until 1996, he was head of the Distributed Multimedia Research Division at the Integrated Publication and Information Systems Institute of the German National Research Center for Computer Science.